THE PRESIDENT AND CONGRESS

Collaboration and Combat in National Policymaking

Lance T. LeLoup
Washington State University

Steven A. Shull
University of New Orleans

Allyn and Bacon
Boston • London • Toronto • Sydney • Tokyo • Singapore

To Pamela and Janice

Vice President, Editor-in-Chief, Communication and Political Science: Paul Smith
Series Editorial Assistant: Kathy Rubino
Marketing Manager: Jeff Lasser
Production Editor: Robert Tonner
Editorial Production Service: Ruttle, Shaw & Wetherill, Inc.
Composition Buyer: Linda Cox
Manufacturing Buyer: Megan Cochran
Cover Administrator: Jenny Hart
Electronic Composition: Omegatype Typography, Inc.

Copyright © 1999 by Allyn and Bacon
A Viacom Company
160 Gould Street
Needham Heights, MA 02194

Internet: www.abacon.com

Library of Congress Cataloging-in-Publication Data

LeLoup, Lance T.
  The President and Congress : collaboration and combat in national
policymaking / Lance LeLoup, Steven A. Shull.
      p.   cm.
  Includes bibliographical references and index.
  ISBN 0-205-26534-0 (pbk.)
  1. Presidents—United States. 2. United States. Congress.
  3. Political planning—United States. 4. Public policy (Law)-
-United States. I. Shull, Steven A. II. Title.
JK585.L45 1998
320'.6'0973—dc21   98-13341
                                              CIP

Printed in the United States of America

10 9 8 7 6 5 4 3 2   04 03 02 01 00 99

CONTENTS

PREFACE

From a budget deadlock that led to government shutdowns to a historic balanced budget agreement between Congress and the President, both collaboration and combat between branches have been in evidence in recent years. With the election of Bill Clinton in 1992, followed by the Republican takeover of Congress in 1994, and the reelection of both in 1996, presidential-congressional relations have been anything but dull. A variant of divided government—Democratic president/Republican Congress—unimaginable only a decade before, has provided new opportunities to examine the conventional wisdom about national policymaking. Not in the modern era has a Congress attempted to lead national government as much as the 104th Congress did in 1995–1996. Yet Clinton's political revival only a year later reminds us as political scientists to avoid the pundits' instant analysis and to look systematically for long-term forces and trends.

Several major themes of *The President and Congress: Collaboration and Combat in National Policymaking* seem even more evident since the publication of our earlier book *Congress and the President: The Policy Connection*. First, the presidency-centered approach to the subject, focusing on the president as the main initiator in policymaking, simply does not reflect reality today. The tandem institutions or separationist perspective, viewing Congress and the president as coequal partners, is much closer to reflecting the way policies are made. Second, it is more evident than ever that no single pattern characterizes presidential-congressional policymaking. The 1990s have witnessed presidential leadership on trade, congressional leadership on cutting taxes, consensus on banning gay marriages, cooperation over welfare reform, and deadlock over health care reform and campaign finance reform. Third, while we continue to believe that divided or unified party control of government matters in many important ways, it neither precludes nor ensures effective policymaking. President Clinton forced a tough deficit-reduction package through Congress without getting a single Republican vote under unified party control in the 103rd

Congress. He won a major victory on NAFTA later in the year, with most of the support coming from Republicans. But the next year, despite Democratic majorities, the Health Security Act—the crown jewel of the first term—failed to even come to a vote. Conversely, under divided government, Clinton and the Republican Congress collaborated over welfare reform and a balanced budget agreement but also engaged in brutal interbranch combat over Medicare, campaign finance, and presidential appointments.

Although the four patterns of presidential-congressional policymaking we identify are still based on which branch shapes policy and the degree of interbranch conflict, we have adopted the terms *presidential leadership* and *congressional leadership* instead of *presidential dominance* and *congressional dominance* that were used in our earlier work. So few occasions arise in national policymaking today where one branch is truly dominant over the other that it seemed more accurate to adopt that change. We include important research on Congress, the president, presidential-congressional relations, and divided government that has been published recently. Our analysis of Congress reflects the more centralized Republican House in 1995–1996 as well as the return to a more normal balance between leadership and committees after the Republicans maintained control in 1997–1999. Cases we include reflect the political and institutional changes that have taken place: same-sex marriage, the Helms-Burton Cuba Sanctions Act, the balanced budget standoff, welfare reform, and others.

In the earlier study, we noted that cases may fall on the boundary between two patterns and that reasonable analysts might disagree how a case should be classified. Based on comments from readers and our own discussions and reevaluation, we have reclassified the 1964 Civil Rights Act from the pattern of consensus to the pattern of presidential leadership. This reclassification also highlights that our goal is not to be able to make precise, definitive categorizations of cases of presidential-congressional policymaking. Rather, we seek to provide a means to examine cases comparatively, identify key variables and relationships, and make conclusions about why certain patterns of policymaking develop and what difference they make.

Nearly a decade after the fall of the Berlin wall and the end of the cold war, the balance of power between Congress and the president continues to evolve. Although the world remains dangerous, with less threat of nuclear annihilation the imperative for presidential leadership in foreign *or* domestic policy is diminishing. Public cynicism and the turn against government has affected both branches but has strengthened the hand of a Republican Congress that wants to devolve more power to the states. This has created near parity in institutional power. Whether collaboration or combat between branches occurs also depends on issues and ideology, short-term political and economic forces, and personal leadership skills in the different branches. We hope that the framework, cases, and analysis in this book will increase understanding of the fascinating and crucial policy relationship between the president and Congress.

ACKNOWLEDGMENTS

The President and Congress: Combat and Collaboration in National Policymaking is the result of a collaboration started in the early 1970s when we were graduate students at Ohio State working under Randall Ripley. We also shared the experience of watching combat in legislative-executive relations when we were Ohio Senate staffers: the Democratic leader banned the Democratic governor's lobbyist from the office and inflicted other indignities. Our collaboration progressed to a *Social Science Quarterly* article, a coedited book in the late 1970s, a *Journal of Politics* exchange, continued with *Congress and the President* in 1993, and culminates (for now) with this book. It has been a rewarding partnership, and we have managed to remain friends throughout.

Many people contributed to this project. We are grateful to Roger Davidson, Steve Smith, Bruce Evans, Donald Freeman, Janet Martin, David Kozak, Harvey Lieber, Conrad McBride, Keith Nichols, and Charles Tidloch for their helpful comments on our framework and approach. Research assistant David Murphy at Washington State University did an excellent job of researching new cases. Research assistants Randy Burnside and Fintan O'Brien at University of New Orleans also provided important help in updating material. Lisa Janowski at Washington State did a fantastic job in pulling the different parts of manuscript together and making it possible to make our deadline. Special thanks to Cynthia Avery and Diane Berger at Washington State, who also helped make it possible to complete the book. We are grateful to Allyn and Bacon for their commitment to the project, including editor-in-chief Paul Smith and his assistant Kathy Rubino, Bob Tonner, and Peg Markow. Finally, we thank our families and our wonderful wives for their love and support.

Lance T. LeLoup
Steven A. Shull

ABOUT THE AUTHORS

Lance T. LeLoup is Professor and Chair of the Department of Political Science at Washington State University. He is a leading authority on the federal budget, congressional-presidential relations, comparative legislative politics, and the relationship between institutions and policies in the United States and abroad. He is the author of *Budgetary Politics* (four editions), *Politics in America* (three editions), *The Fiscal Congress: Legislative Control of the Budget,* and *Congress and the President: The Policy Connection.* He has published numerous articles in scholarly journals, including *The American Political Science Review, Journal of Politics, Polity, Public Administration Review, Legislative Studies Quarterly, American Politics Quarterly, Social Science Quarterly, Public Budgeting and Finance,* and others. He was a Fulbright Senior Scholar at the Budapest University of Economics in 1995 and is currently engaged in research on the transformation of public budgeting in Central and Eastern Europe during the democratic transition. He and his wife Pam enjoy outdoor activities in the beautiful Pacific Northwest, Pac-10 sports, and cooking and wine tasting.

Steven A. Shull is Research Professor of Political Science at the University of New Orleans. He is the author of *Presidential-Congressional Relations: A Kinder, Gentler Racism?; Congress and the President; The President and Civil Rights Policy; Interrelated Concepts in Policy Research; Presidential Policy-Making;* and *Domestic Policy Formation* and is editor or co-editor of five volumes. His articles have appeared in the *Journal of Politics, Western Political Quarterly, Social Science Quarterly, Political Research Quarterly, American Politics Quarterly, Policy Studies Journal, Policy Studies Review, Social Science Journal, Legislative Studies Quarterly, Presidential Studies Quarterly,* and other journals and books. He has served on the editorial boards of *Presidential Studies Quarterly, American Review of Politics,* and *Southeastern Political Review* and was a Fulbright Professor at the Chinese University of Hong Kong. He edits a series of books for Garland Publishing on *Politics and Policy in American Institutions.* He won the University-wide career achievement award for excellence in research in 1986.

1

PATTERNS OF POLICYMAKING: COLLABORATION OR COMBAT?

I learned the hard way that there was no party loyalty or discipline when a complicated or controversial issue was at stake—none. Each legislator had to be wooed and won individually. It was every member for himself, and the devil take the hindmost! —JIMMY CARTER (1982)

INTRODUCTION

No relationship in American politics is more important. For 200 years, the connection between Congress and the president has helped steer the course of American public policy. The course has often been erratic, navigating obstacles created by the founders to ensure competition between executive and legislative branches. How effectively the president and Congress work together to make public policy—whether by the relative leadership of one branch over the other or through cooperation and compromise—has profound consequences. At stake are policies that affect economic prosperity, social justice, and the nation's role in the rapidly changing international arena.

The relationship between Congress and the president has many faces. It may reveal a consensus between branches and swift, concerted action. It may reflect cooperation, tough negotiation, and compromise. It may reflect presidential leadership of a reluctant Congress. It may reflect congressional leadership of the policy process with or without the support of the president. Or it may reveal pervasive stalemate grinding the processes of governing to a halt, requiring some extraordinary means to resolve deadlock over essential policy decisions. Patterns of interbranch relations have fascinated students of American politics for more than 200 years, and today they seem more complex than ever.

Relations between Congress and the president over the past decade present a study in these contrasting patterns. Although elected by a wide margin in the electoral college in the 1988 election, President George Bush faced strengthened Democratic majorities in the 101st Congress. Reacting to the divisiveness of the Reagan era and the knowledge that he faced a legislature with proportionately fewer party supporters than any incoming president in history, Bush called in his inaugural address for a new engagement between president and Congress.

> *We need compromise; we've had dissension. We need harmony; we've had a chorus of discordant voices. . . . We've seen the hard looks and heard the statements in which not each other's ideas are challenged, but each other's motives.*
>
> *When our fathers were young, Mr. Speaker, our differences ended at the water's edge. And we don't wish to turn back time, but when our mothers were young, Mr. Majority Leader, the Congress and the Executive were capable of working together to produce a budget on which this nation could live. Let us negotiate soon and hard, but in the end let us produce.*
>
> *The American people await action. They didn't send us here to bicker. They asked us to rise above the merely partisan, In crucial things unity— and this, my friends, is crucial.[1]*

Eight years later, President Bill Clinton also faced majorities of the other party in both houses of Congress and made a similar appeal:

> *The American people returned to office a president of one party and a Congress of another. Surely they did not do this to advance the politics of petty bickering and extreme partisanship they plainly deplore.*
>
> *No. They call on us instead to be repairers of the breach and to move on with America's mission. America demands and deserves big things from us, and nothing big ever came from being small.[2]*

But far from marking a new era of interbranch cooperation, the Bush and Clinton years were a virtual roller-coaster ride in legislative-executive relations. Only weeks into the Bush administration in 1989, his nominee to become Secretary of Defense, John Tower, was defeated in a Senate confirmation vote that capped a nasty partisan battle. Bush had the ignominious distinction of being the first president ever to not gain approval of an initial cabinet nominee. Nonetheless, a few months later, Bush and Congress reached agreement over two of the most divisive issues of the 1980s: aid to the Nicaraguan Contras and the federal budget. Six months later, however, the budget deal collapsed. In 1990, after a year of haggling over the deficit, a deal backed by both Bush and Democratic leaders was rebuked on the floor of the House. Despite Bush's promise of a "kinder, gentler nation," the president locked horns with Congress over social policy and civil rights as well, vetoing a family leave bill and a controversial civil rights bill.

President Bush's reversal of fortunes was swift and dramatic in 1991 as the United States led a coalition of international forces to expel Iraq from Kuwait. Reflecting continued uncertainties about the war-making power and the president's authority to wage war without legislative approval, the House and Senate debated the use of force in the Persian Gulf. While many Democrats wanted to wait for economic sanctions to work, in the end a majority in both houses authorized the president to use force. In just over forty days, a punishing air war and swift ground invasion produced a stunning military victory over Iraq and a euphoric nation. President Bush enjoyed unprecedented public approval ratings, as high as 90 percent. Yet once again, the pattern was short-lived. Only a year later, his popularity had plummeted, the economy headed into recession, and Bush faced sharp attacks from Congress and would be heading for defeat in the 1992 election.

Clinton's relations with Congress were similarly volatile. With unified party control of government in 1993–94 for the first time since the 1970s, the president convinced Democratic majorities to adopt a tough deficit-reduction package in 1993. But not a single Republican in the House or Senate voted for it. However, later that year, with more Republican votes than Democratic votes, Clinton successfully convinced Congress to pass the controversial North American Free Trade Agreement (NAFTA). After these two major victories and the highest back-to-back success rates on vote positions with Congress ever recorded, his major domestic initiative, comprehensive health care reform, ended in disaster. It not only failed to pass the Congress or even be brought to a vote, but also provided impetus for stunning Republican victories in the 1994 midterm elections.

For the first time in forty years, Republicans captured both houses of Congress, and divided government was the rule once more. Led by Republican House Speaker Newt Gingrich (R-Ga.) and his "Contract with America," the 104th Congress dominated the national agenda in 1995. But congressional ascendancy was short-lived as well. The bruising battle over balancing the budget resulted in government shutdowns, largely blamed on the Republicans. As the economy soared, Clinton successfully won reelection to a second term in 1996, while Republicans held on to slim majorities in the House and Senate. The president faced an aggressive Congress determined to investigate the White House on a range of potential scandals including campaign finance abuses, the Whitewater affair, and sexual harrassment.

How can we comprehend these rapidly changing patterns of policymaking and volatile institutional relationships? What do these sharply divergent trends at the close of the twentieth century mean for future policymaking and the governing of the country?

Today, no single, simple pattern characterizes presidential-congressional policymaking. The days when either the legislative or executive branch could consistently dominate policymaking across a wide range of issues are gone, if they ever truly existed. At any given point in time, depending on the problem and the political environment, different patterns of presidential-congressional policymaking occur. The goal of this book is to provide a framework for better understanding the various patterns that emerge. We will use that framework to analyze the factors that influence the way Congress and the president interact to make national policy—and more important, what difference it makes. Does "better" policy emerge from cooperation or conflict, presidential leadership or congressional leadership? To get a real-world understanding of the dynamics of the policy connection, we will analyze case studies of different patterns across various policy areas. To establish the context of the cases and their implications, we first explore constitutional foundations and the historical development of the presidency and the Congress. In this chapter, we develop a typology of legislative-executive policymaking and an explanatory framework encompassing the political environment, institutional capacity, leadership, and the nature of the policy agenda. We begin by considering various perspectives on legislative-executive relationships.

PERSPECTIVES ON LEGISLATIVE AND EXECUTIVE POWER

Constitutional Principles

The common starting point for studies of presidential-congressional policymaking is separation of powers—the division of executive, legislative, and judicial branches in the Constitution. It is perhaps the most prominent structural feature of American government. Yet the phrase *separation of powers* itself is misleading.[3] The Constitution intermingled powers between branches, overlapping responsibility for governing. It is more accurate to think of separation of powers, as Richard Neustadt has characterized it, as "separated institutions sharing powers."[4] This sharing of powers makes possible the related constitutional doctrine of checks and balances.

How one judges or evaluates separation of powers often depends on what purpose of government one deems most important: the protection of individual liberties, the representation of diverse interests, or the ability to make decisive, effective policy. The founders pursued several conflicting goals in creating a government for the United States. They wanted to devise a national government powerful enough to govern but not so powerful as to infringe on individual liberties and state prerogatives. Protecting liberty was foremost in the minds of the framers of the Constitution. Separate institutions sharing power would prevent tyranny by blocking the accumulation of political power by any one branch. This was accomplished by placing one institution in conflict and competition with the other. James Madison, the principal architect of the Constitution, described it in Federalist #51 as a system in which "ambition must be made to counteract ambition."[5]

This system of separation of powers is in contrast to parliamentary forms of government, where greater emphasis is placed on the ability to make policy. Parliamentary systems, such as in Great Britain or West Germany, are characterized by a fusion rather than a separation of powers. The executive head and cabinet members are drawn from the legislative majority; they have a common and shared political base.

Supported by principles of majority rule and party discipline, the prime minister and cabinet are virtually assured of the enactment of its program by the legislature. For example, British Prime Minister John Major and the Conservatives were able to continue to govern without losing a no-confidence vote, even when their majority was down to a single seat in 1996.

As the scope of government expanded and the institutional capacity of both Congress and the presidency increased, many concluded that, although the separation of powers protected liberty effectively, it often made governing more difficult. Critics of separation of powers, who often look longingly at parliamentary systems, became more vocal in the 1980s as institutional conflict and deadlock became more common.[6] However, parliamentary comparisons are of limited value in analyzing Congress and the president. The question of which branch leads government, appropriate in the American context, lacks relevance in parliamentary democracies. In parliamentary systems, the question of who leads government is answered by political parties and election results. In the United States, with elections that rarely produce clear mandates, the answer often depends on the balance of power between branches; partisan control of the House, Senate, and presidency; and attempts by the two branches to achieve policy objectives autonomously outside of the normal legislative process.

Congressionalist Perspectives

Throughout much of American history, the prevailing view recognized congressional supremacy. Congress, the "First Branch," was the source of legislation and policy leadership. The president's job was to make sure only that the laws were "faithfully executed." This perspective emphasizes a literal reading of the Constitution.[7] It stresses the Madisonian model of checks and balances and the representation of multiple interests and regions, a particular strength of the legislature. This "congressionalist," or literal, view distrusted presidential power and executive leadership and respected congressional prerogatives in taxing and spending, war-making, and domestic policy areas. John C. Calhoun in 1817 expressed the essence of the congressional primacy view: "Congress is responsible to the people immediately, and the other branches of Government are responsible to it."[8]

Does a congressionalist view have any relevance today? It does in several different ways. First, many members of Congress ardently defend their lawmaking prerogatives in the constitutional system. As Charles Jones observes, "A day hardly passes on Capitol Hill without a member expressing the theory of legislative primacy."[9] In recent decades, even members of Congress of the president's own party have not hesitated to challenge the president when they felt the institutional power of Congress was being illegitimately threatened. Second, a somewhat different congressionalist or Congress-centered view comes from recent research on presidential legislative success with Congress. As we will examine in more detail below, some recent studies have shown that the most important explanations of what happens to presidential proposals or positions have to do with the partisan and ideological composition of Congress rather than characteristics of the presidency.[10] That is to say, the outcomes of the legislative process are more a function of the composition of Congress than the president's popularity or margin of electoral victory.

Presidentialist Perspectives

As the policy agenda of government expanded in the twentieth century, perceptions of proper balance between legislature and executive shifted. Concern about the ability of government to solve problems quickly and effectively grew, with less emphasis on restricting majorities to protect liberty. Following the dramatic changes that occurred during the administration of Franklin D. Roosevelt, it appeared to many that the presidency was the institution most capable of providing policy leadership. A "presidentialist," or presidency-centered, view became more prevalent, including among scholars.[11] This perspective was reinforced by the institutionalization of the presidency, greatly expanding its capability in policymaking; by enhanced public expectations for presidential leadership; and by the weakening of political parties after World War II.[12] Presidents became less dependent on political parties for their election with the advent of television and the increased use of primaries and campaign advisers in presidential elections. Yet, at the same time, the weakening of party ties made it more difficult for presidents to build cohesive, sustainable legislative coalitions to support their ambitious agendas.

Serious questions about the potential dangers of presidential government emerged in the 1960s and 1970s in response to an unpopular war, presidential abuses and scandals, and impeachment proceedings against Richard Nixon in 1974.[13] Tension between branches escalated with growing congressional opposition to the War in Vietnam and reassertion of its constitutional prerogatives in foreign affairs. Institutional combat grew fiercer as President Nixon and Congress clashed over the president's impoundment of funds (that is, refusing to spend money appropriated by Congress) and control of the power of the purse. Congress responded by enacting the War Powers Resolution in 1973 and the Budget and Impoundment Control Act in 1974 to strengthen its capabilities in warmaking and budgeting. The Watergate scandal and perceived abuses of the executive branch led to impeachment proceedings and the subsequent resignation of Nixon.

Despite the reassessments of presidential power in the wake of the Johnson-Nixon era, the vast majority of studies of legislative-executive relations still focus on the president and his "success" with Congress. Most research starts with the president's legislative agenda and grades the effectiveness of the legislative process through a box score or other measure of presidential wins and losses. A significant literature exploring how to measure presidential legislative success has developed.[14] This presidency-centered perspective often emphasizes confrontation between branches, suggests that one branch gains power only at the expense of the other, grants permanent ascendancy to the presidency, and implies constitutional reforms that will strengthen the presidency.[15]

The Separationist or Tandem Institutions Perspective

In recent years, many scholars are taking a more balanced and neutral perspective on presidential-congressional power. Mark Petersen, attempting to develop a less distorted framework for examining policymaking in national government, describes Congress and the president as "tandem institutions constituting the major components of the national legislative decision-making system."[16] The notion of tandem institutions conveys the existence of a partnership in which both branches must engage if there is to be a response to policy issues. It diminishes the notion that the two branches are operating in a zero-sum power relationship and acknowledges that both branches have increased their scope and power in the twentieth century. The tandem institutions approach focuses on institutional capability and leadership in both branches, recognizing that policy initiatives may originate in either branch or through both branches simultaneously. Even a policy proposed in broad terms by the president may be largely shaped by the Congress or vice versa.

Jones makes a related set of arguments for a "separationist," rather than congressional or presidential, perspective:

> *Focusing exclusively on the presidency can lead to a seriously distorted picture of how the national government does its work. The plain fact is that the United States does not have a presidential system, it has a* separated *system. . . . I propose a separationist, diffused-responsibility perspective that I find more suited to the constitutional, institutional, political, and policy conditions associated with the American system of governing.* (Jones's emphasis)[17]

Jones believes that, at different periods of time, variations in the constitutional balance of power between branches have existed. He identifies four variations. *Congressional primacy* existed at the turn of the century and during the 1920s when the presidency was particularly weak. *Presidential primacy,* he argues, occurred during the Roosevelt (1930s) and Johnson (1960s) administrations. At other times the balance is more even; Jones calls this "mixed government" which can be cooperative or adversarial. *Mixed government-cooperative* characterized the first two years of the Eisenhower (1950s) and Reagan (1980s) administrations, while both turned to *mixed government-confrontational* in their last six years.[18] Recent work by Steven Shull has expanded the tandem institutions approach by analyzing four aspects of interbranch relations across policy areas and over time.[19] Even actions such as executive orders are conditioned on the broader environment including the president. In looking at a wide range of presidential-congressional interactions, evidence exists that a complex array of factors are necessary to explain outcomes.[20]

We believe that the more balanced tandem institutions/separationist perspective is essential for understanding the complex and changing ways in which Congress and the president interact to make policy today. Going a step further, we doubt it is possible to accurately characterize a two-year congressional or four-year presidential term as a single pattern of legislative-executive relations as Jones does. Certainly there are trends and general swings in the relationship. But at the same time that Congress and the president may be cooperating on balancing the budget, they may be in a confrontational battle over health care or abortion. We will see many such examples from recent years. The move away from the once-dominant presidency-centered approach toward a balanced perspective is particularly important in terms of expectations concerning divided party control of the presidency and Congress and how it affects policymaking.

DIVIDED GOVERNMENT

More than at any other time in U.S. history, elections are resulting in the presidency under the control of one party and the Congress under the control of the other party. This has occurred about two-thirds of the time since 1945.[21] As divided government has become more prevalent, it has been given a more prominent role in analyses of national policymaking. Much of the blame for government "deadlock," "stalemate," "gridlock," "paralyzing partisanship"—and the often combative, ill-tempered atmosphere between Congress and the president—goes to divided government. But recent research has shown that the conventional wisdom, at least in part, may be wrong. Even the nature of divided government is in flux. Before the 1990s, it looked like the Republicans had a lock on the presidency (winning five of six elections between 1968 and 1988) and that the Democrats had permanent control of the Congress (majorities in one or both houses between 1955 and 1995). But the events of the 1990s confounded those assumptions, and in 1996, a Democratic president was easily reelected to face the second straight Republican-controlled Congress. Table 1.1 examines divided government since 1900.

The primary cause of divided government is the weakening of voters' ties to the political parties and their willingness to split their tickets, voting for a candidate of one party for Congress and another for president. Divided government is also a trend in the states. Morris Fiorina has taken a careful look at the causes.[22] He was able to rule out some explanations such as an incumbency advantage for Democrats or intentional gerrymandering of districts to advantage one party or another. Still open is the question of whether divided government is accidental or chosen intentionally by voters. Fiorina has suggested that policy balancing may be taking place: voters feel more secure with the Democrats managing one branch to guarantee delivery of popular benefits, but with the Republicans in control of the other branch to ensure fiscally conservative management. Opinion polls have shown that as many as two-thirds of voters say they prefer divided government, lending some credence to this theory. In 1996, however, only 50 percent of respondents said they favored divided government, and more than 75 percent of voters chose a member of the House

TABLE 1.1   **Divided Government in the Twentieth Century**

President	Party	Congress		House Control	Senate Control
Taft	R	62nd	(1911–1913)	D	R
Wilson	D	66th	(1919–1921)	R	R
Hoover	R	72nd	(1931–1933)	D	R
Truman	D	80th	(1947–1949)	R	R
Eisenhower	R	84th	(1955–1957)	D	D
Eisenhower	R	85th	(1957–1959)	D	D
Eisenhower	R	86th	(1959–1961)	D	D
Nixon	R	91st	(1969–1971)	D	D
Nixon	R	92nd	(1971–1973)	D	D
Nixon	R	93rd	(1973–1974)	D	D
Ford	R	93rd	(1974–1975)	D	D
Ford	R	94th	(1975–1977)	D	D
Reagan	R	97th	(1981–1983)	D	R
Reagan	R	98th	(1983–1985)	D	R
Reagan	R	99th	(1985–1987)	D	R
Reagan	R	100th	(1987–1989)	D	D
Bush	R	101st	(1989–1991)	D	D
Bush	R	102nd	(1991–1993)	D	D
Clinton	D	104th	(1995–1997)	R	R
Clinton	D	105th	(1997–1999)	R	R

of Representatives and a presidential candidate of the *same* political party, the highest rate since 1952.[23]

Whatever the causes, many observers, particularly with a presidency-centered perspective, view divided government with great alarm. A century ago, Woodrow Wilson wrote, "If you want to release the force of the American people, you have got to get possession of the Senate and the presidency as well as the House."[24] More recently, James Sundquist observed that under divided government, "all of the normal difficulties of attaining harmonious and effective working relationships between branches are multiplied manifold."[25] Critics of divided government are particularly concerned that frequent deadlock will hamper the international competitiveness and health of the U.S. economy.

In the mid-1980s, frustration over big budget deficits and persistent conflicts between President Reagan and the Democratic Congress led to some serious efforts to propose constitutional reforms that would lessen the probability of divided government or to break deadlocks if they existed. The Committee on the Constitutional System, a blue ribbon panel of scholars and public officials, reported at the bicentennial of the Constitution that separation of powers and checks and balances had led to "government stalemate and deadlock, to indecision and inaction in the face of urgent problems."[26] One of the members, Lloyd Cutler, former counsel to President Jimmy Carter, argued that budget deficits tend to be much higher under divided government than under unified government. His broader concern is the basic structure of government that allows divided government to form:

> *In parliamentary terms, one might say that under the U.S. Constitution it is not now feasible to "form a government." The separation of powers between the legislative and executive branches, whatever its merits in 1793, has become a structure that almost guarantees stalemate today.*[27]

To prevent divided government or break deadlocks once they exist, the Committee proposed a number of dramatic constitutional amendments, such as electing the president, senators, and representatives on a single ballot; allowing the president to dissolve Congress; or giving Congress the right to give the president a vote of no confidence and force new elections. But is divided government as detrimental to policymaking as critics claim?

The most significant challenge to critics of divided government comes from David Mayhew's study, *Divided We Govern.*[28] In a comprehensive study of major legislation and congressional investigations between 1947 and 1990, Mayhew concluded that divided control has not made a difference in whether important policies are enacted or high-publicity investigations are pursued. Using both contemporary judgments and retrospective judgments by policy experts, Mayhew arrived at a list of 267 important postwar enactments. Comparing across periods of unified and divided government, the results do not seem to indicate meaningful differences in legislative output. Mayhew's study shows that divided government does not inevitably lead to deadlock or preclude policy enactment and has helped turn attention toward evidence more than rhetoric.

This is not to say that divided government is unimportant, however. While Mayhew's analysis adds empirical documentation to the debate over divided government, it is not the final word on the subject. A study by Sean Kelley using a more stringent definition of important legislation found that, in fact, divided government did produce less key legislation.[29] He also found greater conflict on roll call votes under divided government. Mayhew's study also measured only the supply of legislation, not the demand for legislation, so we cannot be certain that divided government, indeed, did not prevent certain major legislative initiatives from being enacted. Other scholars have found that divided government increases the level of institutional conflict between branches.[30] The content of legislation—whether it proved to be good or bad policy—is also not tested by Mayhew's study. One recent study comparing policy content and results concluded that divided government inhibited the executive's ability to conduct free trade policy.[31]

While divided government does not always paralyze policymaking as the constitutional critics claim, it does make a difference in some cases. First, divided government affects the nature of the policy bargaining and hence, the content of legislation. For example, the bipartisan deficit reduction agreements in 1990 and 1997 were very different in terms of the balance of tax increases and spending cuts from the Democratic deficit-reduction plan adopted under unified government in 1993. Second, it appears that divided government has led to greater reliance on extraordinary means of resolving deadlocks, outside the normal procedures of the legislative process. The increased use of bipartisan commissions and interbranch summits is an example. Benjamin Ginsberg and Martin Shefler argue that as national elections increasingly fail to provide coherent governing coalitions, both branches resort to "politics by other means" to influence policy. They argue that growing institutional combat has disrupted the system of shared powers and led politicians to attempt to establish the sovereignty of their respective branches in other ways. They cite growing numbers of examples in which, because of deadlock in the normal legislative process, steps were taken by each branch to circumvent the other.[32] Finally, the extraordinary amount of investigatory activity directed against the White House by the 104th and 105th Congresses under Republican control suggests that Mayhew's earlier findings may need to be updated.

The separationist, tandem-institutions perspective by its very nature embraces a more open-minded approach to divided government. In other words, it simply cannot be assumed *a priori* that divided party control precludes effective policymaking. Since separate elections for Congress and the president so frequently produce different results, policymaking patterns under divided government must not be considered aberrations of the ideal. Yet party and varieties of partisanship remain critical for analyzing presidential-congressional relations. Charles Jones writes, "Rather than expect political party to overcome the constitutional division of the executive and legislative branches, one may anticipate that party will function within its presidential or congressional context to facilitate the functions of each institution." He continues, "Assorted patterns of partisan interaction may be expected, even when there is unified government."[33] Jones identifies several kinds of party interaction that will be useful for our analysis. *Partisanship* is generally the case when both parties are unified and in opposition to each other. *Bipartisanship* is the situation in which divisions on the resolution of an issue do not fall along party lines and members of both parties generally work together. *Cross-partisanship* occurs when the parties are still generally divided but enough members of one party cross over to the other party on an issue to ensure a majority. As we will see in the cases, divided government or unified government is important, but it does not in itself dictate any one particular kind of interaction between the parties or the branches.

EXAMINING POLICYMAKING

Policy Approaches

Given the various perspectives on legislative and executive power and the role of divided government, how do we examine the relationship between Congress and the president? In addition to adopting the separationist, tandem-institutions perspective, we use a public-policy approach, analyze a number of policy cases, and develop a framework to help compare and assess different patterns. Policymaking in national government can be seen as a sequence proceeding from agenda-setting, formulation, and adoption, to implementation and results.[34] With a policy approach, we emphasize not only the process of making decisions, but also the substantive choices themselves, making comparisons across policy arenas. There are any number of ways to categorize policies, from a simple foreign policy–domestic policy dichotomy, to very specific issues such as monetary or water resources policy. We compare four broad policy areas: foreign and defense policy, civil rights policy, economic and budget policy, and social welfare policy. While any set of categories is necessarily arbitrary, evidence supports the importance of these issues on both the presidential and congressional policy agendas in the modern era.[35]

Complementing the policy focus is the use of case studies, which allows us to explore a diversity of patterns without attempting to choose a sample that is representative or typical. Despite the old adage that the plural of "case study" is "data," case studies have sometimes been maligned in political science as insufficient for theory building. However, we believe multiple case studies analyzed systematically not only provide significant pedagogical contributions but also can contribute to increases in cumulative knowledge.[36] We use the case studies to examine a series of explanatory factors, patterns of policymaking, and policy outcomes. To foster comparability, the sixteen cases focus on legislation as opposed to appointments, investigations, oversight, or other forms of presidential-congressional interaction.

Dimensions of Policymaking Relationships

In deciding how to categorize presidential-congressional relations, there are many possible dimensions to consider. More than 105 Congresses and forty-two presidents have managed to engage in nearly every conceivable kind of political relationship over the past two centuries. Relations have ranged from the aggressive post–Civil War Congress that nearly drove Andrew Johnson from office because he opposed its radical agenda, to the quiescent Democratic majorities anxious to be led out of the Great Depression by Franklin D. Roosevelt. Between these extremes lies a wide range of political patterns. Many variables can be used to describe legislative-executive interaction, but two dimensions of policymaking seem particularly useful: one describing the level of conflict over a policy issue between legislative and executive branches and the second indicating to what extent the content of policy was shaped in the legislative or executive branch.

How Much Interbranch Conflict?

In sharing power and responsibility for making national policy, relations between Congress and the president range from consensus and close cooperation to open political warfare. Interbranch conflict can vary along a continuum from little or no conflict to moderate levels of conflict to extreme conflict. Divisions between the two branches may stem from a variety of factors. In some cases, the conflict is institutional, based on protecting constitutional prerogatives, disagreement about the proper role of each, and a perception that the relationship between branches is out of balance.[37] This was particularly true during the Watergate era. In many cases, particularly under divided government, the conflict is partisan, springing from ideological differences, disagreements over policy, and the desire to gain electoral advantage over the opposing party. Because Congress rarely speaks with one voice, we are looking at conflict between the presidency and various substantial factions in the House and Senate. Whatever its source, the level of conflict between the White House and Capitol Hill plays a major role in determining the pattern of policymaking that emerges.

Which Branch Shapes Policy?

Consistent with the view that both branches are more or less equal partners in the policymaking process, the second dimension concerns the relative impact of each branch on policy decisions. This, too, can be conceptualized as a continuum ranging from cases where the presidency and executive branch determines the content of policy, to cases where both branches are approximately of equal importance in shaping policy, to cases where Congress largely determines the result. Many factors affect which branch has more influence in framing issues and affecting outcomes. In some instances it reflects the relative salience of different issues for Congress compared to the president. The president may simply not care about some issues of great concern to legislators and is content to let Congress do as it pleases. Presidents often defer to Congress on many pork-barrel bills, for example, recognizing that the political costs of interference may far outweigh the benefits. Conversely, Congress may care little about certain presidential initiatives or fear the consequences of opposition and therefore acquiesce to the Chief Executive. One branch may defer to the other on legal or constitutional grounds, acknowledging greater legitimacy to act on the part of the other branch. Congressional deference to presidents in the area of foreign policy was common from the 1940s to the late 1960s. Finally, which branch shapes policy is often determined on the basis of power politics: can the president exercise the muscle to ram an initiative through Congress, or can Congress gather the two-thirds majority needed to override a presidential veto? Between the extremes are the more common cases of shared policymaking in which each side wins some and loses some in the political process.

Patterns of Policymaking

Combining these two dimensions across a vertical and a horizontal axis makes it possible to create a typology of policymaking patterns. Of course, we are not suggesting that it is possible to locate points (policy cases) along each continuum with precision. We can, however, make some rough comparative assessments of where a case falls within the two-dimensional space. Dividing the space into four quadrants, we suggest a typology of four general patterns, as illustrated by Figure 1.1. The four patterns are presidential leadership, congressional leadership, consensus/cooperation,

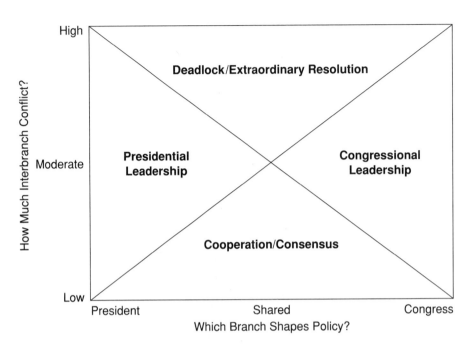

FIGURE 1.1   **Patterns of Presidential-Congressional Policymaking.**

and deadlock/extraordinary resolution. We mean leadership in the context of a shared policymaking relationship: one branch has a greater role in shaping the policy result in a particular case than the other branch. Other scholars refer to essentially the same phenomenon as presidential or congressional "primacy" or "ascendancy."[38] Here, however, we are categorizing individual bills and laws, not entire sessions or time periods. Below, we describe the general characteristics of each pattern. Note, however, that considerable distance can exist between two cases within the same quadrant and close proximity between two cases in different quadrants. We will therefore analyze and compare cases both between different patterns and within the same patterns.

Presidential Leadership

Policymaking shaped more by the president than Congress characterizes presidential leadership. This pattern reflects the presidency-centered view that has prevailed since the era of Franklin D. Roosevelt. It is marked by the executive providing direction and leadership with Congress sharing some part of shaping policy or largely following behind. Presidents can lead policymaking in a highly conflictual environment if they have sufficient power or resources; at the other extreme, presidential leadership can occur where there is relatively little interest or opposition from Congress. Presidential leadership can be partisan if the president controls working majorities in both houses of Congress, cross-partisan if he can attract enough defectors of the other party to win, or bipartisan if a significant number of members of both parties are willing to follow the president. As the figure suggests, moving up the vertical axis as conflict increases, presidential leadership becomes less likely and deadlock becomes more probable. Conversely, at low levels of conflict, the legislation is more likely to fit the pattern of cooperation/consensus than presidential leadership.

Historically, presidential leadership has tended to occur in times of national crisis such as the Civil War when President Lincoln, without the formal approval of Congress, established a draft, appropriated monies, blockaded southern ports, and suspended the writ of habeas corpus. In the 1930s, the economic crisis of the Great Depression, with 25 percent unemployment, widespread bank failures, and pervasive hunger and homelessness, created an environment that invited presidential leadership for awhile. In President Roosevelt's first few days in office, congressional leaders demanded action on legislation that had been submitted only hours earlier. "Vote!" one member exclaimed. "The house is burning down and the President of the United States says this is the way to put out the fire!"[39]

Today, presidential leadership, when it takes place, is much more fleeting and contingent, displaying different kinds of party divisions. President Reagan was successful in getting his controversial economic and budget package in 1981 because of Democratic defections in the House, a pattern of cross-partisanship. President Bush was able to convince a skeptical Democratic Congress to approve the use of force in the Gulf War, also a cross-partisan division. President Clinton was able to pass a tough deficit-reduction plan in 1993, despite unpopular large tax increases, in a partisan vote. Presidential leadership can also occur in less public and controversial cases.

Congressional Leadership

Policymaking shaped more by Congress than the president, either with the cooperation of or over the objections of the president, characterizes the pattern of congressional leadership. As with presidential leadership, the boundaries in Figure 1.1 suggest that as interbranch conflict increases, the possibility of congressional leadership is reduced and the possibility of deadlock enhanced. Conversely, at low levels of conflict, the pattern is more likely to be one of consensus or cooperation. Perhaps the clearest examples of congressional leadership are when both houses override a presidential veto, as the Democratic Congress did to President Reagan with the Civil Rights Restoration Act in 1988 and the Republican Congress did to President Clinton with the shareholders lawsuit bill in 1995. Congressional leadership may be partisan, particularly under divided government. In the case of overriding presidential vetoes, however, whether under unified or divided government, congressional leadership is usually cross-partisan because one party rarely enjoys a two-thirds majority. Or, congressional leadership may be genuinely bipartisan if interbranch conflict is institutional or constitutional, such as with the enactment of the War Powers Resolution in 1973 and the Budget and Impoundment Control Act in 1974 over President Nixon's opposition. At moderate levels of conflict, and with some policy participation from the executive, Congress may still have an edge in determining the content of certain policies.

In the Republic's first century, congressional leadership was the norm for long periods of time, punctuated only briefly by assertions of presidential authority. The post–Civil War Congress that impeached and nearly removed Andrew Johnson was clearly dominant in most instances. Congress continued to lead policymaking in most areas through the late nineteenth century, although it was much more difficult when opposed by the president. President Grover Cleveland vetoed 583 measures during his two terms in the White House in his attempt to block certain congressional actions.

Even in the modern era, with more focus on the presidency, Congress has frequently played a leading role in making domestic policy. Congress led in expanding civil rights and has been influential in shaping economic policy and social welfare policy. In the 1970s, Congress was the force behind the enactment of a number of laws to protect the environment, such as the Clean Air Act and the Water Pollution Control Act. During the Reagan era, a bipartisan coalition of congressional Republicans and Democrats both wrote and enacted comprehensive trade legislation in 1988. While the trade bill could not have become law without the participation and support of the Reagan administration, it was a congressional initiative largely shaped on Capitol Hill.

Cooperation/Consensus

The third pattern of executive-legislative policymaking is marked by moderate or low levels of conflict or the more effective management of conflict. Consensus occurs when opposition in either branch is unorganized, co-opted by informal agreements, or with "motherhood and apple pie" issues where no real disagreement exists.[40] Either branch may play a leading role in formulating the policy or it may be equally shared, but lack of substantial organized opposition is the common characteristic. Important policy innovations can emerge from consensus, such as the National Aeronautics and Space Act of 1958, a reaction to the Soviet Union's successful launching of Sputnik the previous year. Both the Eisenhower administration and congressional leaders helped formulate and enact the space program. More frequently, consensus occurs with more symbolic or less important policy issues.

Cooperation differs from consensus in terms of higher political stakes, more substantial and organized opposition, and higher levels of conflict. Compromise, where neither side gets exactly what it wants, is the common denominator of cases falling in this quadrant. Although bargaining and compromise take place in virtually all cases of presidential-congressional policymaking, it is often more dramatic here, with sides moving significantly from their original positions. While many of the policy conflicts in this pattern reflect ideological or partisan cleavages, cross-partisanship and bipartisanship is the norm. Techniques to moderate conflict and create the basis for reaching compromise are frequently employed including prior consultation and negotiation. Some measures—such as money bills where differences can be split—

are more conducive to cooperation than either/or choices such as school prayer or abortion. While one branch may play a greater role in shaping policy, in most cases both branches work together to formulate and enact public policy.

The enactment of the sweeping Clean Air Act Amendments in 1990 is an example of the cooperation pattern of presidential-congressional policymaking. Although there were sharp differences in positions and competing environmental and economic interests, a commitment was made by both branches to see the process through. While much of the detailed legislating and brokering of the act took place in Congress, it could not move forward without the support and leadership of the president. The legislative process in Congress, from initial consideration through the adoption of a conference report, included consultation with administration officials and a number of closed sessions to facilitate resolution of differences. Cooperation can characterize policymaking in foreign policy as well as domestic affairs. Free trade treaties, most favored nation status, foreign aid, and choices of weapons systems are often settled by constructive negotiation and compromise.

Deadlock/Extraordinary Resolution

The final pattern is characterized by the inability to resolve a policy dispute, or the use of unusual means outside the normal legislative process to break an impasse. Deadlock is the most troubling pattern to students of national policymaking. It is sometimes characterized by political brinkmanship and results in government paralysis, often in the face of urgent problems. The term *political gridlock* became popular in the 1980s as recurrent interbranch conflicts captured the headlines. Yet significant variation can exist within the general pattern as with the other three. As the name implies, this pattern encompasses two distinct phenomena. The first is deadlock: a breakdown of the normal policy process, leading to inaction. This may reflect Congress not acting on or defeating a presidential initiative. It may reflect a presidential veto of congressional legislation in which majorities are insufficient to override. Many proposals remain deadlocked for years because of consistent and concerted opposition in Congress or the White House. Welfare reform was largely deadlocked for decades until 1996 when Clinton and Republican leaders reached an agreement. Partisan disagreement over campaign finance reform, even despite the fundraising scandals of the 1996 elections, has led to a continuing stalemate that goes back to the 1970s.

But some policies, unlike campaign finance or welfare reform, simply cannot remain deadlocked. The inability to resolve differences through normal governing processes can pose severe risks for the nation. The government cannot function without a budget no matter how divergent Republican and Democratic priorities on taxing and spending. The Social Security system cannot be allowed to go bankrupt. It is unthinkable that the federal government default on insurance programs guaranteeing deposits in banks and savings and loans, leaving millions of Americans without their life savings. Such situations characterize the second component of this pattern: extraordinary resolution.

Extraordinary resolution of policy deadlocks is often forced by the imperative nature of the decision. Under these circumstances, Congress and the president look to alternative means or "ad hoc arrangements" to break the stalemate.[41] Summits between leaders of both branches were increasingly employed to resolve divisive budget issues in the 1980s and the 1990s. Bipartisan commissions, with members appointed by the president and congressional leaders, have been created to break deadlocks over contentious issues such as the Social Security system and the closing of military bases. Other forms of extraordinary resolution of policy deadlock include "automatic devices," such as the Gramm-Rudman-Hollings law, which tried to force across-the-board budget cuts if Congress and the president were unable to reach designated deficit targets.[42] When the executive-legislative partnership proves incapable of resolving policy conflict through the normal processes, and deadlock poses unacceptable dangers to the nation, Congress and the president have resorted to extraordinary means to resolve their differences.

Causes and Consequences

The policy connection between Congress and the president over two centuries reflects many variations of these four patterns. The experience of Presidents Bush and Clinton indicate that patterns can change quickly and vary across policies. We believe that the typology provides a useful tool for analysis and comparison, but categorizing complex and multidimensional cases is often difficult. For example, both the Family Leave Act and Motor Voter law passed in 1993 shortly after President Clinton took office. They were legislative priorities for the president. Presidential leadership? Not really. Both had been written in Congress, were important congressional priorities for many years, and had been passed by majorities in both houses but vetoed by the previous president. Some cases may fall between categories, whereas over time other cases may change patterns. Deadlock can become cooperation because of an election, a world event, or other significant change in the environment. Yet many cases share characteristics with other cases. The objective is not to pigeonhole each case but to identify similarities and compare differences to really understand the dynamics of policymaking.

That leaves two essential questions to explore: Why and under what conditions does a case of policymaking fall into one of these four patterns? What difference does it make? Research on legislative-executive relations suggests a number of factors that seem to be important in shaping the way Congress and the president make policy together. Some reflect characteristics of the presidency, some reflect characteristics of Congress, and some are external to both. First, the manner in which Congress and the president legislate together depends on the *political environment,* such as the state of the economy or world events. In addition, elections, the resulting majorities in Congress, and the existence of unified or divided government affect the prevalent pattern of policymaking. Second, decision-making *institutions* in both branches, the ability to formulate and enact policy, is also an important factor. Congressional leadership of policymaking is unlikely, for example, if the institution is constrained by procedural and organizational obstacles. Third, the personal *leadership* skills of the president and congressional leaders are often cited as critical factors in determining policymaking patterns. Fourth, scholars have suggested that *policy agenda* itself affects patterns of presidential-congressional interaction. Certain policies may be more conducive to presidential leadership while others are more conducive to congressional leadership.

What difference do the patterns make? The second crucial question to be explored concerns consequences associated with particular policymaking patterns. This requires identifying characteristics of policies and criteria for judging "good policy." For example, are policies resulting from a dominant president more coherent and timely than policies dominated by Congress? Does a pattern of congressional leadership result in policies representative of more diverse interests and distributing benefits more widely? Are policies adopted through a pattern of consensus or compromise more or less effective than policies that emerge from extraordinary means of resolution? What are the consequences of inaction or deadlock? Figure 1.2 summarizes our analysis of presidential-congressional policymaking from determinants, to patterns, to consequences.

DETERMINANTS OF POLICYMAKING PATTERNS

The Political Environment

The state of the nation, the state of the world, public expectations, and partisan control of government are among the many factors that help define parameters for policymaking and shape presidential-congressional relations.

Public Demand or Expectations for Change

At certain junctures in history, the political environment is conducive to change, such as the periods following the election of Presidents Roosevelt, Johnson, and Reagan. Yet "mandates" for change are elusive and must be translated through the political

Determinants	Patterns of Policymaking		Consequences
Political environment Institutional capability Personal leadership Policy agenda	Presidential leadership Congressional leadership Consensus/cooperation Deadlock/extraordinary resolution		Policy characteristics Policy results and impact

FIGURE 1.2 Presidential-Congressional Policymaking.

process. At other times, the public seems content with the status quo and seeks stability. Some scholars have attempted to discern broader patterns in public expectations for leadership. Arthur Schlesinger, Jr., James David Barber, and James Sundquist all suggest that American political history unfolds in cycles.[43] Schlesinger and Barber argue that public expectations shift from demands for dramatic departures from the past, to a period of consolidation, to a period of reaction and retrenchment. Sundquist emphasizes the existence of particular cycles in presidential-congressional relations. Most studies suggest that the greater the expectations for change, the more dominant the president will be. Conversely, the greater the public desire for consolidation, the greater will be the influence of Congress and the more constraints the president will encounter. Although the evidence supporting the existence of cycles is ambiguous, changes in public expectations clearly can affect patterns of policymaking.

Congressional Elections and Resulting Majorities

Despite national elections being less decisive in setting the direction of U.S. public policy than in parliamentary systems, they remain a crucial element of the political environment. Election results shape the context for presidential-congressional policymaking by establishing partisan majorities in Congress. Based on extensive empirical research, Jon Bond and Richard Fleisher concluded that the size of congressional majorities was the single most important factor in determining a president's success in getting programs adopted by Congress.[44] They found that the president's legislative success is determined by the extent to which the president and members of Congress share policy preferences resulting from the previous election.[45]

Presidents are more likely to have legislative success with unified government than with divided government. This has been particularly true since the early 1980s with the increase in party voting in Congress. Reagan and Bush lost more often than they won. Clinton, on the other hand, had a much higher level of success in Congress in his first two years with a Democratic Congress than in the years following the Republican takeover.[46]

The President's Ability to Claim an Electoral Mandate

Election results also create the basis for a president to claim a mandate. Leverage with Congress is greater for presidents elected by a landslide—Johnson and Reagan, for example—than for presidents elected by a narrow margin—Kennedy and Carter, for example. Reflecting on the political resources gained through landslide elections, one observer suggested:

> *You ought to think of the presidency as an engine. Each president enters office facing the same model—the horse-power is generally stable and the gears are all there. What differs is the fuel. Different presidents enter with different fuel. Lyndon Johnson entered office with a full tank, while Ford entered on empty.*[47]

Presidential Popularity

Using public opinion data and congressional roll call voting patterns, a number of studies have concluded that presidential popularity correlates with increased voting support from members of Congress.[48] During war, the public tends to "rally around the flag," boosting approval of the president and enhancing his influence. The president's popularity tends to increase when the United States is involved in some military action or national security crisis. Following the decisive victory over Iraq, President Bush's public approval ratings were the highest ever recorded. Research has shown, however, that the boost to popularity is often short-lived and does not necessarily translate into increased domestic success. More enduring is the link between the state of the economy and public approval of the president.[49] Inflation, unemployment, and poor economic performance damages public approval ratings. Eisenhower, Reagan, and Bush—all popular presidents—saw their approval ratings bottom out around the time unemployment peaked. How much presidential popularity affects success in Congress has been increasingly challenged by empirical research that suggests the impact is marginal at best.[50]

Public Approval of Congress

Public approval usually has less effect on Congress because of the divergence between public assessments of individual members and the institution as a whole. Except for the period following Watergate and the impeachment proceedings against Richard Nixon in 1974, public approval of Congress has remained low. But as measured by incumbent reelection rates of more than 90 percent, individual members enjoy strong public support. Many members foster this situation by disparaging Congress in their campaigns, in effect running against their own institution. The popularity of incumbents minimizes some of the negative consequences of low approval ratings for the institution and can insulate legislators from a popular president. Even Congress may benefit from the rally-around-the-flag phenomenon. Despite some criticism of members of Congress who initially opposed the use of force, Congress enjoyed higher approval ratings in the wake of the popular Persian Gulf war. The Republican takeover of Congress in 1995 suggests that public support can affect congressional agenda-setting and success. Speaker Gingrich and the Republicans were much more aggressive initially when they enjoyed higher public support than they were in 1996 following the budget deadlock and government shutdowns largely blamed on them.

Mass Media and Interest Groups

The mass media and interest groups are also important components of the political environment. On one hand, presidents attempt to use the media to their own advantage. Using the strategy of "going directly to the people over the heads of Congress," presidents use televised appeals, news conferences, and major addresses to mobilize public pressure on Congress to support the president's program.[51] On the other hand, presidents often see the media as the enemy that is lying in wait for any error or weakness. The media played a major role in the downfall of Richard Nixon. President Clinton turned the tables on adverse media coverage in early 1998. Despite the media engaging in a "feeding frenzy" over his alleged relationship with White House intern Monica Lewinsky, his approval ratings rose to over 75 percent, the highest of his presidency. Congress is more difficult for the media to cover; no single personality can be focused on to dramatize the institution. The legislative process is complicated and often difficult to portray accurately in short broadcasts. Members of Congress also attempt to use the media to their advantage through leaks, off-the-record interviews, and press conferences. For both institutions, the media play an important role in agenda-setting and in creating a context of public expectations about critical issues.

Interest groups have influenced interbranch relations for two centuries and continue to be an important factor. Both branches respond to interest-group pressure and attempt to use groups to build political support.[52] Members of Congress are subject to lobbying and depend on political action committees (PACs) for much of their campaign funding. Presidents claim to be more insulated from interest-group pressure, but it simply may be less visible. Just as Jimmy Carter responded to pressure from organized labor to support pro-labor legislation, George Bush reacted to pressure from business groups in opposing family leave bills and other legislation.

Institutional Capability

The political environment establishes a context for policymaking, but the actual formulation, adoption, and implementation of policy depends on the institutions of national government and how effectively they work. Institutions can be both formal, such as legislative committees or an executive budget process, or informal, such as congressional norms. Institutions and processes help shape individual behavior and collective policy choices. From a public policy perspective, institutional capability refers to capacity to function effectively, to reach decisions and carry them out.[53]

Congressional Institutions

The key question for congressional institutions is how the internal organization, written and unwritten rules and processes, and the distribution of power within the House and Senate affect its ability to legislate and work with the president. As Congress became modernized at the beginning of the twentieth century, many key institutions developed: a stable committee system, party leadership organizations, the seniority system, and other behavioral norms. The degree of centralization/fragmentation of power among members has important consequences for Congress's ability to enact policy as well as the president's ability to lead Congress. It is difficult to build stable coalitions in a highly decentralized, fragmented legislature. A more centralized Congress with powerful leaders is no easier for a president to lead and is generally better able to compete with the president in the policy process.

The distribution of power and institutional capability in Congress has been fluid over the years. In the 1880s, Woodrow Wilson lamented the "impervious authority" of standing committees which decentralized the legislative process.[54] By 1910, power in the House of Representatives had become so centralized that the rank and file revolted against the Speaker, stripping him of many duties and responsibilities. A period of strong committee chairmen characterized Congress from the 1930s to the mid-1960s. Dominance by southern Democrats and midwestern Republicans, according to Roger Davidson, sometimes created "a hostile environment for activist presidents and their ambitious legislative agendas."[55] Beginning in the late 1960s, power in Congress became more fragmented, ushering in an era of "subcommittee" government.[56] By the 1980s, as interbranch conflict intensified, Congress became more centralized through changes in the budget process, more powerful leaders, and the rise of a new "committee oligarchy."[57] This increased the capability of Congress to challenge the president and affected patterns of national policymaking.

Presidential Institutions

The development of presidential institutions enhanced the power of the president and his relations with Congress. Much of the "institutionalized presidency" emerged in the 1940s, increasing the ability of the president to initiate policy, respond to crises, and manage government. The set of permanent institutions in the Executive Office of the President and the White House staff remain important elements in policy-making relationships with Congress. How effectively presidents utilize this "state apparatus" affects an administration's effectiveness in national policymaking.[58] When institutional performance has suffered, reform and restructuring has often taken place. For example, Kennedy reacted to Eisenhower's formal, hierarchical decision-making style with a more wide-open, fluid style. Bush responded to Reagan's detached management style with a more hands-on approach. The president's Office of Legislative Affairs, developed during the Eisenhower and Kennedy years, is particularly important in determining how well the president's agenda is treated on Capitol Hill.[59]

Institutions outside the presidency and Congress can also be important to the policy process. The huge federal bureaucracy is important to both presidency and legislature as a means of achieving policy objectives. The federal courts and particularly the U.S. Supreme Court affect presidential-congressional relations. Court decisions in areas such as abortion, civil rights, and school prayer help shape the policy agenda. The Court also may act as a final arbiter in constitutional disputes between legislative and executive branches and has continued to define the boundaries of separation of powers. The role of the Court in this capacity is explored in Chapter 2.

Personal Leadership

Presidents

Many studies of presidential-congressional relations, particularly those from the presidency-centered perspective, focus on the importance of individual leadership. Social scientists disagree about the importance of leadership in the overall policy-making equation. Many argue that environmental and institutional factors are more critical, but the style, personality, and skills of the president continue to attract attention.[60] For example, some attribute Ronald Reagan's initial legislative success and sustained popularity to personal charisma: that he was more "presidential" and had more "royal jelly" than his predecessor, Jimmy Carter.[61]

Attempts have been made to conceptualize presidential personality and leadership skills. Perhaps best known is James David Barber's fourfold scheme based on style and character to explain presidential performance.[62] Other studies focus on the personal skills needed to succeed, such as selling and management abilities, rather than psychological attributes.[63] Empirical evidence about the effects of presidential leadership skills is mixed. Several studies of roll-call voting have concluded that personal leadership skills have only a slight effect on how members of Congress vote.[64] Personal leadership may be reflected in ways other than final floor votes, however. A skillful president may be able to manage an ambitious agenda and make strategic decisions before bills reach the floor.[65]

Timing is also thought to be important to the effectiveness of individual leadership, although it may have contrary effects. The notion of a presidential "honeymoon" with Congress is widely accepted and premised on the belief that a president has a limited pool of "political capital" on which to draw. James Pfiffner has written of the need for presidents to "hit the ground running." [66] Paul Light argues that presidents must "move it or lose it"; to push the legislative agenda with Congress quickly before their influence is reduced.[67] Lyndon Johnson alluded to this phenomenon after his landslide election over Barry Goldwater in 1964:

> *I was just elected president by the biggest popular margin in the history of the country—16 million votes. Just by the way people naturally think and because Barry Goldwater simply scared the hell out of them, I've already lost about three of those sixteen. After a fight with Congress or anything else, I'll lose another couple of million. I could be down to 8 million in a couple of months.*[68]

Countering this cycle of decreasing influence is the view that delay can help the president because of increasing skill and competence. Kennedy and Bush did not launch major legislative initiatives until they had been in office for some time, and Jimmy Carter had more success in his second year than his first. One study concluded that presidents were no more successful with Congress early in their tenure than later and that the stage of a president's term did not matter.[69] The policy cases in subsequent chapters help shed some light on the question of leadership and timing.

Research provides limited evidence, at best, to support the relationship between a president's personal leadership skills and legislative success. One study found that presidents were slightly more successful when journalists reported favorably about their legislative skills.[70] Another study found evidence of presidential leadership skills influencing support between initial consideration and the final approval of a bill.[71] One scholar found that the more frequently a president mentioned an issue, the more support he would receive with key supporters in Congress.[72]

Members of Congress

Although most of the literature focuses on presidential leadership in Congress, leadership by individual members of Congress is also important from a tandem-institutions perspective. It is much simpler to focus on one president than on 535 members of Congress or even a handful of party and committee leaders. But the personalities, use of resources, and skills of House and Senate members are also instrumental in determining policymaking patterns and results. Norman Ornstein asserts that:

> . . . *individual talent and adaptability matter. Certain eras may call out for strong (congressional) leaders, but for various reasons the individuals who find themselves elected or appointed to leadership posts do not measure up. At other times, clever, assertive, and adaptable leaders may be able to overcome considerable institutional impediments to provide surprisingly strong leadership.*[73]

In the 1950s, Senator Lyndon Johnson was a forceful, assertive majority leader. His successor, Mike Mansfield, in contrast, was restrained and consensual. In the 1980s, four Senate majority leaders—Howard Baker, Robert Dole, Robert Byrd, and George Mitchell—used various styles and skills to influence policy. House speakers also vary in leadership skill and effectiveness, and their personalities can have a profound effect on interbranch policy negotiations. One of the strongest speakers in recent years was Jim Wright of Texas. Before a scandal cut his tenure short, he provided a visible and aggressive counterpoint to the Reagan White House. His willingness to use the Democratic party organization to run the House, to use the Rules committee to set the agenda and limit amendments, and to sidestep committees on crucial bills infuriated Republicans but strengthened Congress in negotiating with the presidency. His successor, Tom Foley (D-Wa.), was much less partisan and more likely to work cooperatively with Republican presidents.

One of the most controversial congressional leaders is Republican Speaker of the House, Newt Gingrich. He helped engineer the stunning Republican election victory in 1994 with his "Contract with America." As a result, a large number of freshmen Republicans entered the House loyal to Gingrich. He centralized power in the House to an extent not seen since Cannon at the turn of the century. He handpicked committee chairs, breaking the seniority system, and weakened their power. He had remarkably high public visibility and, more than the president, established the agenda of government in 1995. As we shall see, however, this period of centralization and dominance was relatively short-lived and by the start of the 105th Congress in 1997, Gingrich was weakened by an ethics scandal and under fire from his own rank and file. Nonetheless, he demonstrated the potential for strong congressional leaders to shape the policy linkages between Congress and the president.

Leadership by members of Congress is not limited to the elected party leaders of the House and Senate. Certain committee chairs and ranking minority members exert significant influence over legislation. Informal groups and caucuses increasingly provide policy leadership in Congress. Certain members, regardless of their seniority or position, act as "issue" leaders, playing a major role in defining the agenda and shaping outcomes.[74] Other members are particularly important as coalition builders because of their expertise, popularity, or personal skills; however, they may work with or against the party leaders. Finally, leadership in Congress takes forms other than rounding up votes. According to Ross Baker, other key leadership activities include attracting policy experts and guiding policy development, providing political cover for members, and enhancing media exposure of members.[75]

The Policy Agenda

Agenda Control

Patterns of policymaking involving Congress and the president also depend on the policy agenda and who sets it. The congressional and presidential agendas may be strikingly different. Even when policy agendas coincide, each branch may have opposing ideological and partisan goals. Since the 1930s, presidents may have had the advantage in setting the national agenda, but with the prevalence of divided government today, Congress increasingly frames, publicizes, and pursues its own agenda. Mark Peterson examined nearly 300 policy initiatives from the Eisenhower to the Reagan administration to determine which branch was more dominant.[76] He found presidential leadership in only 11 percent of the cases, opposition party dominance in Congress 20 percent of the time, compromise 24 percent of the time, and no action 25 percent of the time. This is highly suggestive that agenda control is more equally shared between the two branches than is often assumed.

Agenda Size

Studies have linked the size of a president's legislative agenda to his subsequent legislative success. Presidents seem to pay for ambition: more proposals to Congress result in lower overall success.[77] This result corresponds to popular wisdom in comparisons of Carter and Reagan as well as recent research. Reagan focused almost exclusively on his budget and economic plan in his first year and saw its major provisions adopted. Carter, on the other hand, had a diverse and unfocused agenda in his first year. Reagan focused on 107 issues before Congress compared to 232 for Carter.[78] Looking back, Carter concluded:

> *With the advantages of hindsight, it now seems that it would have been advisable to have introduced our legislation in much more careful phases— not in such a rush. We would not have accomplished any more, and perhaps less, but my relations with Congress would have been smoother and the image of undue haste and confusion could have been avoided.[79]*

Difference among Policies

Issues themselves may help determine the relationship between Congress and the president and which branch is more likely to shape the final result. The most obvious example is the "two presidencies" thesis, which suggests that presidents are much more dominant in foreign affairs than domestic affairs.[80] Since 1965, differences between foreign and domestic success rates have narrowed considerably.[81] Some recent studies conclude that the phenomenon holds only for Republican presidents—who have greater success in foreign policy votes—rather than for Democratic presidents, who do equally well in both. Others suggest that a reemergence of the "two presidencies" phenomenon is due more to presidential weakness than to strength with Congress.[82]

In an earlier study, we compared congressional approval of presidential initiatives across the policy areas we are using in this study. Congressional approval ranged from 55 percent in *foreign and defense policy,* to 50 percent in *social welfare policy,* to 37 percent in *economic and budget policy,* to a low of 26 percent in *civil rights.*[83] While this suggests that policy area is related to policymaking patterns, the variation in overall success between individual presidents was just as great, ranging from a high of 57 percent for Johnson to a low of 31 percent for Ford. Rather than looking at legislative success from only the president's vantage point, we will utilize these four policy areas to examine different patterns of separate institutions making policy.

CONSEQUENCES OF PRESIDENTIAL-CONGRESSIONAL POLICYMAKING

The negotiations, compromises, and battles between Congress and the president help clarify how national institutions work and occasionally make for good political drama. From a policy perspective, however, the ultimate question concerns results and consequences. Did the policy work? Did it solve the problem? Were there unintended consequences? Are there particular kinds of policy results associated with the four patterns of presidential-congressional policymaking?

Michael Mezey, in *Congress, the President, and Public Policy,* provides a useful framework for analyzing public policy results.[84] He distinguishes between contextual and procedural criteria for evaluating policy outcomes. Contextual criteria are subjective evaluations of the goals of public policy based on ideology, history, partisanship, and culture.[85] More appropriate for social scientists are criteria dealing with the procedures and results of policymaking: democratic and managerial criteria. Did the policy achieve what was intended? Was it produced by a democratic process? Mezey suggests that good public policy should be responsive and accountable by democratic standards as well as informed, timely, coherent, effective, and responsible by managerial standards.[86]

These criteria provide an important basis for evaluating policies. The problem, however, is an underlying assumption that only Congress can produce policies that satisfy democratic criteria and only the president can produce policies that satisfy managerial criteria. Mezey notes, for example, that "Congress seems structurally incapable of producing public policy that is informed, timely, coherent, effective, and responsible."[87] This reflects a pronounced presidency-centered perspective. We believe there are examples of congressional policies that are timely, informed, and effective as well as cases of presidential policies that are responsive and accountable. Although there are plausible reasons to suspect that executive and legislative branches have different strengths in the policy process, we are not prepared to judge *a priori* the policy characteristics of any given pattern. Our emphasis is on how they work in tandem because very few policies are produced by the legislative or executive branch alone. Despite this different perspective, Mezey's work is helpful in developing a set of policy characteristics:[86]

Timeliness and responsiveness: Does the policy respond to a popularly perceived problem? Are policies adopted in a timely fashion that respond to immediate problems and needs or does delay cause additional difficulties?

Representativeness: Are a wide range of interests and concerns reflected in the process? Does the final result represent the public interest rather than a narrow special interest?

Symbolic or substantive: Are policies more show than substance, avoiding fundamental issues for the sake of taking some action? Are policies sufficiently informed by expert information and analysis? Are policies adopted primarily for political purposes or to solve problems in a realistic, honest way?

Accountability: Do citizens know who is responsible for policies that are enacted or not enacted, or is responsibility for a policy obscured, limiting the capacity of citizens to hold policy makers accountable.

Nature of benefits: Do policies primarily provide private goods that benefit groups or individuals or public goods that benefit the larger society? Are the costs and benefits of policies targeted to achieve a desired result, or diluted and dispersed so that everyone gets a piece of the pie but overall impact is reduced?

Consistency and coherence: Are policies clear, relatively unambiguous, moving in a single general direction, or are they contradictory and internally inconsistent? Do policies correspond reasonably to government actions in other areas, or do they conflict with other related policies?

Effectiveness: Do policies have the desired impact and results, making progress toward their objectives? Or do they require constant reconsideration and reformulation, often creating undesired, inadequate, or unintended results? Do policies meet long-term needs as well as short-term demands?

CONCLUSION

Although we believe that the nature of policy issues affects the level of interbranch conflict and influences the role that each branch plays in the policy process, our objective in this book is not to test which pattern is most prevalent in each policy arena. Chapters 5 through 8 are divided into substantive policy areas: foreign and defense, civil rights, economic and budget, and social welfare. Each chapter explores the evolution of policy, agenda and major issues, and particular features of the political environment, leadership, and institutional structure. Each of the four general patterns we have identified occur in various forms across each policy area. In nonrandomly selecting cases, therefore, we have chosen one each of presidential leadership, congressional leadership, consensus/cooperation, and deadlock/extraordinary resolution across the four policy areas. This approach demonstrates the wide range of patterns that occur. *It is clearly not meant to imply, however, that each pattern is equally prevalent across policy areas.* We know, for example, that presidential leadership is more common in foreign and defense policy than in social welfare policy. Drawing on the literature and many other cases not reported here, we discuss which patterns are more typical or unusual in a given policy area.

Table 1.2 presents the cases that will be examined in Chapters 5 through 8. At the conclusion of each of these chapters we offer an overview of presidential-congressional interactions in that policy area and the prevalence of certain patterns. In the concluding chapter we assess each of the four patterns across policy areas, summarizing policy characteristics and consequences. Although several cases are drawn from the 1960s, most have been chosen from more recent times. In particular, the prevalence of divided government since 1969 and the increase in institutional conflict in the 1980s and 1990s suggest that recent cases are most relevant for understanding the shifting patterns of collaboration and combat today.

Before the cases are presented, Chapter 2 explores more fully the constitutional foundations of Congress and the presidency and traces the evolution of their relationship over two centuries. Chapters 3 and 4 examine separately the modern Congress and presidency, in particular the environment in which they operate,

TABLE 1.2   Cases of Presidential-Congressional Policymaking, by Pattern and Policy Area

	Pattern of Interaction			
Policy Area	Presidential Leadership	Congressional Leadership	Consensus/ Cooperation	Deadlock/ Extraordinary Resolution
Foreign policy	Gulf War (1991)	Cuba Sanctions Act (1996)	Panama Canal Treaties (1978)	Aid to Contras (1983–1989)
Civil rights policy	Civil Rights Act (1964)	Civil Rights Restoration Act (1988)	Same-Sex Marriage Act (1996)	Civil Rights Act (1991)
Economic and budget policy	Economic and budget plan (1981)	Shareholder Lawsuits Act (1995)	Tax Reform Act (1986)	Balanced Budget Plan (1995–1996)
Social welfare policy	Economic Opportunity Act (1964)	Catastrophic health care insurance (1988–1989)	Welfare Reform Act (1996)	Social Security bailout (1983)

policymaking institutions and processes, changing agendas, and leadership capabilities. Chapters 5 to 8 examine the political environment, institutions, and leadership across policy areas before presenting the cases and their results. In Chapter 9, we review general policy consequences across the four patterns and consider potential reforms designed to increase collaboration and decrease combat in national policymaking. In doing so we hope to expand understanding of the way in which Congress and the president make public policy.

ENDNOTES

1. From the Inaugural Address of President George Bush, January 20, 1989, reprinted in Gerald M. Pomper, *The Election of 1988* (Chatham, N.J.: Chatham House, 1989): 209–210.

2. Inaugural address of William Clinton, January 20, 1997, in *Congressional Quarterly Weekly Report,* January 25, 1997: 252–253.

3. Louis Fisher, *The Constitution Between Friends* (New York: St. Martin's, 1978): 7–13.

4. Richard Neustadt, *Presidential Power* (New York: Wiley, 1960): 26.

5. James Madison, Federalist Paper #51 (New York: Modern Library, 1965).

6. Lloyd Cutler, "To Form a Government: On the Defects of Separation of Powers," in Thomas Cronin (ed.), *Rethinking the Presidency* (Boston: Little, Brown, 1982): 62.

7. Roger H. Davidson, David Kovenock, and Michael O'Leary, *Congress in Crisis: Politics and Congressional Reform* (Belmont, Calif.: Wadsworth, 1969): 17–25.

8. Quoted in Charles S. Hyneman and George W. Carey (eds.), *A Second Federalist* (New York: Appleton-Century-Crofts, 1967): 151.

9. Charles Jones, *Separate But Equal Branches* (Chatham, NJ: Chatham House, 1995): 8.

10. See Jon Bond, Richard Fleisher, and Glen Krutz, "An Overview of the Empirical Findings on Presidential-Congressional Relations," in James Thurber (ed.), *Rivals for Power: Presidential-Congressional Relations* (Washington D.C.: Congressional Quarterly Press, 1996): 103–139; and David W. Brody and Craig Volden, *Resolving Gridlock* (Boulder, CO: Westview Press, 1998).

11. Thomas E. Cronin, *The State of the Presidency* (Boston: Little, Brown, 1975): 25–30.

12. James P. Pfiffner, "Divided Government and the Problem of Governance," in James Thurber (ed.), *Divided Government* (Washington, D.C.: Congressional Quarterly Press, 1991): 39.

13. Arthur M. Schlesinger, Jr., *The Imperial Presidency* (Boston: Houghton Mifflin, 1973).

14. George C. Edwards III, *At the Margins* (New Haven, Conn.: Yale University Press, 1989); Jon R. Bond and Richard Fleisher, *The President in the Legislative Arena* (Chicago: University of Chicago Press, 1990); Douglas Rivers and Nancy Rose, "Passing the President's Program: Public Opinion and Presidential Influence in Congress," *American Journal of Political Science* 29:2 (May 1985): 183–186; and Ken Collier and Terry Sullivan, "New Evidence Undercutting the Linkage of Approval with Support and Influence," *Journal of Politics* 57 (1995): 197–209.

15. Mark A. Peterson, *Legislating Together* (Cambridge, Mass.: Harvard University Press, 1990): 4–6.

16. Ibid., 7.

17. Charles Jones, *The Presidency in a Separated System* (Washington D.C.: Brookings, 1994): 2–3.

18. Jones (note 9): 11.

19. Steven A. Shull, *Presidential-Congressional Relations* (Ann Arbor: University of Michigan Press, 1997).

20. Steven A. Shull and Thomas C. Shaw, *Explaining Presidential-Congressional Interactions* (forthcoming).

21. Lloyd Cutler, "The Cost of Divided Government," *New York Times,* Nov. 20, 1987: C1.

22. Morris Fiorina, *Divided Government,* 2d ed. (Boston: Allyn and Bacon, 1996).

23. Rhodes Cook, "A New Dynamic Splits the Vote," *Congressional Quarterly Weekly Report,* April 19, 1997: 934.

24. Woodrow Wilson, quoted in Pfiffner (note 12): 44.

25. James L. Sundquist, "Needed: A Political Theory for the New Era of Coalition Government in the United States," *Political Science Quarterly* 103 (1988–1989): 629.

26. Donald Robinson (ed.), *Reforming American Government: The Bicentennial Papers of the Committee on the Constitutional System* (Boulder, CO: Westview Press, 1985).

27. Cutler (note 6): 62.

28. David R. Mayhew, *Divided We Govern* (New Haven, Conn.: Yale University Press, 1991).

29. Sean Kelley, "Divided We Govern: A Reassessment," *Polity* 25 (1993): 475–484.

30. George C. Edwards III, Andrew Barrett, and Jeffrey Peake, "The Legislative Impact of Divided Government," *American Journal of Political Science* 41: 545–563; and Shull (note 19).

31. David Epstein and Sharyn O'Halloran, "Divided Government and the Design of Administrative Procedures," forthcoming, cited in Fiorina (note 22): 167.

32. Benjamin Ginsberg and Martin Shefter, *Politics by Other Means* (New York: Basic Books, 1990): 164–165.

33. Jones (note 9): 30.

34. See Charles O. Jones, *An Introduction to the Study of Public Policy* (Pacific Grove, CA: Brooks Cole, 1984) for a description of the process. For an empirical test, see Steven A. Shull and Dennis W. Glieber, "Testing a Dynamic Process of Policymaking in Civil Rights," *Social Science Journal* 31 (1994): 53–67.

35. See Aage R. Clausen, *How Congressmen Decide: A Policy Focus* (New York: St. Martin's, 1973) and John H. Kesse, "Parameters of Presidential Politics," *Social Science Quarterly* 55 (June 1974): 8–24; Steven A. Shull (ed.) *Presidential Policymaking* (Armonk, N.Y.: M. E. Sharp): forthcoming.

36. Bruce M. Russett, "International Relations Research: Case Studies and Cumulation," in Michael Haas and Henry Kariel (eds.), *Approaches to the Study of Political Science* (San Francisco: Chandler, 1970): 425–440; Examples of such integrative case studies include Irving Janis, *Groupthink,* 2d ed. (Boston: Houghton Mifflin, 1982) and Charles Bullock III and Charles Lamb, *Implementing Civil Rights Policy* (Pacific Grove, Calif.: Brooks/Cole, 1984).

37. Peterson (note 15): 9.

38. See Jones (note 9): 11, for example.

39. Quoted in James M. Burns, *Roosevelt: The Lion and the Fox* (New York: Harcourt Brace, 1956): 165.

40. Barbara J. Nelson, *Making an Issue of Child Abuse: Political Agenda Setting for Social Problems* (Chicago: University of Chicago Press, 1984): 27–29.

41. John B. Gilmour, "Summits and Stalemates: Bipartisan Negotiations in the Postre-form Era," in Roger H. Davidson (ed.), *The Postreform Congress* (New York: St. Martin's, 1992): 233–256; Pfiffner (note 12): 82

42. Michael L. Mezey, *Congress, the President, and Public Policy* (Boulder, Colo.: Westview Press, 1989): 147–188: Walter Oleszek, "The Context of Congressional Policy-making," in Thurber (note 12): 82.

43. James D. Barber, *Pursuit of the Presidency* (Englewood Cliffs, N.J.: Prentice-Hall, 1980); Arthur Schlesinger, Jr., *The Cycles of American History* (Boston: Houghton Mifflin, 1986); and James L. Sundquist, *Decline and Resurgence of Congress* (Washington, D.C.: Brookings Institution, 1981); Stephen Skowronek, *Politics Presidents Make,* (Cambridge: Harvard University Press), 1993.

44. Bond and Fleisher (note 14).

45. Bond, Fleisher, and Krutz (note 10): 105.

46. Ibid., 125.

47. Quoted in Charles O. Jones, "Presidential Negotiations with Congress," in Anthony King (ed.), *Both Ends of the Avenue* (Washington, D.C.: American Enterprise Institute, 1983): 102.

48. George C. Edwards III, *Presidential Influence in Congress* (San Francisco: Freeman, 1980); Rivers and Rose (note 14): 183–196.

49. Michael B. MacKuen, "Political Drama, Economic Conditions, and the Dynamics of Presidential Popularity," *American Journal of Political Science* 27 (1983): 165–192.

50. Bond, Fleisher, and Krutz (note 10): 127. Collier and Sullivan (note 14); Shull and Shaw (note 20).

51. Samuel Kernell, "Explaining Presidential Popularity," *American Political Science Review* 72 (June 1978): 506–522; MacKuen (note 49).

52. See Norman Ornstein and Shirley Elder, *Interest Groups, Lobbying, and Policymak-ing* (Washington, D.C.: Congressional Quarterly Press, 1978).

53. Lester M. Salamon and Michael S. Lund, *The Reagan Presidency and the Govern-ing of America* (Washington, D.C.: Urban Institute Press, 1983): 3.

54. Woodrow Wilson, *Congressional Government* (Boston: Houghton Mifflin, 1885).

55. Roger H. Davidson, "The Presidency and Three Eras of the Modern Congress," in Thurber (note 12): 67.

56. Laurence C. Dodd and Bruce I. Oppenheimer, *Congress Reconsidered,* 3d ed. (Wash-ington, D.C.: Congressional Quarterly Press, 1985): 42–45.

57. Laurence C. Dodd and Bruce I. Oppenheimer, *Congress Reconsidered,* 4th ed. (Washington, D.C.: Congressional Quarterly Press, 1989): 49–50.

58. Colin Campbell, *Managing the Presidency: Carter, Reagan, and the Search for Ex-ecutive Harmony* (Pittsburgh, Pa: University of Pittsburgh Press, 1986): 11.

59. Paul C. Light, *The President's Agenda: Domestic Policy Choice from Kennedy to Carter* (Baltimore: Johns Hopkins University Press, 1982); and Ken Collier, *Between the Branches: The White House Office of Legislative Liaison* (Pittsburgh: University of Pittsburgh Press, 1997).

60. Neustadt (note 4) emphasizes individual or personal leadership, for example, whereas Campbell (note 58) emphasizes institutional factors.

61. Campbell (note 58): 10.

62. James D. Barber, *The Presidential Character,* 4th ed. (Englewood Cliffs, N.J.: Prentice-Hall, 1992).

63. Marcia Whicker and Raymond Moore, *When Presidents Are Great* (Englewood Cliffs, N.J.: Prentice-Hall, 1988).

64. Clausen (note 35); Edwards (note 48); Bond and Fleisher (note 14).

65. Terry Sullivan, "Headcounts, Expectations, and Presidential Coalitions in Congress," *American Journal of Political Science* 32:3 (August 1988): 567–589; Peterson (note 15): chapter 2.

66. James P. Pfiffner, *The Strategic Presidency: Hitting the Ground Running,* 2d ed. (Lawrence, Kan.: University Press of Kansas, 1996).

67. Light (note 59).

68. Quoted in Doris B. Kearns, *Lyndon Johnson and the American Dream* (New York: Harper & Row, 1976): 226.

69. Shull (note 19) finds that legislative support does vary by stages in the president's term; also see Pfiffner (note 66).

70. Brad Lockerbie and Stephen A. Borrelli, "Getting Inside the Beltway: Perceptions of Presidential Skill and Success in Congress," *British Journal of Political Science* 19 (January 1989): 97–106; Dennis W. Gleiber and Steven A. Shull, "Measuring the President's Professional Reputation," *American Politics Quarterly* 26 (1998): forthcoming.

71. Terry Sullivan, "Explaining Why Presidents Count: Signaling and Information," *Journal of Politics* 52 (August 1990): 939–962.

72. Patrick J. Fett, "Presidential Legislative Priorities and Legislative Voting Decisions: An Exploratory Analysis," *Journal of Politics* 56 (May 1994): 502–512.

73. Norman Ornstein, "Can Congress Be Led?" in John J. Kornacki (ed.), *Leading Congress* (Washington, D.C.: Congressional Quarterly Press, 1990): 16–17.

74. Susan Webb Hammond, "Committee and Informal Leaders in the U.S. House of Representatives," in Kornacki (note 73): 62–63.

75. Ross K. Baker, "Fostering Entrepreneurial Activities of Members of the House," in Kornacki (note 73): 29–32.

76. Peterson (note 15).

77. Charles W. Ostrom, Jr. and Dennis M. Simon, "Promise and Performance: A Dynamic Model of Presidential Popularity," *American Political Science Review* 79:2 (June 1985): 334–358.

78. Fett (note 72).

79. Jimmy Carter, *Keeping Faith: Memoirs of a President* (New York: Bantam, 1982): 87.

80. See Steven A. Shull (ed.), *The Two Presidencies: A Quarter Century Assessment* (Chicago: Nelson Hall, 1991), which reprints Aaron Wildavsky, "The Two Presidencies," *Transaction* 4 (1966): 7–14.

81. Lance T. LeLoup and Steven A. Shull, "Congress Versus the President: The 'Two Presidencies' Reconsidered," *Social Science Quarterly* 59 (March 1979), reprinted in Shull (note 80).

82. Jon Bond and Richard Fleisher, "Are There Two Presidencies? Yes, But Only for Republicans," *Journal of Politics* 50 (August 1988): 747–767; reprinted in Shull (note 80).

83. LeLoup and Shull (note 81).

84. Mezey (note 42).

85. Ibid., 5–6.

86. Ibid., 8–9.

87. Ibid., 142.

2

THE CONSTITUTION AND SHARED POLICYMAKING

. . . by so contriving the interior structure of the government, as that its several constituent parts may, by their mutual relations, be the means of keeping each other in their proper places.   *—JAMES MADISON, FEDERALIST #51*

To a remarkable degree policymaking between the Congress and the president of the United States still runs along a path laid out by the founders two centuries ago. Throughout history, scores of court decisions, precedents, traditions, and innovations have helped shape legislative-executive politics. Chapter 1 introduced the tandem, separated institutions perspective, the policy and case study focus, patterns of presidential-congressional policymaking, and their causes and potential consequences. In this chapter, the foundations and development of legislative-executive policy making are explored: Why did the founders write the language of Articles I and II as they did? What were the key decisions and the philosophy underlying them? Once the Constitution was ratified, how did relationships between branches evolve and to what ends? How did the political environment, institutional capacity, personal leadership, and the policy agenda affect presidential-congressional relations over two centuries? What role has the Court played as an arbiter of disputes between branches, interpreting the Constitutional boundaries between Congress and the president? Finally, is the Constitution adequate for the governing needs of today?

PRELUDE TO CONSTITUTION MAKING

In the summer of 1787, fifty-five delegates from eleven of the thirteen colonies met to amend the Articles of Confederation. Of course, they did more; they drafted an entirely new blueprint for government—one that was unprecedented in the history of the world. As one eminent historian noted, "The Framers . . . virtually invented both the concept of a written frame of government and the ideal of constitution making by convention."[1] Since 1787, nearly all constitutions around the world have followed the American model of written constitutions produced by a representative assembly. Even more important than the constitution-making process was the unique structure created by the Founders, which shapes policymaking today.

The Colonial Experience

Colonists did not even think of themselves as "Americans" until the 1770s when the prelude to the Revolution began to create a sense of national identity separate from that of the British. When war became inevitable, the Declaration of Independence expressed radical sentiments about the natural rights of citizens relative to government. Influenced by philosopher John Locke, the Declaration proclaimed that government must be based on the consent of the governed.[2] Their experience in the 1770s during the war, and in the 1780s as a confederation of states, had a profound effect on the thinking and actions of the framers.

American colonists had developed a strong distaste for executive powers. For them, King George III was a powerful symbol of an arbitrary, capricious executive. These feelings were enhanced after 1765, when the British Crown became displeased with the role of the thirteen colonies during the French and Indian Wars. The Stamp Act and Navigation Acts were enacted to force the colonies to pay some of the costs of the war. Before 1765, American colonies had been governed relatively loosely, so these measures to exert more control ran counter to the rising tide of American nationalism. Colonial governors were increasingly viewed as extensions of the impervious authority of the Crown; their actions exacerbated resentment of the monarchy. As tensions mounted in the early 1770s, colonial governors often suspended rights previously enjoyed by the colonists: habeas corpus, trial by jury, and the sanctity of private homes. England reacted harshly to the Boston Tea Party in 1773, virtually rescinding the charter of Massachusetts. American political activity increased with the growing hostility.

When independence was declared on July 4, 1776, many of the states took the opportunity to draft new constitutions, completing the task in 1776 or early 1777.[3] Most were predisposed to strong legislatures and weak governors in reaction to the events of the preceding decades. In some states, the governor was little more than the first among equals; terms were as short as six months, with no opportunity for reelection. New York State, which started later than the rest, was an exception. The war was already centered in New York when the state constitutional convention began its work. The delegates had to deliberate literally on the run as British troops followed them up the Hudson River from New York City, where they began, to Albany, where they finished. The need for a stronger executive to direct the conduct of the war had become obvious. The New Yorkers wrote a constitution giving the governor the power to mobilize and direct the militia and exert significant control of state affairs during the war. The provisions of the New York State Constitution would become an important model for the national Constitution, particularly regarding the powers of the presidency.[4]

Government under the Articles of Confederation

Articles of union for the thirteen independent states were drafted in 1777 and submitted by the Continental Congress to the state legislatures for ratification. The Articles of Confederation were not actually ratified until 1781, when seven states relinquished claims on land to their west. It was a weak central government: Each state was guaranteed "its sovereignty, freedom and independence, and every power, jurisdiction and right" not granted to the national government. This nominal national government consisted of a unicameral legislature—the Confederation Congress—consisting of one representative from each state. Congress was granted the power to make treaties, coin money, regulate trade with the Indians, build a navy, and create a post office. Major decisions required unanimous agreement by all the states.

It was at best a feeble union, with severe structural deficiencies. The national government lacked the power to raise revenues because this power had been abused by the Crown; without it a national government could hardly function. There was virtually no head of government or executive branch. John Hanson was elected the first "President of the Confederation Congress of the Confederacy" in 1781. John Hancock was later elected to the post but never bothered to show up! There were no national courts. What little power the states ceded to the national government under the Articles belonged to the legislature.

The United States could barely make policy under the Articles of Confederation in the 1780s. The nations of the world did not know with whom to negotiate and lacked respect for the new country. National finances were in disarray. Each state printed and coined its own money, which caused problems in travel and commerce. Some states had enormous debts from the Revolutionary War, and it became increasingly difficult for the national government to borrow money. The unity forged during the war started to unravel as conflicts began between economic classes and regions. Indebted farmers were jailed, leading to civil unrest. In western Massachusetts, local war hero Daniel Shays led a group of disgruntled farmers into North Hampton and took over the local courthouse. When word of Shays' rebellion spread, citizens were shocked and frightened at the prospect of anarchy. Some wondered aloud if America might need a king.

Efforts to revise the Articles of Confederation gained momentum. Only five states had sent delegates to a convention in Annapolis, Maryland, in 1786 to discuss trade between the states, but those in attendance ended their meeting by calling for a convention in Philadelphia the next year. Congress approved the convention for the "sole and express purpose of revising the Articles of Confederation." However, the delegates would go far beyond their legal mandate, creating an entirely new government structure.

SHAPING THE LEGISLATIVE AND EXECUTIVE BRANCHES

Fifty-five delegates gathered in Philadelphia in the sweltering summer of 1787. It was a distinguished group, including Benjamin Franklin, James Madison, Alexander Hamilton, and James Wilson. The country's most prominent statesman and war hero, George Washington, presided. As a group they were wealthy, politically experienced, and powerful men. They were not only practical politicians but well educated, conversant with the books and dominant ideas of the day. Many had read Locke and Montesquieu, whose ideas helped Madison conceptualize the new government.

The founders' difficult challenge was to create a national government powerful enough to effectively run the country but not so powerful as to infringe on the liberties that the country had won. At the first week of the convention, they agreed to create a national government with three separate branches. The presumption changed from reforming the Articles of Confederation to creating a new national government in which powers were separated. Convention politics and decisions reached in Philadelphia reflected various interests: large states versus small states, slave states versus nonslave states, and advocates of a strong executive versus those who wanted a weak executive. Their choices still influence the course of policymaking today.

The Congress

The dominant branch of the new government would be the legislature, the most democratic creation of the founders. Its preeminence was reflected in its very position as Article I. Determining how seats would be apportioned in the new Congress was one of the thorniest conflicts of the convention. James Madison and the Virginia delegation had arrived in Philadelphia several weeks before the first official session and took that time to develop a series of proposals. The fifteen resolutions proposed by Madison became known as the Virginia Plan, which largely set the agenda for the convention. Madison proposed a strong central government dominated by Congress, which would have the ability to legislate on any matter in which the states were "incompetent." The plan called for a bicameral Congress with both houses apportioned on the basis of population. (Virginia was the most populous state.) The Senate, the upper chamber, would be elected by the House, and the House would be elected by the people.

Delegates from the smaller states were concerned about several aspects of Madison's proposals. They thought the national government would be too strong and that their states would lose too much autonomy. With both houses of Congress apportioned on the basis of population, their voices would be lost in a government dominated by Virginia, New York, and other large states. They wanted each state to have equal voice in the new union, as they had under the Articles of Confederation. The small states offered a set of counterproposals several weeks later, referred to as the

Patterson plan or the New Jersey plan. It called for a unicameral legislature in which each state—regardless of population—had equal representation. The balance of political power would remain with the states.

These fundamental differences over the power of the national government and representation in Congress threatened to cause the collapse and failure of the convention. On the brink of disaster, a committee of one delegate from each of the eleven states in attendance met over the Fourth of July weekend. This committee arrived at the most critical compromise of the convention. The Connecticut or Great Compromise proposed two houses of Congress: the House of Representatives, apportioned on the basis of population elected by the people, and the Senate, with each state having two senators who would be appointed by state's legislature. Delegates agreed that all bills to raise revenues and appropriate monies would have to originate in the House of Representatives. Representatives would be elected every two years, and Senators would be appointed on a staggered basis for six-year terms. The compromise on the shape of the bicameral legislature went a long way toward assuring the success of the convention.

The Presidency

Disagreements over the shape of the executive branch were less threatening to the convention itself, but views were strongly held and passionately debated. Madison's original plan had called for a single executive to be elected by Congress. The New Jersey plan called for a plural executive that would be relatively weak. The debate over the nature of the presidency reflected the founders' uncertainty about government power—more specifically, executive power. Those who wanted a weak executive, subservient to the legislature, were suspicious of anything that smacked of monarchy. As Madison noted in his diary, Roger Sherman of Connecticut argued in debate that the president should be "nothing more than an institution for carrying the will of the Legislature into effect, that the person or persons ought to be appointed by and acceptable to the Legislature only."[5] One delegate proposed a plural executive representing different sections of the country, to lessen the threat of a drift toward monarchy. Other delegates, troubled by the inability to govern under the Articles, favored a strong executive with an independent veto power over the legislature.

Over the course of the summer, the shape of the presidency took form. Delegates finally agreed on a single executive, as advocate James Wilson argued, to ensure "energy, responsibility, and dispatch" in the presidency. The means of selection was extensively debated. Those who wanted a powerful, independent executive argued for direct election. Those who wanted a subservient president lobbied for selection by Congress. In the end, they compromised on the Electoral College, with election by the House of Representatives in case no individual won a majority of electoral votes. The Electoral College was made up of electors chosen by the various states, one for each senator and representative. Not anticipating the rapid development of the party system, the Founders generally assumed that after George Washington, most presidential elections would be decided in the House.

Delegates also disagreed on the term of office for the presidency and provisions for removal. Some favored a single six- or seven-year term, without the possibility of reelection, to put the president "above politics." The convention originally agreed to a single seven-year term but later reversed itself and accepted a four-year term, with no limitation on reelection. The ultimate sanction of the legislature was impeachment and removal of the president from office in cases of "treason, bribery, and other high crimes and misdemeanors." The presidency became more of a national symbol than the founders wanted, and they would be surprised at its modern-day scope.

Dividing and Intermingling Powers

As we saw in Chapter 1, the founders created separate institutions sharing powers. Using the ideas of Montesquieu, James Madison believed that separate branches would prevent the accumulation of political power and tyranny. The result is a complex mix of powers specifically delegated to one branch or the other and many powers divided between the two branches

Congress was granted the power to approve all legislation and to override a presidential veto by a two-thirds vote of both houses. The Constitution grants to Congress a number of economic and budget powers: to raise revenue and appropriate monies (which must originate in the House of Representatives), to borrow money, to regulate commerce with foreign nations, to coin money, and to punish counterfeiting. Congress was also explicitly delegated powers dealing with foreign and military affairs: to declare war, to raise and support an army and navy, to make laws regulating military forces; to mobilize state militias; and to punish piracy. Congress was also granted the power to make laws "necessary and proper" for the execution of their other powers. Over the years, broad interpretation of this provision by the courts not only established national supremacy over the states but made it possible for Congress to legislate in the areas of social welfare policy and to amplify later constitutional amendments—particularly the First and Fourteenth Amendments—by enacting civil rights legislation.

The powers delegated to the president in the Constitution were more restricted. The president was granted the power to recommend measures to Congress, to call special sessions, to provide information on the state of the Union, to veto legislation, and to ensure that the laws are faithfully executed. In the realm of foreign affairs, the president was named Commander-in-Chief of the armed forces and delegated the power to nominate ambassadors, recognize nations, and negotiate treaties. All executive power was delegated to the president. Thus, subsequent executive branch institutions have legal authority but possess no direct constitutional power.

"Separate" institutions actually share intermingled constitutional powers. In a sense, the Madisonian system of checks and balances institutionalized interbranch conflict by dividing responsibility to ensure that ambition would counteract ambition. Congress checks the president through the power to impeach and remove from office, to override vetoes, to confirm nominations, and to ratify treaties (Senate only). The president's veto power checks the legislature. The courts were included in the division of powers as well: The president nominates judges and justices, and the Senate has the power to confirm them. The ability of the Supreme Court to declare an act of Congress or the executive branch unconstitutional, established in the case of *Marbury v. Madison* (1803), became the Court's most potent check on the other two branches.

Over the years, the powers of the national government and both legislative and executive branches expanded far beyond those specifically delegated in the Constitution. In the case of *McCulloch v. Maryland* (1819), the Supreme Court recognized implied powers of national government, which could be exercised even if not expressly enumerated in the Constitution. Today, both branches are engaged in activities beyond the imagination of the founders. The powers of the two branches are not only those formally enumerated in the Constitution and implied by the Constitution (often as interpreted by the courts) but also those that were added by statute or evolved informally through custom and precedent. Table 2.1 compares some of these powers of Congress and the president.

TABLE 2.1   **Executive and Legislative Powers**

Congress	President
Enumerated powers	
Accept or reject legislation	Recommend legislation
Override veto by two-thirds vote	Veto legislation
Accept or reject nominations by majority vote	Nominate executive and judicial officials
	Advise Congress on state of the union
Determine qualifications of members	Call special sessions
Raise taxes and appropriate funds	Enforce the laws
Create and define executive departments	Grant pardons/reprieves
Support army and navy	Negotiate treaties
Ratify treaties	Recognize countries
Declare war	Commander-in-chief
Remove president by impeachment and conviction	
Implied powers	
Instruct agencies	Executive privilege
Legislative veto	Formulate and submit budget
Enact congressional budget	Manage economy and submit economic reports
Produce economic and budget reports	
Review executive agreements	Impoundment, reprogramming
Oversight and investigations	Make executive agreements
Audit federal agencies	Central clearance and submission of legislative program
Send delegations abroad	
Expand legislative staff and agencies	Issue executive proclamation and orders
Coordinate communications and media	Regulatory review
	Expand White House staff
	Media and news management

Despite two centuries of change, the fundamental, inherent competition between branches remains: Madison's system of separation of powers and checks and balances has effectively protected individual liberty by preventing tyranny. However, it has also created a political system that does not make policy through a single dominant pattern of executive-legislative interaction. As a result, leaders sometimes have difficulty in making policy quickly and effectively, and accountability may be obscured by interbranch conflict and opposition. The patterns of interbranch relations today and their consequences depend not only on the constitutional foundation, but on more than two hundred years of customs, precedents, and conflicts between Congress, the president, and the courts.

POLICYMAKING PATTERNS IN THE EARLY REPUBLIC

The Policy Agenda and Political Environment

Government and public policy were so fundamentally different in the 1790s that it is difficult to conceptualize today. The new United States was an agrarian nation with a dispersed population. People had to be self-reliant, independent, and were individualistic; there was simply no other choice. The policy agenda was limited and simple: conducting foreign affairs, facilitating commerce, and providing those few needed services that people could not provide for themselves. Delivering the mail and paying for soldiers were among the most costly expenses of government. Roads and canals were often built with public money. Some of the most important early issues were economic: trade and tariffs, whether to maintain a national bank, and questions of debt.

Yet despite the limited policy agenda, divisions in government may have been deeper in the first twenty years of the Republic than at any other time, with the exception of the Civil War. As George Washington and the early Congresses began the task of governing, the political environment was that of a nation dividing into two camps. The creators of the first political parties disagreed in fundamental terms over the power and scope of the national government. The two emerging political parties, as one expert has noted, "regarded themselves not as parties but as embodiments of the nation's will."[6] Alexander Hamilton's Federalists supported a strong national government as exemplified by the National Bank. George Washington's and Alexander Hamilton's economic programs fostered commerce and attempted to protect domestic manufacturing. The National Bank, authorized in 1791, was a key component.

In growing opposition to the Federalists were Thomas Jefferson's Democratic Republicans, the forerunner of the modern Democratic Party. Jefferson feared that the Federalists would erode federalism (particularly the autonomy of the states) and the entire concept of limited government. Even their choice of name was meant to imply that the Federalists were not "republicans" but rather tilted toward monarchy. The Federalists favored manufacturing over agriculture, whereas the Democratic

Republicans were strongly agrarian in their roots and sentiments. Jefferson's followers supported the French Revolution as an extension of the American Revolution, pitting the common people against their masters—in contrast to Hamilton and the Federalists, who saw it as a dangerous threat to order and society.

Developing Political Institutions

In terms of institutional development, both Congress and the presidency were in their infancy. The House of Representatives was the more active of the two chambers, engaging in lively public debate over the issues of the day. The Senate, in contrast, met in secret, kept no records, and senators spoke quietly and decorously.[7] John C. Calhoun found life in the Senate stifling, choosing to resign and run for the more lively House of Representatives. Neither branch remained in session for long periods. Travel to and from Washington made the job of serving in Congress rather a hardship on family and career. It often took weeks to obtain a quorum. The first Senate, meeting in the Capitol in New York City, was delayed for over a month waiting for enough Senators to arrive. Turnover was high. Most members served for only one or two terms before retiring from public life. It remained a citizen legislature, in which influence was based on individual character rather than longevity. Henry Clay was elected Speaker of the House in his very first term in 1810. However, a few members served for many terms and were among the important early American leaders: Aaron Burr, Hamilton, Madison, James Monroe, Adams, George Clinton, and others. As political parties emerged, party caucuses within Congress became important. Presidents met informally with them, and the caucuses nominated presidential candidates. That nominating system lasted until its malfunction in the election of 1824.

The presidency, too, was in its infancy in terms of institutional development. George Washington created the first Cabinet by assembling the secretaries of the four original Cabinet departments: State, Treasury, Justice, and War. These remain today the most important Cabinet positions, sometimes called the "inner cabinet." Hamilton, Washington's first secretary of the Treasury, originally acted as a de facto Prime Minister in Congress, presenting the administration's program on the floor of Congress, even though he was a member of the executive branch. By 1793, growing animosity led Congress to ban Hamilton from the floor.[8] President Washington knew many of the members of the first Congresses, having served with them in the war and in drafting the Constitution. Madison served as an important legislative adviser to Washington while holding a seat in the House of Representatives.[9] Interpreting the provisions of the Constitution that called for the Senate to "advise and consent" on presidential appointments and treaties, Washington sought input from senators ahead of time. Later, President Washington made a personal trip to the Capitol to consult with Senators concerning an Indian treaty and was not well received. He was furious with his treatment by the Senate and vowed never to go to Congress in person again. This precedent diminished the Senate's role from advising the president to giving or withholding consent after a presidential appointment or treaty had been made.[10] Washington also asserted the power of executive privilege—that the president could withhold certain sensitive information from Congress.

Leadership and Legislative-Executive Relations

Washington made efforts to establish informal ties with Congress and began the long presidential tradition of "wining and dining" members of Congress, initiating the custom of dinners for legislators at the president's residence. One attendee noted, "the president is a cold, formal man; but I must declare that he treated me with great attention."[11] Washington was perhaps more of a statesman than a politician, but his overall record with Congress was relatively successful. Washington cast two vetoes, in both cases on the grounds that the legislation was unconstitutional.

Presidential leadership changed with the election of John Adams in 1796. Divisions had become increasingly bitter, and Adams lacked Washington's status and skills. He would become the only president of the first five to be defeated for re-election and not serve two terms. The Federalist Party was eclipsed by the Democratic Republicans with the election of Thomas Jefferson as president in 1800. Despite being a bitter opponent of the Federalists, Jefferson adopted a position favorable to a strong national government and consummated the Louisiana purchase in 1803. Jefferson was the first president to use the party caucus as a way to lead Congress. Jefferson frequently met with members of his party and submitted legislation through friendly members.

By today's standards, Jefferson was extremely deferential to Congress, which was still seen as the dominant and central branch of the national government. Congressional leadership was the predominant pattern of national policymaking. He cast no vetoes because, by maintaining good relations with congressional majorities, he did not need to. Jefferson placed great emphasis on courting legislative support, holding small dinner parties almost nightly while Congress was in session. It was once observed that, "food and wine were standard accessories of political persuasion [and] the secret of Jefferson's influence."[12] Madison and his immediate successors were not as successful or skillful as Jefferson, but by the end of the War of 1812, the United States had entered a period of one-party politics. The Federalists ceased to be a significant political force, and presidents were content to let Congress handle the main responsibilities for governing. In foreign affairs, however, presidential leadership had already begun to assert itself, such as with the declaration of the Monroe Doctrine.

POLICYMAKING PATTERNS FROM THE JACKSON ERA TO THE CIVIL WAR

The Changing Policy Agenda and Political Environment

Economic issues continued to be a critical part of the policy agenda as the nation expanded and grew. The economies of the North and South headed in different directions, with the South relying on a slave-based plantation economy; the North, on a growing industrial and manufacturing base. The National Bank continued to be a major national controversy thirty years after its original charter. In the area of foreign policy, the Monroe Doctrine helped define the role of the United States in the world and allowed presidents to concentrate on westward expansion rather than European affairs. The question of slavery was never far below the surface of national politics, even after the Missouri Compromise of 1820. Closely related to the question of slavery was that of the power of the national government versus the power of the states. Neither question would be answered until the Civil War.

Until the election of Andrew Jackson in 1828, the national government had little enough to do, and Congress could do most of it. Changes in the political environment and presidential leadership showed the potential power of the presidency. The American electorate expanded dramatically in the 1820s during a period of national growth and democratization. The right to vote had previously been limited to landowners, but as the nation grew and moved west, property qualifications for voting were dropped in most states. Between 1824 and 1828 alone, the number of eligible voters tripled.[13] The sharpening of divisions between political parties also changed the political environment. The era of one-party politics was over; Andrew Jackson and his supporters emerged as the Democratic Party, vociferously opposed by the Whigs and other political factions.

The Potential for Presidential Leadership

Based on his appeal to the expanded American electorate, President Andrew Jackson demonstrated what more aggressive leadership could attain. He claimed coequality with Congress in governing the nation and to be a more legitimate voice of the electorate. He considered himself the "Tribune of the People" compared with Congress, which he claimed, represented local, parochial interests. His opponents branded him a tyrant and labeled him "King Andrew the First." This did little to dim his popularity with the people, demonstrating the importance of public support as a political resource for any president. Jackson was the first president to use the veto for political reasons rather than purely constitutional reasons: He asserted that he had the power to veto any bill passed by Congress, even if he deemed it constitutional. The president, he argued, could not be instructed by either Congress or the Supreme Court. His twelve vetoes were more than double the total of all the previous presidents combined. Jackson was opinionated, stubborn, energetic, and combative, and his relations with Congress were rocky. Forty years after the Constitution was drafted, the potential political separation between branches became clearer, as well as the expansive language of Article II enumerating the powers of the presidency.

However, Jackson's successors did not build on his precedent of a stronger presidency. His political opponents went so far as to promise to reverse Jackson's stance. President William Henry Harrison, for example, in his few weeks in office before succumbing to pneumonia, "foreswore any executive interference in the legislative process."[14] Both he and President Millard Fillmore took legislative positions on the divisive issue of admission of new states, ultimately leading to the Compromise of 1850. A succession of presidents—Tyler, Polk, Pierce, and Buchanan—served only one term and demonstrated little interest in challenging Congress. Only James Polk laid out much of a presidential agenda.

Institutional Development

Institutional development of both branches was modest but steady. The executive branch grew very slowly; presidents relied on the cabinet and a few personal confidants and private citizens as advisors. President James Polk once complained about spending too much time correcting grammatical errors in State Department memos, a presidential task nearly incomprehensible today. In Congress, the committee system began to take shape, although the strong standing committees of later years did not yet take form. Presidents found themselves facing more numerous power centers when dealing with the legislative branch.[15] The decentralizing impact of the emerging committee system was in part countervailed by developing party organizations within Congress. The Senate gained in stature during this period, reducing the preeminence the House of Representatives had enjoyed in the early years of the Republic. But both branches would take a back seat to the presidency during the Civil War.

Presidential leadership of national government may have saved a nation torn apart by the Civil War. Abraham Lincoln, though elected by only 40 percent of the vote in a four-way race, was probably the most powerful president in American history. As other presidents would discover during crisis situations, the political environment was conducive to expanded presidential power. The public supported it and other branches acquiesced in its exercise. Lincoln took a number of unprecedented actions as president, moving decisively to preserve the Union. Without the approval of Congress, he appropriated money, instituted a draft, ordered the blockade of southern ports, closed the post office, and suspended habeas corpus, allowing southern sympathizers to be jailed for the duration of the war without being charged with any crime. As a courtesy to Congress, Lincoln submitted some of these actions for approval after the fact. He based his actions on "popular demand and public necessity" and the "inherent" powers of the presidency.[16]

POLICYMAKING PATTERNS FROM RECONSTRUCTION TO THE DEPRESSION

The Political Environment and Growing Policy Agenda

After the Civil War, the domestic political environment took a very different form. Foremost was the question of reconstruction: how to treat the defeated South. This issue, more than any other, split legislative and executive branches in the 1860s; the hostility between Congress and the president reached historic proportions. Congress, under the control of the Radical Republicans, was determined to punish the South, and no presidential interference would be tolerated. Also, in reaction to the dominance of President Lincoln, leaders of the House and Senate were anxious to reassert their control of policymaking in the postwar era. When the ineffective Andrew Johnson, Lincoln's successor, proved meddlesome, he was impeached by the House and nearly convicted by the Senate in 1868.

The Founders specified that Congress would be able to remove the president in case of "treason, bribery, or other high crimes and misdemeanors." The exact definition of what were impeachable offenses was left vague. The removal process consists of a majority vote by the House to impeach (the equivalent of indictment) and removal by a two-thirds vote of the Senate (the equivalent of conviction). The process had never been used until charges against Andrew Johnson were trumped up by the power-hungry and vindictive Congress. Johnson was accused of violating the Tenure of Office Act, a law of dubious constitutionality limiting the president's removal power. One article of impeachment accused the president of speaking too loudly. Johnson, and to some extent the presidency itself, was saved when the Senate failed by a single vote to remove him.[17] Nonetheless, the presidency was in a weakened state, and national politics was dominated by Congress for decades after.

The policy agenda of Congress in this period focused heavily on civil rights and economic policies designed to promote the growth of private industry. The Thirteenth, Fourteenth, and Fifteenth Amendments to the Constitution, adopted in the 1860s, abolished slavery, guaranteed due process and equal protection to all citizens, and protected the right to vote regardless of race or previous condition of servitude. For the first time, blacks were elected to Congress. However, the Supreme Court in 1873 placed the most narrow possible interpretation on "privileges and immunities" of blacks. Congress responded by passing a series of Civil Rights laws in the 1870s, forbidding discrimination in public accommodations such as hotels and restaurants. The Court unraveled these protections as well and allowed states to pass so-called "Jim-Crow" laws, which reinstituted a system of legal segregation of the races in the South.[18]

Economic policy continued to hold the attention of president and Congress in the late nineteenth century. The Civil War had destroyed the slave-based economy of the South, and the harsh reconstruction policies of Congress prevented a timely recovery. For the rest of the nation, however, it was an era of prosperity. The Civil War provided a direct stimulus to the development of industry; the economy was reshaped in ways favoring industrialization.[19] The Republican party, which dominated national government in this era, passed legislation that promoted the interests of industrial capitalists. The National Bank Act gave favored status to large commercial banks. The Homestead Act helped the railroads by giving settlers free land in the West, thus creating a market and dependency on the railroads. The Morrill Act created the great land-grant universities of the Midwest and West, helping agriculture and encouraging industrialization by increasing the supply of technically skilled manpower. At the same time, economic interest groups became a more prominent part of the national political environment.

Presidential Leadership

Party competition was often fierce in this era. Republicans dominated the presidency; Grover Cleveland and Woodrow Wilson were the only Democrats to win the presidency between 1868 and 1932. However, Democrats often did better in congressional elections, building on the one-party "solid" South and their strength in big cities. Divided government sometimes resulted. Political leadership also continued to influence legislative-executive relations. Grover Cleveland attempted to reassert presidential authority in the 1880s and ran into congressional opposition. In two terms, Cleveland vetoed a record of 583 bills, only seven of which were overridden. Teddy Roosevelt was an assertive leader, using the presidency as his "bully pulpit." Roosevelt believed that the president could engage in any action not expressly forbidden by the Constitution. His successor, William Howard Taft, had a less expansive view of the presidency, believing presidential power should be limited to only what was expressly granted in the Constitution. Teddy Roosevelt was willing to use innovative tactics with Congress. When Congress refused to appropriate enough money to send the U.S. Navy on a muscle-flexing world tour, Roosevelt sent the Navy halfway around the world on available funds and then demanded that the legislature spend the money necessary to bring the ships back.

Woodrow Wilson's notions of leadership in the presidency were heavily influenced by parliamentary forms of government. From early in his career as a professor of government to the end of his political career, Wilson believed in the importance of overcoming the fragmentation caused by the constitutional system. In the 1880s, when Congress still dominated national government, he expressed concern regarding the impervious authority of the standing committees.[20] By the time he was elected president in 1912, Wilson believed in a strong presidency with a Congress that behaved like the British House of Commons. Key to this approach was a strong party system, and Wilson accordingly based his presidency on partisan appeals. He boldly proposed a parliamentary-like transition of power if he were to lose the 1916 election. He suggested that rather than wait months for the inauguration, he would appoint his opponent as secretary of state (then second in line for the presidency) and then he and his vice president would immediately resign. Wilson was a powerful and effective president whose influence was enhanced by World War I. However, his parliamentary and partisan approach ultimately came back to haunt him. Alienated Republican senators blocked ratification of the Treaty of Versailles, which contained his dreams for the League of Nations and his blueprint for the international order after the war. He suffered a disabling stroke and died a broken man.

Maturing Institutions

Institutional development occurred in both branches in this era. The executive branch grew as the functions of government expanded. The Interstate Commerce Commission was created in 1889, making it the first regulatory agency. During the late nineteenth century, a number of reforms were proposed to improve legislative-executive relations. George Pendleton of Ohio introduced legislation to permit cabinet officials to "occupy seats on the floor of the House of Representatives" and respond to direct questions during sessions.[21] Others proposed allowing members of Congress to serve in the president's Cabinet. Overall, however, the presidential office remained limited compared with today. Perhaps the most important institutional development occurred in 1921, with the enactment of the Budget and Accounting Act. This law created the Bureau of the Budget (BOB) and led to a national budget assembled by the president and his budget director.

Significant institutional developments affecting congressional policymaking took place in this era. Between 1865 and 1932, Congress modernized. It evolved from a part-time citizen legislature to a professional legislature. Service in the House and Senate became a career: The average length of service went from two years to eight years. As turnover declined, Congress became a more stable institution, with established rules, norms, and legislative procedures. Workloads and the length of sessions increased.[22] Whereas Congress had met less than six months a year in the nineteenth century, by the twentieth century, it remained in session throughout the year. With less turnover, the committee system became the bulwark of congressional decision making. The seniority system (giving committee chairs to the member of the majority party who had been on the committee the longest) became the key to power within the legislature. Party leadership organizations—floor leaders and whips—were established by 1900. The powers of the Speaker of the House expanded in the 1880s and 1890s, until a revolt by rank-and-file members in 1910 stripped the Speaker of important powers. This further strengthened the committee system and committee chairs—who, along with party leaders, became the key focal point for presidential negotiations with Congress.

The United States had become one of the world's leading economic powers by the end of World War I. With its economic strength came greater military strength and an enhanced role in world affairs. Congress had evolved significantly as an institution, but the strength of the presidency continued to depend largely on the leadership skills and policy agenda of the incumbent. Presidents Harding, Coolidge, and Hoover in the 1920s were relatively weak and unassertive. However, the presidency would be permanently changed when the nation faced its greatest economic crisis and elected Franklin Delano Roosevelt to the presidency.

POLICYMAKING PATTERNS IN THE MODERN ERA

An Altered Political Environment and a Permanently Expanded Agenda

The Great Depression dominated the political environment when Roosevelt was inaugurated president in 1933. The dire consequences of the global economic collapse gripped the nation: 25 percent unemployment, industrial output cut in half, millions of homeless and hungry, and failures of banks and businesses at the rate of hundreds per day. As president, FDR responded to this situation with an ambitious new agenda and proved to be a dominant leader comparable only to Lincoln. When he left office, he not only left a legacy of strong leadership, he also left the presidency permanently changed as an institution.

Roosevelt came into office promising decisive action to make the government a more active partner in reversing the economic decline that had occurred. Confident that Congress would go along, he warned that if Congress failed to act:

> *I shall not evade the clear course of duty that will then confront me. I shall ask the Congress for the one remaining instrument to meet the crisis—broad Executive power to wage a war against the emergency, as great as the power that would be given to me if we were in fact invaded by a foreign foe.*[23]

The environment was more than conducive to such leadership; the public and Congress demanded it. The president was extremely popular and had swept into office with huge Democratic majorities in both houses of Congress. Roosevelt declared a "bank holiday," closing the nation's banks while asking Congress for additional powers to help solve the banking crisis. The new Congress convened a special session to receive the emergency request. After only forty minutes of debate, the bill, which was only partially written, was passed and sent to the president. In his first hundred days, the president led and the Congress followed in a flurry of policymaking activity. Within a few months, the president proposed and Congress enacted the Agricultural Adjustment Act, the Civilian Conservation Corps, unemployment relief, securities and stock market regulations, the Tennessee Valley Authority, emergency railroad legislation, the National Recovery Act, and dozens of other measures.

The policy agenda of government expanded to encompass social welfare legislation for the first time. The centerpiece was the Social Security Act of 1935, which laid the foundation for the nation's social welfare system for the next half-century. It created old age survivors and disability insurance (OASDI), unemployment compensation, Aid to Families with Dependent Children (AFDC), and aid to the blind and disabled. In dealing with the Depression, Roosevelt took a new approach to budget and economic policy. Using the theories of British economist John Maynard Keynes, the government took a much more active role in managing the economy by using deficit spending in the budget to stimulate economic growth. Civil rights did not yet play a prominent role on the policy agenda, but the efforts of such organizations as the National Association for the Advancement of Colored People (NAACP) sowed the seeds of the civil rights movement in the 1950s and 1960s.

When the United States entered World War II, all other issues took a back seat to the task of winning the war. Presidential government emerged; the Commander-in-Chief used emergency powers to direct the war effort through the growing bureaucracy in Washington. Congress kept a watchful eye on the executive branch, overseeing spending and management. Roosevelt died in 1945, shortly before the war ended, leaving a profound mark on the presidency and national government.

The Institutionalized Presidency

As a result of Roosevelt's tenure, the presidency was transformed into the office we recognize today. The White House staff grew from a handful of aides to hundreds of domestic and foreign policy advisors. The Executive Office of the Presidency (EOP) was created in 1939, giving future presidents a permanent organization to assist them. The Budget office was moved to the EOP and became a powerful instrument for presidential influence over economic policy and budget priorities. The 1946 Employment Act made the national government responsible for economic management and created the Council of Economic Advisors to assist the president. In 1947, Congress passed legislation creating the National Security Council (NSC) as part of the institutionalized presidency.

Franklin D. Roosevelt not only helped change the institutions, his personal leadership helped redefine popular conceptions of the presidency as a source of policy innovation. He was a skilled politician, adept at working with Congress. Although he had his occasional problems—such as the ill-fated "court-packing plan" by which he attempted to add justices to the Supreme Court—his legislative record was unparalleled. He was also the first "media president," enhancing his power by effectively communicating with the American people through his fireside chats, broadcast on radio.

Presidential and Congressional Policy Leadership

Roosevelt created expectations for presidential leadership and institutions with which to achieve it. His immediate successors inherited what has been called the "heroic" presidency, based on the view that presidential leadership is the most effective pattern of interbranch policymaking.[24] The postwar policy agenda was darkened by confrontation and the nuclear threat underlying the cold war between the Soviet Union and the United States. In the atomic age, members of Congress increasingly deferred to Presidents Truman, Eisenhower, and Kennedy in foreign affairs. Although the pattern of presidential leadership became more prominent, Congress did not abdicate responsibility in the domestic realm, despite the more powerful presidency. Economic issues also were a key element of the policy agenda as Congress and the president attempted to promote prosperity through economic policies. Federal spending and the budget grew. Congress and the president often battled over economic policies and budget priorities, particularly under divided party control of government.

Civil rights became a critical policy issue during this period. President Truman integrated the nation's armed forces through an executive order, but it was the Supreme Court rather than the legislative or executive branch that took the lead on civil rights. The landmark decision in *Brown v. Board of Education* (1954) declared segregation in public schools to be unconstitutional, marking the culmination of years of struggle through the courts and the commencement of legislative battles to protect the civil rights of blacks. Congress played a leadership role in enacting the 1957 and 1960 Civil Rights bills. The Civil Rights Act of 1964 and the Voting Rights Act of 1965 reflected legislative support for strong presidential leadership.

Social welfare issues, which were so dramatic in the 1930s, were dormant in the 1940s and 1950s. In the 1960s, however, concerns about poverty, health care, and the elderly resurfaced, making social welfare policy once again a high priority on the policy agenda of both Congress and the president. The Economic Opportunity Act of 1964 created a host of antipoverty programs. The Medicare Act of 1965 provided entitlements to pay for health care for the elderly and those below the poverty line.

Institutions developed in response to changes in the political environment and the condition of legislative-executive relations. The war in Vietnam and the Watergate scandal not only shattered myths of the "heroic" presidency but instigated a period of heightened conflict between branches that still prevails at century's end. Vietnam was an undeclared presidential war that ended the bipartisan consensus in Congress and abruptly halted congressional acquiescence to the president. Although President Johnson claimed that the 1964 Gulf of Tonkin Resolution passed by Congress gave him the legal authority to commit ground troops in Vietnam, by the late 1960s a growing number of members believed that the war was not only immoral but illegal. Senate Foreign Relations Committee Chair J. William Fulbright (D-Ark.) held televised hearings that challenged both the wisdom and the constitutionality of the war. Resolutions to stop the war, although never adopted, commanded increasing support and publicity.

Hostility between branches continued after the inauguration of Richard Nixon in 1969. His secret bombing in Cambodia set off a string of protests and riots on college campuses across the nation in 1970. The presidency, in the words of historian Arthur Schlesinger, had become the "imperial presidency": isolated, aloof, above the law, unchecked by Congress.[25] The Watergate scandal and the fall of the Nixon administration seemed to confirm this view. Richard Nixon became the first president to resign from office in the face of certain impeachment by the House and conviction by the Senate for his role in the cover-up and his attack on democratic processes and institutions.

Congressional Resurgence

In response to growing concerns over the imperial presidency, Congress took a number of steps to increase legislative power in both the foreign and domestic realms. The Case Act of 1972 limited the president's ability to use executive agreements rather than treaties to circumvent the need for Senate approval. The War Powers Resolution limited the president's ability to commit troops in hostile situations without congressional approval. It required prior consultation with Congress and notification of the commitment of troops and limited their stay without congressional approval. Congress beefed up oversight of intelligence agencies and limited the president's emergency powers.

In the domestic realm, Congress attempted to increase its influence over budget and economic policy by adopting the Budget and Impoundment Control Act of 1974. This legislation limited the ability of the president to impound monies and created budget committees, the Congressional Budget Office, and a new legislative budget process. Congress increased administrative oversight and scrutiny of presidential nominations for positions in both the executive and judicial branches. The legislative veto—an arrangement giving Congress the opportunity to block certain agency actions—became increasingly popular. Table 2.2 summarizes some of the actions taken by Congress in the 1970s to check the power of the presidency.

Congress succeeded in changing the balance of political power between the White House and Capitol Hill. However, the difficulties of Presidents Nixon, Ford, and Carter made some observers wonder whether the "imperial" presidency had become the "imperiled" or the "impossible" presidency.[26] The political environment seemed to change in 1980 with the election of Ronald Reagan and a Republican Senate. Reagan succeeded in pushing a dramatic economic and budget plan through Congress. However, the process bogged down into recurring stalemate after 1982. Continued budget crises forced President Bush to abandon his pledge not to raise taxes; he compromised with Congress in a budget agreement in 1990.

Presidential-congressional relations returned to unified government with the election of Bill Clinton to the presidency in 1993 after twelve years of divided government under Reagan and Bush. After two years of often hostile relations, the Republicans took over both chambers of Congress as a result of the midterm elections in November 1994. Republicans in the House, who had not controlled that body in forty years, chose Newt Gingrich (R-Ga.) as Speaker. They drew up and campaigned in 1994 on the "Contract with America" as a conservative agenda to counter what many considered to be Clinton's liberal policies. The stage was set for what some feared would be the greatest interbranch controversy ever.

Scholars and journalists continue to debate the role of the two branches in making policy. As we saw in Chapter 1, many observers consider the president better suited for effective leadership, particularly in foreign affairs. They echo Hamilton's view that the president's advantages over Congress include unity, dispatch, representativeness, and secrecy.[27] In the modern literature, advocates of presidential leadership emphasize that the diverse and fragmented nature of Congress is unlikely to produce the needed clarity of policy and speed of action.[28] In recent years, even in the area of foreign policy, a growing number of scholars support an enhanced or even an equal role of Congress and the president, disputing assumptions about the inherent advantages of the presidency.[29] Particularly with the end of the cold war and the breakup of the Soviet Union, arguments about the necessity of presidential leadership are weakened.

TABLE 2.2   Congressional Resurgence in the 1970s

Presidential Action	Congressional Response	Implications for President
Committing troops	National Commitments Resolution, 1969	Sense of the Senate Resolution requires the president to seek the consent of Congress.
War-making	War Powers Resolution, 1973	President must immediately report any use of the armed forces to Congress and must terminate the use of the military within 60 days unless Congress has declared war; the president can get a 30-day extension. After 90 days, Congress can, through a concurrent resolution, terminate the action.
Emergency powers	National Emergencies Act, 1976	President must notify Congress in advance and identify laws intended to be used in a national emergency. Emergencies are limited to six months. Either house of Congress can vote to end the emergency at any time.
Executive agreements as treaties	Case Act, 1972	The secretary of state must submit within 60 days the texts of any executive agreements.
Impoundment	Budget and Impoundment Control Act, 1974	The president must report any delays in implementation of the budget. Congress established the Congressional Budget Office.
Secrecy	Creation of Senate and House Intelligence Oversight Committees, 1975	House and Senate exercise budgetary control over the CIA and other intelligence agencies.
Reprogramming	Increased use of legislative veto	Congress exercises tighter control over executive branch actions.

In the nation's third century under the Constitution, many questions remained unanswered about the balance between legislative and executive institutions and which branch shapes public policy. This review of interbranch relations has suggested that patterns of policymaking have shifted over time, depending on the political environment, the state of institutional development, the policy agenda, and the effectiveness of individual leadership. Policymaking today is not dominated by Congress as it was in the nineteenth century, nor by the president as it was in the mid-twentieth century. We find instead a shifting array of patterns, including cooperation or deadlock as well as clear leadership by Congress or the president. Yet many questions about the constitutional basis for interbranch competition remain unanswered.

On occasion, legislative and executive officials have turned to the courts—the third branch of government—for remedies. Throughout the Republic's more than two hundred years, the Supreme Court has periodically served as the final arbiter in disputes between legislature and executive, defining the limits of power of each branch. Before examining critiques of the effectiveness of the nation's constitutional structure, we consider the role of the courts in helping to define the balance of power between Congress and the president.

THE COURTS: HELPING SHAPE LEGISLATIVE-EXECUTIVE BOUNDARIES

Two important points help describe the role of the courts in shaping the boundaries of legislative-executive power. First, the courts have attempted to avoid getting involved in disputes between the other two branches. They have refrained from ruling on so-called "political" disputes between branches or in any cases that have become moot (already resolved). Second, when the courts have intervened, they have rarely dealt with fundamental issues of presidential and congressional power. Most frequently, court decisions have nibbled at the edges of separation of powers. In cases of national emergency or wartime, the courts have usually deferred to the expansion of presidential power, even when in apparent violation of the Constitution. Despite these limitations, several court decisions have been very important in affecting the constitutional balance between branches and specific policy questions. In addition, now that institutional conflict is on the increase, the courts have been called on to intervene more than ever in the past three decades. Even though courts often try to avoid disputes between Congress and the president, the Supreme Court has become more of an activist in orientation, as it was in the late nineteenth century. Table 2.3 shows the number of statutes and presidential decisions ruled unconstitutional by the Court during various periods. The challenges to Congress have increased since the 1950s and were particularly extensive against Richard Nixon, who averaged nearly five challenges per year in office. Except for Nixon, however, recent presidents generally have fared better than Congress with the Supreme Court.

Appointment and Removal Power

One set of questions that has occupied the courts is the interplay between presidential-congressional appointment, confirmation, and removal powers. Presidents nominate only the very top officials in the executive branch and all federal judges, subject to Senate confirmation. All evidence suggests that the Senate generally defers to presidential appointees in the executive branch. Only two Cabinet nominees have been rejected in the modern era, Louis Straus as Secretary of Commerce under Eisen-

TABLE 2.3   Supreme Court Decisions against Congress and Presidents

Dates	(years)	No.	(no./year)	Presidents	No.	(no./year)
	Legislative Statutes Voided			*Rulings against Presidents*		
1789–1864	(62)	2	(.01)	Washington–Lincoln	13	(.19)
1865–1910	(46)	33	(.72)	A. Johnson–Taft	6	(.13)
1911–1930	(20)	24	(.83)	Wilson–Hoover	8	(.40)
1931–1936	(6)	14	(.43)	F. Roosevelt	8	(.75)
1937–1953	(17)	3	(.30)	Truman	3	(.30)
1954–1968	(15)	25	(.60)	Eisenhower–L. Johnson	5	(.08)
1969–1988	(20)	38	(.53)	Nixon (25)–Reagan	30	(.67)
1989–1994	(6)	3	(.50)	Bush–Clinton	1	(.17)
Totals	(197)	142	(.72)		74	(.38)

Compiled by the authors from the following sources: for *presidents,* Lyn Ragsdale, *Vital Statistics on the Presidency* (Washington, D.C.: Congressional Quarterly Press, 1996): 435; for *Congress,* Harold Stanley and Richard Neimi, *Vital Statistics on American Politics* (Washington, DC: Congressional Quarterly Press, 1996): 286.

hower and John Tower as Secretary of Defense under Bush. Despite the publicity and controversy over the rejection of Robert Bork, Reagan's nominee to the Supreme Court, the Senate was much more likely to reject presidential Supreme Court nominees in the nineteenth than in the twentieth centuries. Lyn Ragsdale recounts just over thirty instances in our nation's history when presidents encountered difficulties with their Supreme Court nominees.[30]

The question over who had the power to remove officials appointed by the president and confirmed by the Senate embroiled the first Congress and many congresses in subsequent years. After a lengthy debate in 1789, it was agreed that the president would have the power to remove Cabinet secretaries.[31] However, this did not mean that the president had the power to remove all executive branch officials, and questions about executive-legislative removal power remained. The controversy broke out again over Andrew Jackson's removal of the Secretary of the Treasury, against the wishes of Congress, in 1833. As we have seen, this issue also lay behind the main impeachment charge against President Andrew Johnson. The Supreme Court finally confronted the issue directly in the case of *Myers v. United States* (1926).[32] The case arose over the removal of a postmaster in Portland, Oregon, by the Postmaster General, with the concurrence of President Woodrow Wilson. The action violated a law passed by Congress in 1876, which required the Senate to advise and consent on the removal of all postmasters. In the decision, the Supreme Court ruled that the president has broad powers to remove executive-branch officials and that the removal power is vested in the president alone.

The Court's unqualified ruling on the removal power was amended a decade later in the case of *Humphrey's Executor v. United States* (1935).[33] Franklin D. Roosevelt removed one of President Hoover's appointees to the Federal Trade Commission

(FTC) on policy grounds, rather than for neglect of duty or malfeasance as specified in the FTC Act. The Court scaled back the broad decision in *Myers,* unanimously ruling against Roosevelt. The opinion noted that the FTC was not purely an executive agency, so Congress had the right to specify conditions for removal.[34]

The removal power has periodically reemerged as an issue between branches in recent years. With interbranch conflict running high during the Nixon administration, the courts stepped in on several cases. In 1973, President Nixon fired Watergate Special Prosecutor Archibald Cox because he was pressing the case against the president too forcefully. The event became known as the "Saturday Night Massacre," because the Attorney General and the Deputy Attorney General resigned rather than carry out Nixon's order. Although Cox never got his job back, the federal court ruled that the president had illegally removed the special prosecutor from his post.[35]

Early in 1997, the Republican-controlled Senate considered a number of measures designed to limit President Clinton from appointing federal judges not to their liking. One of the devices would expand senatorial courtesy, usually reserved for district court nominees, to presidential nominees to the appellate courts. Any Republican senator from states within each of the eleven federal circuits could object to a presidential nominee. Another measure would require advance approval of a nominee's ideological background. Some conservative Republican senators even made efforts to impeach Clinton-appointed judges they deemed too liberal. Part of the motivation for the proposals was to reduce the power over nominations from the Senate Judiciary Committee, where confirmation recommendations have traditionally resided, and place the decisions more in the Republican caucus as a whole.

Recent Court Decisions

In addition to the removal power, courts have intervened in battles between Congress and the president over questions ranging from legislative vetoes to executive privilege. Conversely, they have exercised judicial restraint in other areas, particularly decisions over war powers and control of foreign policy. A Supreme Court decision in 1974 helped force a president from office as the conflict between Congress and Richard Nixon reached its climax. The case arose when the special prosecutor, whose office had been created by Congress, subpoenaed the tapes that Nixon had secretly made of conversations in the Oval Office of the White House. The administration refused to turn them over on the grounds that executive privilege gave the president the right to withhold certain sensitive information. In the landmark case of *United States v. Nixon* (1974), the Supreme Court unanimously ruled that executive privilege was valid in some cases but not to the degree claimed by the president.[36] Nixon finally turned over the recordings and was forced to resign six weeks later because the evidence contained in the tapes proved he had knowledge of and participated in the cover-up of the Watergate break-in. Executive privilege became an issue again in Clinton's second term when top aides, such as Bruce Lindsay, called by the special prosecutor to testify about alleged sexual misconduct by the president, refused to testify on the grounds of executive privilege.

Other recent court decisions have affected presidential-congressional relations. The Supreme Court refused a lawsuit by U.S. Senator Barry Goldwater (R-Ariz.) against President Jimmy Carter, who nullified a defense treaty with Taiwan. Carter took this action in an effort to improve relations with mainland China. The Court determined that the president has the right to abrogate as well as negotiate treaties. Another high-profile case before the U.S. Supreme Court concerned the legitimacy of the line item veto. The Court earlier ruled that legislators could not challenge the veto until it was used, but President Clinton's item veto of three tax items in the 1997 balanced budget agreement sparked new challenges to this law, which many experts believed was of questionable constitutionality.

One of the key separation-of-powers decisions of recent decades arose in response to congressional attempts to exert control over rules and regulations developed by the executive branch. The "legislative veto" is a process whereby an action by the bureaucracy can be negated if it is disapproved by Congress. As the number of legislative veto provisions included in bills increased, provisions were included whereby rules could be disapproved by a vote of both houses, that of a single house, or in some instances the vote of a single committee. In the case of *Immigration and Naturalization Service v. Chadha* (1983), the Supreme Court declared the legislative veto unconstitutional because it blurred the distinction between branches created by the founders.[37] If Congress wants to "veto" a rule or regulation promulgated by a federal agency, a bill must pass both houses of Congress and be signed by the president. The *Chadha* decision invalidated portions of more federal laws in a single stroke than all previous Courts had struck down in history.

Although the legislative veto was overturned, lawmakers continue to use variations of it. For example, members can adopt "report and wait" provisions that require agencies to submit proposed decisions to Congress. Legislators may pass joint resolutions as opposed to regular bills. Vetoes may be imposed through the appropriations process, denying resources to assure compliance with congressional wishes. Finally, informal understandings between the branches preserve the legislative veto. Such accommodation might not be strictly legal, but it may be necessitated by political realities. Therefore, despite the *Chadha* decision, the legislative veto continues in various reconstituted forms.

Several years later, the Supreme Court applied this narrow interpretation of separation of powers to congressional attempts to reduce massive federal budget deficits. The Gramm-Rudman-Hollings mandatory deficit-reduction law had provided that the Comptroller General of the United States—an official removable only by Congress—could order budget cuts in the executive branch. In the case of *Bowsher v. Synar* (1986), the Supreme Court ruled that this provision violated the separation of powers.[38] Some immediately proposed making the Comptroller General removable by the president, but Congress reinstated mandatory deficit reduction by giving final responsibility to the president's Budget Director. Of equal interest in this case was the more basic issue that the Court avoided: Did Congress have the authority to order executive branch cuts in the first place? By focusing on the more narrow question of who could remove the Comptroller General, the Court sidestepped the more fundamental question of the relative power of legislative and executive institutions in national government.

In 1988, the Supreme Court sided with Congress in a separation-of-powers dispute with the president. Under challenge was the law enacted after Watergate, creating special prosecutors (later called independent counsels) to investigate wrongdoing in the executive branch. Several Reagan-era officials who had been investigated and prosecuted under the statute challenged its constitutionality. In the case of *Morrison v. Olsen* (1988), the Court upheld the constitutionality of the independent counsel law. The justices did not accept the administration's claim that the law interfered with the president's authority over criminal prosecution.[39] On January 17, 1998, Clinton became the first sitting president ever to testify as a defendant in a court case, the Paula Jones sexual harassment suit filed against him. The suit was later dismissed.

The separation-of-powers cases rejected by the courts in recent years are as instructive as the cases that they have heard. Particularly in the area of foreign affairs, the courts have steered clear of decisions. During the Vietnam War, the courts consistently refused to hear challenges brought by members of Congress concerning the constitutionality of an undeclared war. Despite the courts' unresponsiveness, legal challenges by members of Congress against the president have proliferated in recent years. A suit seeking to test the legality of U.S. presence in El Salvador was dismissed by a federal appeals court in 1983.[40] A suit challenging the invasion of Grenada was dismissed in 1985 because the invasion was over. Similarly, cases seeking to test the constitutionality of U.S. policy in Nicaragua and sending the U.S. Navy to the Persian Gulf in 1988 were dismissed by federal courts.

How important have the courts been in shaping the boundaries of legislative-executive power? Even though Congress and the president have increasingly turned to the courts in their battles with each other, the courts continue to avoid cases. When they cannot, they tend to decide cases on the narrowest grounds possible. While court decisions have made important impacts, they have not decisively changed the balance of power between branches. That balance continues to be determined by political factors rather than court rulings.

CONCLUSION

Many critics argue that, whatever the genius of the constitutional system two centuries ago, it is inadequate for the governing needs of today. The system of separate institutions sharing powers is blamed for inaction or inadequate policies in the face of urgent problems. Most of the founders saw the Constitution as a good start but an imperfect document. Thomas Jefferson believed that it would essentially be rewritten every generation or so. A century after its drafting, however, the Constitution tended to be seen as nearly perfect, not to be tinkered with. In the late nineteenth century, British Prime Minister William Gladstone called it "the most wonderful work ever struck off at a given time by the brain and purpose of man."[41] Most modern-day observers are less sanguine in their assessment, but there has been little sentiment to change history's most durable written blueprint for government.[42]

After two centuries, separation of powers and checks and balances remain the constitutional foundation on which shared policymaking is based. Whatever the presumed merits of the arguments to amend the Constitution to reduce the separation between branches, the constitutional structure is here to stay. The relationship between Congress and the president is one of separate institutions sharing power and responsibility for both foreign and domestic policy. As the cases in later chapters will show, policy is made through a variety of patterns of legislative-executive interaction. To make the system work effectively, however, Congress and the president must find ways to work together constructively on the most difficult issues. How each branch makes policy through its own institutional arrangements and decision-making processes is the subject of the next two chapters.

ENDNOTES

1. Elmer E. Cornwell, Jr., "The American Constitutional Tradition: Its Impact and Development," in Kermit L. Hall et al. (eds.), *The Constitution as an Amending Device* (Washington, D.C.: American Political Science Association, 1981): 4.

2. John Locke, *Second Treatise on Civil Government* (1690). See also Clinton Rossiter, *1787: The Grand Convention* (New York: MacMillan, 1966).

3. R. R. Palmer and Joel Colton, *A History of the Modern World* (New York: Knopf, 1965): 327.

4. Joseph Kallenbach, *The American Chief Executive* (New York: Harper and Row, 1966): 26.

5. U.S. Congress, "Debates of the Federal Convention of 1787 as Reported by James Madison," in *Documents Illustrative of the Formation of the Union of the American States,* 69th Cong., 1st Sess., 1927: 664.

6. Paul Goodman, "The First American Party System," in William N. Chambers and Walter Dean Burnham (eds.), *The American Party Systems* (New York: Oxford University Press, 1975): 56–89.

7. Robert C. Byrd, *The Senate 1789–1989* (Washington, D.C.: U.S. Government Printing Office, 1989): 28.

8. Louis Fisher, *The Politics of Shared Power: Congress and the Executive* (Washington, D.C.: Congressional Quarterly Press, 1981): 33.

9. Ibid.

10. James D. Richardson (ed.), *A Compilation of Messages and Papers of the Presidents,* Vol 1, (Washington, D.C.: U.S. Congress, 1899): 64–115.

11. William Maclay, *Sketches of Debate in the First Senate of the United States* (New York: Ungar, 1965): 135, 172.

12. James S. Young, *The Washington Community, 1800–1828* (New York: Columbia University Press, 1966): 168.

13. Charles Williamson, *American Suffrage from Property to Democracy 1760–1860* (Princeton, N.J.: Princeton University Press, 1960).

14. James L. Sundquist, *Decline and Resurgence of Congress* (Washington, D.C.: Brookings Institution, 1981): 23–24.

15. Louis Fisher. *Politics of Shared Powers,* 2d ed. (Washington, D.C.: Congressional Quarterly Press, 1987): 43.

16. J. G. Randall, *Constitutional Problems Under Lincoln* (Magnolia, Mass.: Smith, 1964): 58.

17. John F. Kennedy, *Profiles in Courage* (New York: Harper and Row, 1956): Ch. 6.

18. Slaughterhouse cases (1873), Civil Rights cases (1883), and *Plessy v. Ferguson (1896)* essentially disenfranchised southern blacks.

19. Charles Beard and Mary Beard, *The Rise of American Civilization* (New York: MacMillan, 1927) and Louis Hacker, *The Triumph of American Capitalism* (New York: Columbia University Press, 1940).

20. Woodrow Wilson, *Congressional Government* (Columbus, Ohio: Bobbs Merrill, 1885).

21. Fisher (note 8): 37.

22. Nelson Polsby, "Institutionalization in the U.S. House of Representatives," *American Political Science Review* 63 (1969): 787–807.

23. James M. Burns, *Roosevelt: The Lion and the Fox* (New York: Harcourt Brace, 1956): 165.

24. Thomas Cronin, *The State of the Presidency,* 2d ed. (Boston: Little Brown, 1980): 25–30.

25. Arthur Schlesinger, *The Imperial Presidency* (Boston: Houghton Mifflin, 1973).

26. Geoffrey Hodgson, *All Things to All Men: The False Promise of the Modern American Presidency* (New York: Simon and Schuster, 1980) and Harold Barger, *The Impossible Presidency* (Glenview, Ill.: Scott Foresman, 1984).

27. John C. Donovan, *The Cold Warriors: A Policy Making Elite* (Lexington, MA: D.C. Heath, 1974): 57, 70; Dorothy B. James, *The Contemporary Presidency,* 2d ed. (New York: Pegasus, 1973): 179; Robert A. Dahl, *Congress and Foreign Policy* (New York: Harcourt Brace, 1950); James A. Robinson, *Congress and Foreign Policy* (Homewood, IL: Dorsey, 1967).

28. I. M. Destler, *Presidents, Bureaucrats and Foreign Policy* (Princeton, N.J.: Princeton University Press, 1974): 85; Robinson (note 27): 65; Donovan (note 27).

29. Sundquist (note 14); Charles O. Jones, *The Presidency in a Separated System* (Washington, D.C.: Brookings Institution, 1994) and *Separate But Equal Branches* (Chatham, NJ: Chatham House, 1995).

30. *Vital Statistics on the Presidency* (Washington, D.C.: Congressional Quarterly Press, 1996): 422–423.

31. Fisher (note 8): 56.

32. *Myers v. U.S.* 272 U.S. 52, 61, 98 (1926).

33. *Humphrey's Executor v. U.S.* 295 U.S. 602, 618–619 (1935).

34. Fisher (note 8): 68.

35. *Nader v. Bork* 366 F. Supp. 104 (D.D.C. 1973).

36. *U.S. v. Nixon* 418 U.S. 683 (1974).

37. *Immigration and Naturalization Service v. Chadha* 462 U.S. 919 (1983).

38. *Bowsher v. Synar* 478 U.S. 714 (1986).

39. *Morrison v. Olson* 108 SCT 2597, 101 L Ed 2d 569; on remand in resealed case; 857 F2d 801 (1988).

40. *Congressional Quarterly Weekly Report* (January 7, 1989): 14.

41. William Gladstone, "Kin Beyond the Sea," *North America Review* (Sept/Oct, 1878).

42. Donald Robinson (ed), *Reforming American Government: The Bicentennial Papers of the Committee on the Constitutional System* (Boulder, CO: Westview Press, 1985); Lloyd Cutler, "To Form a Government: On the Defects of Separation of Powers," *Foreign Affairs* (Fall, 1980), excerpted in Thomas Cronin (ed.), *Rethinking the Presidency* (Boston: Little Brown, 1982): 62; David Stockman, *The Triumph of Politics* (New York: Harper and Row, 1987): 9; James Sundquist, *Constitutional Reform and Effective Government* (Washington, D.C.: Brookings Institution, 1986): 4; James Q. Wilson, "In Defense of Separation of Powers: in Cronin (1982): 179–182; Arthur Schlesinger, "Leave the Constitution Alone," in Robinson (1985): 53.

3

THE PRESIDENCY
AND POLICYMAKING

The powers of the presidency are often described. Its limi-
tations should sometimes be remembered.
—JOHN F. KENNEDY (1963)

Under what conditions can the president of the United States set the agenda and lead government? Under what circumstances does Congress follow the lead of the president? As we saw in Chapter 2, both institutions have undergone profound changes in character and relative power over two hundred years. The last half of the twentieth century witnessed a dramatic expansion in the American presidency; the president became the focal point of national politics. The dominant military and economic strength of the United States put the president in an even more powerful position.[1] Yet even in their most dominant periods, presidents faced a myriad of constraints. An enhanced presidency did not mean a diminished Congress. The roles of Congress, the bureaucracy, interest groups, and other actors remained important. Today, the ability of the president to dominate the policy process appears to be declining.

This chapter explores several important questions about the president as a partner in national policymaking. First, what is the potential for presidential leadership, and what are the available political resources and the most difficult obstacles and limitations? Second, how do the four factors identified in Chapter 1 (the political environment, the institutionalized presidency, individual leadership, and presidential agendas) shape the president's role in policymaking? Finally, what is the legislative record of modern presidents? How can we measure and compare the relative performance of recent occupants of the White House in getting what they wanted from Congress? What do those findings suggest about a tandem institutions/separationist perspective compared with a presidency-centered approach?

Conclusions about the policymaking role of the presidency may depend on the level of analysis one adopts and the nature of policy outputs at that level. The presidency can be seen at the individual level as a single person occupying the office, with certain strengths and weaknesses, innate abilities, and personal limitations. Presidents, like other actors in the system, act rationally to achieve certain political, ideological, or personal goals. Policy outputs may be in the form of presidential statements, executive orders, or individual decisions. Second, at the institutional level, the presidency can be viewed as a complex office that a president inherits on inauguration day and leaves behind at the end of his term. Presidents are limited and shaped by the office they inherit, but at the same time, they alter it in their own ways. Policy outputs at the institutional level reflect a wide range of actions, administration proposals, and decisions that emanate from the presidency. Third, at the system level, the presidency can be conceptualized as part of the larger constitutional system and international arena. Policy outputs, such as statutes, regulations, and treaties, emerge from shared responsibilities with Congress, the bureaucracy, and other domestic or international actors. Because our emphasis is on the legislative relationship between branches, the system level of analysis is particularly important.

Considerable disagreement exists among presidency scholars over whether to study the office from individual or institutional perspectives.[2] Although it is useful to consider the presidency from different levels of analysis, the lines between these different levels are not always distinct. The president may have multiple goals that sometimes conflict with each other, creating difficult choices. Presidents want to succeed, to improve their standing in the polls, to push their philosophy of government, to enact good public policy, and to establish a historical legacy, but it may not be possible to achieve all of these at the same time. Individual actions by the president always involve various system and institutional variables. Understanding the president's role in policymaking at the system level depends on both personal leadership and institutional characteristics. It also depends on understanding the political resources and constraints of the American presidency.

THE POTENTIAL FOR PRESIDENTIAL LEADERSHIP

Political Resources and Sources of Presidential Power

Although the powers granted to the president in the Constitution were not extensive, they form the foundation for presidential power today. Many of the disputes between branches, as we saw in Chapter 2, still involve fundamental constitutional interpretations. Did George Bush need congressional authorization for the use of force against Iraq in 1991, or did he have the authority as commander-in-chief to order the invasion on his own? Although he claimed to have the authority, the fact that he requested congressional approval suggests that the constitutional question remains unresolved. The presidential powers to appoint officials, to wield executive authority, and to see that the laws are faithfully executed are significant, but they do not assure the president success in the legislative arena. Informal and implied powers have proved more important as resources in shared policymaking with Congress.

Clinton Rossiter, expressing the view that a strong presidency is essential to effective policymaking, described the expanded roles of the president: chief diplomat, chief legislator, party chief, chief of state, voice of the people, and manager of prosperity.[3] How would presidents be able to fulfill these expanded responsibilities? Developments not envisioned by the writers of the Constitution contributed to increases in the president's power. Because of greater governmental scope and complexity and the trend toward federal solutions to problems, the public came to expect more of the president and more of the Congress as well. Presidents were expected to take a greater legislative role and provide more unified policy alternatives.[4] Within a few years after World War II, Congress and the country had come to look to the president to formulate a legislative agenda.[5] As crisis manager, the president was granted a number of emergency powers over the years to deal with foreign and domestic disasters.[6] The president may call up the National Guard in the case of a civil crisis, as Eisenhower did in Little Rock, Arkansas, in 1957. In addition, the dominant global role of the United States in the postwar era, the dangers of the cold war, and the threat of nuclear destruction further strengthened the role of the president.

Most of the president's political resources are not formal ones. Richard Neustadt noted that presidential power was primarily exercised not through the ability to command but through the ability to bargain and persuade.[7] Presidents succeed by consolidating and maximizing personal political power and by managing political resources skillfully. One of the most important resources is the ability to use the mass media to reach the people. Teddy Roosevelt talked about using the presidency as a "bully pulpit," but the advent of television significantly increased the president's ability to command the center stage of politics. Management of the news and public relations became important presidential resources.[8] Whether through an address to Congress, a visit to a foreign capitol, a press conference, or a hike at Camp David, the president can make news instantly by going public.[9]

In addition to a vast public relations apparatus, the presidency has other perquisites that can enhance presidential power. The president controls several thousand appointments to the most important jobs in the executive branch. This can help shape rule making, enforcement, and policy implementation. The president has resources as the head of his political party, including the national party organization and elected members of the party. In addition, the president has tremendous fundraising potential, either for reelection as president or for the election of fellow party members. President Bush, for example, raised nearly $1 million in a single fundraiser in 1991. President Bill Clinton seemingly elevated fund-raising to a new level by rewarding major campaign contributors with intimate meetings and sometimes even overnight lodging in the White House. Both he and Vice President Al Gore were under fire for making solicitation phone calls from their White House offices, a practice that some considered a violation of federal law.

Sitting in the Oval Office in the mansion on Pennsylvania Avenue, the president enjoys the trappings of a chief of state. In the White House, there is a professional staff of some 500 individuals, and several thousand more are close by in the Executive Office of the President. Air Force One, the president's private jet, and scores of helicopters are available. Presidents may try to emphasize the "regal" aspects of office. Lyndon Johnson, for example, raised his desk and chair while lowering the other chairs in the office, noting "it's hard to bargain from your knees."

The Limits of Presidential Power

Presidents may live like kings, but they cannot govern like kings. Despite the ability to command national and international media attention, the power of the presidency to direct the policymaking process in the United States is limited. Constraints became particularly evident after the Vietnam War and Watergate, when Congress was resurgent. Political Scientist Harold Barger described what he called the "impossible presidency": an office whose expectations far exceeded its ability to produce.

> *The presidency has grown impossible because of important changes in American life and because of dramatic alterations in the political and economic balance of power and influence globally. . . . During the post–World War II era, presidential authority over domestic and foreign policymaking increased, but forces leading to fragmentation in American politics already were beginning to chip away. . . .*[10]

Changes in the international system also have radically changed the ability of the American president to shape world affairs. The collapse of Communism and the dismantling of the Soviet Union eliminated the crisis mentality of the cold war, which had favored presidential leadership. In addition, other economic and geopolitical changes have altered the ability of the United States to act independently in the world in recent years. Increasingly, the United States depends for its prosperity on the global marketplace and no longer has a self-contained economy. In foreign affairs, multilateral cooperation and greater reliance on the United Nations, as in the Persian Gulf War in 1991, have replaced unilateral American action. Richard Rose suggests that the modern presidency, which began with the inauguration of Franklin D. Roosevelt in 1933, has ended and a new postmodern presidency has arrived:

> *The difference between the modern and the post modern presidency is that a postmodern president can no longer dominate the international system. . . . While the White House is accustomed to influencing foreign nations, the postmodern president must accept something less appealing: Other nations can now influence what the White House achieves.*[11]

Many efforts at congressional reassertion (described in Chapter 2) had profound cumulative effects on the presidency by increasing the constraints in the policymaking process. This trend was magnified by changes in elections and the decline of political parties in the United States. The growing independence of voters, the tendency toward ticket-splitting, and the decline in electoral competition for Congress have sharply reduced presidential coattails. Republican landslides in the 1972, 1984, and 1988 elections failed to produce any significant Republican gains in Congress. Such gains came only after Democrat Bill Clinton had occupied the White House for two years. Republicans captured both chambers of Congress in the 1994 midterm elections and maintained control even after Clinton's decisive reelection victory over former Senate Majority Leader Bob Dole (R-Kan.) in the 1996 election.

In addition to Congress, other institutions and actors constrain the president. The Supreme Court has become more likely to overrule past precedents. Interest groups remain a potent force in all stages of policymaking. The bureaucracy can be an obstacle to presidential leadership, particularly when the president's goals differ from the dominant norms and direction of an agency. An aide to John F. Kennedy once remarked, "Everyone believes in democracy until he gets to the White House and then you begin to believe in dictatorship, because it's so hard to get things done."[12] In short, although the presidency has expanded far beyond its constitutionally prescribed powers, other competitors for power are also stronger, and the nation is increasingly interdependent in the global system.

THE POLICYMAKING ENVIRONMENT

Presidential Elections

At one time in American politics, a landslide presidential victory at the polls would usually be accompanied by significant gains in Congress by the president's party. In 1936, Roosevelt was overwhelmingly reelected, carrying scores of new Democrats into Congress. In 1952, Dwight Eisenhower's massive electoral victory led to Republican Party control of both the House and the Senate. In 1964, Lyndon Johnson parlayed his landslide victory into expanded Democratic majorities in both houses. Since 1968, however, presidential coattails have diminished significantly.[13] Although Ronald Reagan exhibited coattail effects in 1980, helping the Republicans capture the Senate and reduce Democratic majorities in the House, the trend is clearly for presidential and congressional elections to be decoupled. George Bush had no coattails in 1988, and Republicans lost seats in both the House and Senate. He ended up taking office having a lower percentage of members of his own political party in Congress than any other president in history.

Of course, the problems have been even worse for Democratic presidential candidates, who usually trail their Democratic congressional candidates in vote margin. Since 1932, Democratic candidates for Congress, on average, have won 4.0 percent more of the popular vote than Democratic candidates for president. Table 3.1 ranks

TABLE 3.1   Vote Differential between Democratic Presidential
Candidates and Congressional Running Mates (1932–1996)

Presidential Candidate	Differential
Johnson	+3.8%
Roosevelt	+2.8 (4 elections)
Clinton	−2.5 (2 elections)
Truman	−2.8
Kennedy	−5.0
Stevenson	−7.2 (2 elections)
Humphrey	−7.3
Dukakis	−7.7
Carter	−7.8 (2 elections)
Mondale	−11.5
McGovern	−14.5
Average	−4.0

Source: Adapted from Norman J. Ornstein et al, *Vital Statistics on Congress* (Washington, D.C.: Congressional Quarterly Press, 1996); Lyn Ragsdale, *Vital Statistics on the Presidency* (Washington D.C.: Congressional Quarterly Press, 1996: 155); data for 1996 updated by Shull and Jonathan Knuckey.

Legend: Figures beginning in 1975 are for House Democrats only.

the last eleven Democratic presidential nominees by the percentage they ran ahead or behind congressional candidates of their parties. Only Roosevelt and Johnson ran ahead and by relatively small amounts. Clinton did next best, and his difference figure would have been considerably higher had not Independent Ross Perot cut into his popular vote margin in 1992. However, these generally negative findings have led some to suggest the existence of "reverse coattails"; the popularity of Democratic congressional candidates may actually help increase voter support for the party's presidential candidate.

Although presidential and congressional elections are increasingly independent, there may be some residue of influence, even if not producing a policy-specific mandate. George Edwards suggests that elections still "provide a vehicle through which the public can express its general views to a congressman and can have an effect on congressional behavior without having detailed views on specific policies."[14]

Public Opinion

Public opinion is an important presidential resource, and it often is shaped by the political and economic environment of the country. One of the key elements of public opinion is public support for the president—the approval rating. This has been measured since the 1930s, so it allows comparisons of presidents over time. Approval ratings have proved extremely volatile. In 1991, for example, George Bush's public approval ratings dropped some 40 percent in the nine months between the end of the

Gulf war in March and the bottoming of public confidence in the economy in December. Bill Clinton's popularity was low during his first term but actually improved at the beginning of his second. The volatility of these popular approval ratings may be seen in Figure 3.1.

Studies have shown that certain factors consistently have a positive or negative impact on presidential approval ratings.[15] Presidents gain in popularity during an international crisis or other occasions when the American people seem to "rally around the flag." This phenomenon occurs even in unsuccessful foreign operations: Kennedy gained in the polls after the abortive invasion at the Bay of Pigs, Cuba invasion in

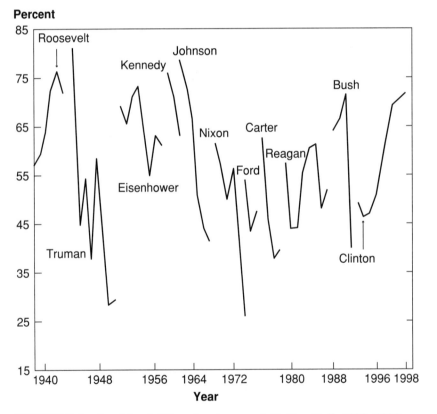

FIGURE 3.1   Presidential Popular Approval, Gallup Poll, 1938–1998. Percent who approve averaged by year. Question: Do you approve or disapprove of the way [president's name] is handling his job as president?

Sources: Harold Stanley and Richard Neimi, *Vital Statistics on American Politics* (Washington D.C.: Congressional Quarterly Press, 1996: 261); figures for 1996 and 1997 updated by Shull and Randy Burnside.

1961. Perhaps the most important factor to shaping presidential approval is the performance of the U.S. economy. Poor economic performance translates into declining presidential popularity, as George Bush, Ronald Reagan, and Jimmy Carter all discovered during their presidencies. Scandal or malfeasance in office can damage a president's standing: Truman's popularity dropped because of scandals involving his staff; Nixon's approval hit a record low for all presidents during Watergate; and Reagan dropped noticeably after the Iran-Contra revelations. On the other hand, Clinton's approval ratings rose to their highest levels after allegations about a relationship with intern Monica Lewinsky. Finally, most presidents simply become less popular the longer they are in office. Although Reagan and Clinton through mid 1998 seemed to be exceptions, the trend holds for most presidents and has important implications for a president's legislative strategies.

Presidents are not passive in the battle over public opinion; today, they actively attempt to bolster their public support and sway public sentiment. The public relations apparatus of the federal government now costs well over $1 billion. Articulate spokespersons often present the president's views to the public. Release of good and bad news from the White House is timed accordingly to hit or miss the nightly television news. Presidents may manipulate economic or budget data to put the best possible face on results. Presidents and their public relations team are often evasive and secretive about information that might have negative political effects. As one of President Carter's spokesmen commented, "Government is not in the truth business. It is the presumed duty of an administration to govern, not to do reporters' work for them."[16]

Public support for the president is critical, because it may affect legislative success with Congress. Research has found that the greater the president's popularity in a congressional district, the greater the likelihood of support from that member on presidential proposals or on measures where the president has taken a position.[17] Edwards found, for example, that increases in a president's popularity of 10 percent increase legislative support by about 1.5 percent.[18] However, other scholars have argued that popularity does not translate directly into enacted legislation; popular support is only one of many important environmental factors.[19] In addition, popularity seems to help presidents more during the earlier years in a president's term compared with later when party majorities in Congress become more important.

Partisanship and Control of Congress

Despite the decline of political parties in recent years, the increase in ticket splitting, and divided government, partisan composition of Congress remains one of the most important aspects of the president's political environment. Partisanship is a key element of presidential support in Congress. Presidents often begin building legislative coalitions with members of their own party, whether in the majority or the minority. Members of the president's party have greater incentives, both in terms of politics and policy, to go along with him. Studies have shown that the party occupying the

White House tends to have more cohesive voting patterns in Congress than the other party, particularly on foreign policy issues.[20]

The alignment in Congress helps determine whether a president pursues a partisan, bipartisan, or cross-partisan approach with Congress. Although party government has worked on occasion in American political history, the legacy of Woodrow Wilson's inability to win ratification for the Treaty of Versailles in 1919 stands as a reminder of the consequences of excessive partisanship in the U.S. system. More often than not, presidents need the votes of members of the other party to succeed legislatively. Even Lyndon Johnson relied on and cultivated Republican help in his civil rights battles because of divisions within the Democratic party. Ronald Reagan, with the help of a small band of conservative Democrats, pursued a cross-partisan strategy in 1981. Although his program was adopted in 1981, the rest of his administration witnessed declining presidential legislative success and increasing levels of partisanship in congressional voting.[21]

Bill Clinton was elected to the presidency as a moderate and, despite a cohesive opposition party, he made numerous efforts to obtain support from Republican legislators. In the 1996 election, he was the first Democrat reelected in 60 years while the Republicans controlled two consecutive Congresses for the first time in 68 years. Many observers speculated greater bipartisanship for the 105th Congress (1997–1999) after the considerable acrimony of the 104th Congress. Moderate Senator John Breaux (D-La.) stated at the outset: "I'm hoping for some cooperation with a president who knows he has to govern from the center and a Congress that knows that compromise is not a dirty word."[22] Reduced Republican majorities in the House seemed to foster the spirit of cooperation. Perhaps the best example of bipartisanship was the 1997 balanced budget agreement (discussed more fully in Chapter 7). Although the budget deal blurred ideological distinctions between the parties, the approval ratings of both branches increased after its adoption.

Of course, party loyalty is rarely certain. Because members of a president's party support him more often than the opposition does, legislative success is related to party control of the House and Senate. Until the mid-1970s, presidents were successful 85 percent of the time when they had majorities in Congress, compared with only 65 percent when their party was in the minority.[23] Since then, presidential success has declined overall, but even Jimmy Carter (who was less popular than either Reagan or Bush) received greater support from Congress because of the partisan Democratic majorities. Of all the factors in the political environment, majorities in Congress remain the single best predictor of presidential support and legislative success.[24] Yet, the influence of party is mediated by other environmental, institutional, leadership, and agenda factors, which we shall consider next.

PRESIDENTIAL INSTITUTIONS

The informal advisory system that had served Presidents Washington through Hoover proved inadequate in the 1930s when government expanded into the areas of social welfare, economic management, regulation, and other new activities. The Brownlow Report of 1937, commissioned by President Roosevelt, issued a number of recommendations for reorganizing the American presidency. The changes that were adopted permanently altered the nature of the office. The institutionalized presidency consists of the president and those who work directly for the president: the inner circle of White House staff and presidential agencies that play a regular and important role in decision making. The presidency is much more than a single individual but much less than the executive branch. Three of the key elements of the presidency are the White House staff, the Executive Office of the President (EOP), and the cabinet.

White House Staff, Executive Office, and Cabinet

Two years after the Brownlow Report, the White House staff and EOP were created. The White House staff includes domestic staff to care for the president and his family as well as the president's top advisors: press secretary, chief of staff, domestic affairs advisor, national security advisor, political affairs advisor, communications director, appointments secretary, congressional liaison, and others. These staff members serve two important functions: They are the president's ambassadors to groups and constituencies in the political system, ranging from Congress to civil rights groups to the business community. In addition, the White House staff is an important decision-making group within the administration, working with the president in formulating foreign policy decisions, a legislative package, a budget, or an economic plan. The White House staff grew from fifty during the Roosevelt administration to around five hundred in the early 1970s. In recent years, the staff has consisted of around 400 individuals.

The EOP forms a second circle around the president. It represents a mini-bureaucracy that works directly for the president. Most employees are located outside of the White House, usually in the Executive Office buildings located nearby. One of the first agencies within the EOP was the Bureau of the Budget (BOB), which played a key role in the institutionalized presidency by compiling the budget for the executive branch. In 1970 BOB was reorganized into the Office of Management and Budget (OMB). Besides formulating the executive budget, OMB helped to manage the vast bureaucracy and, later, to review federal regulations.

The EOP also includes the National Security Council (NSC), created by the National Security Act of 1947. This postwar legislation, based on the lessons of World War II, created the Defense Department (DOD, formerly the War Department), the Central Intelligence Agency (CIA), as well as the NSC. The NSC was designed to better coordinate national security policy and give the president better advice, but oftentimes it has been unable to overcome competition and conflict between DOD, the State Department, and the White House.

The cabinet (the oldest presidential institution, dating back to George Washington) is another source of presidential coordination and advice. The cabinet has long appealed to presidents because of tradition and the hope that the heads of the federal departments can be effectively used to manage the vast federal bureaucracy. However, the cabinet has proved to be of limited value as an advisory body in recent times. Cabinet members have divided loyalty between their job as presidential advisors and their jobs as heads of large executive departments. Cabinet secretaries sometimes "go native"—begin to work more in the interests of the department than those of the president.

Nonetheless, the cabinet remains an integral part of the institutionalized presidency. The composition of the cabinet has symbolic importance, particularly sensitivity to minority concerns through the appointment of blacks, women, and Hispanics. Eisenhower's cabinet was unflatteringly characterized as "nine millionaires and a plumber."[25] Presidents choose between policy generalists and policy specialists associated with a particular constituency such as farmers or veterans. To improve the effectiveness of the cabinet as an advisory institution, some presidents have divided the cabinet into councils, similar to subcommittees, and included members of the White House staff. The vice president, whose role within the White House has increased in importance in all administrations since Carter, also may be part of cabinet councils or work groups.

Central Clearance and Legislative Liaison

One of the most important changes in the legislative role of the presidency was the development of *central clearance:* White House review and approval of all agency program proposals before they are submitted to Congress. Central clearance of programs became institutionalized in the 1950s, helping formalize the president's role as "chief agenda setter."[26] Three separate but interrelated processes are included by program clearance: the approval of departmental legislative initiatives, submission of the president's package of legislative proposals, and coordinating advice on whether the president should sign or veto legislation (called the enrolled bill process).[27] Programs that used to originate within departments and agencies are sent through OMB, which coordinates with the White House staff and the president. This process increased presidential control of a diverse range of policy proposals from the bureaucracy, but it did not ensure greater success. Effective selling of the proposals on Capitol Hill was also needed.

The development of more formal *legislative liaison* operations corresponded with the growth of central clearance beginning with the Eisenhower administration in the late 1950s. The modern Office of Congressional Relations was fashioned to a large extent by Larry O'Brien under Kennedy and Johnson.[28] The liaison office coordinates the legislative efforts of the president, conveying information and carrying messages between the president and congressional leaders. The president's top lobbyists may engage in behind-the-scenes negotiations with key legislative leaders, and other top staff people, such as the chief of staff or OMB Director, also may be involved. Congressional liaison efforts help coordinate the president's lobbying efforts, and most members of Congress perceive them as useful.[29] The experience and quality of the president's appointments to the Office of Congressional Relations influence the administration's legislative success. Jimmy Carter, in particular, suffered because of the inexperience and blunders by his liaison office.

Richard Neustadt observed that "All presidents wish that they could make Congress serve them as a rubber stamp, converting their agendas into prompt enactments, and most presidents will try to bring that miracle about, whenever and as best they can."[30] Nonetheless, direct personal involvement by the president varies considerably. Richard Nixon appointed a staff with extensive Capitol Hill experience and avoided much direct personal contact, since he found personally lobbying Congress distasteful. Ronald Reagan also relied heavily on staff to manage his legislative agenda on the Hill, but to a lesser extent than Nixon. Roosevelt, Johnson, Bush, and Clinton took more active personal roles in lobbying, with differing degrees of success. In 1990, Bush lobbied hard for enactment of the budget summit agreement, personally calling dozens of members. The proposal was defeated anyway. Kennedy, Eisenhower, and Carter fall somewhere in the middle of the scale of personal involvement.

PERSONAL LEADERSHIP

In addition to the political environment and the institutions of the modern presidency, personal characteristics and the leadership abilities of the president influence legislative success. Although presidents inherit essentially the same presidential institutions, they have some opportunities to shape the office and the policymaking process to their liking. Certain presidents have greater management skills and may devise more effective means for coordinating policy. Some presidents have more effective communication skills and may be better able to convince the public and Congress to support their program. Personal leadership is sometimes minimized in political science because it is so difficult to measure objectively. However, it remains important, even from a multiple institutions perspective that does not view all policy originating from the White House.

Marcia Whicker and Raymond Moore developed a typology of presidential leadership based on two main criteria: management skills and selling skills.[31] Instead of focusing on psychological or personality characteristics, they have identified the skills necessary for a president to succeed. A president who is a strong manager can set priorities, assemble qualified people, and take steps to achieve goals. The president who is a good salesperson can communicate, motivate, or even manipulate other leaders, the media, and the public. Both management and communication (selling) skills are important in determining presidential leadership.

Management Style and Skills

Within the parameters of the institutionalized presidency, presidents have an opportunity to tailor decision making to their own personal style. Two basic patterns seem to have emerged since Franklin D. Roosevelt.[32] The first is a more formal, hierarchical organization of the presidency, resembling a pyramid. Directly below the presidents sits a powerful chief of staff who controls the access of people and information to the president. President Eisenhower best exemplified the pyramid management style. As in an army command, his chief of staff, Sherman Adams, served as a deputy president.[33] Adams summarized and initialed all memos going to the president and controlled access to him, even for cabinet members. Richard Nixon also employed the pyramid style of management, having watched it in operation while he was Eisenhower's vice president. His powerful chief of staff, H. R. Haldeman, stood between Nixon and the rest of the political world. The advantages of the pyramid style is that it frees the president from the palace-guard politics that can occur in the White House and that it protects the president's precious time. The danger is that the system is inflexible and the president runs the risk of becoming isolated from diverse points of view and loses contact with people and problems.

The second approach is a much more open management style, with the president in the center, like the hub of a wheel. This approach is characterized by the openness and access to the president by a wide circle of advisors, individuals, and interests. Franklin Roosevelt best exemplified the "hub of the wheel" style, a wide open, freewheeling, conflict-ridden style with overlapping responsibility. John F. Kennedy also opted for this style of management and was not averse to going around official channels, talking directly to officials at all levels of the bureaucracy. The advantages of the hub of the wheel style are its flexibility, its tendency to provide the president with widespread feedback from diverse constituencies, and the greater involvement of the president. The drawbacks are the confusion it can cause within the administration, leading to internal conflicts and wasting valuable presidential time.

Presidents may shift their management style over time. Carter initially opted for a more open administration, without a chief of staff. Two years later, he moved to a more hierarchical system and selected a chief of staff. Regardless of their management styles, every president since Lyndon Johnson thought it necessary to have a chief of staff. Carter tended to immerse himself with many of the details of policy-making and was accused of excessive micromanagement of the presidency. Ronald Reagan, conversely, had a very detached management style, setting the general direction of policy and leaving it to his advisors to fill in the details and implement decisions. The Tower Commission, investigating the Iran–Contra scandal, concluded that the failed policy was in part the fault of Reagan's overly detached management style.[34] Presidents Bush and Clinton, reacting to their immediate predecessors, adopted a more hands-on approach than Reagan, but without being swallowed up in detail as Carter had been.[35]

Communication and Selling Skills

Presidents have varied in their ability to get their message across effectively since the days of George Washington and John Adams. Some, like President John Tyler

(1841–1845), were notorious for having poor relations with Congress and even with their own cabinet. Others, like Franklin Roosevelt, had the reputation for effectively communicating with Congress. Today, communication and public relations are among the most important functions of the White House. A number of formal messages are delivered each year, including the State of the Union Address, the budget message, and the economic report of the president. The president also issues special messages to Congress, letters, reports, and other documents. In addition, the president makes a number of speeches in various forums across the country, usually making the news. Clearly, formal communications between the White House and the Congress have increased over time.

Among recent presidents, John Kennedy, Ronald Reagan, and Bill Clinton had particularly good selling skills and were attractive media personalities. In contrast, Richard Nixon, Jimmy Carter, and George Bush had problems in communicating with the public and with Congress and were less attractive media personalities. Selling skills include more than media skills, however. Lyndon Johnson was not particularly effective on television, but behind the scenes he was a legendary salesman. Timing can be an important aspect of presidential success. A skillful president gauges the appropriate timing of actions or proposals in accordance with the domestic and international environment. All other things being equal, it appears that presidents have a greater chance to see their legislative proposals enacted if they move relatively early in their administration. Several scholars argue that presidents must "move it or lose it," acting boldly to bring clear but limited priorities before Congress early in their terms.[36]

An important element combining management and communication skills is sometimes called the *administrative presidency*. This term was originally coined by Richard Nathan in describing the efforts by Richard Nixon and Ronald Reagan to adopt policy independently from Congress. Other scholars have also written of the use of such devices by presidents to further their policy preferences.[37] Presidents since George Washington have used executive orders as a means of facilitating their tasks as chief executive. However, modern presidents have found the device useful in broader policymaking. According to Gary King and Lyn Ragsdale, "only with Franklin Roosevelt did the use of executive orders extend beyond administrative matters to include major presidential policy initiatives."[38] Although Nathan argued that this device was used to bypass Congress, one recent study observed executive orders actually being used more when presidents are successful with Congress.[39] Thus, administrative and legislative strategies have become intertwined.

THE PRESIDENTIAL AGENDA

In addition to the policymaking environment, presidential institutions, and leadership skills, the president's participation in the legislative process (and ultimate success) depends on the presidential policy agenda. Clearly, presidents anxious to change the world face a greater challenge than those satisfied with consolidating and maintaining the status quo. In addition, we have noted the "two presidencies" thesis—that presidents have more influence and success in foreign affairs than in domestic politics. That proposition is examined in detail in Chapter 5. In the present context, it reinforces the importance of the policy agenda in the relationship between Congress and the president.

Three things are important to know in analyzing the impact of agenda on policy outcomes. First is the nature of the president's agenda: Is it clearly defined? Is it sweeping or narrow? Does it generally advocate the expansion, maintenance, or retrenchment of government as a whole? Second, how much congruence or conflict exists between the president's agenda and the agenda of the party majorities in Congress? Third, how active is the president willing to be to pursue the agenda, to use the resources of the presidency as aggressively as possible, and to take on sharp confrontations with Congress?

Table 3.2 presents a typology based on two general variables: the president's orientation toward government programs and the assertiveness of the administration in pursuing that agenda in Congress. These classifications are judgments based on research; some fit more clearly than others. Also, the classifications are based more on domestic policy than on foreign policy, because strong defense and containment of Communism were hallmarks of U.S. foreign policy from 1945 to 1990 regardless of who was president. Despite some imprecision between categories, we believe that the general orientation of a president's agenda and how aggressively it is pursued have important implications for the patterns of policymaking.

We divide the orientation toward government into three categories. *Expansion* characterizes an agenda that is oriented toward enlarging the size, scope, and responsibility of government. *Consolidation/maintenance* means an agenda that, although including new initiatives, accepts the existing level of government responsibility and proposes modest, incremental changes. *Retrenchment* character-

TABLE 3.2   Presidential Agendas and Legislative Assertiveness

Orientation of Agenda to Scope of Government	Presidents' Legislative Assertiveness		
	High	Moderate	Low
Expansion	Roosevelt Johnson	Clinton (1993–1994)	
Consolidation/ Maintenance	Truman	Clinton (1995–1999) Kennedy Nixon Carter	Ford
Retrenchment	Reagan	Bush	Eisenhower

izes an agenda that is oriented toward reducing the size, scope, and responsibility of government.

Legislative assertiveness is divided into three categories as well: high, moderate, and low. High assertiveness suggests a president's willingness to pursue the agenda aggressively on Capitol Hill. When the agendas of Congress and the president are congruent (more likely under unified party control of government), it means acting quickly and decisively to move the agenda, pulling out all the stops. When the agendas of the president and the Congress are divergent (which is more likely under divided government), a highly assertive president is willing to use all possible means to pressure Congress to go along, confronting and publicly attacking the legislature when necessary. Low assertiveness involves presidential deference to Congress, even when policy preferences are not congruent. Such a president will not use all available resources to assert presidential preferences.

Expansion: Increasing the Scope of Government

Franklin D. Roosevelt and Lyndon Johnson are the two presidents in the modern era most oriented to expanding the size, scope, and responsibility of government. In Roosevelt's case, it meant expansion of social welfare programs, dramatic increases in government regulatory activities, use of the federal government to create jobs directly, use of discretionary fiscal policy, and the introduction of elements of national planning and public ownership. Roosevelt's first one hundred days are legendary for the amount of extraordinary legislation and the speed of its enactment.

The presidency of Lyndon Johnson was also oriented toward a significant expansion of the role of government in people's lives. Strongly influenced by Roosevelt, Johnson launched an ambitious war on poverty, developing new programs for the poor and creating federally funded health care for the elderly and indigent. His agenda included the expansion of the government's ability to protect and enforce civil rights and voting rights, developing hundreds of categorical federal grants to state and local governments, and more aggressive health and safety regulation.

Both Roosevelt and Johnson were highly assertive, willing to pursue their expansive agendas. Roosevelt proved willing to dominate the legislative process, use the veto when necessary, and even threaten to pack the Supreme Court to protect his programs. He spent hours on the phone and in personal contact with members of Congress nearly every day. As a former majority leader, Johnson was intimately knowledgeable about Congress and its ways. He briefed members, twisted arms, made promises, and often held cabinet members personally responsible for particular legislation.[40] Johnson was able to enact legislation that had languished during the Kennedy presidency, in addition to his own priorities. Both Roosevelt and Johnson had dramatic expansive agendas and pursued them assertively and successfully in the legislative arena.

We place Bill Clinton in his first two years in the expansion category but recognize that his agenda was both less ambitious and more moderately pursued than were Roosevelt's or Johnson's. Although all three were consummate politicians, Clinton was less ideological and more pragmatic in pursuit of his policy preferences. He won early victories on moderate NAFTA and deficit reduction during his first term. Clinton's most expansive proposal was health care reform, which never even came to a vote on the floor of Congress (see Chapter 8). He demonstrated his willingness to use government with his plan to bolster the Mexican peso with billions of dollars in loan guarantees. Clinton abandoned efforts to obtain congressional approval and vowed to go it alone with administrative rather than legislative solutions to the problem. All in all, Clinton's agenda was not as expansive as Roosevelt's or Johnson's and sought to return considerable power to state governments. At the same time, Clinton faced much more hostile congresses than either of these Democratic predecessors and had to work more closely, and tread more softly, with the opposition party to achieve his goals. After the Republican takeover of Congress, Clinton adopted a much more moderate, consolidating agenda. His reinventing government proposals resulted in more reductions in federal employees than occurred under either Reagan or Bush. He reached a balanced budget agreement in 1997. Clinton's orientation shifted significantly when party control of Congress changed.

Retrenchment: Reducing the Scope of Government

The mirror image of Roosevelt and Johnson—an agenda of scaling back the size, scope, and responsibility of the federal government—was Ronald Reagan. He is the clearest example of a president oriented toward retrenchment, and he also pursued his agenda aggressively. Reagan confounded the notion that the only presidents who pursue their agendas actively are those who want government to grow. He used the media effectively before key votes on his economic and budget proposals. He used procedural innovations to get controversial measures through Congress. And during the process, Reagan did not soft-pedal his fervent antigovernment ideology or seek consensual solutions to disagreements with Congress.

Reagan did not achieve everything he sought, but he eliminated many programs and clearly slowed the growth of government. Charles Jones concluded that "Reagan did not reduce government to the same extent that LBJ expanded it but he created the policy conditions for contractive politics that had not been played before."[41] However, many critics of Reagan argue that although he clearly wanted to shrink government programs, he was not hostile to using government power to regulate social practices, including opposing abortion, favoring prayer in public schools, and opposing privacy rights.

In our estimation, Eisenhower also had a policy agenda that emphasized retrenchment, although clearly less so than Reagan. Eisenhower is often viewed a moderate, particularly in contrast to Robert Taft, his rival for the Republican nomination in 1952. Although Eisenhower was considered by some to be the architect of modern Republicanism with a more liberal attitude toward social programs, his underlying ideology was strongly antigovernment. John Sloan reveals that Eisenhower's high priority on balancing the budget—a feat he accomplished three times—overrode other policy concerns.[42] This was particularly true during his second term, when he abandoned other domestic policy interests for the sake of cutting spending and balancing the budget.

Eisenhower was clearly not prepared to pursue his goals assertively with the Congress as Reagan later would. He zealously pursued budget-cutting within the executive branch, but he was a strong supporter of separation of powers and was not inclined to confront Congress. One observer wrote that he had a "reluctance to jeopardize his popularity by formulating goals or a distaste for the goals the demands of the system had thrust upon him."[43] He took little advantage of his Republican majorities in 1953 and 1954. He was inclined to work with the leaders of the Democratic majorities in Congress after 1955 rather than to attack them.

George Bush adopted many of the same themes as Reagan while trying to consolidate the changes of the 1980s. His pledge of no new taxes proved hard to maintain, and his willingness to compromise reflects his greater acceptance than Reagan's of the role of government. Some of Bush's behavior, such as in the area of civil rights, was actually more conservative than his predecessor's.[44] Bush did not propose the elimination of several departments as Reagan had, but he did advocate such changes as the development of a national energy policy. His agenda was nonetheless significantly at odds with Democratic congressional leaders, who were anxious for more ambitious domestic programs. Clearly more interested in foreign policy than domestic policy, and facing huge opposition majorities, Bush was only moderately aggressive in pursuing his agenda in Congress.

Other Republicans are considered to be oriented toward retrenchment and shrinking the size of government. In contrast, we believe that Nixon and Ford largely accepted the status quo. These presidents, along with Democrats Truman, Kennedy, and Carter, were more interested in maintaining programs and making them more efficient, rather than significantly changing the scope and responsibility of government.

Consolidating and Maintaining the Scope of Government

In terms of presidential agendas, the evidence suggests that most of the modern presidents seek neither to expand nor to reduce the size and scope of government dramatically. Consolidation/maintenance does not mean that a president has no new initiatives or opposes additional government programs. It means that proposals are less dramatic and more incremental; in general, the president accepts the current level of federal responsibilities. This obviously allows a great deal of variation within the category—lumping together Kennedy and Nixon, for example. However, the nature of these presidents' more modest agendas, and how they assert them with Congress, provide important insights to presidential-congressional relations.

Truman was a product of the New Deal and rarely questioned the directions that had been set by Roosevelt. His agenda was to consolidate the domestic policy changes and defend them from a hostile Congress. The only post–World War II Democratic president to face a Republican Congress until Clinton, his agenda was in sharp conflict with congressional leaders. Truman did make proposals for new programs, such as national health care, but for the most part his agenda represented a holding action. However, he pursued this agenda with Congress vigorously and aggressively. Truman railed against what he called the "do nothing" 80th Congress, calling their bluff by ordering them back into session after the 1948 nominating conventions. He helped institutionalize the practice of submitting a formal legislative package to Congress at the beginning of the term, met weekly with party leaders, and did much liaison work himself.

Kennedy, Nixon, Ford, and Carter are all categorized as presidents whose agendas were oriented to consolidation and maintenance and who pursued them in Congress less aggressively than Roosevelt, Truman, Johnson, or Reagan but less passively than Eisenhower. Kennedy's New Frontier presented a cautious approach to domestic policy, not a major expansion of activities.[45] Many innovative programs, such as the Peace Corps, were developed, but they represented modest changes in policy. Even with unified party control, Kennedy's agenda was not totally congruent with that of Congress. Perhaps because of his narrow election victory and the dominance of conservative Southern Democrats in Congress, he was generally passive in asserting his agenda with Congress. Liberal critics see Kennedy as overly pragmatic, lacking a real agenda to back up his rhetoric.[46] Although he enhanced the effectiveness of the legislative liaison office, it was not until late in his administration that he actively asserted his agenda.

Richard Nixon, despite his conservative anticommunist credentials, was a moderate in domestic policy. He did little to scale back the scope of government, despite occasional rhetoric to that effect. The Nixon administration proposed the Family Support Act, which was a liberal proposal by today's standards. His administration saw the passage of major tax reform, the Clean Air Act, the creation of Amtrak, and the expansion of the food stamp program—none of which were indicative of retrenchment. Conflict between branches grew throughout his six years in office, largely because of politics rather than policy differences. Nixon was more interested in foreign policy, where he had to deal less with Congress; he seemed to lack the conviction to pursue his domestic agenda. Although he bitterly attacked Congress as an institution, it was rarely in an attempt to enact legislation.

Jimmy Carter was elected as a conservative, Southern Democrat, running on a platform of honesty and integrity rather than the expansion of government programs. Charles Jones refers to the Carter administration as the "trustee presidency."[47] The country was already reacting to the rapid expansion of government programs and federal spending. Many of his programs were designed to make government more efficient and effective. Carter promised to cut spending using zero base budgeting and balance the budget. His energy proposals would have expanded the role of government in regulating energy, but the results were modest. Carter, inexperienced in dealing with Congress, was unable to pursue his agenda aggressively. Although Democrats controlled both houses, they had little sympathy for Carter's agenda. In their resurgence following Vietnam and Watergate, congressional Democrats were anxious to pursue their own agenda.

Finally, Gerald Ford shares the general orientation toward the maintenance of existing programs with Truman, Kennedy, Nixon, and Carter. Like Eisenhower, however, he was generally passive in asserting his agenda with Congress. As an interim president taking office under difficult circumstances, Ford had relatively little agenda at all.[48] Nonetheless, what he did propose was moderate and "short on innovative breakthroughs."[49] Recognizing his low popularity after the pardon of Nixon and his status as the only unelected president (even as vice president), Ford seemed reluctant to force his agenda. In addition, although he criticized Congress, he remained a legislative insider, sympathetic to the needs of its members.

The president's agenda; orientation towards expansion, maintenance, or retrenchment of government; and his willingness to pursue the agenda in Congress are important determinants of the policymaking relationship between branches. When the presidential agenda is in conflict with congressional agendas, cooperation is likely to be required to make policy or avoid stalemate. Dominance by either branch is less likely. A president willing to be assertive with Congress is more likely to lead than a more passive president and more likely to risk deadlock when in conflict with Congress. In the cases that begin in Chapter 5, we will see that the nature of the president's agenda and willingness to pursue it help determine which pattern of policymaking occurs.

THE PRESIDENTS' LEGISLATIVE RECORDS

Congressional Quarterly Measures

The political environment, presidential institutions, the personal leadership abilities, and the policy agenda all help determine the nature of policymaking with Congress. This chapter has examined the presidential side of tandem but separated institutions. We will now examine presidential legislative support and success, much in the manner in the presidency-centered perspective, to see how often Congress agrees with or goes along with the president. Two measures compiled by Congressional Quarterly Inc. (CQ) are commonly used to compare congressional agreement with the president. Although the measures are not without flaws, they provide independent, quantifiable, and comparable measures of legislative responses to presidential actions.[50]

Beginning in 1945, CQ introduced the box score measure in an effort to rate presidential relations with Congress. The box score seemingly measured presidential *success* with Congress by recording whether Congress passed legislation that presidents proposed in their public messages. The reasons for success may be serendipitous or otherwise, and sometimes CQ felt the success scores were misinterpreted. The organization subsequently dropped the boxscore but contributed to some confusion by developing another measure of success (the proportion of the president's vote positions upheld by Congress), which Lyn Ragsdale more appropriately labels congruence.[51]

In contrast to success, *support* connotes an alignment with a presidential preference (the percentage of legislators siding with presidential vote positions). The two CQ measures are sometimes confused, and by understanding their different meanings, scholars can more easily clarify what they want to explain. Although success and support scores have proven useful and reliable, further progress can be achieved through hard work and ingenuity. Using multivariate analyses, success or support variables have sometimes been used to infer leadership and influence in presidential-congressional relations.[52]

The CQ support score is not a measure of successful presidential initiatives to Congress (the president's agenda), but rather his preferences on issues before Congress, positions that it supports or rejects. Therefore, it is the congressional rather than the presidential agenda that becomes the focus and scholars should not confuse the two. Like the original success measure (the box score), the support score possesses both advantages and disadvantages. Because a support score is assigned to each member of Congress, it is possible to construct a variety of data aggregations. For example, these individual scores can be combined by state, region, party, ideology, and other groupings. As a result, the support score is more versatile than the success score, which is inherently limited by its high level of aggregation. Of course, support scores are a poorer measure of presidential preferences. Despite problems, legislative support and success provide an important basis for understanding presidential-congressional interactions.

Figure 3.2 shows CQ's success and support scores on presidents' vote positions in the House only. Note that success is nearly always greater than support until the mid-1980s. Reagan and Bush were the exceptions to modern presidents by receiving greater support than success. The early figures for Clinton show dramatic differences in the two measures but similarity later on. One recent study finds support most influenced by the presidents' party margin in Congress, policy area, and the extent to which they take vote positions.[53] Although these findings are interesting, they reflect the inadequacy of a presidency-centered perspective for understanding the relationship between Congress and the president today. Too much is missing from the picture when it is assumed that the president proposes and Congress disposes. Particularly in recent years, Congress has shown legislative independence from the president. Quantifying on the basis of roll call votes also ignores the bargaining relationship involved in shared policymaking. As we will see in the cases, whether Congress and the president agree on a vote is only the last step in a very complicated process.

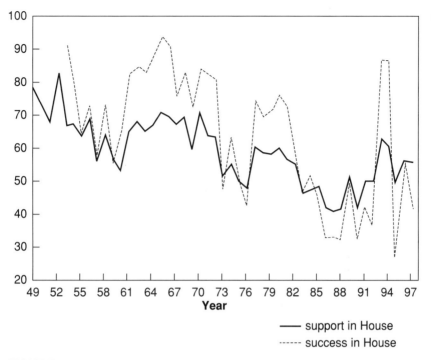

FIGURE 3.2 Comparison of legislative support and success of presidents' vote positions in the House, 1949–1997. *Success* = the percentage of presidential vote positions upheld; *support* = the percentage of Representatives siding with the president.

Source: *Congressional Quarterly Almanac* (Washington D.C.: *Congressional Quarterly Almanac*), annual; figure prepared by Thomas C. Shaw.

The Veto

When collaborative bargaining fails, veto threats, vetoes, and veto overrides characterize combat and competition to set the policy agenda. Between 1970 and 1990, Congress had greater success than earlier in overriding presidential vetoes, particularly with Presidents Nixon, Ford, and Reagan. George Bush and Bill Clinton changed the trend. Despite substantial majorities in both houses, the Democratic Congress was unable to override a single Bush veto until near the end of his presidency. Clinton did not have to use the veto until Republicans took control of both chambers in 1995; even then, like Bush, he was overturned just once during his first term. Table 3.3 compares recent administrations as to the number of vetoes and overrides and the percentage of vetoes overridden.

The veto is a formal mechanism that makes the president an effective participant in the legislative process. This tool provides presidents the opportunity to shape

TABLE 3.3   Regular Presidential Vetoes and Congressional Overrides

President	Vetoes	Vetoes Overridden	Percentage of Vetoes Overridden
Kennedy	12	0	0
Johnson	16	0	0
Nixon	26	7	27
Ford	48	12	25
Carter	13	2	15
Reagan	39	9	23
Bush	46	1	.02
Clinton (through 1997)	19	1	.05

legislation and guarantees congressional consideration of presidential preferences. Robert Spitzer argues that the presidential veto is the president's central domestic resource.[54] We believe the veto is a complex power, best understood by relating it to the other activities in adopting public policy. Understanding the use of the veto can help us uncover presidential influence over legislation and it is an important manifestation of presidential-congressional interactions. However, the considerable scholarly research on the veto has considered the device largely in isolation.[55] Nevertheless, presidential vetoes provide a unique opportunity for directly examining presidential-congressional decision making.

In January 1997, President Clinton obtained a power available to three-fourths of the nation's governors but to none of the forty-one previous presidents—the line item veto. Although long advocated by presidents, budget deficits during the 1980s and 1990s led Republicans in the House to pass such legislation in their "Contract with America" when they took control in 1995. Rather than an actual constitutional amendment, Congress gave the president enhanced rescission authority through a statute. The law allows the president to rescind within five days individual items in appropriations bills not exempted by Congress. These cuts take effect immediately unless Congress passes a disapproval bill within 30 days, which, if vetoed by the president, Congress may override with a two-thirds vote in both houses as with the traditional veto.[56] In the summer of 1997, the Supreme Court declined to rule on the constitutionality of the line item veto because the plaintiffs lacked standing. President Clinton first used the line item veto on August 11, 1997, to eliminate three tax breaks from the fiscal 1998 budget. During the appropriations process he vetoed many additional provisions. In all, he line item vetoed eighty items worth over a billion dollars.[57] Nonetheless, many more provisions could have been vetoed but were not, including projects in Republican leaders' districts. In 1998, Congress overrode 38 of the line item vetos. The Supreme Court heard a challenge to the constitutionality of the line item veto and a decision was expected by mid-1998.

CONCLUSION

When can the president set the agenda and lead government? The political environment must be conducive to presidential leadership in terms of domestic and international events, favorable public opinion, and generally supportive majorities in Congress. Presidential institutions must be used effectively—particularly the White House staff members who deal with Congress on a regular basis. Leadership qualities are also essential; the president must be able to communicate clear priorities, sell Congress and the public on their merits, and manage them effectively. Finally, the president's ability to play a leading role in shaping public policy depends on the presidential agenda: whether it is oriented to expanding, maintaining, or shrinking government; how congruent or divergent it is with relation to the congressional agenda; and how aggressively and quickly the president is willing or able to move it.

The conditions necessary for presidential leadership seem increasingly rare. The constraints on the presidency, both at home and abroad, have increased in recent years. Congressional support and success for the president as measured by roll-call voting shows a steady decline, while veto usage and congressional overrides remain fairly stable. As we have seen, interbranch conflict has led the Congress to strengthen itself vis-à-vis the presidency, in an attempt to compete more effectively to set the direction of government. Even the president's traditional dominance of foreign affairs is disintegrating. The end of the cold war, the collapse of the Soviet Union into sovereign republics, and the growth of multilateralism all suggest a reduction in presidential leadership in foreign affairs and defense. Presidential resources are "at the margins" in influencing Congress, making the president a "facilitator rather than a director of change."[58]

Despite these constraints, the presidency remains a key partner in policymaking. Congress still looks to the president for national leadership even if members are often unwilling to follow it. George Bush received sharp criticism from members of Congress of both parties for failing to provide a clear and decisive domestic agenda, and similar criticism was leveled at Bill Clinton in foreign policy. The presidency remains more unified in policymaking than the legislative branch. The president is still the nation's spokesperson and head of state. In the cases presented in later chapters we will see the many versions of the president's role in policymaking. First, however, we look at the congressional side of the relationship.

ENDNOTES

1. Richard E. Neustadt, "The White House and Whitehall," in Francis E. Rourke (ed.), *Bureaucratic Power in National Politics,* 2d ed. (Boston: Little Brown, 1972): 172.

2. See, for example, Gary King and Lyn Ragsdale, *The Elusive Executive* (Washington, D.C.: Congressional Quarterly Press, 1988); Gregory L. Hager and Terry Sullivan,

"President-Centered and Presidency-Centered Explanations of Presidential Public Activities," *American Journal of Political Science* 38 (1994): 1079–1103; Lyn Ragsdale and John J. Theiss III, "The Institutionalization of the American Presidency," *American Journal of Political Science,* 41 (October 1997): 1280–1318.

3. Clinton Rossiter, *The American Presidency* (New York: New American Library, 1956): 3–24.

4. Bert Rockman, *The Leadership Question: Presidency and the American System* (New York: Praeger, 1984): 86.

5. Richard E. Neustadt, "Presidency and Legislation: Planning the President's Program, *American Political Science Review,* 49 (December 1955): 980–1021.

6. Robert Diclerico, *The American President* (Englewood Cliffs, NJ: Prentice Hall, 1983): 277–278.

7. Richard Neustadt, *Presidential Power* (New York: Wiley, 1960).

8. George C. Edwards, *The Public Presidency* (New York: St. Martins, 1983).

9. Samuel Kernell, *Going Public,* 3d ed. (Washington, D.C.: Congressional Quarterly Press, 1997).

10. Harold Barger, *The Impossible Presidency,* (Glenview, Ill.: Scott Foresman, 1984): 12.

11. Richard Rose, *The Postmodern President* (Chatham, N.J.: Chatham House, 1988): 3.

12. Quoted in Thomas Cronin, *The State of the Presidency* (Boston: Little Brown, 1975): 233.

13. George C. Edwards III, "Impact of Presidential Coattails on Outcomes in Congressional Elections," *American Politics Quarterly,* 7 (January 1979); John A. Ferejohn and Morris P. Fiorina, "Incumbency and Realignment in Congressional Elections," in John E. Chubb and Paul E. Petersen, eds. *The New Direction in American Politics* (Washington, D.C.: Brookings Institution, 1985): 99.

14. George C. Edwards III, "Presidential Electoral Performance as a Source of Presidential Power," *American Journal of Political Science* 22 (February 1978): 152–168.

15. See, for example, John Mueller, *War, Presidents, and Public Opinion* (New York: Wiley, 1973).

16. Hodding Carter III. Remarks made at Washington University, St. Louis, Mo., March 23, 1988.

17. George C. Edwards III, *At the Margins: Presidential Leadership of Congress* (New Haven: Yale University Press, 1989): 152–168.

18. Ibid., 118.

19. Jon Bond and Richard Fleisher, *The President in the Legislative Arena* (Chicago: University of Chicago Press, 1990); Dennis W. Gleiber and Steven A. Shull, "Presidential Influence in Policy Making," *Western Political Quarterly,* 45 (1992): 441–467; Paul Brace and Barbara Hinckley, *Follow the Leader,* New York (Basic Books, 1992); Ken Collier and Terry Sullivan, "New Evidence Undercutting the Linkage of Approval with Support and Influence." *Journal of Politics,* 57 (1995): 197–209.

20. John E. Schwartz and L. Earl Shaw, *U.S. Congress in Comparative Perspectives* (Hinsdale, Ill.: Dryden Press, 1976): 307.

21. *Congressional Quarterly Weekly Report,* January 3, 1998: 18.

22. *New Orleans Times-Picayune,* January 1, 1997: A-10.

23. Charles E. Jacob, "The Congressional Elections and Outlook," in Gerald Pomper (ed.), *The Election of 1976* (New York: David McKay, 1977): 101.

24. Bond and Fleisher (note 19); Edwards (note 17); Steven A. Shull, *Presidential-Congressional Relations* (Ann Arbor: University of Michigan Press, 1997).

25. Nelson Polsby, "Presidential Cabinet Making: Lessons for the Political System," in Steven A. Shull and Lance T. LeLoup (eds.), *The Presidency: Studies in Policymaking* (Brunswick, Ohio: Kings Court, 1979): 83.

26. Richard E. Neustadt, "The Presidency and Legislation: The Growth of Central Clearance," *American Political Science Review,* 48 (September 1954): 646.

27. James F. Hyde and Stephen J. Wayne, "White House-OMB Legislative Relations," in Shull and LeLoup (note 25).

28. Stephen J. Wayne, *The Legislative Presidency* (New York: Harper and Row, 1978), ch 5.

29. Abraham Holtzman, *Legislative Liaison: Executive Leadership in Congress* (Chicago: Rand McNally, 1970): 284; Ralph K Huitt, "White House Channels to the Hill," in Harvey C. Mansfield (ed.), *Congress Against the President* (New York: Praeger, 1975): 83.

30. Neustadt, "Politicians and Bureaucrats," in David Truman (ed.), *Congress and America's Future,* 2d ed. (Englewood Cliffs, N.J.: Prentice-Hall, 1973): 136.

31. Marcia Whicker and Raymond Moore, *When Presidents Are Great* (Englewood Cliffs, N.J.: Prentice Hall, 1988).

32. Steven Hess, *Organizing the Presidency* (Washington, D. C.: Brookings Institution, 1976); Charles Walcott and Karen M. Hult, *Governing the White House* (Lawrence, Kan.: University Press of Kansas, 1995).

33. Frank Kessler, *The Dilemma of Presidential Leadership* (Englewood Cliffs, N.J. Prentice Hall, 1982): 59.

34. *Congressional Quarterly Weekly Report,* February 27, 1987.

35. William Safire, "Bush's Cabinet," *New York Times Magazine,* March 25, 1990: 32.

36. Paul Light, *The President's Agenda* (Baltimore: Johns Hopkins University Press, 1982); James Pfiffner, *Strategic Presidency,* rev. ed. (Lawrence, Kan.: University Press of Kansas, 1996).

37. Richard P. Nathan. *The Administrative Presidency,* 2nd ed. (New York: John Wiley, 1983); Richard A. Waterman, *Presidential Influence and the Administrative State* (Knoxville: University of Tennessee Press, 1989); Robert F. Durant, *The Administrative Presidency Revisited* (Albany: State University of New York Press, 1992).

38. Gary King and Lyn Ragsdale, *The Elusive Executive* (Washington, D.C.: Congressional Quarterly Press, 1988): 122.

39. Brad T. Gomez and Steven A. Shull, *Presidential Decision Making: Explaining the Use of Executive Orders,* presented at the Southern Political Science Association, Tampa, Fla., November 2–5, 1995.

40. Richard A. Watson and Norman C. Thomas, *Politics of the Presidency* (Washington, D.C.: Congressional Quarterly Press, 1988): 253.

41. Charles O. Jones, *The Reagan Legacy* (Chatham, N.J.: Chatham House, 1989): 86.

42. John Sloan, *Eisenhower: Manager of Prosperity* (Lawrence, Kan.: University Press of Kansas, 1991).

43. Nelson W. Polsby, *Congress and the Presidency,* 3d ed. (Englewood Cliffs, N.J.: Prentice Hall, 1976): 29.

44. Steven A. Shull, *A Kinder, Gentler Racism?* (Armonk, N.Y.: M. E. Sharpe, 1993).

45. Randall B. Ripley, *Kennedy and Congress* (Morristown, N.J.: General Learning Press, 1972).

46. Bruce Miroff, *Pragmatic Illusions* (New York: David McKay, 1978).

47. Charles O. Jones, *The Trusteeship Presidency: Jimmy Carter and the U.S. Congress* (Baton Rouge: Louisiana State University Press, 1988).

48. Light (note 36): 133.

49. *National Journal,* June 21, 1975: 928.

50. The CQ measures do not distinguish between major and minor proposals and qualitative measures may be just as important. See Steven A. Shull, *Domestic Policy Formation: Presidential-Congressional Partnership* (Westport, Conn.: Greenwood Press, 1983): 195–199; Shull (note 24), chapter 6; John Bond, Richard Fleisher, and Glen S. Krutz, "Empirical Findings on Presidential-Congressional Relations," in James A. Thurber (ed.), *Rivals for Power* (Washington, D.C.: Congressional Quarterly Press, 1996): 103–109.

51. Lyn Ragsdale, *Vital Statistics on the Presidency* (Washington, D.C.: Congressional Quarterly Press, 1996).

52. Shull (note 24); Bond, Fleisher, and Krutz (note 50); Edwards (note 17); Bond and Fleisher (note 19).

53. Steven A. Shull and Thomas C. Shaw, *Explaining Presidential-Congressional Interactions,* forthcoming.

54. *The President's Veto* (Albany: State University of New York Press, 1988): 25.

55. Richard A. Watson, *The President's Veto Power* (Lawrence: University Press of Kansas, 1993); David W. Rohde and Dennis M. Simon, "Presidential Vetoes and Congressional Response," *American Journal of Political Science,* 29 (1985): 397–427; Sam B. Hoff, "Presidential Support and Veto Overrides," *Midsouth Journal of Political Science,* 13 (Summer 1992): 173–190; Shull and Shaw (note 53): ch.6.

56. *Congressional Quarterly Weekly Reports,* March 23, 1996: 780.

57. Lance T. LeLoup, Carolyn N. Long, and James N. Giordano, "President Clinton's Fiscal 1998 Budget: Political and Constitutional Paths to Balance," *Public Budgeting and Finance* 18, 1 (Spring 1998): 3–32.

58. Edwards (note 17): 223.

4

CONGRESS AND POLICYMAKING

Congress has the strength of the free enterprise system; it multiplies the decision makers, the points of access to influence and power, and the creative moving agents. It is hard to believe that a small group of leaders could do better. What would be gained in orderliness might well be lost in vitality and sensitiveness to the pressures for change.
—*RALPH K. HUITT (1964)*

When can Congress set the agenda and make public policy? Under what circumstances does Congress cooperate with or follow the president? The answers depend not only on the political environment, the policy agenda, and what the president does, but also on the capability of the legislature itself: its membership, its institutions and processes, and its leaders. On the congressional side of policymaking is, according to many experts, the world's most powerful legislative body. Yet Congress is popularly perceived as being disorganized and fragmented—and often as an obstacle to effective policymaking. This is not a misperception or a contradiction but reflects that *Congress has multiple personalities as a policymaker.*

This chapter explores several important questions about Congress as a partner in national policymaking. First, what is the potential for congressional leadership? What are its resources and strengths as well as its limitations and constraints? Next, how does Congress make policy and what determines its performance? What role does the political environment, particularly election results, play in determining the membership, defining the policy agenda, and establishing the parameters for legislative-executive relations? How has Congress evolved as an institution? How have recent institutional developments concerning the legislative process, committees, and rules and procedures affected Congress's decision-making capacity and influence in government? Are congressional leaders actually able to lead senators and representatives? Finally, in the face of increased institutional conflict, how has Congress attempted to achieve its own policy agenda? The answers to these questions will help us to characterize policymaking on Capitol Hill and understand the different roles Congress plays in the policymaking process.

Judgments about Congress partially depend on whether one is looking at individual members, Congress as an institution, or Congress as a part of the constitutional system.[1] As with the presidency, Congress can be examined on three levels of analysis, each focusing attention on certain aspects of the legislature and producing different kinds of policy outputs. At one level are *individual members of Congress,* 535 individuals each elected from his or her own constituency. Members, by virtue of their election, control substantial resources and help shape their own political destiny. They usually behave as rational, goal-oriented people, motivated by reelection, the enhancement of political power, and the achievement of certain ideological and policy goals. It is at this level that leadership, whether from party or committee leaders or from rank-and-file members, is important in determining patterns of policymaking with the president. Policy "outputs" at the individual level include casework and constituent service, "pork-barrel" projects, and the creation of a personal political base.

A second level of analysis focuses on *Congress as an institution:* committees, subcommittees, caucuses, leadership organizations, and the formal and informal rules that produce collective action (or inaction). The behavior of individual members helps shape the institution, determining how power and resources are distributed and how rules and procedures for doing business are developed. At the same time, Congress as an institution is more than the mere sum of its parts. Congress has developed its own traditions and identity over two centuries, so congressional institutions constrain individual members and help shape their behavior.[2] Policy outputs at this level are most familiar: legislation in the form of public or private bills, resolutions, confirmation of nominees, committee reports, as well as codes of ethics and other norms. Institutional arrangements are critical in determining the congressional role in policymaking. For example, institutions that strengthen rank-and-file members and weaken leaders may enhance reelection chances and the delivery of benefits to constituents to the detriment of timely, decisive action. Conversely, other rules and procedures may empower congressional leaders, streamlining decision making and emphasizing collective action rather than individual outputs.

The third level of analysis looks at *Congress as part of the larger political system,* one crucial cog in the constitutional framework of government. This level includes systemic factors that help determine patterns of policymaking with the president. Congress responds to the international arena, to the state of the national economy, to the actions of the president and courts, and to events and changes in American society and the world. In this book, we are particularly concerned with the system-level question stemming from constitutional structure and political environment: How do Congress and the president interact to make policy and what difference does it make?

The lines between individual, institutional, and system questions are often blurred. Members want to be reelected, help constituents, make good policy, have strong legislative leaders, and sometimes support the president, but these goals are often incompatible. For example, spending money on pork-barrel projects in the district promotes reelection but conflicts with the policy objective of keeping taxes low and keeping the budget in balance. Congressional behavior may appear paradoxical because the legislative process seeks various goals and operates under complex internal rules and external constraints. Recognizing congressional performance at each level of analysis is key to understanding legislative-executive relations and the overall governing capacity of the political system.

THE POTENTIAL FOR CONGRESSIONAL LEADERSHIP

Congress was the dominant institution of government throughout the early years of the Republic. As we saw in Chapter 2, only in rare cases was the president able to dominate Congress during the nineteenth century. The transition to the modern era strengthened the president and ushered in a period of presidential government. Yet even the most powerful presidents from Franklin D. Roosevelt to Lyndon Johnson had to confront a legislative branch that was sometimes assertive. The war in Vietnam and Watergate triggered a resurgence in congressional power as the House and Senate attempted to restore a more favorable balance with the president. Paul Light has observed that, in policymaking today, "the congressional agenda increasingly competes for agenda space."[3] Spurred by the globalization of the economy, the end of the cold war, the reduced ability of the president to control world events, and the prevalence of divided government at home, the legislative role in the shared leadership of national government appears to be growing rather than shrinking.[4] The assertive 104th Republican Congress in 1995–1996, the first GOP majority in forty years, proved that the legislative branch could dominate the agenda of government, at least for a period. It also proved that the legislative branch, just like the president, could overreach and make serious political mistakes.

Congress remains a powerful partner in policymaking by virtue of a number of factors, ranging from original constitutional powers to its ability to adapt to a changing political environment. Yet many citizens, journalists, and scholars remain skeptical. Is "congressional leadership" an oxymoron? Not always, as many of the cases in subsequent chapters show. In reality, Congress, like the president, has certain advantages and disadvantages, possessing certain resources while facing a number of constraints. Congress's effectiveness in policymaking depends on how it manages to build on its strengths and minimize its weaknesses.

Constraints and Limits on Congressional Power

Tending to restrict congressional policymaking are factors that empower the president or constraints that reduce the potential for congressional leadership. The president's constitutional powers and informal powers, greatly enhanced in the twentieth century, check the exercise of congressional leadership. The veto power, when legislative and executive branches are in direct conflict, requires a two-thirds majority for Congress to exercise its will. Despite the end of the cold war, war powers still favor the president in times of international crisis such as in the Persian Gulf War, and even in unpopular peacekeeping missions such as in Bosnia.

Perhaps the greatest constraint on congressional leadership in national policy-making is the individualistic and fragmented nature of Congress. The House and Senate remain a cross-section of 535 individuals, each with his or her own motives, interests, and goals. They are largely self-selected and responsible for their own election to Congress, not dependent on their political party. The committee system fragments power by dividing up the political turf, creating independent sources of expertise and legislative authority. The devolution of power to subcommittees in the 1970s further fragmented congressional power.[5] With weaker rules and opportunities for obstruction of the majority by a minority, the Senate is particularly decentralized and difficult to lead for anyone—inside or outside of the legislature.[6] Regionalism and competing sectional interests often make collective decisions difficult.

Some of the changes in the nature of elections in recent years limit the capability of Congress. Despite electoral security and a stable membership, some point to a growing timidity and reluctance by members to confront controversial issues and face up to tough policy choices.[7] To foster their reelection, members tend to emphasize noncontroversial district service, pork-barrel projects, and "credit-taking."[8] Campaigns are increasingly negative and dominated by 30-second television commercials. Congressman David Obey (D-Wis.) laments:

> *When the main question in a member's mind every time he votes is, "what kind of a thirty-second spot are they going to make out of this vote?" then truly the ability of the political system to make complicated and tough decisions in the long-range interest of the United States is atomized.*[9]

Congress's ability to lead government is also constrained by the low esteem in which its members and leaders are held by the public. Except during the Watergate scandal in the early 1970s, the public has consistently evaluated presidents equally with or more highly than Congress. Members often contribute to the problem by running against the institution themselves. On closer inspection, public attitudes about Congress are complex. Voters generally love their own representatives and reelect them at record rates.[10] In fact, people disapprove of the collectivity of members and Congressional leaders but overwhelmingly approve of the institution of Congress.[11] That information is shown in Figure 4.1 from a study by Hibbing and Theiss-Morse. Attitudes such as these help explain the strong public support for term limits in the 1990s.

Percent approve

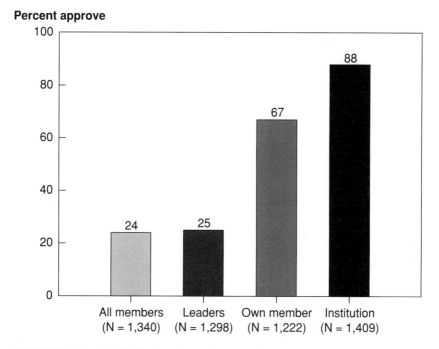

FIGURE 4.1   Public Evaluations of Congress and Its Members.

Source: John R. Hibbing and Elizabeth Theiss-Morse, "What the Public Dislikes about Congress," in Dodd and Oppenheimer (1997): 63, taken from Perceptions of Congress Survey, 1992.

Political Resources and Sources of Congressional Power

Despite the limits and constraints, Congress has significant political resources and is considered to be the most powerful legislative body in the world. The Constitution remains the wellspring of congressional power in national government. The "First Branch" of government detailed in Article I has formal powers that are superior to those of the presidency. Article I, section 8 gives Congress the power to raise revenues, to borrow money, to regulate commerce, to coin money, to establish the post office, to create courts, to raise and support an army and navy, to declare war, and to make the laws necessary and proper to carry out the Constitution. Under checks and balances, many of Congress's formal powers are "negative" in the sense that they impinge on executive prerogatives: veto overrides, confirmation of appointees, oversight, ratification, and investigation. Yet constitutional powers alone cannot explain the ebb and flow of congressional power or variations in effectiveness in the policymaking process.

Recent trends in national elections—the reduction of presidential coattails and decoupling of elections for Congress and the president, and the resulting prevalence of divided government—tend to enhance the policymaking role for Congress. Divided party control of government results in disparate policy priorities between the two branches, which increases congressional resistance to presidential leadership and promotes a more independent, assertive role. But active pursuit of the congressional agenda is not limited to divided government. Party decline may make it more difficult for legislative leaders to build lasting coalitions in Congress, but it also allows congressional independence even when the presidency and Congress are controlled by the same political party.

The stability of membership in the House and Senate is a resource that can enhance congressional power. The decline of electoral competition and increase in incumbency in the postwar period was troubling to many but did create a secure and stable membership able to sustain an agenda over time. With the shift in power in Congress from Democrats to Republicans in 1994, maintained in 1996, it remains to be seen whether the Republican Congress will be in office for a long period as well.

Congress also possesses institutional resources that enhance its policymaking role. Despite cuts in congressional staff under the Republicans in 1995, the legislative branch still spends billions of dollars on staff and agencies that support its policymaking capability.[12] Congress has thousands of employees working for members in their home districts and Washington, committee staff, and agencies such as the Congressional Budget Office, the Legislative Research Service, and the General Accounting Office. These resources give Congress information capabilities that allow it to compete with the presidency. Policy leadership in Congress may come from committees and subcommittees (policy specialists) or from the party leaders (policy generalists) with a perspective more comparable to the president's.

In recent years, expanded party leadership organizations and strengthened party leaders have facilitated congressional policymaking. In some ways, congressional leaders have adopted some of the techniques of the presidency, using national media campaigns to push their policy positions. More visible, activist leaders, such as House Speakers Newt Gingrich (R-Ga.) and Jim Wright (D-Tex.) or Senate Majority Leaders George Mitchell (D-Me.) and Trent Lott (R-Miss.), were regulars on television and radio programs, promoting the congressional agenda.[13]

Congressional rules and procedures that foster collective decision making increased notably in the 1980s and 1990s, providing additional capacity for a more assertive congressional leadership. The congressional budget process, particularly reconciliation, has enhanced the power of congressional majorities to act decisively and comprehensively.[14] Compared with the domination of subcommittees and the fragmentation of power in the 1970s, by the late 1980s and 1990s, more congressional policy responses and strategies were developed centrally by the party leaders. Under the Democrats in the 1980s, party task forces drafted a number of important bills that bypassed the committee system. Under the Republicans in the 1990s, many of the party's most important legislative initiatives were formulated by the Speaker and party leaders. Although the power relationships between leadership and committees has proved fluid (for example, committees were much more powerful in the

105th Congress than in the 104th), the experience of recent years has proved that, under the right political conditions, Congress can overcome its political fragmentation and move with clarity and decisiveness.

What can we conclude about the potential for congressional leadership in the policy process? No simple answer exists, and many recent developments have contrary or unintended effects. Today, Congress clearly is a roughly equal partner with the presidency in policymaking, but the particular relationships vary widely depending on the issue. In recent years, the political environment of the nation has changed Congress. At the same time, its institutions have gone through a continuing series of reforms and adaptations. These have had effects on the nature of congressional leadership and the ability of leaders to develop and promote a policy agenda.

THE POLICYMAKING ENVIRONMENT

Congressional Elections: The Changing Membership

In a fundamental sense, the environment for policymaking in Congress is determined by the outcome of elections, which determine the nature of the membership. In recent years, both the nature of elections and the resulting membership have undergone dramatic change. Congress is more diverse, with a higher proportion of women, blacks, and Hispanics. Despite the power of incumbency and some very senior members, by 1997, a majority of members of the House and Senate had been elected in the 1990s. Perhaps the most important change was in the party and ideology of members, with conservative Republicans replacing both moderate and liberal Democrats. Congress has proved to be more responsive to national trends than many feared a decade earlier.

Turnover was high in the early Congresses because of low pay, difficult travel to Washington, a modest policy agenda, and the norm of a citizen legislature. Beginning after the Civil War, turnover began to decline as more members sought and won reelection. The average length of tenure in Congress grew from around two years in the 1870s to ten years by the 1970s.[15] The stabilization of the membership and the growing responsibilities of government led to a process of institutionalization within Congress: the development of a strong committee and seniority system, party leadership organizations, formal rules, and informal norms of behavior.[16]

After World War II, competition in congressional elections began to decline. Incumbents won reelection more frequently and by larger and larger margins. Traditionally, certain congressional districts were regarded as "swing seats" that reflected national political sentiments and presidential election results, not just local concerns. In 1948, one in five congressional districts were considered marginal swing seats (defined as the winner receiving 55 percent of the vote or less). By 1970, the number of swing seats had declined to one in thirteen districts.[17] This trend continued through the 1980s. In both 1986 and 1988, a record 98 percent of members seeking reelection to the House of Representatives were returned to office, with 96 percent reelected in 1990. Only one Senate incumbent was defeated in 1990. Incumbent success was attributed to changes in the behavior of members, who expanded their salaries, increased their staff located in the district, and enhanced travel allowances and other perquisites of office worth more than a million dollars.[18] Incumbents increasingly emphasized casework, helping constituents deal with various problems. They worked to "bring home the bacon," providing a host of pork-barrel projects in their districts such as hospitals, military bases, dams, and other projects that boost the local economy. Table 4.1 examines incumbent reelection rates since 1946.

Electoral change and turnover increased in the 1990s, despite reelection rates only slightly below those of the previous two decades. Much of that change came in

TABLE 4.1   **Reelection Rates of House and Senate Incumbents, 1946–1996**

Year	Percent Reelected of Those Seeking Reelection to the House	Percent Reelected of Those Seeking Reelection to the Senate
1946	82	57
1948	79	60
1950	91	69
1952	91	65
1954	93	75
1956	95	86
1958	90	64
1960	93	97
1962	92	83
1964	87	85
1966	88	88
1968	97	71
1970	95	77
1972	94	74
1974	88	85
1976	96	64
1978	94	60
1980	91	55
1982	90	93
1984	95	90
1986	98	77
1988	98	85
1990	96	97
1992	93	85
1994	91	92
1996	94	95

the South, culminating a regional realignment that began in 1964. In the 1994 elections, Republicans outpolled the Democrats in every state of the old Confederacy and gained a majority of congressional seats in the region.[19] Incumbency advantages did not disappear, but reapportionment and redistricting, higher rates of voluntary retirement, and increased electoral competition all combined to create dramatic changes in the composition of the Congress. In 1992, 110 new members were elected to the House and 14 to the Senate. In the 1994 Republican sweep, 86 new representatives and 11 new senators were elected. In 1996, the Democrats made a modest comeback, gaining 10 seats, but not enough to wrest control from the Republicans, who won back-to-back congressional elections for the first time since the 1920s. Eighteen Republican incumbents and three Democratic incumbents were defeated as more than 75 new members were elected in the House.

One of the most notable changes in the 1990s was the attempts by the political parties in 1994 and 1996 to nationalize the election. After years of emphasis on local issues and noncontroversial district service, the Republican "Contract with America" articulated a national agenda for congressional candidates. Although fewer than half of the voters had even heard of the "Contract," it may have resonated with enough voters to shift the two-party vote nationally. In 1996, the Democrats turned the tables and tried to nationalize their campaign, running against the "Contract" and Newt Gingrich, who had become the most unpopular national political leader, according to opinion polls. With the help of their allies in organized labor, the Democrats also attempted to tarnish the Republicans for their proposed Medicare cuts. In comparison to the congressional elections before 1994, the most recent elections reflect greater attention to national issues and party differences, as well as to the state and local concerns and political personalities that remain important.

Campaign Finance

The system of campaign finance has also affected the environment for Congress as a policymaker in many important ways. The cost of getting reelected has grown astronomically in recent decades, to an average of nearly a million dollars every two years for a House election and several times as much for a Senate seat. Expensive races in either body can double or triple these averages. Serious challengers—experienced politicians with their own political base—can be discouraged from entering a congressional race because of the financial advantages of incumbents.[20] A large portion of contributions come from political actions committees (PACs)—the financial arm of interest groups and organizations. PACs, wanting to back winners, give overwhelmingly to incumbents, further increasing the gap between incumbents and challengers.

In the 1990s, however, plenty of candidates were available and willing to do what it took to finance a serious congressional campaign. In 1994, for the first time, Republicans fielded a candidate in every congressional district in the country. The money scramble is getting even more intense as candidates focus more attention on media campaigns and television than more old-fashioned, grass roots, door-to-door campaigns.

The continued growth of the cost of campaigns for Congress has several important consequences. First, legislators spend more and more of their time "dialing for dollars"—actively fund-raising. This often reduces the time spent legislating or talking to regular constituents. Second, as the Obey quote suggests, members are more cautious about what they say and do, fearing the vicious attack ad that takes their words and actions out of context. Third, the money chase can affect how party leaders are selected. Members now consider a potential leader's fund-raising abilities along with their leadership skills and media presence.[21] Finally, the unwillingness of the two parties to give up their own particular fund-raising advantages for the sake of campaign finance reform has fueled continued public cynicism about Congress and undermined its public approval as an institution.

Ideological Swings

Congressional elections reflect the political mood of the country into a specific ideological environment for making policy. Roger Davidson recently described four eras of Congress since the 1930s and tried to characterize their different overall ideological perspectives:[22]

> *Bipartisan Conservative Era* (1937–1964), when interparty divisions among Democrats between Northern and Southern wings often resulted in conservative Republican–Southern Democrat coalitions.
>
> *Liberal Activist* (1965–1978), when solid Democratic majorities provided strong support for government programs regardless of who was in the presidency.
>
> *Postreform Era* (1979–1994), when moderate and conservative members became more dominant in confronting the problems of sagging productivity and growth, higher taxes, and a perception that government had gotten too big.
>
> *Partisan Conservative Era* (1995–   ), when Republican majorities press more aggressive antigovernment economic policies and conservative social policies.

Capturing sweeping historical epochs with short, simplistic descriptions is difficult, but these four eras are helpful in suggesting the cumulative effect of congressional elections as a reflection of the larger political environment. Electoral patterns and trends obviously have important consequences for defining congressional policy goals and setting the context for executive-legislative relations. Members need a strong and effective legislature to achieve these goals. From the War Powers resolution and the Budget and Impoundment Control Act in the early 1970s, to the "Contract with America," the postmodern Congress has increasingly challenged presidential leadership with its own policy agenda. How effectively it can pursue that agenda often depends on the capability of its institutions. We begin that assessment with a brief review of the legislative process in Congress.

CONGRESSIONAL INSTITUTIONS

An Overview of the Legislative Process

Congress makes policy in a very different manner from the president. The most familiar congressional product is public laws, but its policy outputs also include private bills; simple, concurrent, or joint resolutions; confirmation of presidential nominees; ratification of treaties; instructions to agencies; oversight; and a variety of other actions. Because our focus is on legislation involving Congress and the president, we concentrate on that process.

Introduction of Legislation

Bills must be introduced by a member of Congress, even if drawn up in the executive branch. The number of bills introduced in a Congress varies considerably and has declined significantly over the past two decades. In the mid-1970s under President Gerald Ford, for example, 24,283 bills were introduced in a two-year period, 2870 were reported by committee, and 588 passed. In the first two years of the Reagan presidency, when the White House more effectively controlled the policy agenda, 13,240 bills were introduced, 1877 reported, and 473 passed.[23] Only a few dozen of those statutes that are ultimately enacted address major national policy issues. Figure 4.2 looks at bills introduced since the late 1940s. Some of this decline reflects change in cosponsorship rules, but clearly, legislators today simply find it less useful to introduce a lot of bills than they did a generation ago.[24] Fewer bills are passing as well. As we will see, however, this does not mean that Congress is less powerful, but that members are concentrating on more important legislation that is often omnibus, encompassing multiple bills.

Referral to Committee

Most bills are referred to committee in the House and the Senate by their respective parliamentarians. This process is now largely automatic compared with earlier times, when sending a bill to a favorable or unfavorable committee made the difference between success or failure. Multiple referral of House bills became more common in the 1980s but was sharply reduced by the Republicans in 1995. Committee chairs refer bills to subcommittees, which do most of the work in holding hearings and writing legislation. In the 1991–1992 Democratic Congress, the House had 22 standing committees with 138 subcommittees, compared with 16 standing committees and 86 subcommittees in the Senate. Republicans streamlined and reduced the independence of committees after taking control of Congress. In 1997–1998, the House had 18 standing committees with 83 subcommittees, compared with 17 standing committees and 67 subcommittees in the Senate.

Committee Review and Markup

Committees vary considerably in terms of their power and prestige, internal rules and procedures, reliance on subcommittee or full committee markup, and the role

**Measures
(thousands)**

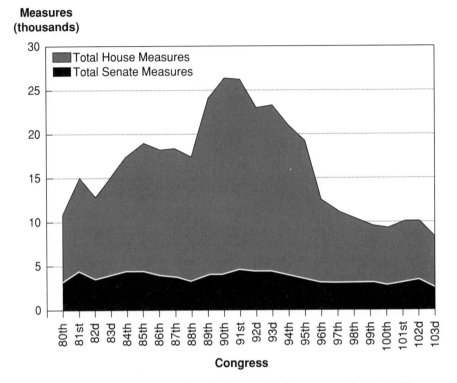

FIGURE 4.2   **Measures Introduced, 80th–103d Congresses (1947–1995).**

Source: Rozanne M. Barry, "Bills Introduced and Laws Enacted: Selected Legislative Statistics, 1947–1994," *CRS Report* 95-233C (February 2, 1995), 2.
Note: Measures include all bills and joint resolutions and exclude simple and concurrent resolutions, which do not have the force of law when enacted.

of minority party members.[25] Committee chairs help shape the agenda, determining which bills will be heard, although this is less true in the case of major legislation. The committee or subcommittee process begins with public hearings, in which testimony is taken from a variety of witnesses, particularly proponents. Administration officials play an active role in testifying for and against legislation, whether it had been initiated in the executive branch or in Congress. Hearings are designed to build support for legislation as much as to provide new information. *Markup* is the process of amending a bill line by line; it is characterized by the active participation of legislative staff. Markup can be exceedingly complex with legislation such as a tax reform bill or a crime bill that can encompass thousands of pages. The president's congressional liaisons monitor the markup process carefully, attempting to clarify the president's stance and intentions. Once markup is completed, a bill must be reported by a vote of the full committee, which occasionally makes substantial changes in the subcommittee version or may simply decline to vote it out at all. The margin of passage and the partisan or regional split on a committee vote send an important signal and can influence the outcome on the subsequent floor vote.

Rules and Floor Consideration

In the House, bills reported by committees go to the Rules committee, a panel appointed by and loyal to the Speaker.[26] The majority party leadership controls the agenda of the House, determining which legislation will be heard at what time. In the Senate, bills are scheduled for floor consideration by unanimous consent agreements between the majority and minority leaders. Rules for floor consideration are much more restrictive in the House than in the Senate. Time for debate is strictly allocated between supporters and opponents, and amendments are often limited by the use of *closed* and *modified-closed* rules. Debate is unlimited in the Senate, but a filibuster can be broken by a cloture vote of sixty members. In the House, legislation may be subject to an up or down vote with no amendments allowed, may be changed significantly through amendments offered on the floor, or may be replaced completely by a substitute version of the bill. Floor debate provides an opportunity to make a public record and clarify legislative intent, but it is rarely instrumental in determining the outcome of the vote.

Voting

Members of the House vote by "electronic device" and can watch the progress of the vote on a large tote board during the voting period, usually fifteen minutes. The Senate still conducts its recorded votes by calling the roll. Although many minor issues are approved by voice vote in both houses, major votes, particularly in the House, are usually recorded. Members sometimes hold back their vote to watch patterns unfold. Attempts by party leaders and administration lobbyists to shape the outcome begin long before the vote and continue through the waning minutes as the vote is completed. Leaders use their party whips and whip organization to get approximate head counts beforehand and may delay a vote until more support can be generated. Senators tend to be more independent, less influenced by leadership pressure, and more informal and consensus-oriented in procedures. In the House, party leadership is more powerful, rules are more formal, and the minority party plays a lesser role than in the Senate.

Party leaders in both chambers are limited in the rewards and sanctions that are available to them to generate support. Even when the leadership pulls out all the stops and makes a vote a test of party loyalty, success is not guaranteed. Nonetheless, *party remains the most important single predictor of floor voting,* although party discipline is much less in Congress than in other parliaments. The Republican Congress in 1995–1996 was extremely partisan and witnessed a degree of party leadership and discipline that had not been seen in the United States in many decades. Yet even in sharply partisan legislative periods, regional and other splits that cut across party lines are often apparent, particularly concerning issues such as agriculture, energy, or natural resources.

The policymaking process in Congress is complex, confusing, messy, and often chaotic. Coalitions shift, key leaders change, and the influence of the president waxes and wanes. Of course, many of these characteristics are inherent in a powerful legislative body. As Huitt suggests in the quotation that opens this chapter, certain benefits are derived from an open legislative process. However, to participate fully with the president in the policy process, Congress must not only represent various interests but also must be capable of clarifying an agenda and acting collectively in a timely fashion.

Centralization versus Decentralization of Power in the Legislative Process

The distribution of power within the House and Senate is a critical determinant of how effectively Congress makes policy and shares leadership of government. Throughout history, Congress has gone through cycles of relative centralization or decentralization. The distribution of power within Congress has varied among committees and their chairs, party leaders, and rank-and-file members. More centralized power is normally associated with the ability to make policy decisions more quickly and decisively. Decentralized, fragmented power is associated with deliberation rather than speed or decisiveness. Writing in the 1880s, Woodrow Wilson lamented the great power—what he called the "impervious authority"—of standing committees that dominated Congress.[27] Two decades later, in the early twentieth century, party leaders had grown more powerful, particularly the Speaker of the House. The House finally revolted against the excesses of "Czar" Joseph Cannon in 1910, stripping the Speaker of many powers.[28] In the decades that followed, the entrenchment of the seniority system—giving committee chairs to majority party members who had been on committees the longest—led to a Congress again dominated by powerful committees.[29] By the 1960s, there were serious reform efforts underway that would affect not only the distribution of power but also ethics and openness.

The Subcommittee System and Reforms of the 1960s and 1970s

The 1960s and the 1970s were a period of a number of important congressional reforms that affected the ability to make policy. At least three distinct reform themes were apparent in the late 1960s and early 1970s. They had different objectives, and the results were often inconsistent and unintended.[30] The first thrust for reform was to democratize Congress, breaking down the hierarchical structures and existing power bases in the House and Senate. For example, the seniority system was weakened through the subcommittee bill of rights and changes in the committee assignment process. These reforms were pushed by younger, more aggressive members, who wanted to be able to influence policy early in their legislative careers. A second set of reforms focused on ethics and openness in Congress. These issues were pressed by members concerned with low public evaluations of the morality and capability of their institutions. Open-meeting requirements (sunshine laws), ethics codes, and financial disclosure rules are examples. These efforts were inspired by the Watergate investigation and congressional scandals. A third set of reforms, running somewhat counter to the other two, had the objective of protecting the constitutional prerogatives of the legislative branch, increasing congressional power vis-à-vis the president, and strengthening party leaders. The Budget and Impoundment Control Act and the War Powers Resolution are prime examples.

Perhaps the most crucial change in the House was the devolution of power from committees to subcommittees.[31] The new rules limited the discretion of the committee chair in assigning bills to subcommittee and in delaying referral. Subcommittees were given the right to select their own chairmen, write their own rules, hire their own staff, schedule their own sessions, and have complete control of their own budgets. In 1974, the House Ways and Means Committee was forced to organize and use subcommittees. Significant changes in the process of committee and subcommittee assignments were made in the early 1970s as well. A bidding procedure was established by House Democrats, allowing all members to secure desirable assignments and limit the number of plum assignments any single member could hold. Democratization took place within the caucus as well.

These reforms had a profound impact in just a few short years, democratizing the House, and to a lesser extent, the Senate. Congress was no longer dominated by a few powerful "whales" but by a large school of "minnows." For individual members, the benefits were immense and they gained obvious advantages for securing reelection. With nearly 150 subcommittees available to chair, members did not have to wait for years to gain an independent power base with control of agenda, staff, and budget. The grip of autocratic, conservative committee chairs was loosened. Cracks appeared in the century-old seniority system. But while a more democratic Congress may have been inevitable after the 1960s, it was a two-edged sword for the institution as a whole. Greater democracy and the subcommittee government it brought did not improve Congress's capability to lead government or share leadership with the president. Power became more fragmented, and greater interest group access made the task of coalition building more difficult. Lawrence Dodd and Bruce Oppenheimer summarize the impact:

> *Subcommittee government created a crisis of interest aggregation. It largely removed committees as arenas in which interests would be compromised, brokered, and mediated; and it led to increased dominance of committee decision making by clientele groups, to narrowly focused policy leadership, and to confusion in policy jurisdictions.[32]*

In addition to a more democratic Congress, reformers promoted greater openness. The Legislative Reorganization Act of 1970 allowed television cameras in congressional hearings for the first time. Later in the decade, C-SPAN would begin broadcasting gavel-to-gavel coverage of the House of Representatives. By the mid-1980s, the Senate finally accepted television coverage of its sessions. One of the most important changes was the sunshine requirement adopted by the House in 1973.[33] All subcommittee and committee sessions would be open to the public, including markup and conference committees, which previously had been closed. The Senate followed suit in 1975. Voting was made public: recorded roll calls were required in committee and conference committee for the first time.

Reforms that promise greater democracy and openness would seem to be an unmitigated good for the political process, and in many cases, their objectives were achieved. But unintended consequences were less desirable, particularly for the ability of Congress to make policy. Interest groups and the media—with their own particular agendas—were the prime beneficiaries of many of the reforms. Sunshine requirements and greater accessibility to congressional decision making made the task of congressional leaders more difficult. Members became less likely to trade votes openly, to help out committee chairs, party leaders, or even the president when they really needed a vote. Under close public scrutiny, members are less likely to take a public position against the interest of the district in support of a broader national interest.

The predominant impact of the reforms of the 1970s was to create a Congress dominated by subcommittees. In 1970, only 35 percent of all bills were initially heard in subcommittee. By 1980, 80 percent of all initial hearings were in subcommittee.[34] Ironically, democratization made policy influence more difficult for members. The workload increased substantially, and staff assumed more power and responsibility. Members became prisoners of their own success: the constancy of fundraising and courting of PACs made members more vulnerable to interest groups and less effective as legislators. The costs of fragmentation became more apparent during the 1980s in the midst of divided government, an ideological president largely hostile to Congress, and an unprecedented deficit crisis that placed severe strains on the legislative process. As a result of both external and internal forces, Congress adapted by strengthening both its leadership and rules and procedures.

Party Leadership and Budget Rules in the 1980s

Other reforms in the 1970s, running contrary to the democratization process, were intended to strengthen party leaders who manage and organize the legislative process. The goal of these reforms was to streamline legislation, enhance majority rule, and reduce opportunities for minorities to block or dilute legislation. The Democratic caucus became an agent of a more disciplined party apparatus in the House of Representatives. In 1973, the Democrats established the Policy and Steering Committee to take control over the process of making committee assignments. The caucus also attempted to strengthen the Speaker of the House in addition to giving him an important role on the Policy and Steering committee. The Speaker was given the right to nominate Democratic members of the Rules Committee subject to caucus approval. The objective was to make the crucial Rules panel, with its control over the House agenda and rules for debate and amendment, loyal to the leadership. The Speaker was also given greater influence in determining the referral of bills to committees, including multiple referrals, in creating special ad hoc committees, and in setting time limits on consideration.

Deficits and budget issues dominated Congress in the 1980s and were a major battleground between President Reagan and Congress. Although there were problems with the congressional budget process, and the Reagan administration was able to use it to their advantage in 1981, the process proved to be a powerful tool that contributed to more centralized control of the legislative process by congressional leaders. Reconciliation—a procedure from the 1974 act that instructs committees to cut appropriations or even deauthorize programs—provided a means to shape the budget from the top down in a single bill.[35] After the 1982 elections, which restored larger Democratic majorities in the House, reconciliation and the budget process provided the congressional leadership with the means to gain greater control of budget totals and compete with the president. But the process was both messy and disruptive to the normal legislative flow of business.

Between 1981 and 1985, the budget process was increasingly characterized by delays, with fewer and fewer appropriations bills passed on time. As a result, more spending bills—both authorizations and appropriations—were lumped together in huge omnibus packages. This "must-pass" legislation became the vehicle for scores of nongermane amendments, but it strengthened those in Congress who controlled them: party leaders and a handful of chairs of the money committees. The House adopted what some called the "four bill" system, which encompassed most legislation: the budget resolution, continuing appropriations, supplemental appropriations, and the reconciliation package.[36] The Senate was also drawn into the process of relying on megabills, both under Republican and Democratic majorities. As more and more legislative time was devoted to the budget, the number of roll calls and bills passed declined. At the same time, the fewer bills that passed were longer, tripling in average length between the early 1970s and late 1980s.

Omnibus taxing and spending bills provided an instrument for more centralized budgeting and more effective negotiation with the White House. The result was a "new oligarchy" of party leaders and chairmen of the money committees.[37] With the help of a loyal Rules Committee, there were stricter limitations on amendments when legislation came to the floor. Table 4.2 shows the increase in restrictive rules for bills coming to the floor either limiting amendments (restrictive or modified-closed rules) or prohibiting all amendments (closed rules) between the mid-1970s and 1980s. Another technique was greater use of bills written by the leadership that had not gone through the regular committee channels. Critics complained that fully one third of the bills passed in 1988 were written by the leadership and had never been reported by a standing committee.[38]

Major changes in budget rules in the 1980s continued the process of strengthening congressional majorities and their leaders while reducing committee power

TABLE 4.2   The Move to More Restrictive Rules in the House,
94th Congress–99th Congress

Congress	*Type of Rule*			
	Open	Restrictive	Closed	Total
94th (1975–1976)	84.3	11.3	4.4	100.0 (248)*
95th (1977–1978)	83.9	12.4	3.8	100.1 (186)
96th (1979–1980)	68.9	20.0	11.1	100.0 (180)
97th (1981–1982)	71.2	22.1	6.7	100.1 (104)
98th (1983–1984)	64.0	22.4	13.6	100.0 (125)
99th (1985–1986)	55.4	33.7	10.9	100.0 (101)

Source: Stanley Bach and Steven S. Smith, *Managing Uncertainty in the House of Representatives: Innovation and Adaptation in Special Rules* (Washington, D.C.: Brookings Institution, 1988): Table 3-3.
*Number of measures subject to a rule.

and discretion. In addition to providing automatic across-the-board budget cuts, the Balanced Budget and Emergency Deficit Control Act of 1985—better known as Gramm-Rudman-Hollings—tightened control within Congress.[39] Totals in the congressional budget resolution were made binding, placing stricter limits on the actions of committees and subcommittees. Bills that violated the targets were subject to points of order on the floor, often requiring supermajorities to waive the budget rules. These new rules affected virtually every aspect of national policy: any legislative provisions affecting the authorization of programs, revenues, or spending. The new rules placed restrictions never seen before in Congress. In the Senate, for example, the enforcement provisions provided time limits on debate and restrictions on amendments on a regular basis for the first time in the chamber's 200-year history. In 1990, Congress abandoned the mandatory deficit reduction process but adopted the Budget Enforcement Act, which further reduced discretion by including strict appropriations caps for committees to follow.

In the 1970s and again in the 1980s, Congress underwent a remarkable series of transformations as an institution. The strengthening of the congressional budget process along with a more powerful party leadership in the 1980s weakened subcommittee domination and removed many obstacles to majority rule. John Gilmour summarizes the result:

> *The budget reforms adopted since 1974 have increased the power of congressional majorities: helping overcome a lack of coordination in budget-*

ing that weakened Congress vis-à-vis *the executive; providing Congress with procedures that permit adopting a far more coherent budget policy than previously possible; and enabling Congress to exercise more deliberate control over the budget and deficit. Now, what majorities want to accomplish in the budget, they can.*[40]

Even more dramatic changes would occur in the 1990s, however, as Republicans captured Congress for the first time in forty years. They would not only further change the balance of power between committees and party leadership but also pursue the most well-defined congressional policy agenda in history.

The Republican Challenge to Committee Power in the 1990s

The elections of 1994 and 1996 brought back-to-back Republican Congresses to power for the first time since the 1920s. It is an important period for scholars of Congress not only because of the ambitious policy agenda of the Republican Congress but also because of the numerous institutional reforms and the power exercised by the Speaker and congressional party leaders. The Republicans were emboldened in part by their massive victory in 1994, especially in the House. In picking up 52 seats, the Republicans defeated 34 Democratic incumbents, including the Speaker of the House, while not a single Republican incumbent in the House lost. They picked up eight seats in the Senate, to take control there as well. This fostered dramatic institutional changes by bringing in a number of new Republicans extremely loyal to Speaker Newt Gingrich, who was credited with engineering the victory. Perhaps the most important institutional change of the 104th Congress was the weakening of the committee system while strengthening the centralized party leadership.

Gingrich served notice that committees would be servants of the majority party, not vice versa. The Speaker had such strong initial support that the Republicans allowed him to hand-pick committee chairs, sometimes disregarding the principle of seniority. Major House committee reforms adopted in the 104th Congress included the following[41]:

- limiting committee and subcommittee chairs to one six-year term
- reducing committee staff by one-third
- limiting members to two committees and four subcommittee assignments
- limiting members to chairing one committee or subcommittee
- giving chairs the power to appoint subcommittee chairs
- limiting most committees to five subcommittees
- abolishing three committees and transferring their jurisdiction
- eliminating joint referral of bills to committees
- prohibiting proxy voting (members must be present to vote)
- opening all committee sessions to media

Such reforms would have been unthinkable for the powerful committee chairs—the "old bulls"—of an earlier generation. These sweeping changes were possible because the Speaker was backed by a tightly disciplined majority party reminiscent of parliamentary systems. Many bills were written by party task forces rather than commitees, and on several occasions, the Speaker and party leaders rewrote legislation reported by committees. Term limit legislation was sent to the floor despite the opposition of the committee chair. The philosophy of the Republican leadership was expressed by one of Gingrich's lieutenants: "We're trying to get away from the idea that all these committees are fiefdoms over which the chairmen have complete control and are jealous of each other's prerogatives."[42]

Committees are traditionally weaker in the more individualistic Senate than the House. But even the Senate adopted some major committee reforms under Republican rule. Six-year term limits for committee chairs were adopted, as well as secret balloting for chairs and limits on the number of committees a senator could chair. Even with Republican reforms, committees chairs could sometimes still exercise considerable power. In 1997, Senate Foreign Relations Committee Chair Jesse Helms (R-N.C.) was able to prevent the nomination of fellow Republican William Weld as ambassador to Mexico from being heard in committee or coming to a vote.

The changes in the committee system were part of the broader changes in party leadership, and the desire of the new freshman Republican class to make major policy changes contained in the Contract with America as well as erase the legacy of forty years of Democratic control of the House. Aided by record levels of party voting in 1995, Republican party leaders were able to take a much more aggressive leadership role in setting the agenda of the nation.

CONGRESSIONAL LEADERSHIP AND THE POLICY AGENDA

The ability to set the agenda and make policy means Congress must be able to consistently forge majority coalitions. This is achieved primarily through the party leaders, although it does not mean that majorities necessarily pit Republicans against Democrats. The most interesting development in terms of congressional leadership has been the speakership of Newt Gingrich in the mid-1990s. In a short period, he has swung from exercising what some called "Czarlike" powers in 1995, to barely holding on to his job and avoiding a coup by his own supporters in 1997. His record and its lessons and the long-term consequences of Republican reforms are considered after examining House and Senate leadership.

Party Leaders

The chief party leader of the House is the Speaker, who is elected by the 435 members. He is supported by the majority leader, majority whips, and several assistants.

The minority party is led by the minority leader, who is assisted by minority whips. The forty-year string of Democratic speakers began in the 1950s with Sam Rayburn (Tex.) and continued through Mike McCormack (Mass.), Carl Albert (Okla.), Tip O'Neill (Mass.), Jim Wright (Tex.), and ended with Tom Foley (Wash.) who was defeated in November 1994. The prevalence of leaders from Texas and Massachusetts reflects two traditional areas of Democratic party strength—the so-called Boston-Austin axis—that has broken down in recent years with Republican gains in Texas and the South. These speakers differed considerably in their personal leadership style, from the more reserved, conciliatory style of Tom Foley to the more aggressive, partisan style of Jim Wright. After the Republicans captured the Congress in 1994, Richard Gephardt (D–Mo.) was elected minority leader.

Newt Gingrich was the first Republican Speaker since the 1950s and perhaps the most powerful speaker of either party since Cannon just after the turn of the century. Frustrated with years out of power, beginning in the late 1980s, Gingrich led a group of younger, more conservative members who rebelled against their own leaders and pushed for a more confrontational style. Gingrich and his allies were considered "bomb throwers" by the Democrats and contributed to the growing partisanship in Congress. Gingrich led the ethics probe that eventually toppled Speaker Jim Wright in 1988, and he has remained anathema to many Democrats ever since. His strategy of nationalizing the election in 1994, using the Contract with America, helped propel the Republicans into the majority and himself into the Speakership. He was assisted by Dick Armey (R-Tex.) who would become majority leader.

Leadership is important in the Senate, but as we have noted, party leaders tend to be weaker than their House counterparts. The chief party leader of the Senate is the majority leader who is elected by the majority party. He has the responsibility for setting the Senate agenda and building majority coalitions. After the 1994 elections, Senator Bob Dole (R-Kan.) was chosen as majority leader. He had also served as majority leader in the last Republican Senate in 1985–1986. Dole resigned in May 1996 to devote full time to his campaign for president, which he lost to President Clinton in November. Trent Lott (R-Miss.) was elected majority leader after Dole's resignation and he was reelected in the 105th Congress. Tom Daschle (D-SD) served as minority leader in the 104th and 105th Congresses. The Republican leaders in the Senate were nearly as important as the House leaders but did not enjoy the degree of party loyalty or support and had to develop different strategies.

Congressional leaders of both parties must work constantly to build or maintain successful coalitions. Unlike parliamentary systems, leaders cannot simply count on party discipline. The speaker has a number of formal and informal powers to help lead: he presides over sessions, recognizes members to speak during debate, has influence on committee assignments, can direct reelection campaign funds to certain measures, and chooses members to take trips, and to serve on conference committees. Party leaders can help a member get a bill on the calendar, or conversely, to block it. Yet leadership is more than using formal powers. It also depends on personal leadership skills and the existence of common policy preferences within a party and how effectively a leader can respond to those preferences.

Leadership is more informal in the Senate, where power is more equally divided, leaders have fewer formal powers, and they must rely on persuasion. Majority leaders Dole and Lott had a more difficult time than Speaker Gingrich in maintaining party discipline. That was reflected in the fact that in 1995–1996, many of the House-passed elements of the Contract with America were derailed by the Senate. Nonetheless, the agenda set by the House put pressure on the Senate, which also showed record levels of party voting. Figure 4.3 shows the percentage of partisan roll calls in the House and Senate from 1954 to 1996. Note that the levels around 70 percent in both houses in 1995 were the highest during the period.

Speaker Gingrich and the Congressional Agenda

The case of Newt Gingrich and the Contract with America is revealing of both how far Congress can go in driving the agenda in government and of how quickly political fortunes can turn. On September 27, 1994, 367 Republican incumbents and challengers for seats in the House met on the steps of the Capitol to sign the Contract

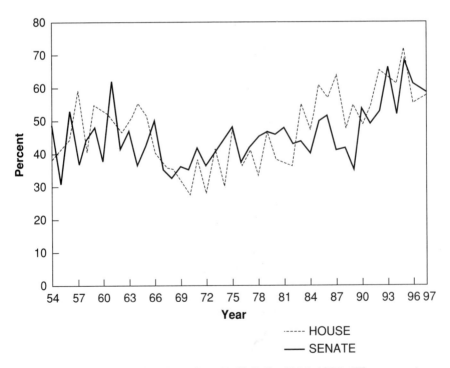

FIGURE 4.3 Proportion of Partisan Roll Calls, 1954–1997. (The percentage of recorded votes in which a majority of one party votes against a majority of the other party as computed by *Congressional Quarterly*).

with America.[43] It was a promise that if Republicans gained control of the House, ten major pieces of legislation would come to a vote within the first 100 days of the 104th Congress. It was a carefully crafted agenda designed to appeal to disaffected voters, giving Republican candidates a national platform. Table 4.3 shows the promises included in the Contract.

After the election, Gingrich and Armey claimed an unprecedented mandate for Congress, even though few Republican Senate candidates backed it. Of course, it was only one of many factors responsible for the election, which was as much a rebuke of the Democrats as it was an endorsement of the Contract. Nonetheless, it resulted in an unprecedented case of congressional leadership of the agenda. House Republicans kept their promise by voting on all major provisions within 100 days. They were heady times for the Republicans: the House was in session for 487 hours during the first three months compared with an average of 123 hours over the prior 20 years. The Senate was another matter, however, because only one and part of another provision passed both houses in 1995.

How quickly things changed through late 1995 and 1996. Gingrich and the House Republicans may have been guilty of hubris and overreaching. The most protracted battle of 1995 was with President Clinton over the Republicans' balanced budget plan (this case is profiled in Chapter 7). Democrats began to attack the Republicans on their planned Medicare cuts, and refused to give in to Republican demands on the budget. Clinton threatened and used the veto, and a budget stalemate ensued, marked by two separate government shutdowns. The Democrats won the public relations battle if not the policy battle: voters largely blamed the Republicans for the shutdowns. Clinton's rating climbed while Gingrich's plummetted. The Democrats carried those winning issues with them to the 1996 elections, getting Clinton reelected and reducing the Republican majorities.

Gingrich won reelection as Speaker of the 105th House in 1997, but with far less enthusiasm and more intrigue than would have been expected. Only two years after his initial triumph, Gingrich faced ethics charges and defections within Republican ranks. Republicans had learned in 1996 that they could achieve far more by compromising with President Clinton than by confronting him. But this angered some of the more conservative Republicans who wanted Gingrich to stay the course. In July 1997, a cabal of Republican leaders planned a move to remove Gingrich. It was reportedly foiled only when Armey learned that he would not succeed Gingrich.

There are several important lessons to be drawn from the 1994 elections, the Contract with America, and the Gingrich speakership. The Contract shows that under certain extraordinary environmental conditions, Congress can dominate the policy agenda. But those conditions can change quickly, and power relationships between the branches remain very fluid. Because of miscalculations by the Republicans, it took the presidency less than a year to recover from the devastating 1994 elections and effectively counter congressional attempts to lead government. Under the Republican Congress, the institutional changes in terms of the balance of power between committees and party leaders were profound but not necessarily transforming and permanent. By 1997, with a weakened Speaker, committees were moving quickly toward their more traditional important role in the legislative process. However, as long as rules on committee chair term limits stay in place under the Republi-

TABLE 4.3   Republican "Contract with America" (1994)

Preface   Congressional Process
  * Require that Congress end its exemptions from 11 workplace laws.
  * Revise House rules to cut committees and their staffs, impose term limits on committee chairmen, end proxy voting, require three-fifths majority for tax increases.

1. Balanced-Budget Amendment and Line-Item Veto
   * Send to the states a constitutional amendment requiring a balanced budget.
   * Give president line-item veto power to cancel any appropriation or targeted tax break.

2. Crime
   Require restitution to victims; modify exclusionary rule; increase grants for prison construction; speed deportation of criminal aliens; create block grants to give communities flexibility in using anti-crime funds; limit death row appeals.

3. Welfare
   Convert nutrition programs into block grants to states, end payments to mothers under age 18 who have children out of wedlock, require proof of paternity to receive welfare, require work after receiving two years of welfare benefits, impose a lifetime five-year cap for most welfare benefits, end payments to most non-citizens, allow states to impose other restrictions and cap welfare spending.

4. Families and Children
   * Require parental consent for children participating in surveys.
   * Offer tax credits for adoptions and home care of the elderly.
   * Increase penalties for sex crimes against children.
   * Strengthen enforcement of child support orders.

5. Middle-Class Tax Cut
   Add $500-per-child tax credit; ease "marriage penalty" for filers of joint tax returns; expand individual retirement account savings plans.

6. National Security
   Prohibit use of U.S. troops in U.N. missions under foreign command; prohibit defense cuts to finance social programs; develop a missle defense system; cut funding for U.N. peacekeeping missions.

7. Social Security
   Repeal 1993 increase in Social Security benefits subject to income tax; permit senior citizens to earn up to $30,000 a year without losing benefits; give tax incentives for long-term insurance.

8. Capital Gains and Regulations
   * Cut capital gains tax rate; accelerate depreciation on equipment.
   * Reduce unfunded mandates.
   * Reduce federal paperwork.
   * Require federal agencies to assess risks, use cost–benefit analysis, reduce paperwork, and reimburse property owners for reductions in value due to regulations.

9. Civil Law and Product Liability
   * Establish national product liability law with limits on punitive damages, other restrictions.
   * Make it harder for investors to sue companies.
   * Apply "loser pays" rule to certain federal cases.

10. Term Limits
    Send to the states a constitutional amendment limiting congressional terms.

cans, the committees are not likely to achieve former levels of power. In just two years, the fundamental legislative strategy of the Republicans had changed from confrontation and deadlock to cooperation and negotiation. This was demonstrated by the passage of the balanced budget agreement in 1997, requiring many concessions but giving the Republicans many policy changes that they had wanted for decades, such as the capital gains tax reduction.

CONCLUSION

In the 1990s, Congress has emerged as a coequal with the presidency, yet engages in numerous, often contradictory patterns of policymaking. As an institution, it has continued to strengthen its ability to pursue its own agenda while checking the prerogatives of the executive branch. It has bolstered its own agencies such as the Congressional Budget Office and the General Accounting Office. Despite the loss of the legislative veto, Congress has found other ways to control the actions of federal agencies. Increasingly detailed statutes constrain agency discretion and enhance legislative influence. Congressional investigations have been mounted to discredit and blunt presidential policies. The 1997 hearings into campaign finance were a challenge to President Clinton and the Democrats. Congress is now more assertive in foreign policy as well as domestic policy. Led by Speaker Jim Wright's independent initiatives in Central America a decade ago, and followed more recently by legislation such as the Helms-Burton act against Cuba (profiled in Chapter 5), Congress displays a growing determination to pursue its own policy objectives, even in foreign policy.

Despite efforts on both sides, *neither branch can govern autonomously.* The apparent increase in cooperation in some key areas like welfare reform in 1996 and the balanced budget agreement in 1997 seem to reflect a greater recognition of that fact. When deadlocks do occur, both legislative and executive branches have increasingly turned to extraordinary means for resolving conflicts. Bipartisan commissions consisting of members appointed by the president and congressional leaders have played a more prominent role in policymaking in recent years. A bipartisan commission played a critical role in restoring the fiscal integrity of the Social Security system in 1983 (see Chapter 8).[44] Commissions were also used to make controversial decisions on the closing of military bases, the basing of MX missiles, and Central American policy. A bipartisan commission on Medicare opened hearings in 1998.

Summits between the two branches have become more common, particularly in attempting to resolve intractable budget disputes. In five of the years between 1982 and 1990, some form of interbranch summit was attempted. Summits are not popular with either side. For the president, they represent a diminution of his power and an undermining of the entire executive budget process. For the rank-and-file members of Congress, they represent a severe reduction in their ability to amend, legislate, and put their imprint on policy.

When can Congress set the agenda and take a leading role in shaping public policy? For major policy initiatives, it can rarely govern alone except in cases of presidential acquiescence or veto-proof majorities. Only in rare cases, such as the Civil Rights Restoration Act of 1988, enacted over Reagan's veto, can Congress overcome concerted opposition by the president (see Chapter 6). But even if it can rarely dominate, Congress plays an increasingly important role in defining issues and shaping policies. What has emerged is a Congress better equipped to challenge and confront the president in the 1990s than in previous decades. There remain areas where Congress may do its will, such as the distribution of pork-barrel projects within spending limits agreed on by both branches. Even in areas where Congress plays a leading role, presidential cooperation rarely comes without concessions. Facing a very difficult congressional situation, Clinton became a master of winning major concessions during his second term.

Congress's success in achieving the policy goals of members depends on the external environment, elections that determine its membership, and the institutions and processes that shape policymaking. In the subsequent chapters, we explore shared policymaking in the areas of foreign and defense policy, civil rights policy, budget and economic policy, and social welfare policy. Some patterns are more prevalent than others, but we will examine cases of presidential leadership, congressional leadership, consensus/cooperation, and deadlock/extraordinary resolution across all four policy areas.

ENDNOTES

1. Christopher J. Deering (ed.), *Congressional Politics* (Chicago: Dorsey, 1989): 1–13.

2. See Donald R. Matthews, *U.S. Senators and Their World* (New York: Wiley, 1962); and Roger B. Davidson, *The Role of the Congressman* (New York: Pegasus, 1969).

3. Paul Light, *The President's Agenda* (Baltimore: Johns Hopkins University Press, 1982): 205.

4. See, for example, L. Gordon Crovitz and Jeremy A. Rabkin (eds.), *The Fettered Presidency* (Washington, D.C.: American Enterprise Institute, 1989).

5. Lawrence C. Dodd and Bruce I. Oppenheimer, "The House in Transition: Partisanship and Opposition," in Dodd and Oppenheimer (eds.), *Congress Reconsidered,* 3d ed. (Washington, D.C.: Congressional Quarterly Inc., 1985): 43–46.

6. Norman J. Ornstein, Robert L. Peabody, and David W. Rohde, "Change in the Senate: Toward the 1990s," in Dodd and Oppenheimer (eds.), *Congress Reconsidered,* 4th ed. (Washington, D.C.: Congressional Quarterly Inc., 1989): 13–38.

7. See Morris P. Fiorina, *Congress: Keystone of the Washington Establishment* (New Haven, Conn.: Yale University Press, 1974). For a critique of congressional "timidity" in the 1988 elections, see *New York Times,* March 18, 1990: 16.

8. See David R. Mayhew, *The Electoral Connection* (New Haven, Conn.: Yale University Press, 1974), for a discussion of "credit taking."

9. Congressman David Obey, quoted in *New York Times,* March 18, 1990: 16.

10. See Gary C. Jacobsen, *The Politics of Congressional Elections* (Boston: Little, Brown, 1987).

11. John R. Hibbing and Elizabeth Theiss-Morse, "What the Public Dislikes About Congress," in Lawrence C. Dodd and Bruce I. Oppenheimer, *Congress Reconsidered,* 6th ed. (Washington D.C.: Congressional Quarterly Press, 1997): 61–80.

12. For a discussion of the growth of staff, see Michael J. Malbin, *Unelected Representatives: Congressional Staff and the Future of Representative Government* (New York: Basic Books, 1980).

13. Norman J. Ornstein, "Can Congress Be Led?" In John J. Kornacki (ed.), *Leading Congress: New Styles, New Strategies* (Washington, D.C.: Congressional Quarterly Inc., 1990): 22–23.

14. John Gilmour, *Reconcilable Differences?* (Berkeley, Calif.: University of California Press, 1990).

15. See Randall B. Ripley, *Congress: Process and Policy* (New York: Norton, 1983): 41–75.

16. Nelson W. Polsby, "Institutionalization in the U.S. House of Representatives," *American Political Science Review* 62 (1968): 144–168.

17. Mayhew (note 8).

18. Roger H. Davidson and Walter J. Oleszek, *Congress and Its Members* (Washington, D.C.: Congressional Quarterly Inc., 1981): 123–124.

19. Walter J. Oleszek, "The New Era of Congressional Policymaking," in James Thurber (ed.), *Rivals for Power: Presidential-Congressional Relations* (Washington D.C.: Congressional Quarterly Press, 1996): 51–53.

20. Gary C. Jacobsen and Samuel Kernell, *Strategy and Choice in Congressional Elections* (New Haven, Conn.: Yale University Press, 1983).

21. Oleszek (note 19): 53.

22. Roger Davidson, "The Presidency and Congressional Time," in Thurber (note 19): 19–44.

23. Walter J. Oleszek, *Congressional Procedures and the Policy Process,* 2d ed. (Washington, D.C.: Congressional Quarterly Press, 1984): 74.

24. Davidson (note 22): 23.

25. See Richard F. Fenno, Jr., *Congressmen in Committees* (Boston: Little, Brown, 1973).

26. See Walter J. Oleszek, *Congressional Procedures and the Policy Process,* 3d ed. (Washington, D.C.: Congressional Quarterly Press, 1989), for an overview.

27. Woodrow Wilson, *Congressional Government* (Boston: Houghton Mifflin, 1885): 318.

28. White L. Busby, *Uncle Joe Cannon* (New York: Henry Holt, 1927).

29. Roger H. Davidson, "The Presidency and Three Eras of the Modern Congress," in Thurber (note 19): 66.

30. Leroy N. Reiselbach, *Congressional Reform* (Washington, D.C.: Congressional Quarterly Press, 1986): 41–78.

31. Norman J. Ornstein, "Causes and Consequences of Congressional Change: Subcommittee Reforms in the House of Representatives," in Norman Ornstein (ed.), *Congress in Change* (New York: Praeger, 1975): 88–114.

32. Dodd and Oppenheimer (note 5): 47.

33. Reiselbach (note 30): 52–57.

34. Ibid., 82.

35. See Lance T. LeLoup, "After the Blitz: Reagan and the U.S. Congressional Budget Process," *Legislative Studies Quarterly* 7 (August 1982): 321–339.

36. Lawrence C. Dodd and Bruce I. Oppenheimer, "Consolidating Power in the House," in Dodd and Oppenheimer (note 5): 48.

37. Ibid., 48–49.

38. Steven Smith, "Taking it to the Floor," in Dodd and Oppenheimer (note 5): 338–340.

39. Lance T. LeLoup, Barbara L. Graham, and Stacey Barwick, "Deficit Politics and Constitutional Government: The Causes and Consequences of Gramm-Rudman-Hollings," *Public Budgeting and Finance* 7 (Spring 1987): 83–103.

40. John B. Gilmour, *Reconcilable Differences?* (Berkeley: University of California Press, 1990): 224.

41. C. Lawrence Evans and Walter J. Oleszek, "Congressional Tsunami? The Politics of Committee Reform," in Dodd and Oppenheimer (1997): 193–211.

42. Representative Robert Walker (R-Pa.), quoted in *Congressional Quarterly Weekly Report,* Supplement to no. 12 (March 25, 1995): 10.

43. James G. Gimpel, *Fulfilling the Contract* (Boston: Allyn and Bacon, 1996).

44. See Paul C. Light, *Artful Work: The Politics of Social Security Reform* (New York: Random House, 1985).

5

FOREIGN POLICY

I make American foreign policy.
—PRESIDENT HARRY S TRUMAN

*If you want us (Congress) in on the landings, you have to
have us in on the takeoffs.*
—SENATOR ARTHUR VANDENBERG
TO PRESIDENT HARRY TRUMAN

After World War II, in the dawn of the nuclear age and cold war, many scholars and political leaders argued persuasively for presidential leadership in foreign affairs.[1] Most presidents preferred foreign policy. There was less competition, and they could deal with lofty issues such as world peace rather than welfare checks. This dichotomy led Aaron Wildavsky to assert that there were two presidencies in the United States: one for foreign policy and one for domestic policy.[2] British scholar Marcus Cunliffe wrote of this imbalance that "the presidency works badly. . . . there is not enough leeway in domestic affairs. . . . and in foreign affairs he possesses too much capacity to commit the nation to disaster."[3]

More than any other single event, the Vietnam War caused a reassessment of the presumption of presidential superiority and led Congress to reassert an independent, substantive role in foreign policy. Numerous studies have confirmed and supported the expanded role of Congress; yet others question whether Congress has increased its influence substantially.[4] Constitutional ambiguity with regard to congressional war powers and the president's power as commander-in-chief became an "invitation to struggle" over control of foreign policy in the post-Vietnam era. The past three decades have witnessed a search for an appropriate balance between the two branches.[5]

Officials at both ends of Pennsylvania Avenue have been dissatisfied with the balance that has emerged. Historically, Congress played a significant role in shaping the defense budget and deciding issues related to foreign aid, weapons systems, base locations, and other aspects of military policy that had local and regional implications.[6] In the post-Vietnam era, however, congressional influence extended into numerous other foreign policy areas. Critics argued that Congress was guilty of excessive micromanagement, which made American foreign policy less coherent than the policies emerging from unified parliamentary democracies. When asked what struck him most about the American political system, a former British ambassador pointed to the "extraordinary power of Congress over foreign policy."[7]

Defenders of Congress's independent role point to its positive influence in ending the Vietnam War, making the CIA more accountable, canceling arms sales, amending treaties, and helping block military aid to the Contras in Nicaragua. With divided government and growing interbranch conflict, judgments about the relative roles of Congress and the president are increasingly made on partisan grounds rather than constitutional grounds. Elliot Abrams observed:

> *What makes the system not only different but much worse is the infusion of ideology and partisan politics into the struggles between the branches. . . . This ideological venom in the relations between Congress and the executive makes it particularly difficult to conduct a sensible foreign policy.[8]*

How has U.S. foreign policy evolved in the postwar era? Despite the enlargement of Congress's role, is the president still more capable of leadership in foreign affairs? Can the United States make coherent policy under separation of powers and divided government? How does the changing domestic and international environment affect the patterns and results of making foreign policy? This chapter explores these questions and examines recent cases that exemplify the four patterns of presidential-congressional policymaking. We begin by considering in more detail how U.S. strategies for foreign policy and national defense have evolved since the end of World War II.

THE EVOLUTION OF U.S. FOREIGN POLICY

From its earliest years as a nation, the United States attempted to avoid what George Washington called "foreign entanglements." Located on a continent distant from their European ancestors, Americans attempted to stay out of European affairs if European nations in turn would not meddle in the Western Hemisphere. Although the United States participated in World War I, American isolationism remained strong until the bombing of Pearl Harbor by Japan in 1941. After World War II, isolationism was seen as no longer possible or desirable in American foreign policy. After World War II until the late 1960s, foreign policy competed about equally with domestic policy as the American public's "most important problem" (Figure 5.1).

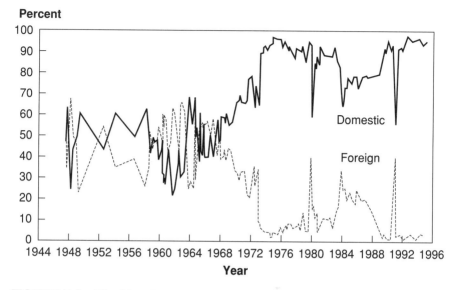

FIGURE 5.1 The Most Important Problem: Domestic or Foreign, 1947–1995.

Source: Harold W. Stanley and Richard G. Niemi, *Vital Statistics on American Politics,* 4th ed. (Washington, D.C.: Congressional Quarterly Press, 1996):156.

Note: Typical question: "What do you think is the most important problem facing this country today?"

THE COLD WAR AND CONTAINMENT OF COMMUNISM

Although the United States and the Soviet Union had fought as allies to defeat Germany and Japan, the alliance was one of necessity. American leaders felt a strong distaste for Communism, and once victory was assured, the alliance collapsed. The nation derived an important lesson from World War II: Never again would the United States be a passive bystander in the international arena in the face of massive aggression.[9] The nation's worst fears were realized when Soviet troops occupied Eastern Europe, setting up puppet communist regimes loyal to Moscow. Former British Prime Minister Winston Churchill warned that the Soviets had built an "iron curtain" across Europe. Cold war tensions divided the world in two. The bipolar international system would dominate the world order for nearly fifty years until the collapse of the Soviet Union.

President Harry S Truman played an important role in defining postwar foreign policy, announcing that the United States would "support free peoples who are resisting attempted subjugation."[10] The economy of a devastated Europe was of great concern: Economic chaos and poverty bred unrest, which American leaders feared would open the door to communist disruption. In addition, economically weak nations would be unable to defend themselves from an attack by the Soviet Union. To prevent these eventualities, Secretary of State George Marshall proposed a plan for rebuilding Europe. The Marshall Plan poured billions of dollars of aid into Europe, to achieve the "revival of a working economy in the world so as to permit the emergence of political and social conditions in which free institutions can exist."[11]

The cornerstone of postwar foreign policy was articulated within weeks of the announcement of the Marshall Plan. State Department Soviet affairs expert George Kennan described the doctrine of containment: "The main element of any United States policy toward the Soviet Union must be that of a long-term, vigilant containment of Russian expansive tendencies."[12] In 1949, the United States finalized its first modern peacetime military alliance with the nations of Western Europe. The North Atlantic Treaty Organization (NATO) committed the United States to stationing troops abroad and protecting the nations of Western Europe with its nuclear weapons. In response, the nations of Eastern Europe and the Soviet Union formed their own military defense treaty, the Warsaw pact.

The first major application of the containment doctrine came in Korea in 1950, when communist North Korea invaded South Korea. Even though Korea had not earlier been defined as within the network of U.S. security interests, the Truman administration saw it as a test of the nation's will to stand up to communist aggression. Fighting under the banner of the United Nations, U.S. forces initially achieved military successes. This encouraged them to expand the aims of the war by entering North Korea, with the objective of reuniting it with the South. The United States ignored warnings from China, which had been under communist rule since 1949, not to invade North Korea.[13] The Chinese surprised American forces, driving them back. A bloody stalemate followed.

President Dwight Eisenhower forced a settlement in the Korean War by threatening to use nuclear weapons against North Korea. He would use the doctrine of "massive retaliation" to back up the strategy of containment. Secretary of State John Foster Dulles explained that to counter communist aggression, the Unites States would "retaliate instantly, by means and at places of our own choosing."[14] This emphasis on the potential use of nuclear weapons had two consequences. First, it heightened world tensions through "brinksmanship," escalating conflicts to the brink of nuclear war. Second, it spurred the Soviet Union to increase its weapons development to expand its nuclear arsenal so as to equal or pass that of the United States.

U.S. foreign policy had important domestic consequences. During the 1950s, anticommunist hysteria swept the country, fanned by demagogues such as Wisconsin Senator Joseph McCarthy. Billions were spent to build an interstate highway system designed for the rapid transportation of troops and equipment. The success of the Soviet's earth-orbit satellite, Sputnik, prompted the United States to increase spending for education and scientific research. More money went to defense after the Soviet Union developed long-range intercontinental ballistic missiles (ICBMs). The success of communism in appealing to newly independent third world nations also caused growing concern in the United States. The most troublesome such development was the 1959 Cuban revolution that brought to power Fidel Castro, who installed a communist regime only ninety miles off the U.S. coast.

John F. Kennedy made few changes in the containment doctrine. Early in his administration, Kennedy was persuaded by the CIA to approve a clandestine invasion to liberate Cuba. The operation was a fiasco, not only failing but also embarrassing the administration at home and around the world.[15] A more serious crisis developed in 1962 during the thirteen-day Cuban missile crisis, when the world came closer to nuclear war than previously. In the words of Graham Allison, "there was a higher probability that more human lives would end suddenly than ever before in history."[16] The Soviet Union had placed offensive nuclear missiles in Cuba, and a confrontation was averted only after Premier Nikita Khrushchev backed down and agreed to remove the missiles. The event had a chilling effect on Kennedy, who later softened his rhetoric and favored detente—normalization of relations between the superpowers and reduction of tensions in the world.

By the 1960s, the Soviet Union had reached nuclear parity with the United States. In the continuing arms race, both sides possessed massive arsenals of nuclear weapons, capable of destroying the world many times over. If containment was the cornerstone of postwar foreign policy, the doctrine of deterrence was the cornerstone of U.S. strategic defense policy. The premise was that if neither superpower can destroy the other in a first-strike nuclear attack without suffering unacceptable damage itself, both sides will be deterred from attacking. The doctrine is also known as *mutually assured destruction* or MAD. Throughout this period, containing communism and managing nuclear arsenals fell largely to the president. When South Vietnam was threatened by the communist regime in North Vietnam, it was also the president who took action.

The Vietnam War and Its Aftermath

In 1964, based on a disputed incident involving U.S. and North Vietnamese ships in the Gulf of Tonkin, Congress passed a resolution giving President Johnson the go-ahead to use military force against the Vietnamese Communists. Although Johnson promised in the 1964 presidential campaign not to expand U.S. participation in Vietnam, he used the Gulf of Tonkin Resolution to send thousands of Americans to fight for South Vietnam: 550,000 troops by 1967. The Johnson administration justified U.S. intervention using the "domino theory": If Vietnam were to come under communist rule, the other nations of Southeast Asia would fall as well. Although a majority of Americans supported the war at first, a large and vocal segment of society vehemently opposed U.S. involvement. Opposition grew as the war dragged on. A growing coalition in Congress tried to end the war by cutting off funds and withdrawing U.S. troops. Under siege, Johnson withdrew from the 1968 presidential election, paving the way for the election of Republican Richard Nixon.

Two dimensions emerged in Nixon's foreign policy. The first conformed to the containment doctrine that had dominated the postwar period, but the second was a reaction to Vietnam, based on a more pragmatic view of the United States's role in the world. Nixon first attempted to gain a military victory in Vietnam, secretly bombing Cambodia and escalating the war. When it became clear that military victory would not occur, the administration began turning over responsibility to the South Vietnamese and withdrawing U.S. troops. Nixon and his Secretary of State, Henry Kissinger, recognized that the Vietnam War had been a tactical disaster, even though they supported its aims.

Although they did not challenge the basic doctrine of containment, they did question what strategy was best to achieve it. What emerged was the Nixon doctrine, which stressed indirect military assistance to friendly governments rather than direct intervention with American troops. Nixon announced that

> *The postwar period in international relations has ended. The United States will participate in the defense and development of allies and friends but . . . America cannot—and will not—conceive all the plans, design all the programs, execute all the defense of the free nations of the world.*[17]

Nixon also pursued a policy of detente with the Soviet Union and China, opening up and improving relations. Despite détente, a restive Congress took a much closer look at foreign policy, national security, intelligence gathering, and arms control. Hostility between Congress and Nixon spilled into the realm of foreign policy. The bipartisanship and interbranch cooperation that had characterized the making of foreign policy through the late 1960s declined notably. The change in strategies in applying containment may have begun to reduce international tensions, but Democratic President Jimmy Carter hoped to go further and eliminate the containment doctrine altogether.

Carter believed that the containment era was at an end and that U.S. foreign policy should be based on greater international cooperation, arms reduction, and an emphasis on human rights.[18] U.S. foreign policy goals during the Carter administration included promoting peace in the Middle East through the Camp David agreements and negotiating the Panama Canal Treaties. However, his human rights policy proved difficult to apply fairly, particularly in cases of abuses by important allies. Containment was hard to banish. The USSR had launched a massive military buildup in the 1970s, and when the Soviet Union invaded Afghanistan in 1980, the cold war intensified once again. The United States boycotted the Moscow Olympics in 1980 and canceled a massive grain sale to the Soviet Union, angering many farmers and other Americans. The feeling of U.S. weakness in the world was further exacerbated by the Islamic fundamentalist revolution in Iran and the seizure of American hostages in the U.S. embassy in Teheran.

Ronald Reagan capitalized on this feeling of weakness in U.S. foreign policy in the 1980 presidential campaign, promising a massive defense buildup and a tougher stance toward the Soviet Union, which he called the "evil empire." The rhetoric of U.S. foreign policy sounded much like it had in the 1950s. The United States invaded the tiny Caribbean nation of Grenada in 1983 after a left-wing coup. Marines were sent to Lebanon. Containment was applied in Central America by assisting the Contra rebels in Nicaragua against the Marxist Sandinista regime. By the mid-1980s, the United States had rapidly expanded its military capability, and U.S. foreign policy looked much as it had forty years before. However, when Mikhail Gorbachev assumed power in the Soviet Union in 1985, events unfolded that would end the cold war, permanently altering the international system and U.S. foreign policy. George Bush became the first post–cold war president, and the United States attempted to provide leadership in a transformed world.

THE NEW INTERNATIONAL ENVIRONMENT

The End of the Cold War

Mikhail Gorbachev served as president of the Soviet Union from 1985 until December 1991, when the USSR broke up into separate Republics. The reform process began slowly. Gorbachev launched a gradual campaign to restructure the Soviet economy, called *perestroika,* and a policy of greater openness, called *glasnost.* The Reagan administration was cautious but began to see that the changes were real. Significant progress was made in achieving arms reductions, including the intermediate nuclear force (INF) treaty, signed in 1987. The Soviets pulled out of Afghanistan in 1988, recognizing the limits of their power in much the same way as the United States had after Vietnam.

Dramatic changes occurred in 1989 after Gorbachev signaled to Eastern Europe that the Soviets would no longer use force to prop up communist governments or oppose democratic reforms. A tide of reform swept through Eastern Europe, toppling the old guard and undertaking experiments in democracy and market capitalism. The end of the cold war and the demise of the Soviet empire had dramatic implications for U.S. foreign policy. After years of confrontation in the Mideast, for example, the United States and the USSR found themselves on the same side in opposing Saddam Hussein's invasion of Kuwait. In the new world order, multilateralism and the United Nations play a much more important role. Because of the reduction in world tensions and the globalization of the economy, foreign policy has begun to blend more with domestic economic policy.

Defense Spending and Fiscal Constraints

In this new environment, U.S. military and diplomatic needs are different. The United States entered the 1990s with defense spending at record levels for peacetime, along with huge budget deficits and debt accumulated in the 1980s. Figure 5.2 shows defense spending since 1962 in current and constant dollars projected through 2002. Rapid changes in the international system have increased the pressure for cuts in defense spending—the "peace dividend"—to finance deficit reduction, domestic programs, and tax relief. The chronic deficits also constrained foreign policy options.

Billions of Dollars

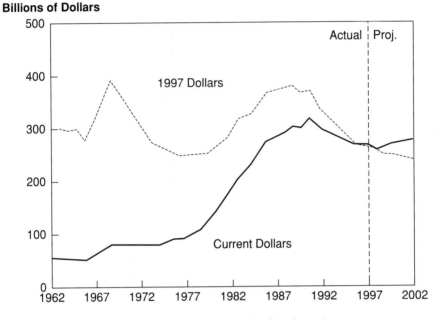

FIGURE 5.2   **Outlays for national defense (by fiscal year).**

Source: Congressional Budget Office (1997), based on data from the Office of Management and Budget and the Department of Defense.

Because of the large deficits, the United States was limited in responding to unforeseen international needs. Much of the cost of U.S. military operations in the Gulf War was paid by allies. Because of fiscal constraints, the United States was unable to respond to developments in Eastern Europe and the Soviet republics as effectively as Germany and Japan did. Recession and domestic economic problems influence foreign policy—from proposals to cut spending on defense and foreign aid, to pressure to limit the immigration of foreign workers, to protectionist trade restrictions.

Unlike Bush's acknowledged penchant for foreign affairs, Bill Clinton appeared much more interested in domestic policy. However, he inherited several pressing international problems from the Bush administration, including rectifying human rights violations in Somalia, Haiti, and Bosnia. Although members of Congress and others criticized Clinton's lack of foreign policy experience, at least the first two crises were resolved satisfactorily. The third was more difficult, and legislation was considered in opposition to Clinton's expressed desire to handle such conflicts more through UN auspices. Another Clinton decision controversial in Congress was his recognition of the communist government of Vietnam. Clinton also encountered some congressional opposition over whether to expand NATO (the North Atlantic Treaty Organization) to include three former eastern bloc nations (Poland, Hungary, and the Czech Republic) into the western military alliance.

Free Trade Issues

Despite attention to these military and diplomatic problems, Clinton appeared most interested in trade matters within the realm of foreign policy. During the fall of 1997, trade was high on the Clinton foreign policy agenda, just as it had been with NAFTA (North Atlantic Free Trade Agreement) earlier in his administration. Clinton asked for expanded authority to make "fast track" trade deals overseas that Congress could not amend. He requested this power, which had been granted to prior presidents, despite opposition from organized labor and from Democratic congressional leaders. In a major foreign policy speech at American University, Clinton stated: "It will promote peace; it will promote freedom; it will promote stability; it will raise the level of living standards in other parts of the world even as it maintains America as the world's most prosperous nation."[19]

But Democratic legislators, such as House majority leader Dick Gephardt (D-Mo.) and Senate minority leader Tom Daschle (D-S.Dak.), were not so sure. They became part of the same coalition that had opposed Clinton's earlier bipartisan trade success, NAFTA, the impact of which is still being hotly debated. Even the American public was unpersuaded that free trade deals improve U.S. wages. Opponents contend that NAFTA actually lost U.S. jobs and that any expanded authority to the president should protect both U.S. labor rights and the environment in the effected countries. Clinton and Vice President Al Gore had big business and most Republican legislators on their side, but Democratic support remained elusive. This was despite the healthy U.S. economy, which gave Clinton more trade and other foreign policy options than Bush had experienced under weaker economic conditions. Congress refused to extend "fast track" in 1997 and the administration would have to try again. Trade emerged as a major area of dispute between Congress and the president, cutting across party lines.

MAKING FOREIGN POLICY

Executive Branch Institutions

The executive branch's system for foreign policy, defense, and national security was designed to meet the needs of the cold war era. The State Department and the Defense Department (originally the War Department) were two of the first four federal departments, dating back to George Washington's first cabinet. After World War II, several changes in the executive branch were adopted. The National Security Act of 1947 created the Department of Defense (DOD), the National Security Council (NSC), the Central Intelligence Agency, and the Joint Chiefs of Staff. Despite efforts to avoid conflict and duplication, the making of foreign policy in the executive branch has often been plagued by bureaucratic infighting and competition. If not managed effectively by the president, the national security staff can get out of control, as Reagan's NSC did in the Iran–Contra scandal. These formal institutions have not always suited the needs of presidents in making foreign policy decisions. Thus, the roles of the secretary of state, national security adviser, and secretary of defense have fluctuated markedly in different administrations. For example, national security adviser Henry Kissinger dominated foreign policymaking in Nixon's first term. Eisenhower, Bush, and Clinton, in contrast, relied heavily on their secretaries of state.

In crisis situations, when presidential power is greatest, presidents often rely on ad hoc decision-making groups rather than formal bodies such as the NSC. Presidents are most comfortable with manageable groups that include advisors in whom they have personal trust. The Bush foreign policy apparatus placed particular emphasis on informal channels and close personal relationships. In making routine, noncrisis foreign policy decisions, the State Department is usually in charge. However, presidents have often been critical of State for its rigid hierarchy, caution, inefficiency, and traditionalism.[20] Rivalries periodically arise between Defense and State over diplomatic or military solutions to problems. Some argue that the DOD is more pragmatic and adaptable to the president's needs.[21] As the international environment changes, presidents will probably be making fewer crisis decisions; instead, they will need executive institutions that can plan and implement foreign policy effectively over the long run.

Legislative Branch Institutions

Traditionally, the Senate, with its constitutional powers to ratify treaties and confirm ambassadors, has been more prominent in foreign policy than the House of Representatives. In recent years, however, House members have actively sought more input into foreign policy, and the Senate Foreign Relations committee has declined in effectiveness and prestige. As some of the cases that follow will suggest, greater congressional participation in foreign policy is part of the general assertiveness of Congress and reflects many of the institutional changes of the 1970s and 1980s. As policy differences with the White House became more pronounced, the Democratic Congresses in the 1980s used whatever techniques were available to contest presidential policy. For example, the Reagan administration's policy in Nicaragua was checked by the enactment of the Boland amendments, which restricted assistance to the Contra rebels.

House Speaker Jim Wright (1987–1989) asserted himself in foreign policy to a greater extent than previous congressional leaders, traveling around the world. His independent peace initiatives in Central America and use of the media to highlight policy differences infuriated the Reagan administration. His successor, Speaker Tom Foley, did not follow Wright's lead, nor did Speaker Newt Gingrich (R-Ga.), who focused more on domestic matters. Nor did the Senate under Majority Leader Trent Lott (R-Miss.) seek to wield much foreign policy authority in a relatively peaceful international environment. Apart from congressional party leaders, Senate Republican committee chairs, such as Jesse Helms (R-N.C.) and Richard Luger (R-Ind.), exerted considerable influence in foreign policy matters. Thus, as world tensions ease and foreign policy increasingly affects the domestic economy, Congress is likely to become even more involved. How will this tilt the legislative-executive balance?

Is the President Still Dominant in Foreign Affairs?

Despite the reassertion of congressional power after the Vietnam War and the continuing struggle between branches, the president retains certain advantages over Congress. This remains true despite the 1973 War Powers Resolution and other restrictive legislation. Presidents can shape foreign policy by recognizing foreign governments, by making international agreements and negotiating treaties, by appointing key personnel to conduct foreign policy, and by using military force when necessary.[22] Many aspects of presidential power in foreign affairs go beyond votes in Congress.[23] Also one or two critical votes—such as the 1991 vote to authorize the use of force in the Persian Gulf—may be far more important than half a dozen lesser measures that a president loses. Acting as commander-in-chief of the armed forces, President Reagan invaded Grenada in 1983, and President Bush invaded Panama in 1989, both without prior congressional approval. Although he sought House and Senate approval before launching Operation Desert Storm in 1991, Bush asserted his right to use force against Iraq even without it. Bill Clinton also asserted his role as commander-in-chief in Haiti and Bosnia despite some opposition in Congress.

This discussion leads us to the question of just how different presidential influence is in domestic and foreign policy. Do "two presidencies" still exist? What evidence can help us clarify the relative power of Congress and the president in foreign affairs? Wildavsky argued in 1966 that presidents rarely lost on any major initiatives in foreign affairs and defense. In looking at presidential initiatives, he found that Congress approved 70 percent of foreign policy proposals compared with only 40 percent of domestic proposals.[24] These differences seemed to decline over the next decade, when foreign policy issues took on more domestic implications. Between 1966 and 1975, the gap in presidential success narrowed to 55 percent support for foreign policy proposals and 46 percent for domestic policy proposals.[25] As we noted in Chapter 3, this measure of "success" for the president was discontinued in 1975, and researchers have since focused on "support" (the percentage of members in Congress who vote in accordance with the roll-call vote position taken by the president.)

Using the support measure, recent findings clarify some of the differences between foreign affairs and domestic affairs. One of the important factors determining whether a president has significantly greater support in foreign policy votes is the president's party. Fleisher and Bond found that the "two presidencies" phenomenon occurs only for Republican presidents.[26] The difference stems from the tendency of congressional Democrats to support Republican presidents substantially more on foreign policy issues than on domestic votes. Conversely, congressional Republicans are just as likely to oppose Democratic presidents on foreign policy as on domestic policy. Table 5.1 compares the differences in support on the two kinds of votes since the Eisenhower administration. Support was significantly greater on foreign policy votes for Presidents Ford and Reagan (and somewhat less so for Eisenhower and Nixon), when compared with the records of Carter and Clinton. These two Democrats actually fared better in the domestic policy realm, whereas Kennedy and Johnson revealed almost no differences in support. However, much of the difference simply reflects the lower levels of support that Republican presidents have on domestic issues. The findings in Table 5.1 lead us to agree with Fleisher and Bond, who concluded that "there may be two presidencies, but the phenomenon is limited and conditional."[27] All in all, the gap in support exists only for Republican presidents.

With the globalization of the economy and dramatic changes in the international environment, foreign policy issues are increasingly subject to the same political forces as domestic issues.[28] As these differences narrow, and as divided government and interbranch conflict spread to foreign policy, the "two presidencies" phenomenon may decline further. Although the president retains some inherent advantages in crisis decisions, these instances are relatively rare. In foreign as well as domestic policy, Congress and the president usually operate as tandem institutions to make decisions. The new foreign policy agenda on which they must cooperate includes trade, competitiveness, immigration, base location, terrorism, foreign and military aid, and international environmental issues. Regarding these issues, like others, the president must bargain and persuade to put his imprint on policy.

Figure 5.3 compares three types of presidential actions in foreign policy and national defense since 1957: taking a position on legislation before Congress, casting

TABLE 5.1 Average Percent Agreement (Support) in the House (Two Presidencies: by Presidential Party and Individual President) 1953–1994

President	Mean Overall	Foreign	Domestic	Difference
Eisenhower	57.7	62.1	55.9	−6.2
Kennedy	66.3	70.5	64.3	−6.2
Johnson	69.2	68.1	69.8	+1.7
Nixon	61.1	61.6	61.1	−.5
Ford	56.9	57.9	47.0	−10.9
Carter	59.7	57.3	61.2	+3.9
Reagan	47.7	53.6	42.9	−10.7
Bush	48.7	51.8	46.3	−5.5
Clinton*	61.3	59.0	62.1	+3.1
Republican	53.8	57.3	50.8	−6.5
Democrat	64.9	64.2	65.2	+1.0
Totals	57.4	59.9	56.0	−3.6

*Through 1994

Source: Adapted from Steven A. Shull, *Presidential-Congressional Relations* (Ann Arbor: University of Michigan Press, 1997): chapter 6.

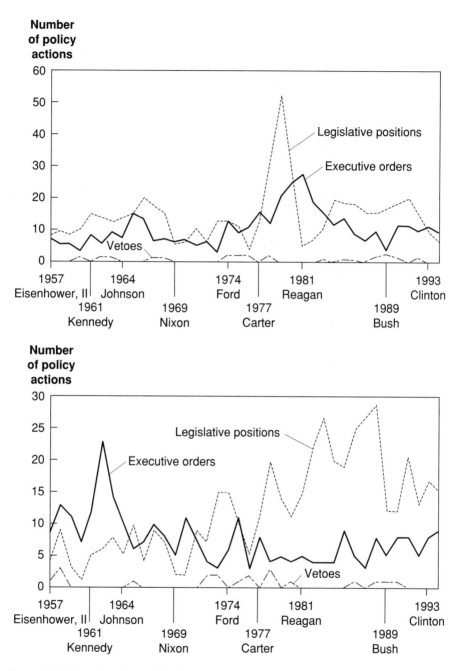

FIGURE 5.3 Presidential Behavior on *Foreign* Policy, Eisenhower, II, to Clinton (top). Presidential Behavior on *Defense* Policy, Eisenhower, II, to Clinton (bottom).

Source: Lyn Ragsdale, *Vital Statistics on the Presidency* (Washington, D.C.: Congressional Quarterly Press, 1996): 406–407.

vetoes on foreign policy measures, and issuing executive orders. Of the three, legislative position taking shows an upward trend for both diplomatic and defense issues. Executive orders appear to be declining slightly (especially on diplomacy), and vetoes remain stable at a low level. This suggests the growing importance of Congress and the greater importance of legislation to the president's success and influence in foreign policy. The cases that follow provide some examples of the changing dynamic between Congress and the president in legislation within the realm of foreign policy.

PRESIDENTIAL LEADERSHIP: THE PERSIAN GULF WAR (1991)

On January 16, 1991, President George Bush's Press Secretary, Marlin Fitzwater, announced to the nation, "The liberation of Kuwait has begun." The president of the United States had succeeded in leading the country and the international community to act against the aggression of Iraq's Saddam Hussein. Bush dominated policymaking internationally by forging an unprecedented coalition of nations, composed of Arab and Western countries. He dominated policy domestically by successfully urging Congress to give him the formal authorization to use force in the Persian Gulf. After weeks of a punishing air war, followed by a lightning ground war, the United States and its allies won. The jubilant nation gave President Bush the highest public approval ratings ever recorded.

The outcome of the war overshadowed a number of questions about earlier U.S. support for Iraq, which may have encouraged the invasion of Kuwait to occur in the first place. U.S. policymakers seemed to ignore ominous Iraqi troop movements until it was too late. By the last week in July, American intelligence judged that Iraq was preparing to seize a small part of Kuwait. The Bush administration was unprepared when Iraq launched a massive invasion early in August, and its tanks rolled over Kuwait in a matter of hours. Saddam Hussein announced to the world that Kuwait had become Iraq's nineteenth province.

After joining the world in denouncing Iraq's aggression, the Bush administration's most immediate concern was the security of Saudi Arabia and its oil reserves. The large Iraqi army was in a position to continue its advance across the Saudi desert; if the Iraqis chose to do so, they would control a huge proportion of the world's oil supplies. Unwilling to risk becoming an energy hostage to Iraq, Bush announced that U.S. troops and naval forces would be deployed immediately in Saudi Arabia and the Persian Gulf. Operation Desert Shield would attempt to deter further advances by Iraq. Many Arab nations, although they had historically been opposed to a U.S. military presence in the Middle East, supported the move.

The president received strong bipartisan support for the deployment of U.S. troops to the gulf. Both houses of Congress passed a resolution in support of the president by nearly unanimous margins. The administration's other main strategy was diplomatic, urging the United Nations to impose economic sanctions on Iraq. Very quickly, the UN Security Council passed several resolutions condemning Iraq and implementing a virtual economic blockade around it. The administration also worked to build a multinational force in Saudi Arabia, including troops from Egypt and other Arab states.

Within a matter of weeks, the Unites States had deployed over 200,000 troops and tons of equipment and materiel. Back home, the invasion was having severe economic effects. Oil prices doubled at one point, to over forty dollars a barrel. Growing impatient with economic sanctions, the administration made a crucial change in policy in November 1990, after Congress had recessed. The administration doubled the number of U.S. troops in the gulf to over 400,000. This constituted a move toward an offensive posture, because that number of troops could not be rotated out over a prolonged period. At the same time, the administration successfully pushed a UN resolution that authorized the use of force if Iraq did not withdraw from Kuwait by January 15, 1991. Dissent in Congress grew steadily, as the earlier bipartisan consensus eroded. Democrats and some Republicans warned the president that only Congress had the power to commit the nation to war. A confrontation was developing; the administration claimed that, as commander-in-chief, the president did not need congressional authorization.

Congress reconvened in January 1991, as the UN deadline approached. Although partisanship was restrained in public, support for the president had split Congress, largely along party lines. On January 8, the administration switched gears. In a letter to congressional leaders, Bush requested that Congress adopt a resolution backing UN Security Council Resolution 678, which authorized the use of "all necessary means" to expel Iraq from Kuwait. Such a congressional resolution, the president wrote, "would help dispel any belief that may exist in the minds of Iraq's leaders that the United States lacks the necessary unity to act decisively."[29]

An emotional but solemn debate on the resolution began on Capitol Hill on January 10. Over the next three days, over 300 speeches would be given on the House floor, and 94 of 100 senators would rise to speak. The administration worked hard behind the scenes to ensure a majority in both houses. The biggest problem was in the Senate, where the opposition was led by Majority Leader George Mitchell (D-Me.) and Senator Sam Nunn (D-Ga.), the influential Chairman of the Armed Services Committee. Two Republican Senators defected from the president's position, meaning that at least seven Democratic votes were needed for a majority.

Democrat Joseph Lieberman of Connecticut cosponsored the resolution in the Senate and helped Bush round up the needed Democratic votes. On January 12, the Senate passed the resolution by a vote of 52 to 47. Minutes later, the House of Representatives voted 250 to 183 for the same resolution. The administration's task was much easier in the House, where Armed Services chairman Les Aspin (D-Wis.) and Rep Steven Solarz (D-N.Y.), an influential northeastern liberal, worked hard for passage. House Republicans voted in favor 164 to 3, and 86 of 265 Democrats supported the resolution—a more comfortable margin than in the Senate. In the end, the debate was remembered as one of Congress's finest hours, and the vote represented a crucial political victory for the Bush administration.

On January 16, Desert Shield became Desert Storm as the air attack on Iraq began. Days later, both the House and Senate passed nearly unanimous resolutions supporting the president and U.S. troops. Within weeks, coalition forces had expelled Iraq from Kuwait, in the process destroying much of Iraq's vaunted military might. The United States stopped short of occupying Baghdad and forcing Saddam Hussein from office—a decision that would later be subjected to considerable second-guessing. Chaos gripped Iraq for weeks, with Kurds rebelling in the north and Shiite Moslems rebelling in the south. Saddam Hussein regrouped and reestablished control of the country. In the United States, the nation was euphoric. A jubilant George Bush said, "By God, we've kicked the Vietnam syndrome once and for all."[30]

How was President Bush able to lead policymaking? Although the presidency has a number of political advantages in foreign and military affairs, congressional support in the crucial vote was far from guaranteed. The United States itself had not been attacked, and many people questioned how essential it was to restore Kuwait's ruling royal family to power. In addition, there was a clear alternative to military action. The economic sanctions initiated by the administration had not had time to work, and there was strong sentiment among many members of Congress to give them more time.[31] Bush prevailed because he made his case and effectively sold it to Congress. The administration skillfully used the United Nations to its advantage, bringing international pressure on Congress. Although later evidence suggested that the administration was not as unified as it had appeared, it was clear and unwavering in defining its goals and ways to achieve them.[32]

The Gulf War had a number of constitutional, political, and policy impacts. With respect to the issue of war powers, some scholars considered that Bush's letter to Congress requesting authorization was important. Yale law professor Harold Koh noted that "the president blinked" in the "constitutional face-off."[33] Senate Majority leader Mitchell commented, "His request clearly acknowledged the need for congressional approval. The Constitution of the United States is not and cannot be subordinated to a United Nations resolution."[34] In terms of immediate political effects, the war was a bonanza for the administration. Immediately after the war, more Americans reported themselves as Republicans than Democrats for the first time ever.[35] The president's approval ratings approached 90 percent.

The war had several immediate policy consequences. It restored confidence in the American military and proved the capability of many of the advanced weapons that had been procured during the 1980s. The main objective of the policy—the expulsion of Iraq from Kuwait—was achieved. Much of Iraq's offensive military capacity seemingly was destroyed, including chemical and nuclear weapons. The process strengthened the United Nations and established important precedents for multilateral cooperation in the post–cold war world. Middle East peace talks between Arab nations and Israel began. The war also affected oil prices; a year after the war, gasoline prices in the United States were 20 percent lower.

Despite these achievements, questions about the impact of the war remained. Saddam Hussein managed to cling to power, build weapons of mass destruction, and defy the UN resolutions. The balance of power in the region remained in doubt. The progress of democratic reforms remained questionable in Kuwait and other Gulf states. Further study showed that American weaponry had been less accurate than originally reported. Many returning American soldiers suffered from an ill-defined illness known as "gulf war syndrome" that some claimed resulted from poison gas. Finally, the president's political advantages proved fleeting, as public attention turned from the war to an economy mired in recession. A year later, Democrats once again had a 10 percent lead over Republicans in party identification, and Bush's approval ratings had plunged below 40 percent as he entered the election year.

CONGRESSIONAL LEADERSHIP: CUBA SANCTIONS LEGISLATION (1996)

On February 24, 1996, Cuban fighter pilots shot down an unarmed U.S. registered aircraft that had entered Cuban airspace, killing four American citizens of Cuban ancestry. This confrontational act forced President Clinton and moderates in Congress to support controversial legislation that greatly expanded economic sanctions against Cuba. The legislation, known as the Helms-Burton bill, would also sanction U.S. allies whose international companies were doing business with Cuba. Indeed, the White House and Congress reached agreement on the bill just four days after the incident. Castro had only himself to blame for making it politically impossible for the president to oppose the Republican Congress on this issue. The Cuban pilots who shot down the U.S. plane touted their manhood. However, the U.S. Ambassador to the UN, Madeline Albright, questioned that very manhood in stating their act displayed "not cajonnes, but cowardice." Both events greatly limited Clinton's options and allowed Congress to gain the upper hand.

The sanctions legislation was the culmination of a long festering disaffection with the single remaining communist dictatorship in the Western Hemisphere. In the United States, the Cuban vote was a powerful force in Florida, a state critical to winning the presidential election. In October 1995, conservative Republicans in the Senate, led by Jesse Helms (R-N.C.), Bob Dole (R-Kan.), and Phil Gramm (R-Tex.), opposed President Clinton's plans to increase cultural exchanges and travel with Cuba. The latter two senators were candidates for the Republican nomination for president and sought to strengthen their conservative foreign policy credentials by embarrassing Clinton for easing such restrictions. They accused him of seeking to limit a boycott of Cuba that had been in place for thirty years and pushed for a heavily modified sanctions legislation that had passed the House overwhelmingly the previous month. The tactic these leaders used was to cut off debate by White House supporters by invoking cloture, which would have ended the filibuster against House Bill 924. They failed in this endeavor by a mere four votes on October 12, 1995. Clinton had threatened a veto if the bill did pass, and even some Republicans feared that the legislation "could strain relations with U.S. allies, spawn a flood of costly litigation and trigger a backlash against U.S. companies abroad."[36] Although Clinton prevailed, he brought forth the wrath of conservatives who wanted even stronger sanctions.

This vote revealed the deep ideological divisions in the Senate, particularly among Democrats, over how best to deal with the Castro regime in Cuba. A short time later, the Senate passed more moderate sanctions legislation that contained fewer provisions objected to by the White House. Even this scaled-back version, passed by a fifty-vote margin, was opposed by many Democrats and two Republicans. But Clinton and his democratic allies in Congress were undercut by the shoot-down of the plane. Four days later, the revised legislation passed both chambers on February 28, 1996, by veto-proof margins (larger than two-thirds majorities) after conferees agreed on a compromise version.

The Senate adopted the conference report to HB 927 on March 5, 1996, by a vote of 74 to 22, which had passed the House the previous day by an also lopsided vote of 336 to 86. Highlights of the resulting Cuban Liberty and Democratic Solidarity Act (PL 104-116) included the following provisions. It (1) urged the president to seek an international embargo against Cuba through the United Nations; (2) codified existing embargoes until Castro is replaced; (3) prohibited the extension of loans and credits involving confiscated property until a democratically elected government appears in Cuba; (4) authorized the president to encourage democracy building efforts in Cuba; and (5) withheld U.S. assistance to any nation supporting completion of nuclear facilities in Cuba. In addition to condemning the attack of February 24, 1996, the most controversial provision sought to protect the property rights of U.S. nationals whose property had been confiscated by making the perpetrators liable for damages.

The Cuban Liberty and Democratic Solidarity (or LIBERTAD) Act, nicknamed for its chief sponsors Senator Jesse Helms and Representative Dan Burton (R-Ind.), was signed into law on March 12, 1996. Despite earlier presidential opposition, President Clinton felt compelled to present a unified front against Castro. In signing the legislation, he made the following remarks:

> *Today I sign with a certainty that it will send a powerful unified message from the United States to Havana, that the yearning of the Cuban people for freedom must not be denied. This bill continues our bipartisan effort to pursue an activist Cuba policy, an effort that began some four years ago with the Cuban Democracy Act.*[37]

Rhetoric was hot in the Senate when Foreign Relations Committee Chairman Helms said, "there is no mistaking the bill's intent. 'Farewell Fidel,' that's the message of this bill."[38] The law was in the political interests of all sides to present a unified front against Castro. Before the legislation, the president had been able to lift embargoes on his own, but now that authority was transferred to Congress. The administration had obtained a provision that empowered the president to delay implementation of suits against foreign businesses. Still, the resulting law was more strict than the previous efforts and limited the president's discretion. As one Republican stated: "This means he can't do what he did on Vietnam," referring to Clinton's initiating diplomatic relations with the Communist nation over congressional objections.

The case of sanctions legislation shows the political intricacies and interrelationships among domestic, economic, and foreign policy in presidential-congressional relations. It also shows in dramatic fashion how an international event can change the political environment and, as a result, negotiations between Congress and the president. Its elements of international intrigue and diplomacy might appear at first to be solely in the realm of foreign policy. After the attack on American citizens, Congress and President Clinton made retaliatory threats against Castro. However, the legislation greatly heightened tensions with U.S. allies in both the Americas and the European Community. The case also contains elements of trade and economic matters because the new law places sanctions on any nation "trafficking" in Cuban money expropriated (confiscated) from U.S. citizens. Additionally, the Cuban sanctions law involved a heavy dose of domestic politics, pitting candidates for the presidency against one another in 1996. Although its future remains uncertain, the legislation shows an interesting example of relationships, shifting from initial congressional leadership to the presidential viewpoint and back to Congress taking the predominant leadership position.

In addition to military implications, the legislation likely will inflict further economic hardship on the Cuban people, who remain among Latin America's most impoverished. Castro and his brother Raul blasted Helms-Burton as "a monstrous plan . . . to make Cubans surrender to hunger and need." During the annual celebration of the Cuban revolution, the Castro brothers claimed it would have little effect and that tourism would increase by nearly 20 percent during the year.[39] Clinton suspended all charter air travel from the Unites States to Cuba indefinitely. Helms-Burton raised potential complications with U.S. allies who resented having conditions placed on their trading relations. These nations threatened retaliation, stating that the lawsuits provision could "expose U.S. businesses to similar claims in foreign courts."[40] Private businesses were also subject to its provisions wherein any economic involvement with Cuba that encompassed expropriated U.S. property was subject to legal action. In addition, foreign governments and companies involved in such "trafficking" would be barred from entering the United States except for medical conditions. Thus, the provisions were very wide ranging, and several foreign governments, Mexico and Canada among them, hinted at retaliation against U.S. companies in their countries.

Congress had largely ignored objections from U.S. allies in its efforts to punish Castro. Canada and Mexico suggested they would challenge the new law under NAFTA provisions, and European Community members also objected. Even the World Trade Organization (WTO), an organization largely set up by the United States, expressed concern over the legislation. One member stated: "You don't export your laws and your principles to other countries."[41] Several European diplomats considered filing a complaint with the WTO but feared such a move would further worsen tensions. International businesses waited anxiously to see how the law would be enforced. One investor stated, "This law is going to make an investment here [Cuba] a little more difficult perhaps, but it will not stop it."[42] Although more than 650 companies have some presence in Cuba, most find doing business in the undeveloped country difficult.[43]

The Helms-Burton Act has generated much controversy, not only among the international trade community but also among scholars of international law.[44] Numerous lawsuits sought to clarify the vague or unresolved issues of the law, such as the liability of foreign citizens in U.S. courts or subjecting foreign countries to retroactive liability. Some provisions of the Act, such as the definition of "trafficking," seemed inconsistent. Mexico announced that it would consider inducements to its companies to ignore the Act. Such actions and confusion over the law prompted President Clinton to name a special envoy to deal with criticisms and seek to promote Cuban democracy.

Clearly the legislation shifted the balance of presidential-congressional relations in terms of Cuba policy toward Congress, at least in the short run. The president obtained the authority to suspend the rights of claimants to file lawsuits for six months if he asserted that delays would be in U.S. interests. Clinton, in effect, refused to implement the law. He suspended the law for the third time on July 20, 1997, thereby not allowing U.S. citizens to sue foreign firms using confiscated property in Cuba. He stated that he would continue to do so as long as progress was being made in organizing other international actions against Castro's regime.[45] However, the legislation had codified all U.S. embargoes against Cuba under congressional rather than presidential auspices and gave presidents no latitude in barring foreign executives who "traffick" from entering the United States; they and their families would be barred automatically. International negotiators postponed a clash over the law because of Clinton's suspensions, but the case represents the problems associated with efforts to extend U.S. laws outside the country. Regardless of the intentions, such actions likely will increase international tensions and, thus, the long-term impacts of this policy remain uncertain.

CONSENSUS/COOPERATION:
THE PANAMA CANAL TREATIES (1978)

On April 18, 1978, with only one vote to spare, a two-thirds majority in the United States Senate ratified the treaty that would turn over operation of the Panama Canal to the nation of Panama in the year 2000. This followed an identical 68 to 32 vote in March over the neutrality treaty with Panama. Ratification of these two treaties was a victory not only for President Jimmy Carter, but also for Senate leaders who had navigated through a legislative mine field for two months. Immediately after the vote,

Carter said, "These treaties can mark the beginning of a new era in our relations not only with Panama but with the rest of the world."[46]

There may be constitutional ambiguity about the war power, but responsibility for treaties with foreign nations is clear: The president negotiates treaties, and the Senate ratifies by a two-thirds vote. Since the days of George Washington, treaty negotiation has been an executive prerogative, with the Senate limited to approval or rejection of the final document. That approval has not always been easy to get. The defeat in the U.S. Senate of the Treaty of Versailles, negotiated by President Woodrow Wilson at the end of the First World War, was a devastating blow to his presidency. As a result of difficulties with treaties, presidents in the modern era increasingly turned to executive agreements (which do not need Senate ratification), as shown in Table 5.2.

Renegotiating the control of the Panama Canal, however, could not be disposed of by executive agreement. A treaty with Panama had existed since 1903, revised in 1936 and 1955. By the 1960s, U.S. control of the canal had become a sore point between the United States, Panama, and the nations of Latin America. It was seen as a vestige of U.S. colonialism: "Yankee imperialism." In 1964, a riot about flying the American flag left twenty-five dead and led Panama to break diplomatic relations with the United States. Talks over a new treaty began under President Johnson and continued under President Nixon. In 1974, Secretary of State Henry Kissinger signed an agreement with Panama establishing the principles for new negotiations. Throughout the process, there was strong congressional opposition to giving up

TABLE 5.2   Treaties and Executive Agreements, 1789–1994.

Years	Number of Treaties	Number of Executive Agreements	Executive Agreements as Percentage of Total
1789–1839	60	27	34
1839–1889	215	238	53
1889–1932	431	804	65
1933–1944 (Roosevelt)	131	369	74
1945–1952 (Truman)	132	1324	91
1953–1960 (Eisenhower)	89	1834	95
1961–1963 (Kennedy)	36	813	96
1964–1968 (Johnson)	67	1083	94
1969–1974 (Nixon)	93	1317	93
1975–1976 (Ford)	26	666	96
1976–1980 (Carter)	79	1476	96
1981–1988 (Reagan)	117	2837	96
1989–1992 (Bush)	67	1350	95
1993–1994 (Clinton)	41	594	94

Source: Adapted from Harold W. Stanley and Richard G. Niemi, *Vital Statistics on American Politics,* 4th ed. (Washington D.C.: Congressional Quarterly Press, 1996): 260.

control of the canal. Ronald Reagan made the canal an emotional national issue in his bid for the 1976 Republican presidential nomination.

Early in his first year in office, Jimmy Carter promised the Organization of American States that he was "firmly committed to negotiating . . . a new treaty which will take into account Panama's legitimate needs as a sovereign nation."[47] Over the course of the year, the administration finalized work on two separate treaties: one establishing the neutrality of the canal zone, and the second turning over control of the canal to Panama on December 31, 1999. The treaties were signed on September 7, 1977. In October, the Panamanian people approved the treaties in a national plebiscite. Now the challenge for the president would be to work with congressional leaders to secure the necessary votes for ratification. Given Carter's unspectacular legislative record in his first year, the prospects for getting a two-thirds majority seemed slim at best.

Lobbying was intense. Proponents and opponents battled both for Senate votes and public opinion. In late 1977, the Gallup poll indicated that most Americans opposed the treaties. Conservative groups attacked what they called "giving away our canal." Senate Minority Leader Howard Baker (R-Tenn.) was lobbied at a University of Tennessee football game by a plane flying overhead with a banner that read "Save our Canal."[48] The American Conservative Union launched a massive grassroots campaign against ratification, spending hundreds of thousands of dollars. Mail to Sen. Charles Percy (R-Ill.) was running 95 percent against the treaties. However, pro-treaty groups and the Carter administration were active as well. The president concentrated on elite opinion, inviting influential people from around the country to the White House for briefings. An impressive bipartisan group of former officials was brought in to tout the treaties, including former President Gerald Ford, former Vice President Nelson Rockefeller, and former Secretaries of State Dean Rusk, Henry Kissinger, and William Rogers. Even conservative actor John Wayne was enlisted to publicize his support for the treaties.

Much of the work in building support for the treaties was done in the Senate itself. Minority Leader Baker and Majority Leader Robert Byrd (D-W.Va.) both announced their support in early 1978 and formed a bipartisan team to win ratification. The debate in the Senate began on February 8 and was carried nationwide on National Public Radio. As more and more senators announced their intentions, vote counters estimated that there were sixty-two senators in favor, twenty-eight opposed, and ten undecided.[49] Each side needed only a handful of votes to reach their goal. Opponents were led by James Allen (D-Ala.), one of the Senate's old guard, who challenged the treaties on both substantive and procedural grounds. The main fear of congressional leaders was the possibility of "killer amendments"—changes mandated by the Senate that would force Panama to resubmit the treaty to its voters. For over a month, Allen offered amendment after amendment, but all were defeated. Finally, opponents agreed to a vote on the neutrality treaty on March 16. Neither side knew whether it had the votes.

As the dramatic vote unfolded, all 100 senators sat at their desks. The administration had been busy in the hours leading up to the vote, sending 30 State Department officials to meet with senators and providing expensive maps and information packets. Vice President Mondale, well known and respected in the Senate, worked the Hill tirelessly. To secure the votes of those senators who still had major concerns, the administration and congressional sponsors agreed to accept several major "reservations" by the Senate. Unlike amendments, reservations do not change the text of the treaty but, according to international law scholars, would carry the same weight.[50] In the end, Byrd and Baker got 68 votes for the treaty and claimed to have four in reserve (members who would have voted yes if they were needed to provide the decisive vote). This was a tremendous victory for proponents, but was no guarantee of victory on the more controversial treaty that would turn over the canal to Panama.

The debate on the second treaty resumed in April. One of the most compelling arguments concerned the effect that a defeat of the treaty would have on the nation's ability to conduct foreign policy. Reluctant supporter Herman Talmadge (D-Ga.) reasoned that "we do not want to destroy the bargaining power or diplomatic credibility of the United States."[51] Still, the treaties remained unpopular with the American people. A Harris poll in April indicated that, by 44 to 37 percent, a plurality of Americans believed the treaties were "not a good thing" for the United States.[52] Despite the polls, Senator Byrd appealed to the Senate to do what they knew was right rather than what was popular:

> *There's no political mileage in voting for the treaties. I know what my constituents are saying. But I have a responsibility not only to follow them but to inform them and lead them. I'm not going to betray my responsibility to my constituents. I owe them not only my industry but my judgment.[53]*

Opponents tried several last-ditch maneuvers to defeat the treaties. Senator Orin Hatch (R-Utah) offered an amendment requiring the House to approve the transfer of U.S. property to Panama even if the treaties were ratified. The Senate rejected the amendment and the constitutional interpretation behind it. Dozens more amendments were tabled or defeated. As the final vote approached, the Senate adopted another sensitive reservation, giving the United States the right to keep the canal open. The vote was in doubt until the final hour, and this time the leadership had no votes in reserve. The result was the same, 68 to 32, with fifty-two of sixty Democrats and sixteen of thirty-eight Republicans voting for the treaty. Although most Republicans opposed it, bipartisan cooperation had been a key to success.

How were the legislative and executive branches able to cooperate effectively to gain ratification for such a controversial treaty? Clearly, the political environment was unfavorable for such an outcome, with deep public fears fanned by opponents of the treaty. The president's congressional liaison efforts, much maligned in the previous year, were given high marks by senators. Individual leadership played a crucial role both in working the intricate rules of the Senate and in setting a high moral tone in the debate. Despite the interbranch conflict that characterized the 1970s, Congress evidenced a respect for the prerogatives of the executive branch in negotiating treaties. At the same time, the administration compromised by accepting a number of reservations to help alleviate congressional concerns. Cooperation emerged when both branches acted responsibly on a measure they believed was in the broad national interest.

What were the policy impacts of the Panama Canal treaties? Although it is impossible to say exactly what would have happened if the treaties had been defeated, Latin American experts agree that it would have been very damaging to U.S. relations with that region. In the years since ratification, the canal has remained open to shipping as responsibility is gradually shifted to Panamanians. Without the treaties, the canal might have been subject to sabotage, targeted for terrorist attacks, or shut down by local protests. Ratification also helped relations with Third World nations and was supported by U.S. allies. The treaties did not do anything to improve the government in Panama; the United States intervened there militarily in 1989. This was not primarily to safeguard the canal, however. Although the treaties did not solve all the conflicts between the United States and its Latin American neighbors, they represented a step toward that goal.

DEADLOCK/EXTRAORDINARY RESOLUTION: AID TO THE NICARAGUAN CONTRAS (1982–1989)

In November 1986, the American people first learned of a Reagan administration initiative to sell arms to Iran in hopes of winning the release of American hostages held in Lebanon. Soon thereafter, it was disclosed that some of the profits from those sales had been diverted to aid the Contra rebels in Nicaragua, in direct violation of a law passed by Congress. The Iran–Contra scandal became one of the top political events of 1987. Televised congressional hearings featured Lieutenant Colonel Oliver North, who, along with the late CIA Director William Casey, had masterminded the scheme. This episode, which tarnished the reputation of the Reagan administration, was the outgrowth of five years of bitter confrontation between Congress and the president over policy toward the Sandinista government in Nicaragua. It is an example of the inconsistent and disastrous policy results that can emerge from a pattern of institutional combat and deadlock.

For many years, Nicaragua had been ruled by the dictator Anastasio Somoza, who had the support of the United States. In 1979, Somoza was toppled in a revolution, which brought to power Daniel Ortega and his cadre of Sandinista rebels. The Carter administration cut off assistance to the Sandinistas as the new Marxist government tilted toward the Soviet Union and Cuba. Anti-Sandinista rebels (the "Contras"), many of them loyal to the old dictatorship, still occupied some rural areas of Nicaragua. The United States offered the Contras humanitarian and military aid until Congress, citing the need for self-determination in Central America, cut off aid in 1980.

The inauguration of Ronald Reagan in 1981 brought into the White House a president firmly committed to checking the spread of communism in the Western Hemisphere and a strong advocate of military aid to the Contras. Over the next half-dozen years, Reagan would make scores of emotional speeches against the Sandinistas—scathing attacks on their human rights abuses, exporting of revolutionary violence throughout Central America, and ties to the Soviet Union. Reagan referred to the Contras as "freedom fighters" and patriots, deserving of significant aid from the United States in their struggle. Despite this rhetoric, Reagan was never able to convince even a plurality of the American people to support aid to the Contras.[54]

Public skepticism about the Contras reinforced congressional opposition to the policy, particularly in the Democratic House of Representatives. Opponents pointed to some of the problems associated with the Contras, particularly the lack of unity among rebel groups and the strong association of some of the rebels with the Somoza regime. Military aid to the Contras began in 1982 through the CIA, which delivered arms, uniforms, and equipment to the rebels. The Reagan administration requested additional aid to fund these activities, but congressional opponents wanted to limit the use of these funds to strictly nonmilitary purposes. One of the leading opponents to Contra aid was Rep. Edward Boland (D-Mass.), who chaired the subcommittee responsible for funding. He authored a number of amendments through the 1980s—the *Boland amendments*—to limit aid to the Contras.

The first Boland amendment was enacted on December 21, 1982 and extended through December 1983 as part of the Defense Appropriation Act. It provided that no funds from the Defense Department or the CIA could be used to "furnish military equipment, military training or advice for the purpose of overthrowing the government of Nicaragua or provoking a military exchange between Nicaragua and Honduras."[55] The policy continued to seesaw back and forth, as the administration pushed for more aid, and congressional opponents sought the means to block it. In 1983, the second Boland amendment was adopted, giving the administration a partial victory. It provided $24 million (less than Reagan wanted) for direct and indirect support for paramilitary operations in Nicaragua.

The next year, interbranch conflict continued to result in inconsistent policies. When it was revealed that the CIA had been involved in mining the harbor in Managua, Congress banned all military aid to the Contras. The third Boland amendment, which was in force from October 1984 to September 1985, prohibited spending any money that would "have the effect of supporting, directly or indirectly, military or paramilitary operations in Nicaragua by any nation, group, organization, movement, or individual."[56] The fourth Boland amendment brought another change: Congress authorized $27 million in humanitarian assistance to the Contras. In 1985 to 1986, the fifth Boland amendment represented yet another reversal, authorizing secret direct aid to the Contras.

During the 1980s, the issue of aid to the Contras consumed months and months of time in the White House and Congress. Congress debated and voted on the same basic issue over and over again. If one side lost a battle, its leaders knew that they would have another chance in a few months. The administration was frustrated because its foreign policy was undermined and because it was unable to deliver military aid with any consistency. Congressional opponents were frustrated that they could not stop the U.S. indirect intervention completely. This policy was a high priority for both branches, and emotions ran high. Toppling the Sandinistas, according to later testimony, was almost a daily preoccupation in the White House. This preoccupation and frustration with congressional opponents led to an attempt by key administration officials to develop an extraordinary resolution to the policy deadlock.

In 1984, National Security advisor John Poindexter, his aide Oliver North, and CIA Director William Casey decided to divert to the Contras profits from the sale of arms to Iran, despite the Boland amendments. The president maintained "deniability"; testimony from his staff asserted that he was not informed of the illegal actions. When the scandal broke, it further inflamed the debate over aid to the Contras. Reagan's popularity plunged, and the percentage of the public who supported military aid to the Contras diminished. President Reagan appointed former Sen. John Tower to head a commission to investigate the affair. The Tower Commission report in early 1987 was highly critical of the organization of the White House and the National Security Council. It concluded that President Reagan was not sufficiently in control of policy in the White House.

Congress used its investigatory powers to explore the case further. The televised testimony of North and Poindexter was avidly watched around the country. Congressional reactions ranged from comparing the administration's actions to a junta seizing power in the White House to justifying them as an appropriate response to congressional interference in foreign policy. North and Poindexter were later prosecuted, but their convictions were overturned because the appeals courts held that material revealed in their congressional testimony under a grant of immunity had influenced the verdicts in the trial courts. Reagan's popularity rebounded after a time, but it never reached the levels he had enjoyed previously.

The conflict between Congress and the president over aid to the Contras was not resolved until 1989. President Bush was committed to developing a compromise with Congress to prevent the disastrous process that had led to the scandal. In March 1989, Secretary of State James Baker and congressional leaders agreed to approve a package of nonmilitary aid to the Contras through early 1990. In return, the president promised to request no further military aid and to make diplomatic overtures to the Sandinista government. The agreement allowed Congress to halt the aid within six months if any of four congressional committees believed that the peace process was being undermined. In reaction to the deal, Bush noted that for the first time in years, both parties "were speaking with one voice."[57] Critics, however, argued that Bush had caved in to Congress, weakening the president's power in foreign affairs. Columnist David Broder wrote, "This evasion of the Constitution was so smelly it had to be accomplished through a side agreement, embodied in a letter from the Secretary of State."[58] The real resolution of the issue came soon after. In a democratic election, Violeta Chamorro defeated Sandinista Daniel Ortega for the presidency of Nicaragua. Within a matter of months, the Contras disbanded.

What explains the emergence of such a pattern of policy deadlock and attempts at extraordinary resolution? The divisions between branches arose from deep differences in ideology with regard to U.S. responsibilities for checking the spread of communism in Central America. The differences erupted into intense partisan conflict between the branches and grew worse as relations between Reagan and Congress deteriorated because of budget battles and other issues. Both sides were more concerned with winning the policy battle than with protecting the integrity of the nation's foreign policymaking institutions and processes. In the political environment, there was no strong public support for aiding the Contras, but the public sentiment was too ambivalent to be decisive either way. Frustrated ideologues in the White House, disgusted with Congress, decided to take extraordinary measures to achieve their policy goals, regardless of the constitutional consequences. A severe failure of institutional performance and presidential leadership occurred.

What were the consequences of this episode? Aiding the Nicaraguan Contras in the 1980s was a policy fiasco of the highest order. The policy was inconsistently applied because of the tug of war between branches. Neither side could win a complete victory, and the policy that emerged was the worst of both worlds. The aid did not succeed in overthrowing the Sandinistas. Although the flow of arms from Nicaragua to the communist rebels in El Salvador was reduced, it was not eliminated. U.S. policy was criticized around the world—particularly in Latin America—even though there was little sympathy for the Sandinistas. Finally, the policy was damaging to the process of governing. The episode highlighted the worst consequences of divided government and interbranch combat.

CONCLUSION

The four cases in this chapter demonstrate a remarkable range in policymaking patterns in the realm of foreign affairs. Although the president retains certain advantages in conducting the foreign policy of the nation, Congress is increasingly influential. If presidential leadership is still the most prevalent pattern in the making of foreign policy, Congress does play an important role, even in cases such as the Gulf War. In the post–cold war era, presidential leadership appears to be less likely on issues that are of great concern to members of Congress. Cooperation, by which both branches help shape policy, may become increasingly prevalent in the future. In a few foreign policy issues that have strong domestic consequences, such as the Cuban sanctions bill, Congress can play a leading role. However, in foreign policy in general, the pattern of congressional leadership is likely to be rare. Fortunately, deadlock to the extent seen in the case of aid to the Contras is also not common. The severe negative consequences of deadlock suggest that even when sharp policy differences exist, mechanisms to resolve the differences must be found, so as to protect the integrity of U.S. foreign policy.

No single model is appropriate to characterize presidential-congressional relations in foreign affairs. Several factors help explain the patterns of policymaking that emerged in the four cases. The political environment was instrumental in the cases of the Gulf War and particularly the Cuban sanctions bill. In the first case, it strengthened a Republican president against a Democratic Congress. In the second, it weakened a Democratic president against a Republican Congress. Presidential leadership was the result in the Gulf War, congressional leadership in the Cuban sanctions case. The environment was much more complex and probably less decisive in the other cases, in which public opinion was either ambivalent or negative. Regarding the Panama Canal Treaties, leaders made their case despite public doubts. On the issue of aid to the Contras, the administration failed to make the case to the public.

Compared to domestic policy, the foreign policy agenda has been remarkably stable for much of American history. Except for an early preference for isolation, the general public has come to accept a greater world leadership role for the U.S. during the last half of the twentieth century. Despite growing military alliances, public opinion since the late 1960s has considered foreign policy a less important problem than domestic policy. Except for the Gulf War military crisis, the general public expressed little interest in the other foreign policy cases covered. With the change from George Bush to Bill Clinton, the foreign policy agenda shifted more from defense matters (given the growing defeat of communism) toward international trade (with the growing globalization of the world economy). Thus, changes in policy preferences and agendas are important.

Individual leadership was also a factor in the patterns that emerged. Bush provided clear and consistent direction to U.S. policy following Iraq's invasion of Kuwait. In winning ratification of the Panama Canal Treaties both branches showed responsibility and leadership, as well as a concern for the integrity of the policy process. Strong congressional leaders prevailed over more ambivalent presidential views on Cuban sanctions. On the other hand, the failure of leaders in both branches led to a failed policy in Nicaragua. Whatever changes may be adopted in the coming years to improve the policy connection between Congress and the president, strong and responsible personal leadership in both branches will remain an essential component of successful public policy.

ENDNOTES

1. See Robert A. Dahl, *Congress and Foreign Policy* (New York: Harcourt, Brace, Jovanovich, 1950); James A. Robinson, *Congress and Foreign Policy Making* (Homewood, Ill.: Dorsey Press, 1967); Louis W. Koenig, *The Chief Executive* (New York: Harcourt, Brace, Jovanovich, 1975); John C. Donovan, *The Cold Warriors: A Policy Making Elite* (Lexington, Mass.: D.C. Heath, 1974); I. M. Destler, *Presidents, Bureaucrats and Foreign Policy* (Princeton, N.J.: Princeton University Press, 1974).

2. Aaron Wildavsky, "The Two Presidencies," *Transaction* 4 (December 1966): 7–14; reprinted in Steven A. Shull (ed.), *The Two Presidencies: A Quarter Century Assessment* (Chicago: Nelson Hall, 1991): 11–25.

3. Marcus Cunliffe, *American Presidents and the Presidency* (New York: McGraw-Hill, 1972).

4. See Gary Orfield, *Congressional Power* (New York: Harcourt, Brace, Jovanovich, 1975); Hugh G. Gallagher, "The President, Congress, and Legislation," in Thomas E. Cronin and Rexford G. Tugwell (eds.), *The Presidency Reappraised* (New York: Praeger, 1977); James L. Sundquist, *Politics and Policy* (Washington, D.C.: Brookings Institution, 1968); John Johannes, *Political Innovation in Congress* (Morristown, N.J.: General Learning Press, 1972); Randall B. Ripley and James M. Lindsay (eds.), *Congress Resurgent* (Ann Arbor: University of Michigan Press, 1993); Barbara Hinckley, *Less Than Meets the Eye* (Chicago: University of Chicago Press, 1994).

5. Cecil V. Crabb and Pat M. Holt, *Invitation to Struggle* (Washington, D.C.: Congressional Quarterly Press, 1989); Paul Peterson (ed.), *President, Congress, and the Making of Foreign Policy* (Norman, Okla., University of Oklahoma Press, 1994); James A. Thurber (ed.): *Rivals for Power* (Washington, D.C.: Congressional Quarterly Press, 1996); Steven A. Shull, *Presidential-Congressional Relations* (Ann Arbor: University of Michigan Press, 1997).

6. Samuel Huntington, *Common Defense* (New York: Columbia University Press, 1961): 124.

7. Quoted in William D. Rodgers, "Who's in Charge of Foreign Policy," *New York Times Magazine* (September 9, 1979): 49.

8. L. Gordon Crovitz and Jeremy A. Rabkin (eds.), *The Fettered Presidency* (Washington, D.C.: American Enterprise Institute, 1989): 38–39.

9. Stephen E. Ambrose, *American Rise to Globalism: American Foreign Policy, 1938–1980* (New York: Penguin, 1980): 13–14.

10. Harry S Truman, "Special Message to the Congress on Greece and Turkey," *Public Papers of the President* (Washington, D.C.: Government Printing Office, 1963).

11. George C. Marshall, "European Initiative Essential to Economic Recovery," *Department of State Bulletin* 16 (June 1947): 1160.

12. George F. Kennan, "The Sources of Soviet Conduct," *Foreign Affairs* 25 (July 1947): 566–582.

13. See Irving Janis, *Groupthink,* 2d ed. (Boston: Houghton Mifflin, 1982): chapter 3.

14. John Foster Dulles, "The Goal of Our Foreign Policy," *Department of State Bulletin* 31 (December 1954): 892.

15. Janis (note 13): 14.

16. Graham Allison, "Conceptual Models and the Cuban Missile Crisis," *American Political Science Review* 63 (September 1969): 689.

17. Richard M. Nixon, *United States Foreign Policy for the 1970s: A New Strategy for Peace* (Washington, D.C.: Government Printing Office, 1970).

18. Jimmy Carter, *Department of State Bulletin* 76 (June 1977): 622.

19. *New Orleans Times-Picayune* (September 10, 1997): A-9.

20. John Campbell, "The Disorganization of State," in Martin B. Hickman (ed.): *Problems of American Foreign Policy* (Beverly Hills: Glencoe Press): 168.

21. Steven A. Shull, *Presidential Policy Making: An Analysis* (Brunswick, Ohio: Kings Court Inc., 1979): chapter 9.

22. Richard A. Watson and Norman C. Thomas, *The Politics of the Presidency* (New York: Wiley, 1983): 334.

23. Duane M. Oldfield and Aaron B. Wildavsky, "Reconsidering the Two Presidencies," *Society* 26 (July 1989): 54–59.

24. Wildavsky (note 2): 10.

25. Lance T. LeLoup and Steven A. Shull, "Congress Versus the Executive: The 'Two Presidencies' Reconsidered," *Social Science Quarterly* 59 (March 1979): 704–719.

26. Richard Fleisher and Jon R. Bond, "Are There Two Presidencies? Yes, But Only for Republicans," *Journal of Politics* 50 (August 1988): 747–767.

27. Ibid., 766.

28. Steven A. Shull, "Presidential Policy Formation: Substance and Process," *Policy Perspectives* 2 (1982): 412–429.

29. *Congressional Quarterly Weekly Report* (January 12, 1991): 70.

30. *Newsweek* (March 11, 1991): 30.

31. *Washington Post National Weekly Edition* (March 18–24, 1991): 30.

32. Bob Woodward, *The Commanders* (New York: Simon and Schuster, 1991).

33. *Congressional Quarterly Weekly Report* (January 12, 1991): 70.

34. Ibid.

35. *Washington Post National Weekly Edition* (February 18–24, 1991): 25.

36. *Congressional Quarterly Weekly Report* (October 14, 1995): 3156.

37. *Weekly Compilation of Presidential Documents,* 32 (March 18, 1996): 478.

38. *Congressional Quarterly Weekly Report* (March 2, 1996): 565.

39. *New Orleans Times-Picayune* (July 27, 1997): A-2.

40. *Congressional Quarterly Weekly Report* (March 2, 1996): 566.

41. *New York Times* (March 15, 1996): D-3.

42. *New York Times* (April 6, 1996): A-3.

43. *The Economist* (April 6, 1996): 12.

44. See, for example, *American Journal of International Law,* 90 (1996): 419–434; 641–644.

45. *WashingtonPost.com/WP-SER/WPlate* (July 17, 1997): 2.

46. *Congressional Quarterly Weekly Report* (April 22, 1978): 917.

47. *Weekly Compilation of Presidential Documents,* 13 (1977): 526.

48. *Congressional Quarterly Weekly Report* (January 21, 1978): 135.

49. *Congressional Quarterly Weekly Report* (February 4, 1978): 317.

50. *Congressional Quarterly Weekly Report* (March 18, 1978): 676.

51. Ibid.

52. Reported in *New Orleans Times Picayune/ States-Item,* (April 27, 1978).

53. Quoted in David Vogler, *The Politics of Congress* (Boston: Allyn and Bacon, 1980): 82.

54. *Congressional Quarterly Weekly Report* (March 15, 1986): 601.

55. *Congressional Quarterly Weekly Report* (November 26, 1983): 2487.

56. *Congressional Quarterly Weekly Report* (March 15, 1986): 602.

57. Ryan Barrileaux, "Presidential Conduct of Foreign Policy," *Congress and the Presidency* (Spring 1988):1–23.

58. *Washington Post National Weekly Edition,* (May 15, 1989): 4.

6

CIVIL RIGHTS POLICY

*Segregation is no longer the law, but too often separation
is still the rule.* —*PRESIDENT BILL CLINTON (1997)*

Civil rights—the ability of all citizens to share fully in the nation's political, economic, and social system—is a critical element of the policy agenda. The heritage of
slavery and racial discrimination in the United States remains at the root of many
current political disputes. Since the abolition of slavery in 1863, civil rights has followed an erratic course as a policy. Reconstruction Congresses in the 1870s and
1880s enacted legislation to protect civil rights of blacks, but they were swept aside
by the courts and southern politicians. Not until the 1950s, after decades of struggle,
did civil rights once again feature prominently on the nation's agenda. At that time,
it was the Supreme Court, not Congress or the president, that took the lead.

When the legislative and executive branches became involved in the late 1950s
and 1960s, more often than not they worked in tandem to enact legislation. Fervent
opposition came from Southern Democrats, who used every tactic available to block
civil rights bills. The 1960 Civil Rights Act reflected this pattern of policymaking.
Eighteen die-hard Southern senators vowed to block the bill. A bipartisan coalition
of northern Democrats and moderate Republicans was assembled by Majority
Leader Lyndon Johnson (D-Tex.) and Minority Leader Everett Dirksen (R-Ill.). They
had the tacit if not active support of President Eisenhower. Faced with filibusters,
quorum calls, and other delaying tactics, Johnson kept the Senate in session around
the clock for months. Cots were set up for weary senators. Finally, Johnson and Dirksen wore down the opposition, and the bill was passed.

Other major civil rights legislation in this era (notably the Civil Rights Act of
1964 and the Voting Rights Act of 1965) resulted from presidential leadership but
with legislative cooperation. In recent years, however, the environment for civil
rights politics has changed, and so have the prevalent patterns of policymaking.

Growing Republican strength in the South and sharp cleavages in the voting behavior of blacks and whites have increased partisanship and interbranch conflict under divided government. Both Presidents Reagan and Bush had confrontations with Democratic Congresses over civil rights legislation, and the issue took on new political overtones. Democratic President Bill Clinton faced much the same challenge from a Republican Congress and a more conservative Supreme Court. Today, race is increasingly related to differences between the two parties.[1]

This chapter examines civil rights policy and patterns of presidential-congressional policymaking. We begin with a history of the evolution of civil rights policy, examine the new environment for civil rights policy, and then look at how Congress and the president make civil rights policy. We also look at the importance of leadership and agenda change. The four cases present examples of each of the four patterns of policymaking and their causes and their consequences.

THE EVOLUTION OF CIVIL RIGHTS POLICY

Slavery, the Civil War, and Segregation

The economic system of the southern states, based on plantations and black slaves, became the dominant issue of the first half of the nineteenth century. Some early presidents and congressional leaders actively opposed slavery: James Monroe proposed making the importation of slaves a capital offense; John Q. Adams challenged the institution of slavery as president and, later, in the House of Representatives.[2] Other presidents, however, avoided the increasingly controversial issue by suggesting that it was a problem that should be left to the states.[3]

A series of compromises kept the Union together through the 1850s, but the *Dred Scott* decision in 1857 helped push the country into civil war. In *Dred Scott,* the Supreme Court ruled that slaves were property and as such had no political rights, even in nonslave states. The high court also struck down the Missouri Compromise of 1820, because it had banned slavery in certain states. The justices were out of touch with a nation, in which opposition to slavery was growing. Four years later, the war started. The question of slavery would not be settled until hundreds of thousands of lives had been lost. On January 1, 1863, the Emancipation Proclamation decreed that "all persons held as slaves within any State or designated part of a State the people whereof shall then be in rebellion against the United States shall be then, thenceforward, and forever free."[4]

To guarantee the civil rights of freed slaves, Congress proposed three amendments to the Constitution, which were ratified by the states. The Thirteenth Amendment banned slavery in the United States, but it was quickly circumvented. Southern states passed "black codes," restricting the rights of freed slaves. Congress responded by passing the Fourteenth Amendment, which was ratified in 1868. It contained seemingly clear language: "No state . . . shall deprive any person of life, liberty, or property without due process of law; nor deny . . . the equal protection of laws." The Fifteenth Amendment was intended to ensure the voting rights of blacks, stating that the right to vote could not be abridged because of a person's race, color, or condition of previous servitude. The growing women's suffrage movement argued that the amendments should apply to women as well, but in 1875 the Supreme Court ruled that the protections of the Fourteenth and Fifteenth Amendments did not extend to women.

Despite the constitutional guarantees in these three amendments, any semblance of equal rights for blacks was wiped out within twenty years. In the *Slaughterhouse* cases in 1873, the Supreme Court chose the narrowest possible interpretations of what it meant to abuse the "privileges and immunities" of blacks. Congress responded by passing a series of civil rights laws that forbade discrimination in public facilities and accommodations. In 1877, the last of the federal troops were removed from the South. The Reconstruction governments, dominated by Republicans and including a number of blacks, were swept out by conservative Democratic regimes. The Supreme Court helped these new governments undermine civil rights once more with the 1883 *Civil Rights* cases. The justices ruled that Congress could not ban discrimination in privately owned establishments. This opened the door to a series of "Jim Crow" laws (named for a slang expression for blacks), which systematically denied them equal access and opportunity.

The sanctioning of a separate, segregated society of blacks and whites in the deep South was completed in 1896 in the case of *Plessy v. Ferguson.* In this case, the Supreme Court upheld a Louisiana law that required those of "colored races" to ride on separate Pullman cars on the train. The Court ruled that such a law was constitutional as long as "separate but equal" facilities were provided. Now public as well as private facilities could be segregated. The rollback of civil rights for blacks was not limited to Pullman cars and schools; the right to vote guaranteed by the Fifteenth Amendment was taken away as well. Between 1880 and 1900, most black voters in the states of the old Confederacy had been taken off the rolls of eligible voters.[5]

The disenfranchisement was accomplished through the use of a series of exclusionary devices. One was the "grandfather clause," which allowed a voter to register easily if his grandfather had voted before 1865. Those whose grandfathers had not voted were often required to pass a literacy test to vote. In one state in which no white ever failed the test, three blacks with doctorates were determined to be too illiterate to vote.[6] Another exclusionary device was the poll tax, which kept poor whites as well as blacks out of the voting booth. Finally, the white primary was another form of Jim Crow law. Because political parties were ruled to be private organizations, it was legal for them to restrict their membership to whites only. In the one-party South of that era, winning the Democratic nomination to an office was tantamount to being elected. Two generations after the Civil War, virtually all facilities in the South were segregated—from bathrooms to drinking fountains to the court Bibles used to swear in witnesses.[7] Segregation and racism also existed in the North, but not to the same extent as in the dual society of the South.

The Civil Rights Movement

The movement to provide civil rights for blacks began quietly at the beginning of the twentieth century. In 1909, a group of black and white activists formed the National Association for the Advancement of Colored People (NAACP). Two years later, the Urban League was formed to improve the lives of blacks living in big cities. Voting rights for women were long in coming, perhaps because paternalism and protection were more characteristic of discrimination against women than discrimination against blacks. The national movement to give women the right to vote had gathered momentum after the turn of the century and would achieve its goal in 1920 with the ratification of the Nineteenth Amendment.

Most of the activity in the civil rights movement in the first half of the century took place in the courts rather than in the White House or Congress. Presidents, including Franklin D. Roosevelt, were unwilling to push civil rights legislation, and Congress was stymied by the power of the southern bloc in the Senate.[8] The House of Representatives passed an antilynching bill in the late 1930s and several bills banning the poll tax in the 1940s, but all died in the Senate. Meanwhile, lawsuits brought by the NAACP were chipping away at the legal basis of segregation. In 1938, the Supreme Court ruled that giving a qualified black student a scholarship to attend law school out of state rather than allowing him to attend Missouri's all-white law school did not meet the "separate but equal," test.[9] In 1950, the Court ruled that a separate law school for blacks did not meet constitutional tests. Although the justices stopped short of overturning the principle of "separate but equal," the doctrine was on its last legs. Harry S. Truman was the first president to push for civil rights legislation to promote equality.[10] He issued an executive order integrating the nation's armed forces and urged the 1948 Democratic convention to adopt a civil rights plank in its platform.[11] This drove a number of southern Democrats out of the party.

On May 17, 1954, the U.S. Supreme Court struck a landmark blow for civil rights in overturning the "separate but equal" doctrine. The case of *Brown v. Board of Education* was a combination of cases from seven cities brought on behalf of black students by the NAACP. In the unanimous decision, Chief Justice Earl Warren's opinion attacked the basic nature of segregation in public education: "separate is inherently unequal," the Court declared. School districts were ordered to desegregate "with all deliberate speed." Reaction to the *Brown* decision was predictable: civil rights advocates were elated, and southern politicians denounced the decision and pledged to disobey it. The implementation proved difficult and often ugly. President Eisenhower was forced to order federal troops into Little Rock, Arkansas, when the state's governor refused to integrate the schools.

The civil rights movement did not stop with school integration; the system of segregation still prevailed throughout the South. In Montgomery, Alabama, a black seamstress named Rosa Parks refused to move to the colored section in the back of a public bus and was arrested. In protest, the Reverend Martin Luther King, Jr., organized a boycott of the Montgomery bus system.[12] A year later, the Court ruled that segregation on public transportation systems was illegal. Economic sanctions such as the bus boycott became increasingly important to the civil rights movement. Some northern activists, including whites, came to the South to participate in protests. One of the most effective techniques was the sit-in. Although blacks could shop in department stores, they could not be served food at lunch counters. In Greensboro, North Carolina, in 1960, a group of black and white college students refused to leave the lunch counter seats until all of them were served. They were arrested by the local sheriffs but were soon replaced by hundreds of other protesters. Within a year, more than 70,000 people had participated in sit-ins, and hundreds of facilities previously closed to blacks were opened to them.[13]

The Civil Rights and Voting Rights Acts

Because of actions by the courts and the growing protest movement in the South, civil rights became a more important component of the policy agenda of Congress and the president. President Eisenhower requested extension of the Civil Rights Commission and the abolition of literacy tests and the poll tax, but remained extremely cautious on civil rights.[14] In 1957, he signed a civil rights bill initiated by Congress. Although the bill was weak, it was an important milestone for the bipartisan pro–civil rights coalition in Congress in overcoming the opposition of the southern bloc. After the monumental battle over the 1960 civil rights bill (described in the introduction to this chapter), it was signed into law by Eisenhower. However, neither bill went very far in eliminating discrimination in public accommodations, voting, housing, and other areas.

During the 1960 campaign, John F. Kennedy voiced strong support for civil rights. After the election, however, he faced a Congress in which Democratic majorities were slim and the southern contingent was powerful. Fearing for the rest of his legislative agenda, Kennedy held back on civil rights legislation.[15] By 1963, President Kennedy was convinced that strong action had to be taken, regardless of the political consequences. Ugly racial incidents such as the murder of Medgar Evers and three civil rights workers in Mississippi helped strengthen his resolve. In June, he sent Congress the most sweeping civil rights bill ever. In August 1963, Martin Luther King led a march on Washington; many people in the country were growing impatient for meaningful change. The bill had emerged from committee in November 1963, when Kennedy was assassinated.

Despite being a Southerner and former civil rights opponent, Lyndon Johnson became a fervent civil rights supporter.[16] As president, he used his legislative skills and the lingering sympathy for John Kennedy to push through the 1964 Civil Rights Act. As we will see in the case that follows, it still took a major legislative battle in the Senate to enact the legislation. For the first time, Congress enacted strong provisions promoting open accommodations and protecting the rights of blacks and women in employment and other areas. The passage of the 1964 Civil Rights Act reveals presidential leadership and had an important effect on the nation's political alignment. Johnson's landslide victory in the 1964 presidential election reflected a significant partisan realignment among the nation's black voters.[17] Richard Nixon attracted over 30 percent of the black vote in the 1960 presidential election, but in 1964 and subsequent elections, Republican candidates garnered around 10 percent of the vote. At the same time, 1964 marked the first time in generations that the South—once solidly Democratic—voted for a Republican presidential candidate.

In 1965, enjoying large Democratic majorities in both the House and the Senate, Johnson helped usher through the Voting Rights Act of 1965. Despite the elimination of many of the old exclusionary devices, southern blacks still had difficulty registering and voting. In Mississippi, for example, fewer than 7 percent of eligible black voters were registered. This would jump to 60 percent a few years after the implementation of the Voting Rights Act.[18] The law took positive measures by providing that registration of less than 50 percent of eligible voters in any state represented *prima facie* evidence of discrimination. It authorized federal registrars to enter those states and oversee voter registration and the conduct of elections. The act made it possible to take legal action against an entire county or state, rather than taking each occurrence of discrimination on a case-by-case basis.[19] In addition, it removed all remaining tests and devices used to prevent blacks from voting. The results were dramatic; in just a few years, there was a significant increase in the number of blacks— and whites—registered and voting in the South.

Achievements had been made in guaranteeing political rights, but the civil rights movement was changing. Protections had been granted to women in the 1964 Civil Rights Act, and the women's movement became more prominent, seeking greater employment opportunities, demanding equal pay for equal work, and campaigning for the elimination of protective gender-based distinction in state and federal law. Dissatisfied with the pace of change, blacks in many American cities erupted in violence in the late 1960s. Militant groups opposed the nonviolent approach of Martin Luther King. The political victories felt hollow to those African Americans who were unemployed and trapped in poverty. When King was assassinated and further violence erupted in 1968, the civil rights movement entered a new phase. By the late 1960s, polls showed that a majority of whites believed that enough change in civil rights had occurred.

THE ENVIRONMENT FOR CIVIL RIGHTS POLICY

The political environment in which Congress and the president made civil rights policy began to change around 1970; by 1980, a new environment was firmly established. One of the changes was that more groups were seeking additional protection for their civil rights. In the 1950s and 1960s, the focus was clearly on the plight of blacks, who were the victims of institutional racism and discrimination. In the years since then, the focus of civil rights has been more diffuse, encompassing new groups: women, Hispanics, Native Americans, the disabled, and homosexuals. On certain issues, these different groups come together with a common interest, but in many cases, the expansion of the civil rights agenda created competition between groups.

In the early 1970s, the Equal Rights Amendment (ERA) became the highest priority for the women's movement. Passed by Congress in 1972, the amendment read, "Equality of rights under the law shall not be denied or abridged by the United States or by any state on account of sex." Its primary objective was to remove the presumption that women should be treated differently under the law. The amendment would have affected thousands of state and federal laws that make gender-based distinctions, such as those dealing with property and inheritance, child custody and support, and equal pay. The ERA gained an initial surge of support that brought it within a few states of the number needed for ratification. As the 1970s progressed, however, the political environment changed, and conservative attacks on the ERA began to take their toll. Charges that it would lead to unisex bathrooms, homosexual marriages, and women in combat concerned state legislators. Several states that had ratified it earlier tried to rescind their approval. Congress extended the period for ratification in 1979, but the amendment died in 1982, three states short of the three-quarters needed for ratification.

The political environment for black civil rights changed in the 1970s and 1980s as well. By 1970, schools in the North were more segregated than schools in the South; this represented *de facto* segregation (based on housing patterns) rather than *de jure* segregation (required by law). In 1971, the Supreme Court authorized the use of a "transportation plan" to reduce racial segregation, and the issue of forced busing sharply divided the nation. Many northern whites who had supported the civil rights movement in the 1960s were opposed to busing. Thousands of whites moved away from the cities rather than see their children bused across town. This left many inner-city schools even more racially unbalanced than before.

Republicans and Democrats began to move in different directions on civil rights. Democrats, with their nearly unanimous black support, continued to press for more aggressive enforcement of existing laws and whatever remedies were needed to desegregate schools. Republicans, although emphasizing that they still supported civil rights, resisted many new changes. The Nixon administration criticized the Supreme Court and announced its opposition to busing.[20] Nixon's 1972 reelection campaign incorporated a "southern strategy" to capitalize on southerners' growing discontent with the Democratic party. More and more, the two parties disagreed on what measures to apply in overcoming the effects of past discrimination against women and blacks. Some Democrats argued that it was not enough simply to provide equal opportunities for minorities; more positive actions were necessary to make up for the effects of past discrimination.[21] Affirmative action—giving preference to target groups—became increasingly controversial. The public supported affirmative action when defined as insuring a broad pool of applicants, but large majorities opposed affirmative action when defined as preferential treatment or quotas.

The differences between Republicans and Democrats on civil rights, which were striking during Nixon and Ford administrations, drew less attention during the Carter administration, when Democrats controlled both legislative and executive branches. Carter was a civil rights advocate; he took unprecedented steps to appoint blacks and women to positions in the executive and judicial branches (Table 6.1). He also urged the bureaucracy to enforce existing laws aggressively. He was not particularly active in the legislative arena, however.[22] As affirmative action became more controversial, the courts became increasingly involved in defining acceptable standards. In the *Bakke* decision in 1979, the Supreme Court allowed race to be considered as a factor in admission to medical school but ruled against setting up quotas for minorities.

The shift in the environment for civil rights policy was reflected in different policymaking patterns after Ronald Reagan was inaugurated in 1981. In the 1980 election, he had received the lowest proportion of the black vote of any Republican candidate in history. Public opinion polls indicated that popular support for civil rights among whites, which had increased until the early 1980s, began to decline.[23] Reagan was opposed to busing, affirmative action, and aggressive enforcement of civil rights laws. He eased the enforcement of existing laws through the appointment of conservatives, executive orders, budget cuts, program changes, and reorganizations.[24] When called on to defend his civil rights record, Reagan simply noted that his actions in civil

TABLE 6.1   **Characteristics of Federal District and Appellate Court Judges (percent)**

							Appointing President							
	Johnson		Nixon		Ford		Carter		Reagan		Bush		Clinton*	
Characteristics	D	A	D	A	D	A	D	A	D	A	D	A	D	A
Political/government experience	21	10	11	4	21	8	4	5	13	6	11	11	11	3
Judicial experience	34	65	35	58	42	75	54	54	47	60	50	62	50	69
Public law school	40	40	42	38	44	50	51	39	42	40	48	41	43	41
Same party	84	95	93	93	79	92	93	82	97	94	95	95	91	86
Past party activism	49	58	49	60	50	58	61	73	59	55	63	70	54	48
White	95	95	97	98	90	100	79	79	92	97	93	89	72	72
Male	98	98	99	100	98	100	86	80	92	95	81	81	70	69
Millionaires	—	—	—	—	—	—	5	10	22	18	35	43	32	38
Exceptionally or well qualified	7	28	5	15	—	17	4	16	55	59	59	65	64	83

Source: Adapted from Sheldon Goldman, "The Clinton Imprint on the Judiciary," *Judicature,* 78 (September–October 1994): 72; *Judicature* 80 (1997): 254–273; values for presidents before Carter appear in earlier editions of this journal.
Legend: D, district court; A, appellate court appointments; —information unavailable
*through first term

rights were consistent with his general objective of reducing the scope and intrusiveness of government in all policy areas. Reagan appointed conservatives to the Supreme Court and the federal bench. Within a few years, court decisions were becoming more conservative with regard to affirmative action standards.

The conflict over civil rights became increasingly bitter and partisan in the late 1980s and early 1990s, pitting the Democratic Congresses against the presidency, and increasingly, the courts. The racial element in voting became more pronounced as well. In 1984, two of three whites voted Republican in the presidential election, and nine of ten blacks voted Democratic.[25] Congress sought to reverse the 1984 Supreme Court decision of *Grove City College v. Bell,* in which the justices ruled that the college did not have to provide equal athletic opportunities for men and women based on title IX of the 1964 Civil Rights Act. In the case discussed later in the chapter, Congress amended the act in order to reverse the Grove City decision, finally succeeding in doing so over Reagan's veto.

The partisan pattern was repeated in the Bush administration as well, beginning during the 1988 presidential campaign, when the Bush campaign ran the infamous Willie Horton ads. These campaign commercials accused Democratic candidate Michael Dukakis of allowing dangerous criminals out on the street. They specifically mentioned Willie Horton, a black man who had raped a white woman while out on furlough from a Massachusetts jail. These ads infuriated many civil rights leaders and Democrats. Congress and President Bush clashed over the issue of "quotas" in the 1990s, as Congress attempted to overturn Supreme Court decisions that limited protection from job discrimination. In one of the cases treated later in this chapter, the administration and Congress were deadlocked for two years until the quota issue was finally resolved. One study finds Bush being even more assertive and conservative on civil rights than was Reagan.[26]

When Bill Clinton was elected president in 1992, he promised a government that looked like the American people, and he made even greater efforts than Carter in appointing women and minorities to the executive branch and federal judiciary.[27] Clinton claimed to be a "new Democrat" and seems to have persuaded voters than he was genuinely moderate on most domestic issues. On the issue area of civil rights, however, Clinton expressed classically liberal views on affirmative action programs, although opposing quotas. In a major speech in San Diego in June 1997, Clinton stated: "I want to lead the American people in a great and unprecedented conversation about race." He wanted to be remembered for fundamentally altering black–white relations by persuading Americans to change the way they view one another. Clinton began a year-long series of town meetings to soothe racial tensions and appointed a presidential advisory board headed by historian John Hope Franklin.

In promising to "mend it, don't end it," the President Clinton was bucking growing opposition to affirmation action programs. Critics, such as governor Pete Wilson (R-Cal.), criticized the president as being out of touch because public opinion polls showed growing opposition to affirmative action. Conservatives in Congress pushed legislation that would prohibit the use of "preferential treatment" in the awarding of federal contracts. However, moderates, such as Representative Tony Hall (D-Ohio) and a dozen other white cosponsors in both parties, introduced legislation that would issue a formal apology for slavery, much as the United States had done for mistreatment of Japanese Americans interred during World War II. Clinton not only defended affirmative action and stepped up fair housing laws, but he became the first president to back measures to end bias against homosexuals (see case later in this chapter). Thus, the climate was ripe for hostile relations with Congress on several fronts.

The environment for civil rights has changed significantly since the 1970s, becoming more politicized and partisan. A significant gap between black and white public support for the president developed in the 1980s. Figure 6.1 shows the trends since 1953. The greatest gap appeared during the Reagan administration, when white support for the president was sometimes as much as 30 percent higher than black support. Although Bush initially received higher black support than Reagan, the gap in support remained. As might be expected, blacks and whites expressed very different views of President Clinton. Thus, the gap between the races in how they view the president remains large.

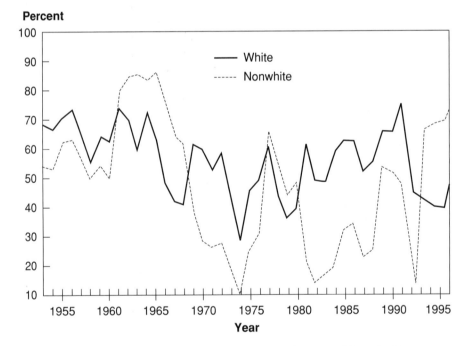

FIGURE 6.1   **Average Public Approval Rating of the President, by Race (1953–1996).**

Source: From George C. Edwards III, *Presidential Approval: A Sourcebook* (Baltimore: Johns Hopkins University Press, 1990). Figures updated by authors from *Gallup Poll Monthly.*

MAKING CIVIL RIGHTS POLICY

Congress has taken more of a leadership role in civil rights since 1980, partially in response to the actions of presidents since Carter. As occurred in recent years, Congress can reverse Supreme Court decisions if those decisions are based on interpretations of statutes enacted by Congress rather than on the Constitution itself. The Supreme Court in *Adarand Contractors Inc. v. Pena,* (1995), restricted the use of race as a consideration in awarding federal contracts. This 5–4 decision was more in line with conservative Republicans, who gained control of Congress in 1995. Congress also can use its power of the purse to thwart proposed cuts in civil rights agencies and their budgets. In 1986, Congress threatened to cut off all funds to the Civil Rights Commission because Reagan had weakened it dramatically. House and Senate Judiciary Committees often use hearings and testimony from prominent civil rights advocates to influence public opinion.

The president has a variety of means for shaping civil rights policy: appointments to the courts and the bureaucracy, executive orders, budget, administrative changes, and using the presidency to influence public opinion. Over the years, legislation has been an important vehicle for policymaking, although the number of bills has varied much more than for other policy areas. This is a function of the presidential and congressional policy agendas and the political environment of the time. Table 6.2 compares civil rights legislation on which the president took a position, listing the percentage of times that the vote in Congress was in support of the president's position. Position taking and executive order issuance illustrate presidential assertiveness, whereas percent support reveals legislative independence.

TABLE 6.2   **Presidential-Congressional Actions in Civil Rights, 1953–1996**

President	No. Positions Taken on Roll-Call Votes	Average No. Vote Positions Taken per Year	Percent Success on Presidential Positions	Executive Orders/Year
Eisenhower	6	1.5	50	0.3
Kennedy	3	1	67	1.0
Johnson	101	20.2	98	0.6
Nixon	38	6.9	66	0.4
Ford	0	0	—	0
Carter	7	1.8	71	2.5
Reagan	23	2.9	52	2.1
Bush	19	4.8	65	1.0
Clinton	4	1.0	75	2.8
Average		5.0	71	1.2

Source: These data are taken from *Congressional Quarterly Almanac* and from *Public Papers of the Presidents,* annually, and were collected by Shull and Randy Burnside.

These data suggest differences in presidential support in Congress as well as in the number of vote positions. The political alignments through 1963 restricted the legislation before Congress. The surge of activity during the Johnson administration stands alone in the postwar period. Not only was the volume of legislation obviously greater, but working with both northern Democrats and Republicans, the administration received record levels of support. Legislative activity remained higher than average during the Nixon administration before declining through the rest of the 1970s. As the environment for civil rights changed in the 1980s, the number of positions taken on roll calls increased under Reagan and Bush. Reagan's support on these votes was lower than the other presidents with the exception of Eisenhower. Bush took more positions on civil rights votes than did Reagan and also received higher levels of support. Very few roll-call votes occurred during the first Clinton term, and they were not very controversial. His level of support on the few votes on which he took positions was higher than for any president except Johnson. This lesser attention in the mid-1990s seems to reflect the diminished attention paid to civil rights in the legislative arena.

Presidents average about fifty-seven executive orders per year but just over one per year on civil rights matters. There is no clear trend in order issuance evident from Table 6.2, but it does reveal that Ford was just as nonassertive administratively as he was legislatively. The higher than average order issuance for Reagan and Carter is consistent with earlier judgments about their more general efforts to deregulate government and also their relatively strong views on civil rights.[28] Clinton issued slightly more orders per year than any president, including orders regarding historically black colleges, education for Hispanics, and environmental justice.

Although these comparisons are interesting, they provide only part of the picture. The civil rights agenda, political leadership, and the environment are highly changeable and important. Policy initiation today comes as much from Capitol Hill as from the White House. Although civil rights is a highly discretionary policy area, neither branch can lead on its own. The cases that follow show different patterns in different eras and some of their results.

PRESIDENTIAL LEADERSHIP: THE CIVIL RIGHTS ACT (1964)

On July 2, 1964, President Lyndon Johnson signed the Civil Rights Act of 1964 into law. It was the most far-reaching protection of civil rights in U.S. history. Johnson called the law "a major step toward equal opportunity for all Americans." On hand for the signing were both Republican and Democratic members of Congress who had worked with the president in successfully enacting the historic legislation. The signing culminated a legislative process that took a year from the time that President Kennedy first submitted a comprehensive bill until its final passage.

Despite his strong support for civil rights voiced in the 1960 presidential campaign, Kennedy had proved reluctant to introduce controversial civil rights legislation. Strong opposition from southern Democrats, who still controlled many of the key committees, could threaten his entire legislative agenda. Some liberals accused him of "abdicating leadership" on civil rights. This pressure, an increase in racial violence, and a sense that the public was impatient, spurred Kennedy to action.[29] In June 1963, he submitted the most comprehensive civil rights bill ever proposed. It was the result of extensive efforts of the Justice Department, led by his brother, Attorney General Robert Kennedy. Because of its expansive interpretation of the interstate commerce clause of the Constitution, it promised real remedies for discrimination in areas such as public accommodations. The bill moved slowly through the legislative process in 1963, with southern legislators vowing to do whatever necessary to defeat the bill. The bill had not yet reached the floor when Kennedy was assassinated. Shortly afterward, Lyndon Johnson stated that no memorial would honor his memory more eloquently than the passage of his civil rights bill.

Previous civil rights legislation in 1957 and 1960 had made only limited progress in protecting the rights of blacks and minorities. The new civil rights bill would go far beyond the earlier laws. Among the most important sections of the bill were Titles II and VI, which prohibited discrimination in public accommodations such as hotels and restaurants. The potential constitutional problems with these provisions went back to the *Civil Rights* cases of the 1880s, when the Supreme Court overturned open-accommodation laws, based on the fact that the Constitution did not allow the government to ban discrimination in the private sector. Working closely with Congress, Attorney General Robert F. Kennedy and his staff devised a way to avoid that potential problem. Using the constitutional power of the federal government to regulate interstate commerce, the bill prohibited discrimination in any business that served people who crossed state lines or used any products that came from out of state. Virtually all businesses would be covered.

The bill made other important changes in the law. It banned various forms of discrimination (Title VII), created the Equal Employment Opportunity Commission, strengthened enforcement of laws against discrimination in voting, and provided more enforcement of school desegregation. The bill empowered the Justice Department to sue violators and to deny federal grants and contracts to any firms that were not in compliance. The bill was amended and strengthened as it went through Congress; the administration worked closely with congressional leaders. In the House Judiciary committee, the ban on employment discrimination was expanded from covering only federal contractors to encompassing all businesses and unions with more than twenty-five members or employees.

Lobbying and political infighting were intense. Outside of Congress, a coalition of seventy-nine civil rights, church, and labor organizations united through the Leadership Conference on Civil Rights. On the other side, the Coordinating Committee for Fundamental American Freedoms was created in 1963 to defeat the bill. The group was headed by the arch-conservative editor of the Manchester (N.H.) *Union Leader,* William Loeb. Inside Congress, bipartisan leadership teams worked in both the House and the Senate to enact the bill. Senate Minority Leader Everett Dirsken (R-Ill.) was a crucial leader in the process. He had worked closely with Johnson in enacting the 1960 civil rights bill.[30] Senate Majority Leader Mike Mansfield (D-Mont.) was assisted by Senators Hubert Humphrey (D-Minn.) and Thomas Kuchel (R- Calif.). The southern legislators, although outnumbered, had certain institutional advantages. Congressman Howard Smith (D-Va.) chaired the crucial House Rules Committee, and James Eastland (D-Miss.) chaired the Senate Judiciary Committee. They were aided in their efforts to obstruct the bill by other powerful members such as Sam Ervin (D-N.C.) and Richard Russell (D-Ga.). Senators had the procedural advantage of the filibuster, by which a small minority could thwart the will of the majority for prolonged periods.

When the bills reached the House and Senate floors, a careful bipartisan strategy was adopted by President Johnson and proponents in Congress. Dirksen orchestrated an approach in the Senate in which one Democratic and one Republican senator would argue each of the bill's ten titles. The southern bloc in the Senate was determined to defeat the bill through the filibuster. The filibuster eventually lasted ninety-three days before the Senate voted to invoke cloture (ending debate) by a vote of 71 to 29, five more votes than needed. President Johnson and his Senate allies did not press for cloture because they knew that many supporters of the civil rights bill remained opposed to limiting debate in any way. Finally, after three months, senators realized that the filibuster could be broken only through cloture. Senate opponents were not done, however. They forced 106 separate roll calls on various amendments after cloture. Most were turned down, although some compromise changes were adopted. Opponents forced a separate vote on each of the bill's titles, failing in each case to delete them. Finally, the Senate adopted the bill by a vote of 73 to 27.

Passage was somewhat easier in the House, where leaders had tighter control of floor procedures and restrictions on debate. Still, southern opponents introduced amendment after amendment, in an effort to weaken or scuttle the bill. The House turned down 122 amendments in a debate that also lasted several months. Finally, the House passed the bill by a vote of 290 to 130. Most of the nay votes came from southern Democrats; 104 of 113 of them opposed the bill.

What factors explain this case of presidential leadership in one of the most explosive issues of its day? The administration, led by Attorney General Robert Kennedy, were primarily responsible for shaping a bill that for the first time gave government real power in enforcing civil rights. Outside of the South, the political environment was increasingly supportive of civil rights legislation. Horror at scenes on television of civil rights marchers being hosed or attacked by dogs, and the deaths of others, helped create growing sympathy for the cause. Martin Luther King's march on Washington in 1963 also helped galvanize opinion. The death of Kennedy certainly provided some impetus for Johnson's efforts and a reservoir of support. The bipartisan leadership contributed to the outcome, building on the coalitions that had formed in 1960. Parliamentary maneuvering by the skillful opponents was matched by the skill and the numbers of civil rights proponents. The president and Congress knew that success depended on both branches and members of both political parties working closely together. In the end, it was a successful combination, but it could not have happened without Johnson's strong efforts.

What effect has the 1964 Civil Rights Act had? Without doubt, it remains the most important and effective civil rights legislation. Soon discrimination in public accommodations had largely disappeared.[31] Compliance with other provisions, such as open housing, was more difficult to achieve, but some progress was made. Efforts at reducing discrimination in the workplace were significantly improved. Today, the bill remains a wellspring for blacks, women, and other emerging groups fighting for their civil rights.

CONGRESSIONAL LEADERSHIP: THE CIVIL RIGHTS RESTORATION ACT (1988)

A bipartisan coalition in the House and Senate won a decisive political battle on March 22, 1988, overriding President Ronald Reagan's veto of the Civil Rights Restoration Act. The House voted 292 to 133 to override, and the Senate voted 73 to 24 (eight votes more than the two-thirds needed). Reagan had vetoed the bill only a week earlier, claiming that it would "vastly and unjustifiably expand the power of the federal government."[32] Despite a desperate, last-minute lobbying effort, members voted for the bill to become law over the president's objections.

The genesis of this legislative battle occurred four years earlier when the Supreme Court limited the application of four federal civil rights laws in the case of *Grove City College v. Bell* (1984). Grove City College was a four-year private institution that did not receive any direct federal assistance, although a number of students individually received Pell grants or other federal assistance. One of the laws in question was the 1972 Education Act amendments, whose Title IX banned sex discrimination. Before the 1984 decision, the law was interpreted to mean that all programs and activities at a college or other institution must comply with sex discrimination prohibitions if any programs received federal aid. Grove City College, a small school, did not provide the same athletic teams for women that they did for men. College officials did not believe that they had to assure compliance with Title IX in their athletic programs or in any other activities that did not receive direct federal aid. They took their case to court, and it ended up in the U.S. Supreme Court.

In their 6–3 ruling, the Court agreed with Grove City College that only its financial aid programs had to comply with Title IX.[33] The effect of the decision was to restrict three other civil rights laws that dealt with discrimination on the basis of race, age, and disability. The decision was extremely unpopular with women's groups and members of Congress, who blasted the Court for undermining civil rights. A group of legislators immediately moved to introduce legislation that would reinstate the old interpretation, so that failure to comply in any program or activity would lead to elimination of all federal aid.

Enacting the Civil Rights Restoration Act would not be easy. President Reagan praised the decision and promised to veto any attempt by Congress to circumvent it. Proponents failed in 1985 and 1986 to get legislation through. More than forty separate hearings were held on various versions of the bill. A number of unrelated issues became entwined with the civil rights debate, including the divisive issue of abortion. Catholic hospitals feared they might be required to permit abortions under the new law, which added to the conservative opposition. Reagan succeeded in blocking the legislation, primarily because of Republican control of the Senate. Although a number of Senate Republicans supported the Restoration Act, there were enough votes to support the president.

The 1986 midterm elections produced an important change in the Senate: The Democrats captured a majority of seats for the first time in six years. Many of the elections, particularly in the South, had been close; strong support from black voters had made the difference. These new Democratic senators were strong supporters of the Civil Rights Restoration Act. In addition, after the Iran–Contra revelations, President Reagan's standing dropped in the opinion polls. He did not appear to be as formidable an opponent as he neared the last year of his presidency. Sensing victory, congressional leaders such as Senator Edward Kennedy (D-Mass.) showed greater willingness to compromise so as to enlarge the base of support. Partial exemption of religious organizations, farmers, and food stamp recipients help diffuse some of the opposition inside Congress.

The debate between the president and the Congress continued into 1988. Proponents continued to argue that the bill did nothing more than restore the interpretation of the statutes that had applied before 1984: It would eradicate discrimination subsidized by federal money. Some attacked the administration's anti–civil-rights stance, noting Reagan's opposition to the landmark Civil Rights Act of 1964 at that time.[34] As the congressional vote neared, Reagan continued to threaten a veto. He charged that the bill

> . . . dramatically expands the scope of federal jurisdiction over state and local governments and the private sector. . . . It diminishes the freedom of the private citizen to order his or her life and unnecessarily imposes the heavy burden of compliance with extensive federal regulations and paperwork on many elements of American society. The bill poses a particular threat to religious liberty.[35]

The stage was set for a showdown. There was never much doubt that the bill would pass; the question was whether the margin would be large enough to override the promised veto. The Senate passed the bill on January 28 by a vote of 75 to 14, with seven co-sponsors missing the vote. In the House, Speaker Jim Wright helped speed passage of the bill by restricting all amendments. The House passed the bill on March 2 by a vote of 315 to 98. Both the House and Senate margins were more than enough to override the veto, but victory was by no means assured. In many previous cases, the president had successfully pressured enough Republicans to switch their votes and uphold his veto. Reagan vetoed the bill on March 16, setting the stage for the override votes.

In a last-ditch effort to sustain the veto, the Reverend Jerry Falwell and the Moral Majority made the extreme claim that the bill "could force churches to hire a practising (sic) homosexual drug addict with AIDS to be a teacher or youth pastor."[36] Even congressional conservatives who opposed the bill felt Falwell went too far and was hurting rather than helping their cause. Finally, on March 22, the override vote was taken. In the Senate, all 51 Democrats voted to override, and Republicans split 21 to 24. Eight Republicans who had originally voted for the bill switched, voting to sustain the veto in the second vote. Although they wound up eight votes short, opponents of the bill claimed that they had actually been only two votes short of sustaining the veto. When they could not get the needed one-third plus one, leaders allowed several Republicans to vote in favor of overriding the veto. The margin was close in the House as well—292 to 133, only eight votes more than needed. Democrats voted 240 to 10 to override, and Republicans voted 52 to 123 against the override. Six Democrats and twenty-nine Republicans switched their original vote to support the president. Nonetheless, congressional sponsors had dealt the administration a blow and successfully orchestrated the enactment of the Civil Rights Restoration Act.

How was Congress able to lead the policymaking process? The political environment was generally supportive, because voting for a civil rights bill is usually considered positive, especially in an election year. The administration failed to mobilize opinion against the bill. Congressional sponsors were determined, working four years before succeeding. The 1986 elections were crucial, changing the composition of the Senate, so that a veto-proof majority for the bill became possible. Streamlined floor consideration in the House helped ease passage. In addition, President Reagan's diminished popularity, and his status as a lame duck in 1988, reduced the negative consequences for Republicans who voted to override the president's veto. Even though there was a strong partisan element in the vote, Congress could not have succeeded without bipartisan support—half the Senate Republicans, led by Minority Leader Robert Dole, voted to override.

What were the consequences and results of the Civil Rights Restoration Act? Congress clearly achieved its goal of reversing the Grove City decision. Colleges that received any federal aid once again had to prove compliance with antidiscrimination statutes dealing with blacks, women, older Americans, and the disabled. The federal courts subsequently have upheld the need for more equal athletic facilities for college women. The act had political consequences as well, setting the tone for a Congress anxious to assert its leadership against the lame-duck president. It also raised support for the civil rights bill as a possible campaign issue in 1988. George Bush, who supported the president, would have his own battles with Congress over civil rights.

COOPERATION/CONSENSUS:
SAME-SEX MARRIAGE LAW (1996)

During the 1992 election campaign, Bill Clinton emerged as the first presidential candidate to openly seek the political support of gays and lesbians. Why then would he cooperate with congressional Republicans on a bill vehemently opposed by the gay community? In one of his first acts as president, Clinton directed the Secretary of Defense to review the existing policy of barring homosexuals from the military. He supported the resulting recommendation of "don't ask, don't tell," wherein homosexuals could stay in the service if they did not announce or practice their sexual preference. Clinton took considerable political heat from conservatives in Congress and elsewhere for this decision, but supporters called it courageous. With this background, Clinton might be expected to oppose legislation restricting homosexual activities, but he did not challenge a 1996 law to discourage gay marriages. The upcoming election campaign moderated Clinton's position on what was a hot button issue for social conservatives. In recognition of strong public opinion against gay marriage, Clinton accepted the consensus and expressed support for the measure on several occasions during the campaign. Clearly Clinton was not anxious to hand this issue to challenger Bob Dole (R-Kan.), an early cosponsor of the legislation.

Identical legislation was introduced in May 1996 in both the House and Senate. The federal action intervened in an area of public policy normally left to the states. The rhetoric was heated on both sides of the issue, in what was called by proponents the "Defense of Marriage Act." In the House, supporters argued that legalizing gay marriages might encourage children to become homosexuals and was contrary to what marriage had always meant in the United States. Judiciary Committee chairman Henry Hyde (R-Ill.) claimed that "the institution of marriage is trivialized by same-sex marriage. It legitimates something that is essentially illegitimate." Opponents, including openly gay Representative Barney Frank (D-N.Y.), stated: "How can you argue that a man and woman in love . . . are somehow threatened because two women down the street are also in love?"[37] These opponents said that the legislation was not needed because no state had legalized gay marriages and that it was a constitutional infringement on states' rights. After defeating several amendments by Frank and others, the House Judiciary Committee approved the bill (HR 3396), voting along party lines. On the House floor, the only Republican voting against the bill was Steve Gunderson (Wis.), a publicly announced gay lawmaker, who said he was not opposing the marriage ban but sought to preserve certain legal rights for gay couples.

Less discussion occurred in the Senate over the same-sex marriage legislation and focused on the definition of marriage, the rights of states to make that definition for themselves, and whether federal benefits would apply to gay spouses. Edward

Kennedy (D-Mass.) led the opponents and sought separate votes on the marriage bill and other legislation to prohibit job discrimination against homosexuals (S 1056). Kennedy prevailed in this effort when a bipartisan agreement allowed separate votes on these two measures. According to *Congressional Quarterly,* the compromise "allowed senators to take an election-year stand against gay marriages but show their tolerance directly thereafter with a vote to outlaw workplace discrimination."[38] This position seemed identical to President Clinton's, who expressed opposition to the former but support for the latter. The votes in the Senate were 85 to 14 in passing the same-sex marriage prohibition but a much narrower defeat (49 to 50) for the job rights bill. Republicans gained back-to-back victories on a sensitive social issue important to the conservative agenda.

The congressional votes reflected a general legislative consensus on same-sex marriage. All the no votes on passage of the same-sex marriage ban in the Senate on September 10, 1996, were cast by Democrats and included only one southerner (Charles Robb, D-Va.). The legislation became PL 104-99 on signing by President Clinton on September 21, 1996. The new law barred federal recognition of gay marriages and specified that states need not recognize same-sex marriages even if legal in other states. In that sense, the legislation did not place a federal ban on homosexual marriages per se but gave states the right not to recognize them either. The law anticipated that Hawaii might allow same-sex marriages. Proponents stated that if Hawaii or any other state passed such legislation the other states were obligated by the Constitution "to 'recognize the public acts, records and judicial proceedings' of all the other states."[39] They charged that the Constitution allows Congress to limit that "full faith and credit" requirement. Fifteen states bar same-sex marriages and others are considering such legislation; two conservative Republican governors have banned them through executive orders. All of this action was in response to a Hawaii Supreme Court ruling in May 1993 challenging such a ban as discriminatory. Three gay couples sued the state for the right to marry, and the legislature was considering legalizing such marriage when Congress acted.

Democrats claimed that Republicans were seeking to cause a rift in the Democratic Party ranks in both chambers and also to embarrass President Clinton. Senator Kennedy stated: "We all know what is going on here. I regard this bill as a mean-spirited form of Republican legislative gay-bashing cynically calculated to try to inflame the public eight weeks before the November 5 election."[40] President Clinton stated at the signing that "I have long opposed government recognition of same-gender marriages and this legislation is consistent with that position." He also stated in the same message that "I want to make clear that the enactment of this legislation should not, despite the fierce and at times divisive rhetoric surrounding it, be understood to provide an excuse for discrimination, violence, and intimidation against any person on the basis of sexual orientation."[41]

Although disappointed with Clinton's stand on the same-sex marriage ban, gay rights groups had no alternative but to support his reelection effort. David Smith of the Human Rights Campaign stated: "this is a wedge issue, but we're too smart to fall for that." Patricia Ireland, president of the National Organization for Women, concurred: "The president is first and foremost a politician and his duty is to get re-elected. A lot of people are willing to give him a pass."[42] Proponents, like Dole, said that it was a huge victory for the pro-family movement, whereas Ralph Reed, then executive director of the Christian Coalition, stated: "These are the bricks in the wall that allow you to build a turnout of religious conservatives."[43]

Numerous legal implications can be drawn from this case regarding what the "full faith and credit" provision of the Constitution actually means. Supporters of the law argue that Congress does have the right to limit the applicability of one state's laws to other states. Majority Leader Trent Lott (R-Miss.) stated: "This is not prejudiced legislation. . . . It is a preemptive measure to make sure that a handful of judges in a single state cannot impose a radical social agenda upon the entire nation." Opponents, however, expressed concern that the law undermines federalism. University of Chicago legal scholar Cass Sustein feared that "a good deal of the entire federal system could be undone . . . Congress could simply say that any law Congress dislikes is of no effect in other states."[44] Some question arose over just how much power Congress has to limit "full faith and credit" between the states. The fact that so many states reacted so quickly to only a potential policy change in Hawaii shows the popularity of the ban, even among legislators who favor considerable homosexual rights (e.g., Paul Welstone, D-Wis., and John Kerry, D-Mass.).

Part of the background for the case was the U.S. Supreme Court decision on May 21, 1996 (*Romer, Governor of Colorado, et al. v. Evans et al.* [116 S. Ct. 1620]) striking down a Colorado amendment banning laws that protect gays and lesbians from discrimination. One area that is not protected by the federal government from discrimination is sexual orientation. Eight states and more than 100 municipalities ban such discrimination, and such issues have appeared in many forums. Homosexual organizations around the country held rallies while opponents vowed to keep fighting. Another argument voiced is that allowing such unions would "cause a run on the federal treasury by gay couples seeking federal benefits."[45] Thus, conservatives found an economic reason to support the legislation as well as what they considered a moral one.

Obviously, antagonists disagreed over whether the legislation would strengthen or weaken the institution of marriage. Proponents of the legislation included the Christian Coalition. In reference to same-sex marriages, Representative Tom Coburn (R-Okla.) stated: "The fact is, it is morally wrong . . . grounded in lust and perversion." Senator Robert Byrd (D-W.Va.) argued that "the permanent relationship between men and women is a keystone to the stability, strength, and health of human society."

Opponents of the legislation included the American Civil Liberties Union (ACLU), the Gay and Lesbian Rights Project, both of whom testified before the Senate Judiciary Committee. The former called PL 104–99 unconstitutional and bad public policy. "For two hundred years, Congress has left it to the states to decide who they will marry and to the courts to make sure they respect each other's decision on that. That is a fine tradition, which ought to be respected." Representative John Lewis (D-Ga.) said that "you cannot tell people they cannot fall in love." Senator Edward Kennedy stated, "America will only be America when we free ourselves of discrimination."

The White House announced early on in May 1996 that Clinton would sign the same-sex marriage ban. Presidential "spokesman Mike McCurry stated: 'the president has very strong . . . personal views' on the subject." However, McCurry stated that the president also "believed the measure was politically motivated . . . it is gay-baiting, pure and simple."[46] Soon thereafter, the Justice Department expressed the opinion that the bill was constitutional. On signing the law late at night, spokesman McCurry confirmed that "the President believes that the sooner he gets this over with, the better." All of these actions were conciliatory and, of course, probably had their own political motivations. It is clear that Clinton would not have taken this conservative position had he not been running for reelection.

This case of consensus involved federal intervention in the area of homosexual rights, a group that has been unprotected by federal antidiscrimination legislation. Over the years, civil rights have been expanded to many other groups by the national government but not to gays and lesbians. By large margins, majorities in both chambers coalesced on an issue defined in terms of traditional family values. This position struck a responsive chord during the 1996 reelection campaign of a Democratic president with a liberal record on homosexual rights. In fact, Democrats, including President Clinton, were able to have it both ways by supporting the marriage ban but also pushing to end employment discrimination against homosexuals. The legislation was initiated by Congress, but the president's role reflects a consensus between the branches that Americans do not want to sanction gay marriages. The case was heavily influenced by election year politics.

DEADLOCK/EXTRAORDINARY RESOLUTION: THE CIVIL RIGHTS ACT (1991)

On November 21, 1991, President George Bush signed the Civil Rights Act of 1991, reversing the effects of Supreme Court decisions that had made it harder for workers to bring job discrimination suits. This followed a bitter, partisan two-year deadlock with Congress, during which political symbols and strategies for the 1992 elections were as important as civil rights policy. A year before, Bush had vetoed a similar bill, insisting that it would have forced companies to use hiring quotas. In a showdown before the 1990 elections, Congress failed by a narrow margin to override Bush's veto. In the end, extraordinary means were necessary to break the deadlock, centering on closed-door negotiations between moderate Republicans and Bush, who were faced with sudden changes in the political environment.

Like the Civil Rights Restoration Act of 1988, this case had its impetus in overturning an unpopular Supreme Court decision. In this case, however, neither branch could dominate, and they remained deadlocked until a means for resolution could be found. Legislation was introduced in response to a series of decisions that limited employee recourse in the case of discrimination on the job. One of the court decisions the proponents found most objectionable was the 1989 case of *Wards Cove Packing v. Antonio.* This decision reversed a 1971 ruling that required employers to justify employment practices that were detrimental to the employment opportunities of women and minorities; employers had to prove that there was a "business necessity" to justify practices that resulted in the exclusion of target groups.

The *Wards Cove* decision reversed the presumption: The Court ruled that the burden of proof now fell to the employee to prove that the company had no legitimate reason for its hiring criteria. Several other adverse decisions were targeted by the 1990 civil rights bill. One provision of the act would overrule a decision that made it harder to punish racial harassment on the job. The bill also would permit women and religious minorities to be awarded monetary damages in the case of discrimination. Under the old law, they were entitled only to back pay.

Legislation was introduced on February 7, 1990, by Senator Edward Kennedy (D-Mass.) and Representative Augustus Hawkins (D-Calif.). The White House indicated its opposition and was represented in the Senate by Orrin Hatch (R-Utah), a staunch opponent of Kennedy on civil rights. The bill caused much consternation in the Senate, particularly among Republicans, who were split on the issue. The bill was reported by the Senate Labor and Human Resources Committee on April 4 and moved to the Senate floor for debate. In the tradition of civil rights legislation, opponents filibustered. Minority Leader Robert Dole (R-Kan.), originally a supporter of the bill, split with the Democratic leadership over the timing of a cloture vote. "If we're going to be treated like a bunch of bums on this side of the aisle," Dole complained, "there won't be any agreements on anything."[47] On July 17, cloture was adopted, and the debate ended. The next day, the Senate approved the bill by a vote of 65 to 34, just short of the two-thirds needed to override. Divisiveness was present on the House side as well; Republicans walked out of several committee meetings to protest the Democrats' tactics. The bill was marked up by both the Education and Labor Committee and the Judiciary Committee, and it was passed on August 3 by a vote of 272 to 154—also just short of a two-thirds majority.

The White House remained opposed to the bill, despite the support for the legislation from influential Republicans such as Senator John Danforth (R-Mo.) and members of the president's own cabinet such as Health and Human Services Secretary Louis Sullivan. With elections approaching, the civil rights bill became a political football. Democrats accused the president of trying to use the quota issue to drive white voters further into the Republican camp. The president accused the Democrats of favoring racial quotas. The confrontation would come to a head in October, after the House–Senate conference report passed both houses and was sent to the president's desk. On October 22, Bush vetoed the bill, saying, "I deeply regret having to take this action with respect to a bill bearing such a title."[48] Two days later, the Senate voted to override. Both sides knew it would be close. By a single vote, 66 to 34, the president's veto was sustained, and the deadlock continued.

When the 102nd Congress opened in 1991, proponents made the Civil Rights Act the first bill introduced. It looked as if 1991 would be a replay of 1990: The House passed the bill in June by a vote of 273 to 156. Meanwhile, President Bush continued to rebuff efforts by Danforth to negotiate a compromise, insisting the bill would still result in quotas. Democrats continued to promote the president's opposition as a campaign issue, and many Republican supporters of the legislation felt caught in the middle. After passing the bill, House leaders left it to Senate Republicans to try to make a deal with the president. The deadlock continued through the summer, until several changes in the political climate helped facilitate a resolution.

The confirmation hearings over Clarence Thomas's nomination to the U.S. Supreme Court exploded into controversy when a former subordinate charged him with sexual harassment. Suddenly the issue of sexual harassment and discrimination against women in the workplace was foremost in voters' minds. Bush was leery of a backlash from the hearings. In addition, he owed a political debt to Danforth, who was instrumental in orchestrating the narrow confirmation victory for Thomas. Second, former Ku Klux Klan leader David Duke, campaigning for governor of Louisiana as a Republican, raised many of same issues as Bush in opposition to quotas. Suddenly, mainstream Republicans, including the president, wanted to distance themselves from Duke. Many Republicans now feared that a nay vote on the civil rights bill would be more damaging than before.

In this context, several moderate Republican senators who had previously supported the president on the civil rights votes, including Virginia's John Warner, notified Bush that they now felt compelled to vote for the bill and override a veto. Based on the one-vote margin in the Senate the year before, this switch appeared to foreshadow what would have been the first override of Bush's presidency. Instead, the president decided to cut a deal. A week of backroom meetings between the administration, Danforth, and several other Republican senators finally produced a compromise. They agreed to leave one of the most divisive issues for the courts to decide, thus allowing both sides to claim victory. Although Bush made concessions, he argued that "We didn't cave. . . . I can say to the American people that this is not a quota bill."[49] Some Democrats scoffed at this. Senate Majority Leader George Mitchell said that Bush had "found a fig leaf to cover a hasty retreat." In any event, the deadlock was finally broken. On October 30, the Senate passed the bill by a vote of 93 to 5. The House passed the bill on November by a 381 to 38 margin, and President Bush signed it on November 21.

What caused this pattern of deadlock to emerge, and why was it finally resolved? The key elements behind this case are divided government and the more partisan environment for civil rights that developed in the Reagan era. Congress was able to dominate in 1988, overriding Reagan's veto of an earlier bill, but lacked the votes to override President Bush. Clearly, political calculations were all-important, causing a division within the Republican ranks. The Thomas hearings and the Duke candidacy helped tip the balance among Republicans toward resolution. Personal leadership by Senator Danforth and several of his colleagues was instrumental in resolving the deadlock, which was accomplished in private meetings rather than the open atmosphere of congressional hearing rooms.

What were the results and consequences of the Civil Rights Act of 1991? It may be too early to gauge the long-term impact on employee discrimination, the criteria for employment, and the ease of proving bias on the job. Several changes were clear, however—particularly the ability of women and religious minorities to collect punitive damages in cases of discrimination. On perhaps the most important issue surrounding the *Wards Cove* decision, both branches agreed to disagree and let the courts decide. A more conservative judiciary, due in large measure to Reagan and Bush appointees, did begin to chip away at some previous employment discrimination decisions. This compromise by Congress may not have been decisive or effective policymaking, but it did allow a resolution of many other issues. Perhaps more important, it helped defuse the volatile issues of race and gender discrimination. Whether the politics of civil rights maintains the divisiveness of the last decade or moves back to the more cooperative patterns of the 1960s remains to be seen.

CONCLUSION

Patterns of presidential-congressional policymaking have evolved through several distinct stages since the *Brown* decision in 1954. Neither branch took a leadership role in civil rights at first, leaving it to the courts to change public policy. When Congress and the president became more involved, the Democratic Party found itself deeply divided between its powerful southern wing and the rest of its members. A substantial moderate wing of the Republican Party also strongly supported civil rights and became the ally of northern Democrats in their civil rights battles. Congressional leadership of policymaking characterized the 1957 and 1960 Civil Rights Acts. By the mid-1960s, the most dominant pattern was presidential leadership with bipartisan support, as displayed in the 1964 Civil Rights Act and the 1965 Voting Rights Act.

Those patterns changed in the 1970s and 1980s. Civil rights policy receded somewhat from the legislative arena to the bureaucracy and the courts. At the same time, the political alignment over civil rights began to change during the Nixon administration. Unified party control of government during the Carter administration left both branches largely in agreement, although very little legislation was enacted during Carter's four years. He used administrative reforms and executive orders to restructure the civil rights bureaucracy. Nonlegislative tactics reemerged somewhat under President Clinton, who was the only modern Democratic president to face a Republican Congress. Clinton's willingness to compromise, even on his deeply held views on civil rights, allowed the same-sex marriage law to become a case of consensus/cooperation rather than of congressional leadership. A prevalent pattern in the

1980s and 1990s is interbranch conflict, as reflected in the cases of the 1988 and 1991 Civil Rights Acts. In the former case, congressional leadership emerged when unified Democrats were able to attract enough Republican votes to override Reagan's veto. In the latter case, deadlock emerged when Bush was strong enough to have his veto sustained in his confrontation with Congress. As long as divided government continues and the racial divisions in voting remain, the pattern of conflict punctuated by periodic resolution is likely to continue.

Despite the interbranch conflict of recent years, the divisions are sometimes more subtle than in other policy areas. Civil rights policy has an important symbolic dimension. Unlike the 1960s, when southern politicians were outspoken against integration of the races, today, politicians of all stripes claim to support civil rights. This apparent consensus masks serious policy differences and the importance of race as an element of party politics. Differences between the two parties over the appropriateness of racial quotas have diminished as even President Clinton has disavowed any minority set-asides; virtually all citizens oppose reverse discrimination. Even such long-accepted remedies as affirmative action based on race alone are being challenged, with suggestions that women and even economically disadvantaged white men should be eligible for government remedies. The changing attitudes in the late 1990s appear in the proposed Civil Rights Act of 1997, which would prohibit "any preferential treatment based on race, sex, or ethnicity."

Civil rights differs from other policy areas in several notable respects. The importance of civil rights groups, instrumental in prompting government action thirty years ago, has weakened considerably. The federal courts play a more important role in defining the civil rights agenda than in foreign policy, economic policy, or social welfare policy. The courts' importance helps shape the agenda and relationship between Congress and the president. Given the transformation of the Supreme Court by the Reagan and Bush appointments, the direction in civil rights decisions is clear: restricting applications of affirmative action, limiting minority preferences, and narrow interpretations of civil rights laws. This was challenged by a Democratic Congress and president elected in 1992, but Republicans of a particularly conservative nature gained control of both chambers just two years later. Under such circumstances, voices supporting civil rights may be crying in the wilderness. The predominant pattern in civil rights in the future will be closely tied to presidential-congressional election results in the new political climate.

ENDNOTES

1. Edward G. Carmines and James A. Stimson, *Issue Evolution* (Princeton, N.J.: Princeton University Press, 1989): 14.

2. See James D. Richardson (ed.), *A Compilation of the Messages and Papers of the Presidents 1789–1897* (Washington, D.C.: U.S. Congress), 10 volumes.

3. See R. Bardolpf (ed.), *Civil Rights Record* (New York: Thomas Crowell, 1970).

4. Ibid., 20.

5. Charles E. Silberman, *Crisis in Black and White* (New York: Vintage, 1964): 23.

6. U.S. Commission of Civil Rights, *Voting 1961* (Washington, D.C.: Government Printing Office, 1961): 91–97.

7. Harrell R. Rodgers, Jr., and Charles S. Bullock, *Law and Social Change* (New York: McGraw Hill, 1972): 17.

8. Barbara Sinclair, "Agenda, Policy, and Alignment Change from Coolidge to Reagan," in Lawrence C. Dodd and Bruce I. Oppenheimer (eds.), *Congress Reconsidered,* 3d ed. (Washington, D.C.: Congressional Quarterly Press, 1985): 291–314.

9. *Missouri ex rel. Gaines v. Canada,* 305 U.S. 337 (1938).

10. *Congress and the Nation I: 1945–1964* (Washington, D.C.: Congressional Quarterly, Inc., 1965): 1597.

11. P. H. Vaughn, "The Truman Administration's Fair Deal for Black America," *Missouri Historical Review* 70 (March 1976): 291–305.

12. See Martin Luther King, Jr., *Stride Toward Freedom* (New York: Harper, 1958).

13. Joel B. Grossman, "A Model for Judicial Policy Analysis: The Supreme Court and Sit-in Cases," in Joel B. Grossman and Joseph Tanenhaus (eds.), *Frontiers of Judicial Research* (New York: Wiley, 1969): 247.

14. See Stephen E. Ambrose, *Eisenhower* (New York: Simon and Schuster, 1984).

15. Theodore C. Sorensen, *Kennedy* (New York: Harper and Row, 1965): 535.

16. Eric F. Goldman, *The Tragedy of Lyndon Johnson* (New York: Knopf, 1969): 515.

17. Carmines and Stimson (note 1): 56–58.

18. Rodgers and Bullock (note 7): 271.

19. Ibid., 62.

20. See Jonathan Schell, *The Time of Illusion* (New York: Vintage, 1975): 40–44.

21. See Paul M. Sniderman and Michael G. Hagen, *Race and Inequality: Study in American Values* (Chatham, N.J.: Chatham House, 1985).

22. J. H. Shattuck, "You Can't Depend on It: The Carter Administration and Civil Liberties," *Civil Liberties Review* 4 (5) (1978): 10–27.

23. Steven A. Shull, *The President and Civil Rights Policy* (Westport, Conn.: Greenwood Press, 1989): 186.

24. Steven A. Shull, "Presidential Influence versus Bureaucratic Discretion," *American Review of Public Administration,* 19 (September 1989): 197–215.

25. *National Journal,* November 12, 1988.

26. Steven A. Shull, *A Kinder, Gentler Racism?* (Armonk, N.Y: M. E. Sharpe, 1993).

27. *The New York Times* (November 13, 1996: 1) reported that in his first term, Clinton appointed more women and minorities to the cabinet and federal courts than any prior president.

28. Shull (note 26).

29. Keith Hindell, "Civil Rights Breaks the Cloture Barrier," *Political Science Quarterly,* 36 (April–June, 1965): 143.

30. B. Muse, *The American Negro Revolution* (New York: Citadel Press, 1968): 89.

31. See Bullock and Rodgers (note 7).

32. *Congressional Quarterly Weekly Report,* (March 19, 1988): 709.

33. *Grove City College v. Bell,* 465 US 555 (1984).

34. *National Journal* (March 19, 1988): 757.

35. *Public Papers of the President* (March 1, 1988): 287.

36. *Congressional Quarterly Weekly Report* (March 19, 1988): 709.

37. *Congressional Quarterly Almanac* (1996): B-27.
38. Ibid., B-29.
39. *Washingtonpost.com*/wp-sv/digest/daily (September 11, 1996: A01).
40. *Congressional Quarterly Almanac* (note 37): B–29.
41. *Weekly Compilation of Presidential Documents,* 32 (1996): 1829.
42. *Congressional Quarterly Almanac* (note 37): B-29.
43. *Washingtonpost.com* (note 39).
44. *Congressional Quarterly Weekly Report* (September 14, 1996): 2599.
45. *Congressional Quarterly Weekly Report* (July 13, 1996): 1976.
46. *cnn.com.con*US/9605/21/gay.reax/indx (July 12, 1996: 1).
47. *New Orleans Times/Picayune* (July 18, 1990): A-3.
48. *New York Times* (October 23, 1990): A1.
49. *Congressional Quarterly Weekly Report* (October 26, 1991): 3124.

7

ECONOMIC AND BUDGET POLICY

When the leadership of Congress insists on going it alone,
one party alone, we get gridlock, stalemate, vetoes, gov-
ernment shutdowns.   —PRESIDENT BILL CLINTON (1996)

A sign that read, "It's the economy, stupid," was pasted on the wall of Bill Clinton's 1992 campaign headquarters. Its blunt message conveyed a fundamental truth of politics: no issue is more important to the president and members of Congress than the health of the economy. It was as true for Herbert Hoover as for Bill Clinton. Congress and the president try to manage the economy, not only to promote the nation's prosperity but also to get reelected. As a result, economic and budget issues remain among the most contentious in Washington: how much should the government spend, who should bear the tax burden, should more go to defense or social programs? Beginning in the first year of the Reagan administration in 1981, budget deficits—the gap between what the government spends and what it takes in—became an annual battleground between the two parties and the two branches.[1] This chapter examines economic and budget policy, the environment in which it operates in, and patterns of policymaking that have prevailed in recent years.

In the late 1960s, President Lyndon Johnson faced not only growing discontent over the war in Vietnam, but also an inflationary economy overstimulated by defense and domestic spending increases. The fiscal policy prescription needed to cool the overheated economy was not a popular one: Raise taxes while holding the line on spending. Johnson, the former Senate majority leader, believed that he understood some of the fundamental differences between Congress and the president in making tough economic choices:

One major source of conflict between the legislative and executive branches
is the difference in constituency. The president is concerned with the eco-

nomic well-being of the entire nation. Congress, by contrast, is the product of 50 states and 435 local constituencies, each representing only one piece of the national jigsaw puzzle. Many congressmen and senators understood my concern for the economy as a whole, but each legislator had one over-riding need—to make a record with the people who sent him to office. On the subject of taxes, the people were extremely vocal. Mail on the Hill was running heavily against a tax increase. On many days in 1966, one or an-other congressman would call me to say that he was with me in spirit—he understood my predicament and sympathized with me, but it would be po-litical suicide for him to support a tax increase.[2]

Congress finally adopted a tax increase in 1968, two years after the president first proposed it—too little and too late to check the inflationary surge.

LBJ's characterization—the presidency unified and coordinated, and Congress torn between protecting local benefits and acting in the national interest—is still commonly accepted, but is less true than thirty years ago because of the congressional budget process and other institutional changes. Economic choices are particularly difficult for legislators. They are concerned with promoting national prosperity—and want to remain an equal partner with the president in doing so—but these objectives are often at odds with the short-term concerns of the local constituency. Legislators struggle with the budget because of the difficulty of making the many desirable parts fit into a responsible whole.[3] However, the dichotomy between the perspectives and capabilities of the two branches is too simplistic today. Presidents do not escape the dilemmas and difficulties of economic policy. Political goals and campaign promises clash with responsible but unpopular decisions. Information is imperfect for both branches. The presidency is not always unified; squabbles between factions within the administration may become public, undermining the president. Economic policy is a difficult challenge for both branches.

THE DEVELOPMENT OF U.S. ECONOMIC AND BUDGET POLICY

From Agrarian to Industrial Society

American political economy is still based on principles of market capitalism, just as it was at the time of the founding. As society and the economy changed over two hundred years, however, public policy evolved to include an expanded role for government in the economy. The nation's first economic policies concerned trade and tariffs to protect developing industries, the establishment of a national bank, and the assumption of debts of the states by the federal government.[4] In its first century, the nation and the economy grew rapidly. The country was being transformed from an agrarian nation to an industrial nation. Millions moved from farms to work in factories in the cities. Revolutions occurred in transportation, communication, energy, and production. With these fundamental changes in the economy came new problems: monopolies and trusts, growing disparities between rich and poor, harsh working conditions, slums, and crime. The social consequences of unregulated market capitalism proved to be unacceptable, and government intervention into the economy became more widespread.[5] Congress created the Interstate Commerce Commission (ICC) in 1887, when it became apparent that it was necessary to regulate the chaotic railroad network spreading across the country. Congress enacted the Sherman Antitrust Act in 1890, and "trust busting" presidents Teddy Roosevelt and Woodrow Wilson continued the fight against monopolies.

As the economy modernized and the demands on government grew, the policy agenda became broader. New institutions and processes were needed to deal with the growing complexity of problems. In the case of monetary policy, Congress and the president created an independent body, more removed from the political fray, empowered to regulate credit, interest rates, and the money supply.[6] In response to the panic of 1907 and the bank failures that followed, the Federal Reserve System was created in 1913. Originally intended to consist of only twelve regional banks, the Federal Reserve Board (the Fed) evolved into the equivalent of a national bank.

Despite the changes in the late nineteenth and early twentieth centuries, U.S. economic policy remained restrained. Reliance on private business, not government, to spur the economy inspired the 1920s view that "what's good for General Motors is good for America." That view would change after the stock market crash in 1929 and Great Depression that followed.

Roosevelt and the Great Depression

The Depression had a devastating effect on the economy of the United States.[7] Total production of goods and services fell by half. Home construction declined by 90 percent. One of four Americans were unemployed, and wages for those who were working fell to as little as five cents an hour. Grassroots pressure began to build for the federal government to take positive action to deal with the economic crisis. Inaction by President Herbert Hoover helped Franklin D. Roosevelt win the 1932 presidential election in a landslide. Roosevelt moved quickly to restore confidence and to change the role of government in managing the economy. The most important change was discretionary fiscal policy: using taxing and spending to stimulate economic activity and growth in accordance with the theories of British economist, John Maynard Keynes. Preventing depressions through the management of surpluses or deficits in the budget would become a critical part of the policy responsibility of Congress and the president.[8] The use of budget deficits to help stimulate the economy would also become the most controversial part of Keynesian economics.

The revolution in the institutions and responsibilities of American government during the remarkable twelve-year presidency of Franklin D. Roosevelt was closely connected to economic policy. The Bureau of the Budget (BOB), created in 1921, was originally located in the Treasury Department.[9] As part of the creation of a presidential bureaucracy, BOB became part of the Executive Office of the President in 1939. This move implicitly recognized the central role of taxing and spending in managing the economy and the president's increased responsibility for promoting the nation's prosperity. During World War II, the economy was largely run by the executive branch in Washington. Scarce resources were rationed, and production of war materiel was coordinated by government officials. The president's role in a more centralized system of economic planning also helped change public perceptions and expectations.

The Employment Act of 1946 translated the theories of Keynes and the policies of Roosevelt into law. The searing memories of the human tragedy wrought by the Great Depression created a rough consensus between Republicans and Democrats to ensure that such economic collapse would never be allowed to happen again. The original sponsors of the bill wanted to establish the basic right of all Americans to a job and make it the responsibility of the president and Congress to secure that right. As the Employment Act worked its way through the legislative process, a more modest set of requirements was adopted. Congress and the president were mandated to "use all practicable means" to promote "maximum employment, production, and purchasing power."[10]

Although Congress intended to play a major role in economic policymaking, the legislation made more important changes in the power of the presidency. Under the Employment Act, the president was responsible for submitting not only the annual budget to Congress, but also an annual Economic Report of the President. This document would describe both the nation's economic conditions and the president's recommendations for fiscal and monetary policy. To formulate this annual report, the Employment Act created the Council of Economic Advisors (CEA). The president's chief economist became a key advisor and represented the president before Congress. To review the president's policies, the Employment Act created a new Joint Economic Committee in Congress.[11]

Managing the Postwar Economy

The politics of guiding the nation's economy continued to evolve under the presidencies of Harry S Truman and Dwight Eisenhower. Republicans captured Congress in 1946, leading to divided government and partisan battles over taxes and spending; the postwar economic consensus evaporated. Two recessions in the 1950s challenged the skills of economists in prescribing policies to compensate for swings in the private sector. Coordination problems became apparent. The administration often spoke with many voices, including the budget director, treasury secretary, CEA chief, Federal Reserve chair, commerce secretary, and others. The Democrats recaptured Congress in the 1954 elections and challenged the economic priorities of President Eisenhower. He faced political ridicule in 1957 when the secretary of the treasury openly criticized the administration's budget on the day it was released.[12] Eisenhower did succeed in balancing the federal budget three times during his time in office; he was the last president to do so that many times.

Keynesian economics reached its zenith under Presidents Kennedy and Johnson in the 1960s. The dominant approach was on the demand side: policies oriented to increasing consumer demand through greater government spending. The Kennedy-Johnson tax cut, adopted in 1964, was successful in stimulating economic growth while keeping inflation at relatively low levels, but the nation's economic waters were about to become choppy. As mentioned in the introduction to the chapter, rapidly growing expenditures for social programs and the war in Vietnam had an inflationary impact on the economy. The surtax finally adopted in 1968 did little to stem the tide of rising prices. In 1971, Republican Richard Nixon surprised many observers by imposing mandatory wage and price controls. This move, which was controversial within conservative ranks, did not prove effective. When controls were removed, prices quickly jumped, making up for lost time.

Presidents Ford and Carter faced difficult economic problems and a growingly assertive Congress that was anxious to take a lead in economic policy. The Keynesian paradigm that had guided economic policy since the 1930s was crumbling. Ford used the presidency as a platform to urge the country to halt rising prices: "Whip Inflation Now" was the slogan. However, this program, with its infamous "WIN" buttons, became more of a subject of ridicule and satire than an effective economic weapon.

Jimmy Carter became president in a time of *stagflation:* double-digit inflation and unemployment.[13] Democrats in Congress who were concerned about unemployment pushed to revise the Employment Act. The resulting Humphrey-Hawkins Act of 1978 attempted to mandate government policies that would produce full employment, low inflation, and other desirable economic goals. More profound changes were in the making, however. A marked shift in emphasis from fiscal to monetary policy occurred when President Carter selected Paul Volcker as Federal Reserve Chair in 1979.

Monetarism, Supply-Side, and "Reaganomics"

Despite the predominance of Keynesian theory in guiding economic policy in the 1950s and 1960s, conservative critics such as Milton Friedman advocated a different approach.[14] Friedman argued that only monetary policy—not fiscal policy—could ultimately control inflation. By the late 1970s, monetarism was gaining adherents around the world. Newly appointed Federal Reserve Chairman Volcker embarked on a restrictive monetary policy, carefully managing the growth of the nation's money supply. Tightening the screws on monetary growth had an immediate effect, as interest rates soared above 20 percent. Other critics of Keynesian economics favored government economic policies that focused on the *supply side* of the economy: helping entrepreneurs, investors, and businesses, who produce economic growth. Supply-side economist Arthur Laffer argued that high taxes in the United States were discouraging investment and causing the economy to stagnate.[15] Widespread public unhappiness with inflation and astronomical interest rates were among the key factors that set the stage for Ronald Reagan's victory over Carter in the 1980 presidential election. The influence of both monetarism and supply-side economics would be felt strongly in the 1980s.

As we will see in one of the cases that follows, the events of 1981 represented a dramatic departure from the economic policies of the postwar era. The Reagan economic and budget plan included deep across-the-board cuts in income taxes, major reductions in domestic spending, and a huge defense buildup. The 1981 plan, masterminded by Budget Director David Stockman, ushered in a decade of economic growth—but with it came unprecedented budget deficits as well as growing animosity between Congress and the president.

After his landslide reelection in 1984, Ronald Reagan announced that comprehensive tax reform would be the highest economic priority of his second term. The process that led to the enactment of the Tax Reform Act of 1986 (also a case examined in this chapter) was markedly different from what had occurred in 1981. A bipartisan coalition took almost two years to enact the most thorough revision of the nation's income tax system in history. However, confrontation with Congress over the budget remained the rule. A frustrated Congress enacted a plan for mandatory deficit reduction in 1985 and 1987. The stock market crash in October 1987 led to a budget summit and a two-year agreement with Congress, a restrained ending to a tumultuous eight years of interbranch conflict over the budget.

Economic Centrism: Bush, Clinton, Congress, and the Budget

Budget deficits continued to dominate the economic and political debate over the next decade. Both Presidents Bush and Clinton would move to the political center to try and solve the problem, Bush accepting higher taxes, and Clinton embracing entitlement cuts and a timetable to balance the budget. After his election in 1988, George Bush initially adopted a less confrontational approach to Congress in 1989, reaching a budget summit agreement only months into his administration.[16] But the consensus collapsed as the two branches divided over the issue of reducing capital gains taxes. These disputes carried over to 1990, when the deficit situation took a critical turn for the worse. Bush faced one of the most unfavorable budgetary situations in history, as the size of the projected deficits exploded. This was a result of the growing sensitivity of the budget to economic trends, poor forecasting, and the savings and loan collapses that required the government to expend billions of dollars for a bailout. The deficit situation was so serious that President Bush needed to work with Congress on a dramatic deficit reduction package. He also felt compelled to renege on his famous "read my lips; no new taxes" pledge made during the 1988 campaign. The result was a deficit reduction package cutting nearly $500 billion over five years with about a third coming from new taxes, a third from defense cuts, and a third from domestic cuts. The tax increase alienated many Republicans, who believed Bush had sold out on their party's best national issue.

The U.S. economy slumped in a recession in the early 1990s, exacerbating budget deficit problems. Deficits continued at stubbornly high levels despite the 1990 deficit reduction package. Of course, the deficits would have been much worse without the legislation. Focusing on the economy and Bush's sinking popularity after the end of the Gulf war, Bill Clinton won the presidency in 1992. He too faced an immediate deficit crisis and had to abandon his planned tax cuts for a deficit reduction package in 1993. It cut the deficit by $430 billion over five years, with about half coming from new taxes and half from spending cuts. It was a bitter political battle that expended much political capital on the part of the president. It passed by one vote in the Senate, and not a single Republican voted for the package. A year later, his health care reform proposal was blocked by Congress, and the Democrats were turned out of control of Congress in 1994.

Combined with an improving economy, the 1990 and 1993 deficit reduction packages set the deficit on a downward course over the next five years. Figure 7.1 examines the federal deficits projected through 2003. In Clinton's first year, the gap between revenues and spending was $290 billion. By his sixth year in office, the budget was balanced for the first time in thirty years. In 1997, Congress and the president had agreed on a bipartisan plan to balance the budget. Getting there was not easy, however. In 1995 and 1996, facing Speaker Newt Gingrich and the partisan Re-

Percent

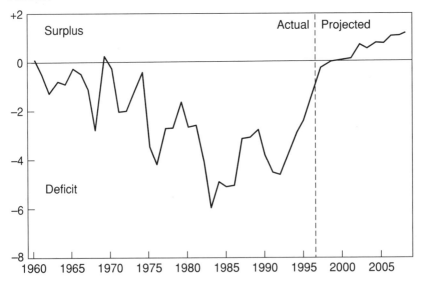

FIGURE 7.1   Deficit (-) or Surplus as a Share of Gross Domestic Product (by fiscal year).

Source: Congressional Budget Office (January 1998).

publican Congress, there was a bitter eighteen-month stalemate over balancing the budget. It was marked by two controversial shutdowns of the government, near default on U.S. debt obligations, and sixteen stop-gap budgets. The last case in the chapter details this episode.

After the Democrats were swamped in the 1994 elections, facing a Republican Congress, Clinton moved to the center. Although he gained politically in claiming the Republicans were savaging Medicare and hurting the elderly, in the end he agreed to accept many Republican positions such as Medicare cuts, tax cuts including capital gains taxes, and a balanced budget by 2002. After sixteen years of conflict over the deficit, both parties were helped by stronger than expected economic growth, using the nation's prosperity to deliver promised tax breaks and new spending programs to constituents.

U.S. economic policy has evolved dramatically since Roosevelt and Keynes. Fiscal policy has become less effective, and monetary policy has become more important. Rather than a tool to stabilize the economy, the economy can destabilize the budget. Federal outlays have become more inflexible because of entitlements (discussed in the next chapter) and other mandatory spending. The globalization of the economy has made the United States less autonomous in making economic policy: Congress and the president are subject to decisions made by governments and traders in Europe and Asia more than ever before. The budget has become one of the central instruments of domestic policymaking, encompassing not only economic consequences but a host of policy goals. All of these trends have made economic and budget making more complicated but not any less important to the president and members of Congress.

THE ENVIRONMENT FOR ECONOMIC AND BUDGET POLICY

Economic Trends

Economic conditions are a crucial aspect of the environment in which Congress and the president operate, affecting public support and policy options in a host of areas. By the late 1990s, the U.S. economy was performing better than it had in three decades. Unemployment dropped below 5 percent, inflation below 3 percent, and the stock market soared, increasing personal wealth. Figure 7.2 shows four major economic indicators between 1980 and 1997, projected through 2008. The economic news was markedly improved over that of a decade earlier, when, although the economy grew, U.S. productivity lagged behind. New jobs were created, but they tended to be low-paying service jobs rather than high-paying manufacturing jobs, which were declining. Inflation, which plagued the 1970s, was brought under control. One of the most troubling trends of the 1980s had been the explosion of debt at all levels: government debt, corporate debt, consumer debt. In addition, the United States

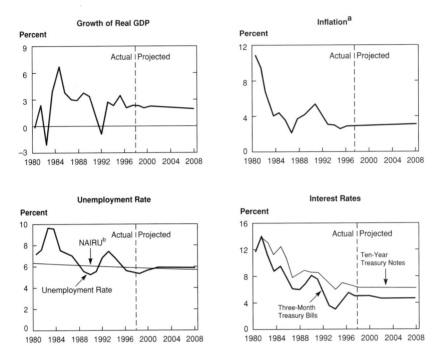

FIGURE 7.2 Economic Trends and Projections

Sources: Congressional Budget Office; Department of Labor, Bureau of Labor Statistics; Department of Commerce, Bureau of Economic Analysis; Federal Reserve Board, (January 1998).

Notes: All data are annual values; growth rates are year over year.

[a]The consumer price index for all urban consumers (CPI-U). The treatment of home ownership in the official CPI-U changed in 1983. The inflation series in the figure uses a consistent definition throughout.

[b]The NAIRU is CBO's estimate of the nonaccelerating inflation rate of unemployment.

had developed a serious trade deficit and, for the first time in nearly a century, became a net debtor to the rest of the world. These economic trends played an important role in establishing the context for battles between Congress and the president.

Between 1982 and 1997, the large budget deficits were a source of recurrent institutional combat as Congress and the president pursued different economic strategies and budget priorities. The performance of the economy has a direct effect on the budget and the deficit; an economic slowdown can quickly undo attempts at reducing the deficit. An increase of 1 percent in unemployment increases the deficit by $33 billion in the first year alone, because tax collections fall by $28 billion, and outlays such as unemployment compensation increase by $5 billion. Similarly, an increase in interest rates expands the deficit because the government must pay more to finance its debt. Economic slumps increased the deficit in 1982 and again in 1991 as the U.S. economy went into recession. It had political consequences for the presidents as well. Reagan's lowest public standing occurred in 1982, when unemployment hit 10 percent. Although the recession was not as severe in 1991–1992, the weak economy contributed to George Bush's defeat in the presidential election. Just as economic trends can hurt the electoral hopes of politicians, positive economic trends can make it easier to reach policy solutions, such as the 1997 balanced budget agreement, and get reelected.

Budget Trends

Trends in government taxing and spending also affect the policymaking environment for Congress and the president. One of the most important changes since the 1960s is the growth of mandatory entitlements such as Social Security, Medicare, and Medicaid. This growing budgetary inflexibility has increased conflict and made the choices all the more difficult. Figure 7.3 compares trends in the four major categories of federal spending as a proportion of GDP since 1960 (projected through 2008). Making up only one quarter of all federal outlays in 1970, entitlements today account for over half of all outlays. With the end of the cold war, defense has declined significantly from 45 percent in 1970 to less than 20 percent today. In addition to the trends in defense and entitlements, nondefense discretionary spending has declined significantly since 1980. This put a squeeze on many government activities and programs. The increase in the national debt from $1 trillion in 1981 to over $5 trillion today has also increased interest costs. With the deficits reduced and a balanced budget achieved, the major budgetary issues at the turn of the century surround Medicare and Social Security, which are discussed in detail in the next chapter.

Tax laws and the government's revenue sources are also an important part of the picture. Federal revenues come from four main sources: personal income taxes, social insurance payroll taxes, corporate income taxes, and excise taxes. Figure 7.4 looks at the trends in federal revenues since 1960. Whereas personal income taxes have hovered around 9 percent of GDP, payroll taxes, which fund Social Security and Medicare, have increased steadily, from 3 percent to 8 percent of GDP, since the 1960s. Corporate income taxes and excise taxes have declined as a source of revenue over the past thirty years. Cutting taxes is a major priority of Republicans. As part of the balanced budget agreement in 1997, Congress and the president agreed to some $90 billion in tax cuts over five years. This package included many provisions of importance to Republicans, including capital gains tax cuts and estate tax cuts. It was the first major tax cut since Reagan's massive tax cut in 1981.

Democrats are not against tax cuts, but they focus more on the issue of who bears the tax burden. Since the initiation of the graduated income tax early in this century, federal taxes have followed a principle of progressivity: wealthier citizens pay a higher proportion of their income than poorer citizens. Social Security (FICA) taxes, however, are regressive in that a taxpayer earning $70,000 a year pays the same as one earning $700,000 per year. The rapid growth of payroll taxes as a source of federal revenue has dampened the progressivity of the federal tax system. This was a major source of contention in budget debates throughout the period. The 1993 deficit reduction package passed by the Democrats made the tax structure more progressive by increasing the top rates paid by higher-income families. But the size of the tax increase made many Democrats nervous about voting for it. The effect of the 1997 tax cuts was less clear: families with children benefited, some provisions benefited low- and middle-income families, and capital gains and estate tax provisions predominantly helped upper-income groups.

Economic and budget trends play a critical role in setting the context for presidential-congressional policymaking. Will the bipartisan agreement to balance the budget reduce the conflict between branches over economic and budget issues? To some extent it already has, allowing both branches to pursue other issues on the policy agenda. But several potential problems could arise. Many experts believe it is probable that the United States will experience an economic recession before 2002,

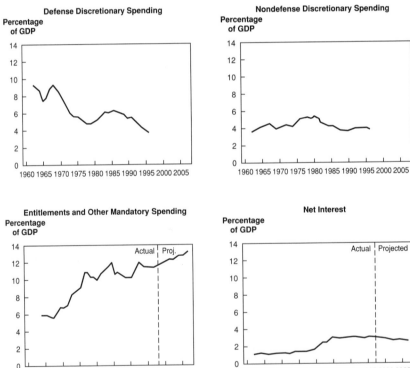

FIGURE 7.3   Outlays, by Category, as a Share of GDP

Source: Congressional Budget Office (January 1998).
Note: Discretionary spending is shown only through 1998 because its future path depends on unspecified reductions necessary to comply with the discretionary cap through 2002.

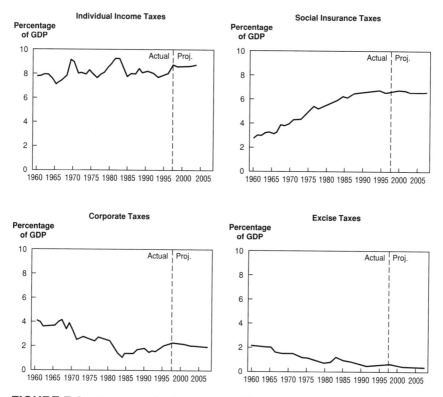

FIGURE 7.4   Revenues, by Source, as a Share of GDP.

Source: Congressional Budget Office (January 1998).

which could make it difficult to maintain balance. This might reopen old cleavages in trying to decide between tax increases or spending cuts to balance the budget. In addition, despite the compromise in 1997, many of the long-term budgetary consequences of the retirement of the baby-boomers were not addressed. Finally, the two parties will still try to distinguish themselves from each other in terms of economic policy and budget priorities. This insures continued conflict, although perhaps more restrained than during the deficit crises of the 1980s and 1990s.

MAKING ECONOMIC AND BUDGET POLICY

Presidential Economic Institutions

How does the presidency make economic and budget policy? The Treasury Department, the BOB, and the Council of Economic Advisors emerged as key organizations for managing the economy in the postwar era. However, these institutions often had different interests and priorities, so presidents needed to develop some means for co-ordinating economic and budget decisions. In the 1960s, Presidents Kennedy and Johnson attempted to coordinate economic policymaking in the presidency by forming the economic "troika": budget director, CEA chair, and treasury secretary. Along with the chair of the Federal Reserve Board, who remained largely independent of the president, this group formed an essential part of what James Anderson called the "economic subpresidency."[17] Broadly speaking, the Treasury Department provides revenue estimates, the Budget Office supplies expenditure projections, and the CEA establishes the economic forecast.

Before he was forced from office by the Watergate scandal, President Nixon had initially attempted to institute a more formal economic policymaking process in the presidency, creating a cabinet committee. Dissatisfied with this system, he then designated Treasury Secretary John Connally as the administration's "economic czar," in charge of all administration economic policy. Nixon also got Congress to agree to his reorganization of the BOB into the Office of Management and Budget (OMB). However, the change in name did little to reduce the importance of the budget office.[18] Ford established an Economic Policy Board within his administration in an attempt to better coordinate policy. Carter also attempted to shuffle responsibilities to improve his control. However, his Economic Policy Group—which added the secretaries of Labor, Housing and Urban Development, and Commerce to the troika—could not prescribe an effective fiscal solution to the country's problems.

Ronald Reagan had a clear economic and budget agenda that made significant departures from past policy. He created a Cabinet Council on Economic Affairs (CCEA) to coordinate policy by bringing together members of the Executive Office of the President, the cabinet, the bureaucracy, and the White House staff. Their mission was less one of policymaking than enforcing a fixed agenda.[19] The budget process became the force driving domestic policy. The deficits created by the 1981 tax cut and defense buildup became the brakes used by the administration to curtail the size and scope of government. Of course, like other modern presidents, Reagan had problems within his administration, and internal disputes became public. At one point late in Reagan's first term, Treasury Secretary Donald Regan told Congress that the economic projections produced by CEA Chair Martin Feldstein were not worth the paper they were printed on!

The Bush administration inherited the big deficits of the 1980s and sought some resolution with Congress through summits. Policymaking was dominated by Budget Director Richard Darman, Chief of Staff John Sununu, and CEA Chairman Michael Boskin.[20] The Clinton administration had a fluid economic policy group, with the president participating actively. Clinton's "pro-business" economic policies were demonstrated by his appointment of Wall Street financier Robert Ruben as secretary of the treasury. Perhaps adhering to his own campaign advice about the economy, the Clinton administration was able to preside over the best economic performance in thirty years.

Congressional Institutions

The presidency was not the only institution of national government during the twentieth century to adapt to a changing political environment and take on new economic responsibilities. However, Congress was more decentralized than the presidency. When the national budget had been created in 1921, Congress attempted unsuccessfully to centralize its fragmented appropriations and revenue processes and consider the budget as a whole.[21] In 1946, at the time of the enactment of the Employment Act, Congress once again attempted to centralize economic decision making by creating a legislative budget.[22] Despite the serious intentions of its creators, this centralized process failed, torn apart by partisanship between the Republican Congress and the Democratic president. Congress was not able to influence monetary policy much either. Even though Congress had oversight responsibility, the Federal Reserve remained substantially independent.[23]

Federal spending expanded rapidly in the 1960s, and Congress seemed incapable of curbing it. Fewer bills were adopted in a timely fashion, and it was more often necessary to rely on stopgap continuing resolutions to fund the government. Because the budget as a whole was never debated, Congress was unable to establish national priorities. Congress also lacked the independent information to challenge the presidency on economic matters. Many of these issues were brought to a head because of the growing antipathy between President Richard Nixon and Congress.[24] He thwarted legislative policymaking by impounding (refusing to spend) billions of dollars that Congress had appropriated. This ultimately led to the passage of the Budget and Impoundment Control Act in July of 1974, only a month before Nixon resigned rather than be impeached. In the ensuing decades, the Budget Act strengthened the capacity of Congress to make economic and budget policy and strengthened its hand in negotiating with the president.

The Budget Act made it possible for Congress to deal with macro-level economic decisions: the overall budget totals.[25] It required the adoption of a budget resolution to set the parameters of the budget and created House and Senate Budget committees to draft the congressional budget. The act specified a strict timetable for congressional action and changed the fiscal year of the federal government. To improve congressional information, the Congressional Budget Office (CBO) was created. One of the most potent elements of the budget process was *reconciliation,* which allowed major taxing and spending changes to be enacted in a single bill. Finally, impoundment controls limited the president's ability to withhold appropriated funds. Over time, the budget process allowed Congress to make decisions on budget totals, to negotiate with the president as coequals in the process, and to use various rules in the budget process to prevent obstructionist tactics that could derail other legislation.

Congress also tried some institutional reforms that failed. In response to the deficit crisis and the growing deterioration of its own decision-making processes, Congress took a dramatic step in 1985 by adopting a mandatory deficit reduction plan. The plan was proposed by Senators Phil Gramm (R-Tex.), Warren Rudman (R-N.H.), and Ernest "Fritz" Hollings (D-S.C.).[26] Their plan was to establish fixed deficit targets for the next five years and establish a procedure for mandatory across-the-board cuts if Congress could not reach the target. Despite reservations about such a mechanical approach to budgeting, the need to reduce the deficit was politically irresistible. Three months of partisan conflict produced a bill that became law in 1985. Although most of the publicity focused on the automatic budget-cutting provisions, Congress took the opportunity to rewrite the 1974 Budget Act. An accelerated timetable was adopted as well as enhanced enforcement procedures on the floor.

Gramm-Rudman-Hollings was eventually abandoned in 1990, and Congress turned to expenditure control through appropriations caps and other devices to reduce the deficit. Congressional budgeting was unstable during the 1980s and 1990s, leading to a great deal of criticism. But despite the improvisational nature of congressional budgeting, it was innovative. Through the use of reconciliation, restrictive rules, and enhanced enforcement procedures, Congress emerged in a stronger position to challenge the presidency than at any time in recent history. The cases that follow show the dramatic range of patterns that take place in making critical choices on economic and budget policy.

PRESIDENTIAL LEADERSHIP: THE ECONOMIC AND BUDGET PLAN (1981)

June 24 and 25, 1981, were dramatic days in the House of Representatives. When they were over, Ronald Reagan had won the biggest battle in the war with Congress over the nation's budget and economic priorities. On the evening of the June 24, the House Rules Committee and Speaker Thomas "Tip" O'Neill had agreed on a rule for the Omnibus Reconciliation bill that forced it to be voted on in six separate sections. This approach would prevent President Reagan's budget package from being offered in the form of a single substitute. Republicans cried foul. "Parliamentary dictatorship," one member screamed; "tyranny of the majority," charged another.[27] But when the day was over, some two dozen conservative Democrats joined with Republicans to defeat the leadership by a vote of 217 to 210.[28] This vote paved the way for the adoption of the president's reconciliation package, guaranteeing that his controversial taxing and spending plan would become law.

Ronald Reagan was inaugurated as the fortieth president of the United States just five days after Jimmy Carter sent Congress his budget for fiscal year 1982. The Reagan administration, in particular Budget Director David Stockman, had already been scrutinizing those figures for potential cuts. During the 1980 campaign, Reagan had promised to restructure national budget priorities and economic policy. After only three weeks in office, the administration sent Congress extensive revisions of the FY82 budget. The plan was composed of three main elements. First, the administration proposed to stimulate savings, investment, and economic growth by cutting income taxes across the board. Second, national defense was to be boosted by a $1.8 trillion infusion over five years. Third, arguing that the federal government had become bloated and wasteful, the administration proposed slashing domestic spending across a range of programs.

Claiming a broad conservative mandate from the 1980 election, the administration moved quickly to sell its proposals on Capitol Hill. The president was helped immeasurably by the surprise capture of the United States Senate by the Republican party after twenty-six years of Democratic dominance. Republican leaders in the Senate stood ready to help the new president in any way they could. Stockman and other high-ranking officials descended on the Congress to argue for the president's program. The president's congressional liaison operation wooed individual legislators, indicating that the president would be willing to dispense specific favors in return for their support. The administration also used procedural innovation. Employing the previously little-used process of reconciliation, Reagan strategists conceived of a plan to put all the elements of their plan to a single vote. Democratic leaders in the House pledged to fight the president, particularly the deep cuts in popular domestic programs.

The first major battle came in May over the budget resolution, the blueprint for the taxing and spending totals in subsequent congressional decisions. The president appeared on television immediately before the vote, appealing to the American people to urge their legislators to support his program. Congress was swamped with letters, calls, and telegrams. House Democrats proposed a plan much like the president's, but protecting some of their sacred cows. It was not good enough for the administration. With the help of a group of conservative southern Democrats—the "boll weevils"—the Reagan administration carried the day on May 7, 1981, by the comfortable margin of 253 to 176.[29] Despite this initial setback, Democratic leaders in the House believed that they could reverse the budget resolution defeat when the reconciliation bill reached the floor in late June. The rule dividing the bill into six parts would maximize their opportunity to defeat all or part of the president's specific proposals. President Reagan again took to the airwaves, appealing directly to the American people to urge their legislators to support him. When the Democratic rule was overturned by a mere seven votes, House Speaker Tip O'Neill was furious:

> *I have never seen anything like this in my life, to be perfectly truthful. What is the authority for this? Does this mean that any time the president of the United States is interested in a piece of legislation, he merely sends it over? . . . Do we have the right to legislate . . . or can he in one package deregulate, delegislate, the things that have taken years to do?*[30]

Seemingly as surprised as the Democrats, Budget Director Stockman hastily put together a final reconciliation bill, which dealt with literally thousands of government programs. The bill that came to a floor vote on June 25 was full of errors, including the phone number of a staff member inadvertently reproduced in the margin of the members' copies. Despite complaints that nobody knew what they were voting on, the president's plan was adopted. In a single bill, the president had succeeded in getting nearly $35 billion in domestic cuts the first year and $100 billion more over the next several years. The final component of the president's plan—a 25 percent across-the-board cut in income taxes—was taken up by Congress in late July. Once again, Reagan made an effective appeal on television shortly before the vote. Lobbying was intense in the House, and both the Democrats and the White House offered special tax benefits to lure potential supporters, but by then there was little they could do. The administration won by a comfortable margin of forty-three votes. In less than six months, Ronald Reagan had changed the direction of government taxing and spending more profoundly than any of his recent predecessors.

How was President Ronald Reagan able to dominate a Congress with a Republican majority in the Senate but a Democratic majority in the House? After all, his predecessor, Jimmy Carter, had had great difficulty with a Congress that boasted sizable Democratic majorities in both houses. The key to the cross-partisan majority was the group of conservative House Democrats that crossed over to vote with the Republicans. The political environment in 1981 was conducive to presidential leadership, despite the assertiveness of Congress over the previous fifteen years. Although public opinion was mixed on the specifics of Reagan's cuts, the president was extremely popular. Surviving the assassination attempt by John Hinckley only made the rugged Reagan more popular. His approval ratings hovered near 70 percent in 1981. The notion that the country was ready for a change was effectively promoted by the administration.

The election results were especially important for Reagan's first year. In an election that pollsters had labeled "too close to call" only days before, Ronald Reagan's 10 percent popular vote margin over Jimmy Carter was magnified in the electoral college to a 489 to 49 vote landslide. The victory was much greater than anyone had predicted, allowing the president-elect to claim a broad mandate. Equally significant for presidential-congressional relations, Republicans picked up twelve seats in the Senate, gaining a majority. Receiving much less attention were the House election results. The Democrats remained in control but saw their majority reduced from 114 to 51 seats. This meant that the Republicans could create a majority with only 26 Democratic defections, compared with 58 before the election.

The Reagan administration used the tools of the presidency quickly and decisively, if not carefully. David Stockman mobilized the administration, in terms of both policy and political strategy. The Reaganites were less concerned about processes and institutions than with achieving ideological objectives. The administration was innovative, moving reconciliation to the beginning of the budget process and using its provisions to force Congress to vote on the cuts in a single package. Congressional institutions were shaken by the Reagan budget blitz.

Leadership and agenda-setting played a significant role in the presidential leadership that resulted. First, Reagan significantly limited the policy agenda of government in 1981. The administration focused attention almost exclusively on the economic and budget package. As a result, the number of recorded roll-call votes in Congress was the lowest in decades. The long list of social issues, such as abortion and school prayer, were deferred until later years. Second, the administration followed the "move it or lose it" strategy, striking quickly. The administration rewrote Carter's last budget only three weeks after taking office and submitted detailed proposals within two months. Third, Ronald Reagan's media appeals were highly effective. Although not well-versed in the details of policy, he was successful at mobilizing public opinion and pressuring legislators.

One explanation was that weakness in the Democratic leadership in Congress contributed to the president's victory, but this is inaccurate. On the key reconciliation vote, nearly 90 percent of Democrats voted with their party, a higher proportion than in any year since the congressional budget process was adopted in 1975.[31] The emergence of the Republican/boll weevil coalition in the House was a result of the 1980 House elections, not weak party leadership by the Democrats. However, the pattern of presidential leadership was fleeting. By late 1981, Reagan's window of opportunity had passed, and relations moved toward institutional combat and deadlock over economic and budget issues.

What were the results of the adoption of the economic and budget plan? Reagan succeeded in two of his objectives. First, defense spending was increased to record peacetime levels—not just in 1981, but until 1985. Second, the tax cut significantly reduced revenues from the income tax throughout the decade. Failure in the third objective—making massive cuts in domestic spending—led to the most negative result: the huge deficits and accumulation of debt that followed.

CONGRESSIONAL LEADERSHIP:
THE SHAREHOLDER LAWSUITS BILL (1995)

The United States has become a litigious society, with lawsuits continuing to proliferate over everything from McDonald's coffee that was too hot to Johnny Carson suing a neighbor for a dog fouling his yard. As the prevalence of coffee room lawyer jokes suggests, the attorneys that bring these suits on behalf of plaintiffs have been subject to growing criticism. One of the less publicized provisions of the Republican's Contract with America was legislation to reduce frivolous lawsuits that hurt emerging, high-tech industries. In 1995, led by the new Republican majority but with bipartisan support, Congress led the policy process by passing legislation limiting lawsuits by shareholders against companies. In doing so, Congress ran into the opposition of President Clinton, who vetoed the bill. Undeterred, both the House and Senate mustered two-thirds majorities to override the veto and pass the shareholder lawsuits bill into law.

Some of the most egregious examples of unnecessary lawsuits in recent years have come in the area of shareholders' suits against companies for securities fraud. A small group of attorneys have made a fortune by watching for companies whose stock price has dropped, reviewing the records for previous optimistic performance projections, then suing on the grounds that the company had defrauded stockholders.[32] Particularly hard hit were high-tech companies, whose stock prices tend to be extremely volatile. Certain attorneys even paid stockholders to join class-action suits. Some investors brought small stakes in companies simply to look for opportunities to sue. Companies usually settle these suits out of court rather than spend the time and money to defend themselves. The CEO of America Online said that "frivolous lawsuits are such a problem that high-tech firms can now be lumped into two groups: those that have been sued and those that will be sued."[33]

On the other side of the issue were several groups, including trial lawyers and consumer rights organizations. The bill was also opposed by a number of state attorneys general and securities regulators. They argued that reformers wanted to go too far to curb the rights of stockowners to protect themselves against fraud and abuse by unscrupulous companies. They noted that there were only about 250 class-action securities suits filed per year and that not all were frivolous. The division of interest groups caused potential problems for President Clinton because it pitted Democratic-leaning trial lawyers and consumers groups against the high-tech industries in California that he was so carefully wooing with the 1996 presidential election coming up.

House Republicans moved quickly on the bill during the ambitious first 100 days of the 104th Congress, their first taste of having a majority in Congress in 40 years. Representative Christopher Cox (R-Calif.) was the prime author of the bill, HR1058. The Telecommunications and Finance Subcommittee of the House Commerce Committee drafted the shareholder lawsuits bill in February and passed it by a voice vote. The full committee passed it on February 16, 1995, by a vote of 33 to 10. It garnered significant Democratic support. The bill prohibited lawyers from paying shareholders for joining a suit and required that the losing party in the suit pay all costs. It placed other restrictions on plaintiffs in terms of how many suits they could be party to and exempted from liability companies that were sued on the basis of projections. Opponents claimed that the bill went too far and was "the stripping of citizens of a mechanism by which they can defend themselves against malefactors of great wealth."[34] Nonetheless, the bill passed the House easily by a vote of 325 to 99 on March 8 with bipartisan support.

The Senate took up the bill in May and scaled back several provisions. To prevent small investors from buying stocks just to sue, the Senate required that the largest investor in a stock be the lead plaintiff in any suit. The bill also included safe harbor provisions to protect companies who wanted to make growth and earnings projections, as long as there was no intent to deceive. During the Senate debate, the lead sponsor, Senator Peter Domenici (R-N.M.), pointed out that most of the damages in these lawsuits went to the lawyers, with stockholders getting only 14 cents of every dollar.[35] He was assisted in getting the bill through the Senate by Christopher Dodd (D-Conn.), who was also general chairman of the Democratic National Committee. Despite his partisan job, Dodd worked with Domenici and other Republicans to get the bill passed. It did so on June 28 by a vote of 70 to 29.

Over the summer and fall, Congress and the president, Republicans and Democrats, were sharply divided on many issues, particularly budget issues. During this time, however, informal negotiations between the House and Senate resolved most of the differences in the two versions of the shareholder lawsuits bills. The conference committee finished work on the bill on November 28 and sent the compromise version to the House and Senate for final approval. It passed the Senate on December 5 and the House on December 6 by comfortable margins and was sent to the president for his signature.

President Clinton and his congressional liaison office had maintained a low profile on the issue during the year as the administration concentrated on other matters. It was clearly a congressional policy initiative with widespread support. But the president was heavily lobbied by interest groups after the bill was passed and sent to him for his signature. The trial lawyers—big Democratic contributors—were strongly against the bill and pressed for a veto. Conversely, high-tech industry lobbyists warned that the bill was so important to California that Clinton might lose that state in 1996 if he vetoed the bill.[36]

Clinton waited until the last possible minute to decide what to do with the bill. The bill would become law without his signature on December 19th at midnight. After meeting with advisors late into the evening, Clinton vetoed the bill. It had been a difficult decision. Clinton claimed that he opposed frivolous lawsuits but felt that the bill had gone too far, particularly with the safe harbor provisions. A White House statement read, "the president supports the goals of this legislation, but he is unwilling to close the courthouse doors on the investors who have legitimate claims."[37] Many on Capitol Hill were stunned at the veto and promised to override it immediately. Even Democrats were surprised given the prominent role played by Dodd, one of the president's most loyal soldiers in Congress. It did not take long for Congress to respond. Only thirteen hours after the veto, the House voted 319 to 100 to override, far more than the two-thirds needed. Two days later, the Senate voted to override by a closer margin of 68 to 30, still enough to enact the bill into law (PL 104–67).

Why did this case evolve the way it did? What does this case tell us about presidential-congressional policymaking, particularly when Congress takes the lead? The political environment in 1995 was exceptional, with the new Republican Congress virtually setting the agenda of the nation for much of the year. As part of the Contract with America, the shareholder lawsuits bill was part of this agenda. Unlike many other provisions, this attracted significant support from the Democratic minority on the other side of the aisle. This case was more typical of inside-the-beltway politics, rather than the highly publicized economic issues such as the budget or proposed Medicare cutbacks. It was fought out by organized interests—high-tech companies, trial lawyers, and consumer advocates in the halls and cloakrooms of Congress. This was also Congress leading, with relatively little input from the administration.

Nonetheless, the administration had stakes in the bill. It was torn, however, between political and policy objectives and divisions between groups that supported it.

His hesitation cost the president the first veto override of his administration, an event with political consequences and a sign of weakness. Although the veto may have shored up the political support among the trial lawyers, high-tech companies were furious with his veto. During the 1996 campaign, some of the CEOs who had supported him in 1992 withheld support. The Republican Congress, however, not only had enacted another provision of the Contract but had won a political victory over the president as well.

CONSENSUS/COOPERATION:
THE TAX REFORM ACT (1986)

The conventional wisdom held that tax reform—especially comprehensive tax reform—was impossible in the American political system. Despite many obstacles, on October 22, 1986, President Ronald Reagan signed into law the most sweeping overhaul of federal income taxes in history. How did Congress and the president work together to make the impossible possible? Jimmy Carter had called the nation's tax system a disgrace during the 1976 campaign, but he never even submitted a comprehensive reform package during his presidency. Tax reform seemed particularly improbable in the partisan, politicized Washington environment after the 1984 election campaign, in which President Reagan had hammered Democratic presidential candidate Walter Mondale on the tax issue. With budget deficits at record levels, Reagan's pledge not to raise taxes had driven legislative and executive branches farther apart.

Tax reform was also seen as highly unlikely because, with fiscal constraints on the spending side in the Reagan years, it had become increasingly popular to deliver benefits through tax preferences or loopholes. Granting special exclusions, exemptions, deductions, deferrals, and lower rates had become an ingenious if costly method for legislators to deliver benefits to constituents. By 1985, these special "tax expenditures" cost the Treasury over $400 billion per year.[38] The decline in fiscal responsibility of the House Ways and Means and Senate Finance Committees— Congress's tax-writing panels—further dimmed prospects for reform. Four years earlier, the Economic Recovery Tax Act (ERTA) looked like a bidding war. David Stockman characterized the process as "pigs feeding at the trough." Legislators were unable to resist the temptation to buy support by creating tax preferences.[39]

Tax reform was also considered impossible because of the array of powerful interest groups lined up against it. Any given group may have benefited from only one or two of the hundreds of special provisions, but as a group would go to any lengths to protect the status quo. Interests ranging from investment bankers to timber companies to university presidents had something to protect in the old tax system. When Congress debated comprehensive reform, hundreds of highly paid lobbyists milled around outside of the hearing rooms. Authors Jeffrey Birnbaum and Alan Murray described the scene:

In the hallway outside the committee room, more lobbyists stand nervously, like so many expectant fathers crowded into the waiting room of a maternity ward. These hallway loiterers include the top ranks of Washington's tax lobbying world—men and women who are paid $200, $300, and even $400 an hour to influence legislators and preserve tax benefits worth millions of dollars to their anxious clients. . . . A few of the lobbyists huddle around the back door of the committee room, hoping to catch a senator coming in or going out, hoping for one last chance to make a pitch before the vote. The desperation in their voices makes it clear that big money is at stake. Their expensive suits and shiny Italian shoes give this hallway its nickname: Gucci Gulch.[40]

Tax reform came into being through a carefully orchestrated collaboration between executive and legislative branches. The tax reform movement in Congress allied two diverse groups. Liberal reformers, such as Representative Richard Gephardt (D-Mo.) and Senator Bill Bradley (D-N.J.), who wanted to eliminate special preferences for the rich, joined with conservative supply-siders, such as Representative Jack Kemp (R-N.Y.) and Senator Robert Kasten (R-Wis.), who wanted lower rates. Both sides agreed that the tax base had to be broadened, which meant eliminating many special tax preferences. The Bradley-Gephardt and Kemp-Kasten bills had received a great deal of attention before 1985 but had never been seriously considered by either house of Congress.

The equilibrium changed when Ronald Reagan announced that comprehensive tax reform was the number one domestic priority of his second term. The building blocks were in place, but the political obstacles remained. In 1984, the president had instructed the Treasury Department to prepare a comprehensive tax reform plan. The details of the plan were carefully guarded until after the election. In December 1984, the Treasury Department unveiled a bold plan. It called for the elimination of many sacred cows in the tax code, so it immediately generated controversy. The Reagan administration was cautious, however, and did not endorse the plan as its own. The White House wanted time to review some of the more controversial provisions before actually submitting a plan to Congress.

The Reagan administration did not submit a plan until June 1985, six months into the second term. Remembering the budget blitz of 1981, many observers felt that the president had failed to capture the momentum of his landslide reelection. The revised plan was dubbed "Treasury II" and retained many of the comprehensive features of "Treasury I." House Ways and Means Chairman Dan Rostenkowski (D-Ill.) quickly pledged Democratic support for the approach of the president's plan, if not all the specifics.

Legislative and executive branch leaders agreed on several ground rules to minimize conflict and make cooperation possible. First, all reform proposals had to be "revenue neutral"—neither raising nor losing revenue—to keep tax reform from being dragged into the bitter deficit dispute. Second, reformers agreed that for strategic purposes, approximately two-thirds of all taxpayers had to pay the same or less in taxes under the new system as compared with the existing system. Third, reformers determined that the number of tax brackets (fifteen at the time) would be sharply reduced, to as few as two or three. Fourth, all sides decided that the effort would be bipartisan, avoiding as much as possible the divisions that characterized most budget and economic issues. These strategic premises did not assure victory but did mean that tax reform would get farther than it had in decades.

The House took up the president's proposal first, reflecting its constitutional primacy in dealing with revenue measures. Rostenkowski confronted the legions of lobbyists in "Gucci Gulch" and watched in frustration as his committee voted to allow a number of the special preferences back into the bill. In October 1985, it appeared that a tax reform was doomed when the Ways and Means Committee voted to reinstate a $7 billion tax break for banks.[41] However, Rostenkowski worked out a deal with members who wanted to retain the deduction for state and local taxes, and the bank loophole was reconsidered and defeated. When the bill finally cleared committee and went to the full House in December 1985, a number of Republicans had grown disenchanted. Feeling left out of the negotiations among the White House, Republican Senate leaders, and Democratic House leaders, they staged a revolt. President Reagan promised to deal with the concerns of the House Republicans when the bill reached the Senate and urged them to support the committee version. However, on December 11, these Republicans joined with several dozen Democrats and defeated the rule under which tax reform was to be debated. It was a major crack in the bipartisanship that had characterized the process, which threatened to kill tax reform. Five days later, the president rescued the process by personally coming to Capitol Hill to convince House Republicans to support the bill. Although not all of them were convinced, the bill passed the House the next day.

The Senate Finance Committee, chaired by Republican Robert Packwood of Oregon, began drafting its version of tax reform in the spring of 1986. The markup seemed to confirm the worst fears and predictions of defeat. One by one, committee members chipped away, voting to restore provisions favoring special interests. After weeks of battering, Packwood withdrew his plan and contemplated giving up, but a key breakthrough occurred. Packwood took his committee members behind closed doors, away from the lobbyists, the reporters, and the glare of television lights of the hearing room. He asked members how low rates would have to drop before they would be willing to give up the special preferences they had already adopted in open sessions. Most members responded that the top rates would have to come down to 30 percent or below. Packwood showed them how it could be done.

Throwing out the decisions made over the previous month, the Senate Finance committee reported a radical tax reform bill, with two brackets and a top rate of only 27 percent. By turning the decision-making process around in private, Packwood succeeded in getting his committee to report the bill to the Senate by a remarkable vote of 20 to 0. This may have been the single most important event in making tax reform a reality. The lobbyists were stunned to see their special tax provisions thrown out. The strong committee vote made tax reform irresistible on the Senate floor, where it passed by a vote of 97 to 3 on June 24, 1986.

The conference committee considering the two versions of the bills ran into its share of problems, but eventually it adopted a plan closer to the more daring Senate bill. The final version contained two brackets, with rates of 14 and 28 percent. The bill was approved by both the House and Senate in September and signed into law by the president in October. The impossible had been accomplished.

Several factors explain the emergence of a pattern of cooperation leading to the successful enactment of tax reform. Both branches worked actively on specific details of the legislation and demonstrated a willingness to negotiate and compromise. Bipartisanship was critical. With the exception of the House Republicans, all participants avoided the temptation to make political hay out of their differences. Tax reform was originally a congressional initiative, but it could not have been enacted without active, aggressive support from President Reagan, whose popularity and landslide election victory helped him to move the legislative process, particularly in the House, when it became stalled. Decision-making processes and individual leadership were exceptionally important in this case. The leadership of Senator Packwood was particularly noteworthy. Private negotiations, in which bargaining and trading could be done honestly, were instrumental in the crafting of the Tax Reform Act of 1986.

What were the results of the Tax Reform Act? One immediate result was that the top rate of personal income taxes fell to its lowest level since the 1920s. Although the revenue code remained complex, the reduction in the number of brackets was a significant improvement. For many supporters, the greatest benefit of tax reform was to restore some of the integrity to the tax system by eliminating hundreds of loopholes. Conversely, many of these loopholes had produced some positive consequences. The new law had a damaging effect on real estate (particularly urban redevelopment), and many critics regretted the elimination of a lower capital gains tax. This would become an issue in the Bush administration. The tax code would be changed again in ensuing years, with top rates being raised as part of the deficit reduction packages in 1990 and 1993. Whatever simplification was enacted was gradually eroded over the next decade. In particular, many new complex tax breaks were added back into the tax code as part of the balanced budget agreement in 1997.

DEADLOCK/EXTRAORDINARY RESOLUTION: THE BALANCED BUDGET STANDOFF (1995–1996)

Perhaps no issue was more important to the new Republican Congress in 1995 than balancing the federal budget. They would approach the issue aggressively, seeking total victory over the repudiated congressional Democrats and a weakened President Clinton. House Republicans would concoct a plan with nearly a trillion dollars in spending cuts over seven years, including sharp reductions in Medicare, enough cuts to allow them to incorporate $350 billion in tax cuts during the same period. They would try to force the president to go along by threatening to shut down the government and default on federal debt if necessary. Although he gradually moved toward their position and agreed to seek a balanced budget, throughout 1995, Clinton stood up to Speaker Gingrich and the Republicans. Clinton's approval ratings soared while the Republicans' tumbled. Eighteen months after the battle over the fiscal 1996 budget started, a truce was called without an agreement on a plan to balance the budget. Both sides decided that the deadlock would best be resolved by the 1996 elections.

As the hectic first 100 days of the 104th Congress were ending, committees in both the House and Senate were getting down to the business of crafting a comprehensive plan to balance the budget. The House Budget Committee, headed by Representative John Kasich (R-Ohio) and the Senate Budget Committee, chaired by Senator Peter Domenici (R-N.M.), began hearings on the budget resolution for FY96. On February 6, 1995, President Clinton, chastened by the 1994 election results, had submitted a cautious budget that included no major initiatives or deficit reduction. Republicans lambasted the president for abdicating leadership, claiming he "took a walk" and "put up the white flag."[42] Not content just to shape the FY96 budget for the fiscal year that would begin on October 1, 1995, the Republicans proposed a package of rescissions (canceling spending already approved) for the current year FY95 budget. In May, Clinton vetoed the rescissions bill and the Republicans lacked the votes to override, a pattern that would be repeated over the next year. A compromise rescissions bill was finally approved in July.

The House balanced budget plan went to the floor in May. It was an ambitious attempt to make major reductions in government, including the elimination of fourteen federal agencies. The House plan would cut spending by $1.04 trillion, including $288 billion in Medicare reductions, and cut taxes by $353 billion.[43] The Senate plan was somewhat more modest, making tax cuts contingent on a plan that would actually balance the budget. Democrats attacked the bills, claiming the Republicans wanted to balance the budget on the backs of the young, the poor, and the elderly. Still on the defensive, however, on June 13, Clinton put out his own plan for a balanced budget over ten years. Some Democrats attacked the president for capitulating to the Republicans, but he argued that his plan would not harm society's most vulnerable. Republicans ignored the president's plan. After House and Senate versions passed by nearly party-line votes, the budget resolution went to conference. The conference committee worked out the differences between the two versions, and on June 29, the budget resolution laying out the Republicans' balanced budget plan was passed. The budget resolution is binding only on subsequent congressional actions and does not have to be signed by the president to take effect.

Implementing the blueprint contained in the budget resolution would take place on two fronts. First, the thirteen individual appropriations bills containing discretionary spending that must be passed by October 1 would provide Republicans an opportunity to make sharp cuts in existing programs. Second, the bulk of the balanced budget package would be contained in a massive reconciliation bill, encompassing multiyear cuts in entitlements and other spending, along with tax reductions. With partisan conflict at every stage, the pace was slow, and the administration's resolve was growing. By October 1, only two spending bills had passed, and Clinton had vetoed one of them. Congress passed a six-week stop-gap spending bill as a big battle was shaping up over the reconciliation bill.

The Republican strategy was to try to force Clinton to approve their balanced budget plan by threatening to shut down the government and default on the debt if he did not sign their bill. The statutory debt ceiling, which gives the government the authority to borrow, was set to expire in mid-November 1995.[44] The Republicans bet that, rather than allow a first-ever default on federal debt, Clinton would accept their budget plan. They were wrong. As the November 13 date for the expiration of the temporary spending bill approached, Clinton stepped up his counterattacks on Congress for trying to blackmail him into signing the bill. The Republicans passed another temporary spending bill and a debt extension with provisions that he had promised not to accept. He vetoed both and on November 14, "nonessential" federal employees were sent home as the government closed down for six days. The Treasury was able to manipulate funds to avoid a default on government bonds.

Republicans did win one important concession from the president. As they were negotiating over another temporary funding bill, Clinton agreed with the seven-year timetable to balance the budget as long as it included his priorities for health care, education, and the environment. Now, both sides wanted a balanced budget—the only question was how to do it. That concession by Clinton would not make compromise any easier. The Republican version of the reconciliation bill passed Congress and was vetoed by the president on December 6. Clinton released a new budget plan of his own on December 7. As the stalemate continued, on December 16, the government shut down again as federal workers were sent home right before the holidays. Voters were getting fed up with the antics in Washington.

It was the Republican Congress rather than the president that paid the political price for the budget deadlock. Clinton's approval rating shot up over 50 percent, the highest rate in two years, as support for Newt Gingrich and the Republicans tumbled.[45] The public saw Clinton sticking to principles and standing up for the little guy. News stories featured unhappy tourists locked out of national parks and monuments and disgruntled government workers not allowed to go to the office. To make matters worse, the stock market dropped over concerns with the budget deadlock. After the holidays, members of Congress returned to Washington and, spurred by rank-and-file discontent over the political consequences of their strategy, the Republicans backed away from their hardball tactics. Robert Dole, worrying about the negative consequences to his presidential bid, said, "Enough is enough. I do not see any sense in what we have been doing, frankly. Maybe I missed the point. . . . If there is any point to be made, I think that point should have been made by now."[46]

Ironically, with concessions by the Clinton administration, the two sides were not as far apart as they had been earlier, and agreement seemed to be within reach.

In November, the White House and Congress were as much as $350 billion apart. By January, this had closed to $66 billion.[47] But as yet another temporary spending bill expired, Republicans were desperate to avoid another shutdown. In essence, the Republicans gave up on getting a budget agreement. Newt Gingrich said, "I don't expect us to get a seven-year balanced budget with President Clinton in office."[48] Meanwhile, no budget had passed, leaving many agencies and departments in financial chaos. In the spring of 1996, halfway into the fiscal year, fewer than half of the appropriations bills had been enacted, and the fourteenth temporary spending bills had to be passed to avoid another shutdown. An increasingly confident White House lambasted the Congress for not completing its work on the budget. Meanwhile, the cycle for the FY97 budget was already starting, although Clinton delayed submission of the plan by over a month and submitted only the rudiments of a regular budget.

The deadlock over the balanced budget plan was not so much resolved as it was postponed. In late April, both sides agreed to a bill that would fund agencies through the end of the fiscal year. Both sides still had their own versions of a balanced budget plan, and both sides planned to use the failure to reach a compromise in the 1996 presidential and congressional elections. There was no extraordinary resolution of the 1995–96 budget deadlock. Instead, it was resolved in part by the mixed message at the election. With the reelection of Bill Clinton by a substantial margin and the trimming of Republican majorities in Congress, the 1996 elections set the stage for eventual agreement on a balanced budget plan in 1997.

This case is an interesting example of how divided government and party differences over economic and budget policy can result in partisan bickering, deadlock, and potentially harmful results. Nothing positive was accomplished by the government shutdowns or threats to default on the federal debt. The case certainly reveals enhanced congressional capacity to lead government in terms of defining issues and formulating solutions. However, it also shows the limits of congressional leadership when there is substantial opposition from the White House. The Republicans were unable to pressure Clinton into accepting their plan, and their tactics backfired politically. In retrospect, many Republicans believe it was a mistake to force the government shutdowns to pressure the president.

The pattern of deadlock that emerged was a result of the unique political environment of 1995, the dramatic election results of 1994, and the strength and unity of the Republican majority in the House. It was possible for Congress to push as hard as it did because of the institutions linked with the congressional budget process that had developed over the past two decades. Personal leadership was also important. Speaker Newt Gingrich and Majority Leader Dick Armey were perhaps too swept up in their own successes and miscalculated the president's resolve and the public reaction. President Clinton, who had been reduced to holding a press conference to deny he was "irrelevant" right after the Republicans captured Congress, boosted his leadership ratings by standing up to the Congress. In terms of policy, despite losing the political battle, Republicans may have won the policy battle by getting the president to commit to a balanced budget by 2002 and bringing him closer to their position in many areas. Undoubtedly, lessons were learned on both sides. In 1996, Clinton was reelected easily and the Republicans held Congress, but narrowly. This created a very different context in 1997, when President Clinton and many of the same Republican leaders were able to negotiate in good faith for the most part, and helped by a booming economy, achieve a plan to balance the budget after all.

CONCLUSION

Both branches know the high stakes involved in economic and budget issues. Accordingly, dominance by either branch is relatively rare. Congressional leadership may be rarer, because the political stakes are so great for the president. In the case of the shareholder lawsuits bill, the president identified his position in the bill too late, and Congress was not willing to let him obstruct their work at the last minute. Congress is more likely to lead on less publicized economic issues, like the shareholder lawsuits bill, or public works and other pork-barrel legislation that distributes local benefits. It is much more exceptional for the legislative branch to try to lead the president on comprehensive national economic and budget legislation, as the 104th Congress did in 1995. This case may be unprecedented in modern times in terms of congressional attempts to dominate policymaking. But despite all their initial political advantages, the result was still deadlock. The case remains instructive, however, in defining both the potential and the limits of congressional power in economic policymaking.

In this era of greater coequality of the branches, strong presidential leadership of Congress may be getting equally rare, occurring only in an unusual political environment. The classic case is Franklin Roosevelt's "Hundred Days" during the depths of the Depression in 1933, when Congress was willing to enact virtually anything the president proposed. This may not occur again absent a comparable economic calamity. In this perspective, Ronald Reagan's 1981 economic and budget blitz was quite remarkable, because there was no economic crisis of the magnitude of the Depression. The political environment was unique in 1981, and Reagan was skillful in exploiting it, as Roosevelt had been in 1933. Interest rates over 20 percent, the double-digit inflation of the 1970s, and relatively high unemployment left the public anxious for a change. The rarity of this pattern is suggested by Reagan's inability to dominate after 1981. What followed, even with a Republican Senate for five more years, was a recurring pattern of partisan conflict. The only comparable recent case was Clinton's 1993 deficit reduction package. The president was able to shape policy, but with the greatest of difficulty. His package was amended by Congress, barely passed, and cost the president dearly in terms of political capital. Clinton's 1993 deficit reduction plan showed that even with unified control of government, Congress is not easy to lead.

If the two branches disagree, and neither can dominate, the alternative is either cooperation or deadlock. Bipartisan cooperation seemed missing on economic and budget policy in the 1980s, making the interbranch cooperation exhibited in the Tax Reform Act of 1986 all the more exceptional. Furthermore, there was no imminent crisis looming to force legislative and executive negotiators to the bargaining table as was the case in the 1983 Social Security bailout (a case described in the next chapter). Tax reform occurred because of an unusual ideological congruence between both branches and both parties, boosted by effective leadership that mustered the political will to stand up to the powerful interests opposing tax reform. The process was also characterized by flexibility and willingness to compromise—avoiding the temptation to draw lines in the sand. Unfortunately, these characteristics are rarely found in combination.

Economic and budget questions have been defining issues for America's two political parties. Because the presidency and Congress have been under divided party control for much of the last thirty years, the most prevalent pattern in budget and economic policymaking in recent years has been interbranch conflict that is predominantly partisan. This conflict has increased the use of extraordinary resolution. Some form of interbranch summit was employed to resolve the budget deadlock five times during the 1980s. In 1993, a unified Democratic Congress and president barely prevailed in the most partisan of atmospheres. The 1995–1996 budget stalemate resulted in multiple government shutdowns and more than a dozen temporary budgets. The question for the future is, will the 1997 balanced budget agreement end two decades of partisan wrangling and interbranch conflict, or is it just a respite? If an economic downturn were to occur, the deficits could start to grow again. Even if budget surpluses continue in the future, the two parties will stake out differences over what to do with excess revenues—shore up Social Security, pay off federal debt, start new programs, or cut taxes.

ENDNOTES

1. Lance T. LeLoup, *Budgetary Politics* 4th ed. (Brunswick, Ohio: King's Court, 1988): chapter 5.

2. Lyndon B. Johnson, *The Vantage Point: Perspectives on the Presidency 1963–1969* (New York: Holt, Rinehart and Winston, 1971): 440.

3. See Allen Schick (ed.), *Congress and the Making of Economic Policy* (Washington, D.C.: American Enterprise Institute, 1983).

4. Louis M. Hacker, *The Course of American Growth and Development* (New York: Wiley, 1970): 55.

5. See Daniel R. Fusfield, *The Age of the Economist* (Glenview, Ill.: Scott Foresman, 1982).

6. See John Wooley, *Monetary Politics* (New York: Cambridge University Press, 1984).

7. Robert Heilbroner, *The Making of Economic Society* (Englewood Cliffs, N.J.: Prentice-Hall, 1962): 122–123.

8. See Robert Lekachman, *The Age of Keynes* (New York: Random House, 1966).

9. See Larry Berman, *The Office of Management and Budget and the Presidency 1921–79* (Princeton, N.J.: Princeton University Press, 1979).

10. Steven K. Bailey, *Congress Makes a Law* (New York: Columbia University Press, 1950): 57–58.

11. The original name of the committee was the Joint Committee on the Economic Report of the President.

12. Richard Neustadt, *Presidential Power* (New York: Wiley, 1960): chapter 4.

13. Congressional Budget Office, *The Fiscal Response to Inflation* (January 1979): 67.

14. Friedman's general political and economic ideas are discussed in Milton Friedman, *Capitalism and Freedom* (Chicago: University of Chicago Press, 1962).

15. D. I. Museman and A. B. Laffer, *The Phenomenon of Worldwide Inflation* (Washington, D.C.: American Enterprise Institute, 1975).

16. *Congressional Quarterly Weekly Report* (April 15, 1989): 804–805.

17. James Anderson, "Managing the Economy: The Johnson Experience," paper presented at the American Political Science Association Annual Meeting, August 27–30, 1980: 6.

18. LeLoup (note 1): 108.

19. Chester Newland, "Executive Office Policy Apparatus: Enforcing the Reagan Agenda," in Lester M. Salamon and Michael S. Lund (eds.), *The Reagan Presidency and the Governing of America* (Washington, D.C.: Urban Institute Press, 1984): 135–168.

20. See *Wall Street Journal* (August 3, 1989): A16.

21. Lance T. LeLoup, *The Fiscal Congress: Legislative Control of the Budget* (Westport, Conn.: Greenwood Press, 1980): 6.

22. Jesse Burkhead, "Federal Budgetary Developments, 1947–48," *Public Administration Review* 8 (Autumn 1948): 267–274.

23. Woolley (note 6): 154.

24. See Louis Fisher, *Presidential Spending Power* (Princeton, N.J.: Princeton University Press, 1975).

25. See Allen Schick, *Congress and Money* (Washington, D.C.: Urban Institute Press, 1980).

26. Lance T. LeLoup et al., "Deficit Politics and Constitutional Government: The Impact of Gramm-Rudman-Hollings," *Public Budgeting and Finance* 7 (Spring 1987): 83–103.

27. *Congressional Record* (June 24, 1981): H3270.

28. Lance T. LeLoup, "After the Blitz: Reagan and the U.S. Congressional Budget Process," *Legislative Studies Quarterly* 7 (August 1982): 321–339.

29. Ibid., 325.

30. *Congressional Record* (June 25, 1984): H3382.

31. LeLoup (note 28): 333.

32. *Congressional Quarterly Almanac 1995* (Washington, D.C.: Congressional Quarterly Inc, 1996): 2–90.

33. Benjamin Weiser, "High-Tech Firms Decry Frivolous Suits," *Washington Post* (March 7, 1995): D3.

34. *Congressional Quarterly Almanac* (1995): 2–91.

35. Ibid., 2–92.

36. Jerry Knight, "A Measure of Security on Securities Suits," *Washington Post* (December 7, 1995): B11.

37. John F. Harris and Sharon Walsh, "Clinton Vetoes Measure to Limit Securities Suits," *Washington Post* (December 20, 1995): A8.

38. Ronald F. King, "Tax Expenditures and Systematic Public Policy," *Public Budgeting and Finance* 4 (Spring 1984): 21.

39. See Catherine Rudder, "Fiscal Responsibility and the Revenue Committees," in Lawrence Dodd and Bruce Oppenheimer (eds.), *Congress Reconsidered*, 3d ed. (Washington, D.C.: Congressional Quarterly Press, 1985): 221–224.

40. Jeffrey H. Birnbaum and Alan S. Murray, *Showdown at Gucci Gulch: Lawmakers, Lobbyists, and the Unlikely Triumph of Tax Reform* (New York: Random House, 1988): 4.

41. Ibid., 124–126.

42. "Clinton's Budget: No Cover for GOP," *Congressional Quarterly Almanac 1995* (Washington, D.C.: Congressional Quarterly Inc., 1996): 2–5.

43. "GOP Throws Down Budget Gauntlet," Ibid., 2–30.

44. See Linda Kowalcky and Lance T. LeLoup, "Congress and the Politics of Statutory Debt Limitation," *Public Administration Review* 53:1 (Jan/Feb 1993): 14–27.

45. Richard L. Berke, "Clinton's Ratings over 50% in Poll as G.O.P. Declines," *New York Times* (December 14, 1995): A1.

46. *Congressional Quarterly Weekly Report* (January 6, 1996): 53.

47. Ibid., 53–55.

48. *Congressional Quarterly Weekly Report* (January 27, 1996): 213.

8

SOCIAL WELFARE POLICY

This day, in the name of reform, this Senate will do actual violence to poor children, putting millions of them into poverty who were not in poverty before.
—SENATOR CAROL MOSELEY-BRAUN (D-ILL.), JULY 1996

I believe history will praise this day, because I believe a system that has failed in every single aspect will now be thrown away, and we will start over with a new system that has a chance of giving people an opportunity instead of a handout.
—SENATOR PETE DOMENICI (R-N.M.), JULY 1996

In addition to crucial matters of war and peace, the promotion of economic prosperity, and the protection of the civil rights of citizens, governments also grapple with questions of the distribution of wealth and the protection of the poor, the elderly, and the sick. From countries in which a small elite barely shares any wealth with the masses to the "cradle to grave" welfare states of Scandinavia, nations adopt policies that affect social welfare and economic equity among their citizens. In the United States, social welfare policies are influenced by values rooted deep in the nation's history and political culture. Although Americans have a more egalitarian tradition and a less rigid class structure than many other developed nations, questions of wealth and poverty and disputes about "fairness" and "social justice" cause intense political division and policy conflict. Those issues frequently divide Republicans and Democrats, presidents and Congresses.

Unlike a budget, which must be approved every year, social welfare policy is periodically the subject of public concern and policy innovation, interspersed with longer periods of relative dormancy. Only extraordinary circumstances, such as the impending bankruptcy of Social Security, can create inexorable pressure to act.

When such forcing mechanisms are absent, social welfare policies require long-term political mobilization to create major changes, much like civil rights. This chapter first explores the evolution of social welfare policies in the United States from the 1930s to today. The most dramatic recent change in social welfare policy occurred in 1996 with comprehensive welfare reform, ending welfare as a federal entitlement after sixty years, and turning responsibility over to the states.

Yet many social welfare issues remain unresolved. The failure of the Clinton administration's health care reform left more than 35 million Americans still without health insurance. And despite the bipartisan balanced budget agreement reached in 1997, the consequences of the impending retirement of the baby boomers on Social Security and Medicare benefits has not been fully addressed. The chapter also examines the policy environment in terms of the existence of poverty, the distribution of wealth and income, public attitudes, and the nature of partisan and ideological cleavages over policies to help the nation's "have-nots." Finally, we look at how social welfare policy is made. The four cases show different patterns of presidential-congressional policymaking and their consequences.

THE EVOLUTION OF SOCIAL WELFARE POLICY

Rugged individualism, materialism, the work ethic, and respect for private property rights were important values in early America.[1] Land was plentiful and cheap compared with Europe. Because there was no nobility in America, there was no sense of "noblesse oblige": the view that the wealthy and powerful had a duty to help the poor. Respect for these values, and ease of access to opportunity, created a general belief that people were largely responsible for their own condition.[2] Accordingly, economic inequality was accepted as part of the natural order. Just as a person could gain great wealth, most people believed that the poor would always be with us. Economic historian Louis Hacker observed:

> *Easy access to property led to . . . acceptance of the uneven distribution of wealth and income and the private decisions made by entrepreneurs. . . . If the man who became wealthy did so because he was an innovator, good for him; . . . the whole society benefited along with him. If the doors of opportunity were open and people could rise, fluidity in the class structure was inevitable.[3]*

The industrial revolution and the transformation of the American economy from agrarian to industrial widened the gap in wealth between rich and poor. Americans were not without sympathy for the elderly, the disabled, and the infirm, who were provided for through private charity. However, not until the Progressive era at the turn of the twentieth century was serious consideration given to the view that poverty may be the result of the social and economic system. Robert Hunter's *Poverty,* published in 1904 and based on his years in the backstreet tenements of New York, suggested that although there is a poverty that "some men deserve," there is also a poverty born of "unjust social conditions which punish the good and the pure."[4]

While Otto von Bismark was establishing a social security system in Germany in the 1880s and other nations in Europe followed suit, the dominant view in the United States continued to be that poverty was a private problem, not a public one. It took the economic ravages of the Great Depression in the 1930s to make the federal government accept the responsibility of protecting the social welfare of its citizens. It was a difficult transition, which required a major political realignment and the emergence of the Democratic New Deal coalition under President Franklin D. Roosevelt. In 1929, Republican President Herbert Hoover proclaimed in his inaugural address that the United States was in sight of the day "when poverty will be banished from this nation."[5] Yet only a few years later, shantytowns populated with the hungry, homeless unemployed were cynically called "Hoovervilles," after the president who opposed any government dole for the poor. Refusing to budge from this view, Hoover was buried in the landslide election of FDR in 1932.[6]

The Social Security Act of 1935

When he took office, Roosevelt did not have a program or specific set of policies in mind. He was clear, however, in his commitment to use the resources of government aggressively to improve the welfare of the millions of Americans who were suffering from the Depression. Roosevelt assembled a group of international scholars and experts—the "brain trust"—to study the experience of European nations that had already adopted more extensive social welfare systems. His Cabinet Committee on Economic Security considered proposals, both evolutionary and revolutionary. Because the Constitution contained no explicit authorization for a comprehensive social welfare program, the administration feared that the Supreme Court might strike down the legislation, as it had other New Deal programs. Roosevelt's advisors disagreed over the issue of whether the national government or the states should have primary responsibility. Labor Secretary Frances Perkins favored state management, and Roosevelt's close personal advisor Harry Hopkins favored national control. In the end, a mixture of both was chosen. The political environment was highly supportive of action, and the president enjoyed huge Democratic majorities in both houses of Congress. Pressure to act was building up; Louisiana's charismatic Governor Huey Long proposed a radical "Share the Wealth" plan that would "soak the rich." Against this backdrop, the administration submitted a Social Security bill to Congress in 1935.

The drafters settled on two kinds of programs, contributory and noncontributory. In the contributory programs, both employers and employees would pay into a trust fund and receive benefits when they retired or were laid off. Anyone who contributed—regardless of income—would be entitled to benefits. Noncontributory programs would provide assistance for people with no means of support, such as the elderly, the disabled, and dependent children. These programs were means-tested: Eligibility depended on income levels. Some critics felt the law would lead to socialism, but the bill was popular on Capitol Hill and sailed through Congress virtually intact. Roosevelt signed the Social Security Act into law in 1935.

The main feature of the law was the program called Social Security: Old Age Survivors Disability Insurance (OASDI). A contributory program, Social Security provided monthly payments to retirees, disabled workers, and their dependents. Determined that the program would not be dismantled by a Republican president or Congress in future years, each contributor was assigned an account (Social Security number) in which their earning history was recorded to assure benefits when needed. Social Security became extremely popular with the American public and remains so, to the point that politicians have found it difficult to modify. A national program, it is administered by the Social Security Administration in Washington. Unlike an insurance program in which contributions are held and accrue earnings, Social Security runs on a "current financing" basis. Benefits are paid out of the trust fund from current contributions, with a reserve in the fund of around six to nine months. Social Security can get into financial trouble if the commitments to pay grow faster than the contributions from those working. It has no means test.

A second contributory program created by the 1935 Act was *unemployment compensation,* designed to provide income to those who lose their jobs. It is administered by the states, and benefits vary from one state to another. The program is funded by state and federal taxes on employers and no means test is required. Benefits usually last for twenty-six weeks. To qualify, recipients must prove that they are actively looking for a job.

The main noncontributory program created in 1935 was *Aid to Families with Dependent Children* (AFDC), commonly called *welfare.* The program was administered by states, which determined benefit levels and eligibility. Benefits varied greatly from state to state. In 1988, benefits were five times higher in Alaska than Mississippi, for example. Originally, eligibility also varied; some states paid benefits only to one-parent families. AFDC was funded jointly by states and the federal government and was means tested. All of this was changed in 1996 with the adoption of comprehensive welfare reform. Unlike Social Security, AFDC was never very popular. It embodied the notion of a "giveaway," and recipients were often called "welfare bums" or worse. Other noncontributory means-tested programs created by the Social Security Act included Old Age Assistance (OAA), Aid to the Blind (AB), and Aid to the Disabled (AD). These were designed to help the elderly and others who were not eligible for Social Security payments. In 1974, these programs were consolidated as *Supplementary Security Income* (SSI), financed and administered by the federal government.

Much of the social welfare system in the United States was established by the landmark Social Security Act of 1935. With a highly supportive political environment, forceful presidential leadership, and a responsive Congress, it was a clear case of presidential leadership in policymaking. Today, Social Security is supported by the single largest expenditure in the federal budget. Although the act was a important policy innovation, it was influenced by traditional values and attitudes about poverty. One observer noted:

> *Poverty was considered a temporary condition due to unemployment, agricultural depression or the dependence of youth, or it was considered a condition due to individual problems such as blindness, or old age. Welfare was assumed to be a temporary measure which would end with rising employment and national income.*[7]

The 1960s War on Poverty

Extraordinary economic circumstances prompted the expansion of social welfare policies in the 1930s. New Deal policies and World War II finally brought the U.S. economy back to full employment, and the 1940s and 1950s were decades of relative prosperity. Poverty and social problems were removed from the public mind and the policy agenda. In the 1960s, however, misery and poverty in America were rediscovered. During the 1960 presidential campaign, John F. Kennedy, traveling though West Virginia while campaigning in that state's crucial Democratic primary, was shocked at the rural poverty he observed. If elected, he promised, something would be done about it. Public awareness of squalor in the midst of plenty was heightened with the publication of Michael Harrington's *The Other America.*[8] Poverty in urban slums became linked to the national struggle for civil rights. By 1964, social welfare issues resumed a prominent place on the national policy agenda.

Once again, presidential leadership was the catalyst. Assuming the presidency after the assassination of Kennedy, Lyndon Johnson declared war on poverty and proposed several "Great Society" programs to eradicate it from the country. The case of presidential leadership in this chapter deals with the Economic Opportunity Act of 1964, an important new initiative that created programs significantly different from the Social Security Act thirty years earlier. Instead of cash transfers through contributory and noncontributory programs, the act established new agencies and services to help the poor directly. Programs created by the Economic Opportunity Act included the Neighborhood Youth Corps, Head Start, the Job Corps, and work-study and literacy programs. The War on Poverty created great expectations, but many of its agencies and programs were under attack only a few years later.

The Great Society program with the most significant long-term financial implications for the nation was the Medicare Act of 1965. By this time, most western industrialized nations had adopted some form of national health care or government insurance to help pay health care costs. Although President Harry Truman had proposed a national health insurance plan in the 1940s, it was strongly opposed by Republicans. The medical establishment, particularly the American Medical Association, opposed any policy that would lead to what they called "socialized medicine."[9] Key congressional leaders, such as House Ways and Means Committee Chairman Wilbur Mills (D-Ark.), had long opposed any national health care programs. However, Lyndon Johnson's landslide election in 1964 and enhanced Democratic majorities in Congress made it possible to enact a program to provide health care for the elderly. Mills's decision to support Medicare legislation helped insure its passage. With growing support in Congress for Medicare, supporters expanded it to include Medicaid—assistance to the poor for paying their medical bills. Medicare, which is not means tested, and Medicaid, which is, have become the fastest growing items in the federal budget.

The Growth of Entitlements

The War on Poverty was short-lived, swept aside in the growing national preoccupation with the Vietnam War in the late 1960s. Many of the Great Society programs were controversial, and social welfare proposals increasingly divided government along partisan lines. Liberal Democrats wanted to see benefits expanded; they complained that eligibility requirements were too restrictive and variations in benefit levels too great. Conservatives charged that the programs were failures, rife with fraud and abuse, and that welfare recipients should have to work for their government checks. Richard Nixon offered a Family Assistance plan to revamp the welfare system. Surprisingly liberal for a Republican president, this plan would have set a minimum level of income below which the government would pay families rather than tax them. But despite some bipartisan appeal, the program bogged down in Congress, where Nixon lacked the clout of Roosevelt or Johnson.

After the failure of the Family Assistance plan, initiatives to restructure health care, Social Security, or the welfare system proved impossible to pass. An attempt to revamp AFDC in 1977 failed to clear Congress. The most important development in the 1970s in social welfare was the rapid growth of entitlements. Entitlements—benefits guaranteed to recipients if they meet certain eligibility requirements—mushroomed from $65 billion in 1970 to $267 billion in 1980, an increase of over 400 percent.[10] As a share of the budget, social welfare entitlements increased from 33 percent of outlays in 1970 to 47 percent in 1980. Part of the increase was a result of high inflation in the 1970s, but much of the growth was attributable to the liberalization and expansion of programs. Large increases in Social Security benefits were approved in the early 1970s, including a 15 percent increase in 1970 and a 20 percent increase in 1972, both election years. Medicare was expanded to include the disabled. Supplemental Security Income consolidated and expanded benefit programs for those not eligible for Social Security. Social Security benefits were "indexed" in 1972: Benefits automatically increased as the consumer price index rose. The expansion of benefits put a financial strain on the Social Security Trust Fund, requiring a major increase in payroll taxes in 1977. Food stamps, an entitlement begun in the late 1960s, rose 1000 percent in a decade. Conservatives became concerned about the exploding costs of social welfare programs.

Attempts to Limit Growth of Entitlements

Ronald Reagan's election in 1980 was followed by a flurry of legislative activity reminiscent of the Roosevelt and Johnson presidencies. As we saw in Chapter 7, plans to curtail entitlement growth were part of the administration's comprehensive budget and economic policy revisions. Yet the president was careful to claim that the "social safety net" would be protected, particularly the popular Social Security program. The administration pledged to eliminate unintended benefits, reduce benefits for middle- and upper-income recipients, and to consolidate and eliminate less crucial programs. House Democrats were able to block some of the cuts, but the administration succeeded in restricting eligibility for food stamps, tightening eligibility for AFDC, eliminating extended unemployment compensation benefits, increasing deductible copayments for Medicare recipients, cutting federal Medicaid reimbursements to the states, and eliminating Social Security benefits for college students. Nonetheless, the administration was disappointed in the reductions it had achieved.[11] Congress rejected most of the subsequent cuts proposed by the Reagan administration through the 1980s, and as deficits grew, budget issues became increasingly divisive.

Democrats accused the administration of trying to balance the budget on the backs of the poor. Despite the tax increase in 1977, the Social Security system was again threatened with bankruptcy in the early 1980s. Congressional Democrats used the Social Security issue in election campaigns, accusing Republicans of attempting to cut benefits to the elderly. A proposal floated by the administration in 1981 to make major cuts in Social Security resulted in an outcry from senior citizens and congressional Democrats. The issue was used against Republicans again in the 1982 midterm elections. The Social Security bailout case in this chapter explores in detail how it took extraordinary resolution, using a bipartisan commission, to break the deadlock and restore the financial solvency of the system. Revamping of the welfare system remained stalled between the Republican presidency and Democratic Congress through most of the 1980s. Not until 1996, when President Clinton and the Republican Congress resolved partisan differences, was the welfare system overhauled. This case of interbranch cooperation is presented in this chapter.

Throughout the 1990s, entitlement spending, particularly for health care, increased far more rapidly than the rest of the budget. However, just as in the 1980s, the issue was politicized and often used to frighten voters. The 1990 deficit reduction package included some proposals that would cut the rate of growth of Medicare, but did little to stop the spiraling growth. With the election of Bill Clinton in 1992, reforms much more ambitious than Medicare reform were put on the policy agenda.

The Failure of Health Care Reform

One of the most important developments in U.S. social welfare policy is legislation that failed to pass—the Clinton comprehensive health care reform proposals of 1994. Despite the existence of unified Democratic party control of both Congress and the presidency for the first time in twelve years, not even a watered-down compromise bill could pass. Advances in medical technology have given the United States the most sophisticated health care system in the world, but also the most expensive. Health care spending, including both public and private, is over 14 percent of GDP and still rising. More and more Americans are living beyond eighty years and 40 percent of all government outlays for health care go to persons in the last six months of their lives. In addition to rising costs, 38 million people or 15 percent of the population have no health insurance at all. All of these factors propelled President Clinton to make health care reform one of his top domestic priorities during the 1992 campaign.

Clinton spent 1993 concentrating on the deficit reduction package that narrowly passed. The budget package was not popular, but public support for health care reform remained high. Clinton named his wife, Hillary Rodham Clinton, to head up the administration task force to formulate health care reform. The process of sorting through all the expert recommendations took over nine months. The range of options ran from a single-payer system (such as in Canada) to more modest reforms, using existing private insurance and Medicare. The administration chose the middle ground and in late 1993 unveiled its 1200-page plan. It would do several things:

- require all employers to provide health care insurance for their workers (75 percent already did)
- create a series of purchasing alliances in the states that would operate like health maintenance organizations (HMOs) to provide competition and reduce costs
- create a National Health Board to monitor the system and impose cost controls if needed
- expand Medicare to cover the poor and unemployed and cover the cost of prescriptions for senior citizens

In his 1994 State of the Union address, Clinton dramatically pulled out a pen and promised to veto any bill that would not provide universal health care coverage. As Congress took up the president's bill, interest groups went into action. Reception on Capitol Hill was lukewarm at best, and Republicans openly attacked the plan. Senator Arlen Spector (R-Pa.) unveiled a huge chart showing the frightening bureaucracy that the administration plan would create. Republicans accused Clinton of nothing less than a "government takeover of health care." A coalition of big insurance companies, hospitals, and doctors launched a massive national media campaign against the plan. The blitz of negative spots featured "Harry and Louise," Mr. and Mrs. Average American, talking about rationing of services, losing choice, and government takeover. Support for the president's plan dwindled. Even Democrats largely ignored the administration's proposal and developed their own alternatives.

The president would never get the chance to veto a compromise bill as he had promised. As summer 1994 arrived, Republicans sensed that the political tide had turned in their favor. They refused to even consider scaled-back health care proposals, and used the filibuster and other dilatory tactics to block administration proposals. By September, the administration conceded that health care reform was dead.

The failure of health care reform is important in the evolution of social welfare policy in the United States. The political environment was initially supportive of health care reform, with the public strongly supporting both universal coverage and mandatory employer coverage. But opponents were able to tap into deep public cynicism and mistrust of government.[12] There were serious flaws in the policy design, a plan that was overly complex and bureaucratic. The process of presidential formulation had been closed, not allowing potential opponents to participate in the process. Because of internal divisions within the Democratic party, Clinton was not able to prevail, even under unified party control of government. The failure of health care reform meant that health insurance in the United States would continue to be dominated by the private sector, that costs for treating the uninsured would fall on providers, and that the costs of medical care would continue to rise.

Health care reform was not only a policy failure for President Clinton, it was a political disaster as well. It contributed to his falling public support and the Republican sweep in the 1994 elections. Ironically, two years later, under the divided government that resulted from those elections, the most significant social welfare policy change in thirty years emerged: comprehensive welfare reform. It eliminated AFDC, the federal guarantee to help the nation's poor that had existed since 1935. Welfare recipients were required to work for benefits, and most of the responsibility for welfare was turned over to the states.

THE ENVIRONMENT FOR SOCIAL WELFARE POLICY

Wealth and Poverty in the United States

The context for presidential-congressional policymaking in social welfare begins with the existence of deprivation in American society: the existence of poverty, hunger, homelessness, and inadequate health care. The gap between rich and poor—measured by the distribution of wealth and income—is another potentially important environmental factor. The federal government has had an official definition of poverty since 1964, when the Social Security Administration computed the "poverty line" at an income level three times the cost of an economy food plan (assuming the poor spend one-third of their income on food).[13] The figure was $3,000 for a family of four in 1964 compared with around $16,000 in 1997. Despite many complaints about the inadequacy of the official poverty measure, the government has not been able to agree on an alternative.

Under the official definition, the percentage of Americans living below the poverty line between 1959 (measured retroactively) and 1995 is shown in Figure 8.1. Some effects of the economic boom of the 1960s and the War on Poverty programs can be seen. Between 1959 and 1973, the percentage of poor was cut in half, from

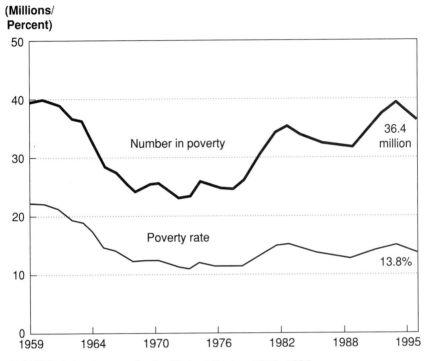

**(Millions/
Percent)**

FIGURE 8.1   **Poverty in the United States, 1959–1995.**

Source: U.S. Bureau of the Census, March Current Population Survey, 1997.

22.4 percent of the population to 11.1 percent. Since 1973, however, the percentage has crept back up, hitting 15 percent in 1983 and again in 1993 after economic recessions. Economic recovery afterwards lowered the figure to 13.8 percent by 1995. That translates into 36.4 million Americans living in poverty, as shown in Figure 8.1.[14]

The incidence of poverty varies in accordance with demographic characteristics such as race, age, gender, and type of family unit.[15] Blacks are three times more likely than whites to live in poverty and Hispanics twice as likely. Since the early 1970s, a feminization of poverty has occurred, measured by the number of single-parent households headed by a female. By the 1980s, almost half of these households were below the poverty line. More than half of the 35 million poor in the United States are children. Conversely, poverty rates for the elderly have dropped sharply since 1970. The elderly now constitute the most affluent age cohort in the country. Approximately one-third of the poor received AFDC benefits before welfare reform in 1996. With welfare reform and a robust economy, the number of welfare recipients has plummeted around the country from 12.8 million to below 10 million. Welfare reform also reduced the 25.8 million Americans who received food stamps in 1996.[16]

At the same time that the incidence of poverty has fallen, the gap between rich and poor in the United States has widened. Wealth (the amount of money and other assets owned) is less equitably distributed than income. The top 10 percent of the population owns one-third of the nation's private wealth and owns 62 percent of all corporate stock. In 1970, the richest 1 percent of families in the United States held 27 percent of the wealth. By 1995, the figure had grown to 36 percent, near the peak share attained in 1929. At the bottom of the economic ladder, the poorest 10 percent of the population had what economists amusingly call "negative wealth": they owed more than they owned. Income is somewhat less skewed. Table 8.1 shows the proportion of income received by Americans divided into fifths (quintiles) from 1950 to 1995. The gap between rich and poor has steadily increased since 1970. By 1995, the bottom fifth received only 4.4 percent of all income compared with 5.4 percent in 1970. At the other end, the top fifth received 46.5 percent of all income in 1995 compared with 40.9 percent in 1970. Annual income for the poorest fifth of Americans has declined in real purchasing power by one-third since 1970, and income for the middle class (the middle three-fifths) has declined in real terms as well. At the same time, the number of top executives earning more than a million dollars per year increased fifty times.

Public Attitudes and Partisan Cleavages

These figures might seem to suggest that the political environment would be highly supportive of social welfare initiatives to help the poor. In fact, the public does *not* generally support welfare programs or policies to redistribute income. Figure 8.2 shows that Americans' views on the responsibility of the government to guarantee a minimum income and policies that would redistribute income from rich to poor remains significantly different from public opinion in other nations. However, support for Social Security is nearly unanimous. Despite growing concern over the underclass, the homeless, and families without health insurance, the vast majority of Americans supported the 1996 welfare reform bill that eliminated AFDC.

TABLE 8.1   Distribution of Income: Percentage Share of Income Received by Each Fifth of Families, 1950–1995

	1950	1960	1970	1980	1984	1988	1995
Poorest fifth	4.5	4.8	5.4	5.1	4.7	4.6	4.4
Second fifth	12.0	12.2	12.2	11.6	11.0	10.7	10.1
Third fifth	17.4	17.8	17.6	17.5	17.0	16.7	15.8
Fourth fifth	23.4	24.0	23.8	24.3	24.4	24.0	23.2
Richest fifth	42.7	41.3	40.9	41.6	42.9	44.0	46.5

Source: U.S. Bureau of the Census, 1997.

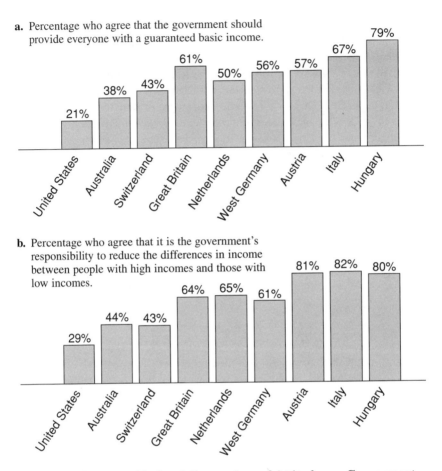

a. Percentage who agree that the government should provide everyone with a guaranteed basic income.

b. Percentage who agree that it is the government's responsibility to reduce the differences in income between people with high incomes and those with low incomes.

FIGURE 8.2 **Cross-National Comparison of Attitudes on Government and Economic Equity.**

Source: The American Enterprise (May/April 1990): 113.

For decades, Republicans and Democrats have had sharply different social welfare agendas. Conservative opposition to the liberal "welfare state" took shape during the implementation of Roosevelt's New Deal. Since the 1930s, social welfare policies have also often reflected deep divisions between the parties. Studies of roll-call voting in Congress showed that partisanship was pronounced on social welfare policy issues.[17] After the 1972 campaign, when Nixon attacked Democratic nominee George McGovern's guaranteed income plan, partisan and ideological cleavages between branches hardened.

The debate heated up in the 1980s, when the failures of the War on Poverty were attacked. Charles Murray created a stir with his book, *Losing Ground,* which argued that the condition of poor people—particularly blacks—had worsened during the 1960s and 1970s despite the rapid increase in federal spending.[18] Murray concluded that the poverty programs of the 1960s created perverse incentives that encouraged idleness, fostered welfare dependency, led fathers to abandon families, and discouraged working. Critics on the left were quick to attack Murray's conclusions. Michael Harrington, who helped launch the War on Poverty, argued that Murray ignored the reduction in poverty among the elderly, improvements in health care, and gains in nutrition.[19] John Schwartz's study, *America's Hidden Success,* concluded that far from causing more poverty, the programs had led to dramatic improvements in a number of areas.[20]

The election of Democrat Bill Clinton in 1992 began to change the nature of partisan divisions on social welfare policy. As governor of Arkansas, Clinton had championed welfare reform, and pledged during his presidential campaign to "end welfare as we know it." As he had with the balanced budget and some other issues, Clinton moved to the center, partially co-opting a traditional Republican issue. As welfare reform was debated in the 1990s, this political shift caused divisions within the Democratic party. Although more moderate Democrats were glad to be on the right side of a popular issue, traditional liberals decried the president's abandonment of the poor. Republicans, however, were alternatively pleased that Clinton was moving in their direction and irritated that they were losing a good issue to the Democrats.

The successful bipartisan collaboration on welfare reform did not depoliticize social welfare issues. Democrats had long played on public fears that Republicans would make cuts in the popular entitlements for the elderly—Social Security and Medicare. In 1996, Democrats and their allies in organized labor accused House Speaker Newt Gingrich and the Republicans of threatening Medicare. In fact, both parties had proposed substantial cuts in Medicare as part of the negotiations to balance the budget. Nonetheless, just as public perception of Democrats as favoring high taxes helps Republicans, public perception that Republicans would favor cuts in entitlements for the elderly helps Democrats and continues to be used as an electoral issue.

The Continued Growth of Social Welfare Entitlements

The fact that Social Security and Medicare are such popular programs has often stifled rational debate and made it more difficult to develop responsible long-term solutions. Although welfare reform in 1996 represented significant savings for the federal government—an estimated $55 billion over five years—welfare spending is only a tiny fraction of entitlement spending. Figure 8.3 compares the amount of projected spending by the federal government in the year 2000 on the popular non–means-tested entitlements compared with the means-tested programs that help the poor. The two largest programs, Social Security and Medicare, will cost nearly $700 billion. This is almost *ten times* more than Food Stamps, Supplemental Security Income, and Family Assistance (welfare) combined.

Despite the balanced budget agreement reached in 1997, the rapid growth of spending for Medicare and Social Security poses a serious problem for policymakers in the twenty-first century. In 1996, spending for these two entitlements was equivalent to 7 percent of the nation's GDP. By the year 2030, Congressional Budget Office projections show that share of the economy doubling to 14 percent.[21] As the baby boomers begin to retire in 2010, demands on both programs will increase dramatically. This means that the younger generations will be required to pay significantly more without much assurance that comparable benefit levels will be available when they retire. Figure 8.4 examines the projected growth in spending in Social Security and Medicare through the year 2070. Dealing with the growth in these programs remains unpopular with the public and difficult for politicians. But if changes are not made relatively soon, more dramatic and radical solutions will likely have to be found later on.

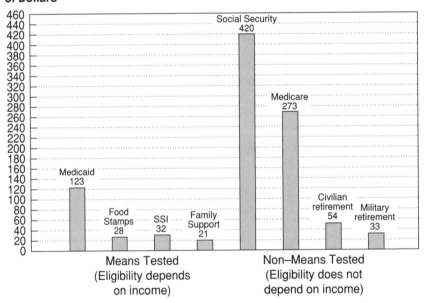

FIGURE 8.3   Projected Social Welfare Spending (Billions of Dollars, FY 2000).

Source: Congressional Budget Office, 1997.

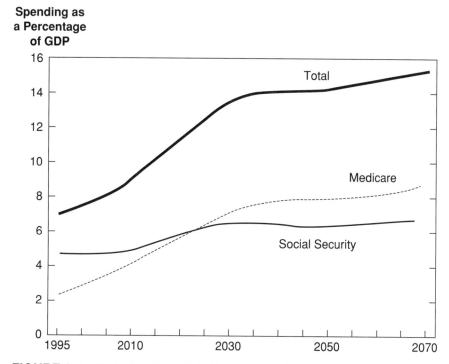

FIGURE 8.4 Projected Growth in Spending for Social Security and Medicare, Calendar Years 1995–2070.

Source: Congressional Budget Office (1997) based on intermediate assumptions from the 1996 reports of the boards of trustees of the Social Security and Medicare trust funds.

MAKING SOCIAL WELFARE POLICY

Which branch shapes social welfare policy? Between 1933 and 1969, four of five presidents were Democrats. Leadership in social welfare emanated most frequently from the presidency, particularly Roosevelt, Truman, and Johnson. In the 1970s, most of the initiatives to expand social welfare responsibilities came from the Democratic majorities in Congress. In the 1980s, the Reagan administration attempted to scale back social welfare programs. In the 1990s, Clinton began by proposing a national health care plan but later worked with congressional Republicans to reform welfare. As in other policy areas, compared with earlier years, today there is more of an equal balance between congressional and presidential initiatives.

Unlike the budget, attention to social welfare issues varies over time, and presidents may create ad hoc organizations within the presidency to accomplish their goals. President Clinton engaged a massive task force to develop his plans for health care reform. President Johnson also assembled a high-powered team to develop the war on poverty. Most frequently, policy initiatives are more modest and handled through a subset of domestic policy advisors. Since the Republican takeover of Congress in 1994, the Clinton White House exerted influence more through negotiating with Congress than by offering new proposals. Clinton administration negotiators tried to shape policy by working with key congressional leaders in defining a set of parameters that the president would accept. The threat of a veto was one of the most important bargaining chips.

Party leaders in Congress have assumed a critical role in formulating social welfare policy and responses to presidential initiatives. Key committees in Congress include the House Ways and Means Committee and the Senate Finance Committee, which have jurisdiction over Social Security, AFDC, Medicare, Medicaid, and most entitlements. Banking committees in the House and Senate, the House Education and Labor committee, and the Senate Labor and Human Resources committee also play important roles in social welfare legislation. In the face of conflict and deadlock, smaller groups of party and committee leaders play an enhanced role in policymaking.

Other actors are important in the social welfare policy process. The growth of social welfare programs since the 1930s created a large bureaucracy in the federal executive branch. The Department of Health, Education, and Welfare (HEW) was created in 1953 to administer programs. It was divided into the Department of Education and the Department of Health and Human Services (HHS, eliminating the politically troublesome word *welfare* from the title) in 1979. In 1997, the two departments had some 140,000 employees and had a combined budget of over $600 billion, most of it in entitlement payments. But the budget's size and scope are no guarantee of influence in the White House or a place on the policy agenda.

Since the 1980s, the states have become key players in making national policy in the area of social welfare. States like Wisconsin were instrumental as policy laboratories in experimenting with various workfare programs and welfare reform. Operating through various organizations, such as the National Governors Conference, states have had significant policy impact.

Social Security and Medicare programs are supported by influential clientele and interest groups. The thirty million senior citizens are well organized and powerful, a potent voting bloc. Groups such as the American Association of Retired Persons (AARP), the National Committee to Preserve Social Security and Medicare, and other seniors' groups are able to flood the Hill with mail and lobbyists. Welfare mothers, in contrast, are fewer in numbers, unorganized, and relatively powerless. Their cause remains unpopular with the general public, which makes legislators skittish about any welfare issues. The four cases that follow show in more detail the changing role and responsibilities of various actors and the different patterns of legislative-executive policymaking in the social welfare arena.

PRESIDENTIAL LEADERSHIP:
THE ECONOMIC OPPORTUNITY ACT (1964)

Weeks after assuming the presidency following the assassination of John F. Kennedy, President Lyndon Johnson wanted to launch his presidency with a bold initiative— one that bore his imprimatur, not Kennedy's. Since Kennedy's domestic agenda was mostly stalled on Capitol Hill, there was a tendency to see Johnson's program as a compendium of unfinished business.[22] Despite facing the same congressional majorities, Johnson recognized that he benefited from a mood of national cooperation. In addition, he brought to the White House his record for effective legislative leadership from his tenure as Senate Majority Leader during the 1950s. With an election only ten months away, members of Congress were mindful of their own electoral fortunes as they considered new social welfare legislation.

Johnson's decision to launch a War on Poverty was signaled on January 5, 1964, only three days before his state of the union address to a joint session of Congress. The White House released a three-page statement on a task force report entitled "One Third of a Nation," promising a "program to attack the roots of poverty."[23] The report was authored by Daniel P. Moynihan, an undersecretary of Labor who had been appointed by Kennedy. Three days later, in his nationally televised address, Johnson declared his antipoverty goals to the nation.

Anxious to get his proposals to Congress, Johnson ordered his staff into high gear to produce a plan. Several Kennedy proposals were still pending in Congress, including the Youth Employment Act and a bill for a domestic peace corps. Johnson wanted a more comprehensive program to attack the roots of poverty and, for political reasons, one that was uniquely his. On January 31, the president named Sargent Shriver to serve as his special assistant to develop the War on Poverty proposals. Shriver, highly successful as head of the Peace Corps, had a "can do" reputation of innovation and effective public relations. Shriver chose Moynihan, Adam Yarmolinsky from the Defense Department, and James Sundquist from the Department of Agriculture to join his task force in drafting the legislation.[24]

John Donovan, who chronicled the passage of the War on Poverty, noted the absence of any Texas influence in the key group, which was a "team of Eastern liberal intellectual-politicians under the leadership of a member of the Kennedy family."[25] Although other agencies and administration figures had input into the process, the Shriver task force took charge. Suspicious of old-line bureaucratic interests, the drafters sought a way to administer the program that would avoid agency turf battles. They suggested creating a new agency—staffed by younger, more aggressive personnel—rather than assigning new functions to an existing department.[26] This was a potential threat to the Department of Labor, HEW, and other agencies, but the task force had strong presidential backing. The poverty program would be administered by a new entity, the Office of Economic Opportunity (OEO), located in the Executive Office of the President and reporting directly to the president.

The Economic Opportunity Act's approach to reducing poverty was fundamentally different from that of the Social Security Act of thirty years earlier. Rather than create entitlements, the act created a number of services and programs to serve the poor directly.[27] Title I created three youth programs that were similar to the Kennedy programs already pending. A new addition was a work-study program to aid college students. Title II, urban and rural community action programs (CAPs), was an entirely new creation and a dramatic policy innovation. Title III of the act was a rural poverty program, authorizing the OEO to make grants to low-income rural families. Title IV allowed the OEO director to make loans to employers to create stable jobs for long-term unemployed and low-income families. Title V, "Family Unity through Jobs," provided for grants to carry out pilot job training and work projects for AFDC recipients. Title VI created the Office of Economic Opportunity to administer and coordinate the programs.

Title II, proposing CAPs, contained the most radical new element of the administration plan. CAPs were programs that (1) mobilized both public and private resources to attack poverty, (2) provided direct services and assistance to the poor, (3) would include "maximum feasible participation" of the poor, and (4) would be administered by a nonprofit group rather than by existing agencies.[28] The concept of a CAP was inherently "anti-establishment," creating competing centers of power in local government to obtain resources and develop new programs. Although easily approved by Congress, CAPs would prove to be the most controversial part of the new law.

The Economic Opportunity Act was conceived of and written in a matter of weeks, and sent to Capitol Hill on March 16, 1964. Congress responded quickly. An ad hoc subcommittee of the House Education and Labor Committee opened hearings on the bill the next day, with Adam Clayton Powell (D-N.Y.) as chair. The bill moved quickly through committee; Republican efforts to make changes in the legislation were turned aside. The committee had a tradition of division between majority and minority factions, but rarely were Republicans completely ignored as they were with this bill.[29] In three weeks of hearings, dozens of witnesses testified in favor of the bill, with only a handful of opponents appearing before the subcommittee. Donovan wrote, "testimony was largely in terms of generalities; the questioning, by and large, was anything but probing."[30] The potentially divisive CAPs received scant attention.

Conservative Congressman Phil Landrum (D-Ga.) was chosen to manage the bill on the House floor. This decision troubled some civil rights and labor groups, but the administration, confident that northern liberals would support the president's program, sought to garner support from southern Democrats. With an election approaching, the Democratic administration was not bothered by Republican opposition to the bill. Congress made some changes in the bill, but in less important titles. Two new programs for adult literacy and assistance for migrant farm workers were added by legislators. In the Senate, some changes were made to the provisions dealing with rural poverty programs.

Aided by aggressive lobbying, the Economic Opportunity Act sailed through the same Congress that bottled up less ambitious programs the year before under

President Kennedy. The Senate adopted the bill on July 23 by a comfortable 61 to 34 margin,[31] and two weeks later, the House passed the bill by 226 to 185. Of the 100 southern Democrats, 60 supported the administration. Republicans opposed the bill 22 to 145. There was a price to be paid for the support of southern Democrats. Adam Yarmolinsky, one of the key architects of the administration program, managed to antagonize several crucial Democrats. To assure southern votes, Shriver had to agree to exclude Yarmolinsky from the Office of Economic Opportunity once it was organized.[32]

What factors produced presidential leadership of policymaking in this case? The Economic Opportunity Act was reminiscent of Roosevelt's hundred days. It was drafted in the executive branch and enacted by Congress within months, with few revisions. Observers of the process concluded, "Congress was asked not to draft the War on Poverty, but rather, to ratify a fully prepared Administration program, and invited, though hardly encouraged, to propose marginal changes."[33] Although the majorities in Congress were the same as they had been in 1963, the political environment and presidential leadership had changed.

What were the results of the Economic Opportunity Act? Clearly, the policy was both timely and decisive. Despite the fact that it was a dramatic new approach to poverty, the bill was written in a matter of weeks and passed with minimal changes in a matter of months. Yet only a few years later, the OEO was under attack and even its most ardent supporters were disappointed. The debate over its effectiveness continues today, including serious questions about the design of the policy.

CONGRESSIONAL LEADERSHIP: CATASTROPHIC HEALTH CARE INSURANCE (1988–1989)

"Older Americans worry about two things—their finances and their health," said HHS Secretary Otis Bowen in 1987, "and wonder which will run out first."[34] As heath care costs spiraled in the 1980s, millions of citizens and their families faced financial ruin in case of catastrophic illness. Five percent of the population (disproportionately senior citizens) account for around 50 percent of all public and private health care costs in the United States. Under Medicare rules, as the costs of acute care for the elderly mounted, the proportion paid by the government would fall. After sixty days in the hospital, in 1987, beneficiaries had to make a copayment of $130 a day.[35] The copayment rose to $260 after ninety days, and Medicare payments ceased altogether after 150 days. Many of the more affluent elderly supplemented their health care coverage with private "medigap" policies, but the majority were vulnerable to catastrophic illness.

Congress had long wanted to do something about the growing problem. The obstacles were the budget crisis of the 1980s and doubt that President Reagan would support the expansion of any social welfare programs. Legislators saw their opening in the president's 1986 State of the Union address. Reagan directed the Secretary of Health and Human Services to develop recommendations "on how the private sector and government can work together to address the problems of affordable insurance for those whose life savings would otherwise be threatened when catastrophic illness strikes."[36] Bowen issued a report on November 20, 1986, recommending an expansion of Medicare coverage to cap at $2000 per year the amount that any recipient would have to pay out of pocket for covered services.

The Bowen report was received more enthusiastically on Capitol Hill than in the White House. The administration was deeply divided over the recommendations; conservatives were adamantly opposed to a government program that would supplant private insurance. Embroiled in the Iran–Contra affair and recovering from prostate surgery, Reagan did nothing to resolve the controversy within his own administration. In his 1987 State of the Union address, he promised only to send legislation to Congress at some unspecified date in the future. Because there was significant Republican and Democratic support for the concept, Congress took the lead on catastrophic health care coverage.

In 1987, Medicare helped 28 million elderly and 3 million disabled persons cope with their health care costs. Medicare part A—the Hospital Insurance program—helps pay for inpatient hospital or skilled nursing care. Anyone over sixty-five eligible for Social Security benefits is automatically eligible for Medicare part A benefits. Persons over age sixty-five not eligible may purchase coverage. The program is financed by an earmarked percentage of the Social Security payroll tax. Medicare part B—the Supplemental Medical Insurance program—is the optional portion of Medicare, in which 98 percent of those eligible choose to participate. Part B pays 80 percent of doctor bills and outpatient charges after an annual deductible is paid. The premium in 1987 was $17.90 per month, which covered only one-fourth of the government's cost. The rest of part B coverage is paid out of general revenues.

Jurisdiction over Medicare in the House of Representatives was shared between the Ways and Means and the Energy and Commerce committees. In hearings and markup during the spring of 1987, both panels significantly expanded the coverage and benefits of the catastrophic illness legislation. HR 2470 provided acute-care coverage, contained a prescription drug benefit, created a "respite care" benefit for families caring for a seriously ill patient, and increased coverage for outpatient mental health, nursing home, home health, and hospice care.[37] The bill would cap out-of-pocket expenses by beneficiaries at less than $1700 per year. Despite some concerns about the long-term costs, the House approved the bill on July 22, 1987, by a comfortable 302 to 127 margin.

The Senate had begun working on its own version of catastrophic health care legislation, S 1127, at about the same time as the House. The Senate Finance Committee version of the bill had one fundamental difference from the House version: It made catastrophic coverage entirely voluntary. By dropping Medicare part B coverage, enrollees could avoid paying any new premiums. In contrast, under the House bill, recipients in higher tax brackets would have to pay extra for part A hospital benefits, even if they dropped part B coverage. Despite some continued concerns about the cost of the bill, the Senate passed the legislation on October 27 by a vote of 86 to 11.[38]

House–Senate conferees appointed to work out differences in the two versions of the bills began meeting in February 1988. Throughout 1987, catastrophic health care coverage had been extremely popular (what some members call a "motherhood" bill) attracting strong bipartisan support with little White House opposition. As the conference committee began work, however, members became increasingly irritated by several intense lobbying efforts launched against the bill. Interest groups representing the elderly split over the issue. Although catastrophic coverage was supported by the AARP, the National Committee to Preserve Social Security, headed by James Roosevelt, son of President Franklin D. Roosevelt, urged its members to oppose the bill. The National Committee already had a nasty reputation on Capitol Hill for using inflammatory tactics to frighten the elderly and fill its own coffers.[39] Opposition also came from the drug industry. Still, members of Congress remained broadly supportive of the concept despite vigorous lobbying efforts on the other side.

By June, conferees had reached an agreement, adopting House provisions instead of making the coverage voluntary. Because of deficit jitters, proponents all along had wanted a program that financed itself. This was accomplished by increasing the Medicare part B premiums over a five-year period and assessing the highest charges on those most able to afford it. The 60 percent of senior citizens who paid less than $150 in federal income taxes per year were required to pay only a small supplemental premium. The 40 percent with higher incomes were required to pay larger premiums. Those with the highest incomes (who paid more than $3,750 a year in income taxes) would pay an extra $800 per year in premiums, increasing to $1,050 per year by 1993. The most affluent group required to pay the maximum fees constituted fewer than 6 percent of all Americans over 65.[40]

Conferees agreed that this financing formula was both fair and fiscally responsible, and House and Senate members overwhelmingly agreed. On June 2, the House approved the catastrophic insurance bill by a vote of 328 to 72. Key Republican leaders, including Minority Leader Robert Michel, urged colleagues to support the legislation. Ways and Means chairman Dan Rostenkowski noted that the bill "strikes a good balance between meeting the medical needs of the elderly and recognizing the limits on their ability for finance additional Medicare costs."[41] A week later, the Senate also ratified the conference report in a bipartisan vote of 86 to 11. In a July 1 ceremony in the Rose Garden, President Reagan signed the bill, noting that it will "help remove a terrible threat from the lives of elderly and disabled Americans."[42]

But the story of catastrophic health care coverage did not end with the signing ceremony. Many elderly citizens wanted the coverage but did not want to have to pay for it. Sponsors of the legislation, after years of effort to enact it, were confused. "I think most of the complaints are from people who don't understand it," one House Democratic sponsor noted.[43] But as the new premiums were assessed, the complaints in 1988 became an uproar from vocal senior citizens in 1989. Several bills were introduced in the 101st Congress to change the financing of catastrophic health care benefits, and others would have repealed the program altogether. Members went back to their districts only to be assailed about the program from every quarter. "It's the only issue out there," said one member after a series of town meetings in his district, which he called his "catastrophic tour."[44] Dan Rostenkowski was confronted by elderly demonstrators after a meeting on the issue at a senior citizens center. Elderly protestors carrying placards blocked his car and called him "Rottenkowski." Coverage of the scene on the national news and photos in the *New York Times* and *Newsweek* magnified public awareness of the controversy.

The tactics of Roosevelt's National Committee continued to infuriate Congress. In its mailings, the group urged its 5 million members to insist that Congress repeal the "seniors-only surtax."[45] By fall, supporters in both parties were in full retreat as repeal bills advanced in both the House and Senate. Members who continued to support the bill were incensed that those who could most afford the premiums were insensitive to the needs of the vast majority of low-income elderly who desperately needed the coverage. Ironically, because of the barrage of negative publicity, even those who paid the smallest premiums were calling for repeal. Many members simply had had enough. Representative Henry Waxman (D-Cal.) claimed that House members ultimately voted to repeal catastrophic coverage because they felt the elderly "were ungrateful, . . . so let them stew in their own juices."[46]

On October 4, 1989, the House voted to repeal the surtax and eliminate the expanded Medicare benefits. Two days later, the Senate voted 99 to 0 to eliminate the surtax but preserve some limited benefits. Six weeks later, the Senate finally gave up on the idea of preserving any of the additional benefits and accepted the House version. At 1:52 A.M. on November 22, 1989, the Senate joined with the House and voted to repeal Public Law 100–360. The Medicare Catastrophic Coverage Act, passed with such fanfare only sixteen months before, was wiped off the books.

How did a pattern of congressional leadership occur? Congress seemed to have bipartisan support to solve a growing policy problem that also seemed to be a good political issue. The Reagan administration was internally divided and content to let Congress work its will. That was even more so during the repeal; the Bush administration, which had taken office six months after the law had passed, stayed on the sidelines, out of the fray. Although HHS Secretary Louis Sullivan tried to preserve some of the benefits, the White House refused to take a position on the repeal, angering some on Capitol Hill. "I guess they don't have a dog in this fight," said one member. "They haven't even been involved enough to be ambivalent," quipped another.[47]

What were the results of the enactment and repeal of catastrophic health care? The case shows that Congress as a representative institution can lead policymaking but remains vulnerable to powerful, vocal interests. Congress lacks the "bully pulpit" of the president that can be used to inform, educate, and lead the public. In the end, Congress took the politically expedient way out. "By repealing the legislation, we have not repealed the problem," said Senate Majority Leader George Mitchell. "The problem is bad and getting worse."[48]

COOPERATION/CONSENSUS: COMPREHENSIVE WELFARE REFORM (1996)

President Bill Clinton's claim to be a "new Democrat" rested in part on his determination to reform welfare—a program developed by FDR and protected by Democrats. In the 1992 campaign, Clinton promised to "end welfare as we know it." Over the next two years, however, welfare reform took a back seat to deficit reduction and health care reform on his domestic agenda. Leadership on welfare reform would change dramatically with the election of a Republican Congress in 1994, which promised to overhaul welfare and turn it over to the states. Over the next year and a half, despite extreme partisanship, two presidential vetoes, and political posturing for the 1996 elections, Clinton and the Congress finally found a way to cooperate. On August 22, 1996, Clinton signed the Personal Responsibility and Work Opportunity Reconciliation Act of 1996, eliminating the federal entitlement to welfare after sixty-one years.[49] It is a case that had all the markings of a political deadlock under divided government, but in the end, both sides found enough common ground to reach a compromise.

Clinton's credentials in welfare reform went back to his days as governor of Arkansas, where as a leader of the National Governor's Association, he lobbied Congress for the passage of the 1988 Family Support Act. Yet as president, he did not introduce a welfare reform plan until June 1994. The administration's bills would require welfare recipients to work for their benefits and limit the amount of time that anyone could remain on welfare. The bill languished during the summer of 1994 as Republican delaying tactics ground legislative business to a halt. During the midterm election campaigns, Republicans would claim that Clinton had done little and had not kept his welfare reform promises.

After the 1994 elections, the Republican Congress put welfare reform at the top of its legislative priorities as part of the "Contract with America." The House moved quickly with a bill that was more radical and comprehensive than Clinton's.[50] The Republican plan would deny benefits to unwed mothers, require states to cut off benefits after a certain time limit, cap spending for other antipoverty programs, and turn welfare over to the states. In his State of the Union address in January 1995, Clinton warned Congress that he would oppose any welfare reform proposal that was too punitive to the poor, especially children. During the first 100 days of the 104th Congress, House Republicans put welfare reform on the fast track. On March 24, the House passed HR 4 by a vote of 234 to 199 that split largely along party lines. It converted AFDC into a block grant for states, allowing them to reduce their own source spending on welfare. The bill required recipients to find work within two years and be limited to five years of payments over their lifetime. Benefits for legal aliens were curtailed, and it would be harder for children with behavioral disorders to qualify for Supplemental Security Income. President Clinton attacked the bill as "weak on work and tough on children." [51]

Progress in 1995 was slower in the Senate, where the approach was somewhat more moderate than in the House. In May, the Senate Finance Committee approved a bill that largely followed the framework of the House bill, but softened some of the provisions. The Labor and Human Resources Committee and the Agriculture Committee also took up parts of the welfare reform package. The Senate did not limit benefits to legal aliens, unwed mothers, and children born to welfare recipients. These differences with the House bill caused internal splits among the Senate Republicans, and Majority Leader Dole delayed bringing the bill to the floor for several months. Warning of a presidential veto of the Republican version, Senate Democrats readied their own welfare reform bill in hopes of having some influence on the legislation. Some of these provisions were included in the Senate bill, providing the basis for more bipartisanship than in the House. After two weeks of floor debate in September, the Senate passed its version of welfare reform 87 to 12.[52] The bill then headed for conference committee.

The conference began on October 24 with Republicans committed to getting a bill to the president's desk by the end of the year. The House and Senate versions shared the same basic premise of ending the federal entitlement and turning welfare over to the states but differed on many significant details. Democrats were largely excluded from the negotiations. Parliamentary maneuvers abounded in the Senate, as the Republican leaders tried to attach welfare reform to the massive reconciliation bill that was working its way through Congress. Democrats, however, were able to use budget rules to strike certain provisions that they opposed.[53] They wanted welfare reform as a free-standing bill rather than under reconciliation, where rules would not permit them to filibuster the bill. Clinton continued to warn Republicans that he would veto a bill that was too punitive. Republicans continued to push welfare reform both through budget reconciliation and a free-standing bill.

On December 6, 1995, Clinton vetoed the massive reconciliation bill, leaving the free-standing bill as the remaining vehicle for welfare reform. Conferees finally reached agreement on that bill in the hectic days before the Christmas holidays. The House passed the bill 245 to 178 on December 21, while Senate approval by a vote of 52 to 47 came the next day. Believing that the Senate had accepted too many of the harsher House provisions, Senate Democrats turned against the conference report. On January 9, 1996, Clinton kept his promise and vetoed the bill, calling it "tough on children and at odds with my central goal of moving people from welfare to work."[54] The issue seemed deadlocked, with prospects for compromise looking dim.

When Clinton gave his State of the Union address in January of 1996, the political environment had changed drastically from the year before. He had survived the Republican onslaught in 1995 and saw his popularity rising after blaming congressional Republicans for the unpopular government shutdowns. He challenged Congress to develop a bipartisan welfare reform bill, promising to sign it immediately. In February, the National Governor's Association endorsed the notion of reforming welfare together with Medicaid—health benefits for the poor jointly financed by the states and federal government.[55] Congressional Republicans picked up on the idea, but the White House opposed it. As the presidential primary season picked up steam, eventual Republican nominee Bob Dole was still Senate Majority Leader. He insisted that welfare and Medicaid reform be linked despite Clinton's repeated veto threats. Dole's view was that a third Clinton veto of welfare reform was more helpful to him in the presidential campaign than sending up a bill that Clinton could sign and take partial credit.

His campaign lagging, Dole resigned from the Senate in June to run for president full time. New Majority Leader Trent Lott (R-Miss.) was under increasing pressure from Republican senators to get a bill passed that they could take credit for in the fall campaign. Republican leaders conceded, dropping their insistence that Medicaid reform be tied to welfare reform. Despite the partisan posturing that prevailed as the political conventions and fall elections neared, the prospects for cooperation and compromise began to improve. Members of both parties believed that actually achieving meaningful welfare reform would help them more than continued deadlock. A new House–Senate conference committee moved toward the more moderate Senate version of the bill, gathering some Democratic support. The House adopted the conference report on July 31 by a vote of 328 to 101. In a last-gasp effort to scuttle welfare reform, liberal Democrats continued to lobby hard for another veto. At a cabinet meeting that day, however, Clinton announced that he would sign the bill despite opposing certain provisions. Knowing that it would become law, the Senate passed the bill on August 1 by a vote of 74 to 24. In both houses, Republicans were nearly unanimous in support, whereas about half of the Democrats voted for welfare reform.

Clinton signed the bill into law on August 22, 1996. It was the most sweeping overhaul of the welfare system since it had been created in 1935. The final version of the bill turned welfare over to the states, with federal assistance in funding coming in the form of block grants. Recipients had to find work within two years or less, depending on state law, and were limited to a maximum of five years of benefits in a lifetime. Clinton signed despite his opposition to limits of benefits to legal aliens and cuts in Food Stamp eligibility. He promised to seek legislation to overturn those provisions. The bill would save the federal government $55 billion over five years, contributing to deficit reduction. At the end of his first term, Clinton was able to tell the voters that he had kept his promise about welfare.

How did the pattern of cooperation working through the regular legislative process finally emerge after a history of partisanship and deadlock? Much of it had to do with the president's and Congress members' perceptions of the political environment and their own political interests. Welfare reform was an extremely popular issue. Both parties ultimately decided that it was better to divide credit for the bill rather than share blame for failure. Clinton had to resist significant pressure within his own party—he was denounced by a number of liberal Democrats. The change in leadership in the Senate also played a role, since Majority Leader Lott proved more willing to clear legislation, despite the campaigns, than Dole had. Congressional Republicans played a greater role in shaping the overall legislation, but through the use of the veto and constant negotiation, the Clinton administration was able to eliminate some of the most onerous provisions. The budget rules also played a role in facilitating passage. The final bill was enacted as a reconciliation bill, providing important procedural safeguards from delaying tactics, particularly in the Senate. In the end, the bill passed because enough of a bipartisan consensus had emerged on the broad outlines of welfare reform.

What are the consequences of comprehensive welfare reform? Although it is still too soon to tell because the two- and five-year limits for millions of recipients have not been reached, initial results were impressive. Within the first year of enactment, welfare rolls around the states had dropped as much as 40 percent. Much of that decline occurred before the bill was actually passed but came in anticipation of sharp new restrictions.[56] By 1997, forty states had submitted new welfare plans to the federal government, thirty-seven of which were approved under the new law. Some of these were even tougher than the federal requirements, requiring less time to find work and less than five years of lifetime benefits. Despite these initial successes, there are still serious concerns about long-term effects. The most employable welfare recipients have gotten jobs first, leaving the more hardcore underclass yet to find work. Many attribute the initial drop in the welfare rolls to the booming economy and worry about what will happen if a recession hits. The Urban Institute warned that the cutoff of benefits could plunge millions into poverty, many of them children. Despite initial encouraging results, it will take a number of years before the long-term impact of welfare reform is clear.

DEADLOCK/EXTRAORDINARY RESOLUTION: THE SOCIAL SECURITY BAILOUT (1983)

In 1981, only four years after Congress and President Carter approved a Social Security rescue plan that promised to put the trust fund on a sound financial basis well into the twenty-first century, the program once again teetered on the brink of bankruptcy. The villains were not deceptive politicians but demographic trends and unforeseen economic developments. The elderly population was increasing, and more Americans were eligible for benefits. At the same time, double-digit inflation drove up Social Security COLAs (cost of living adjustments), while declines in expected wage growth resulted in diminished revenues from payroll taxes. America's favorite social welfare program returned to the center of a political firestorm.[57]

The political battle over the future of Social Security would center on two aging Irish-American politicians: President Ronald Reagan and House Speaker Tip O'Neill. Although personally cordial with each other, they remained ardent political adversaries. President Reagan's "problem" with Social Security went back nearly twenty years. Campaigning for conservative Republican presidential nominee Barry Goldwater in 1964, Reagan urged that Social Security be made voluntary. The charge that he would destroy Social Security dogged Reagan in both his 1976 and 1980 campaigns for the presidency. Carter's claim that Reagan would subvert Social Security did not prevent a strong Republican showing in the 1980 elections, and the political environment in 1981 seemed to favor the president as his budget and economic plan dominated the policy agenda. The high cost of entitlement spending was on the president's mind, but the administration decided against including large-scale cuts in Social Security in the initial plan masterminded by Budget Director David Stockman.[58] By May, after initial successes in its congressional blitz, and growing recognition of deep financial problems with Social Security, the administration decided to switch gears.

In an attempt to distract attention from the president himself, the administration's proposals were offered by Health and Human Services Secretary Richard Schweiker.[59] On May 12, 1981, Schweiker offered a plan to shrink the growing deficit in the Social Security trust fund by reducing benefits for those retiring before the age of sixty-five, phasing out limitations on outside earnings, restricting eligibility for disability benefits, and delaying a scheduled COLA. The last proposal was the most controversial, because it affected all 35 million Social Security recipients. Public reaction and harsh criticism from the Democrats was swift. Representative Claude Pepper (D-Fla.), one of the most outspoken advocates for the elderly in Congress, called the plan "insidious" and "cruel." House Speaker Tip O'Neill called the administration plan "despicable" and promised that "I for one will be fighting this thing every inch of the way."[60] Groups representing the elderly screamed "foul." Save Our Social Security (SOS), a coalition of 83 senior citizen organizations, claimed that the administration plan was a "breach of contract."

Democrats, on the defensive because of the administration's tax and spending cuts, finally had an effective issue to use against Reagan. The House Democratic caucus unanimously adopted a resolution stating that the administration proposals were an "unconscionable breach of faith," pledging to oppose attempts to "destroy the program for a generation of retirees."[61] Congressional Republicans quickly found themselves in a precarious position and lashed out at the Democrats for politicizing the issue rather than dealing constructively with the growing crisis. President Reagan beat a hasty retreat, backing off from the proposals in a May 21 letter to Congress: "I am not wedded to any single solution" to the impending bankruptcy.[62] Congressional Republicans headed for political cover as well, voting for a nonbinding resolution disavowing cuts in minimum Social Security benefits.

Public opinion polls showed that the Democrats had a winning issue; a huge majority of the public opposed Social Security cuts. Some congressional Democrats, such as Senator Moynihan, downplayed the financial problems of the system, calling it an excuse for Republicans to cut benefits. By a large margin, the public perceived the Democrats as the party more likely to take care of the needs of the elderly. In late summer, Congress voted to restore minimum Social Security benefits by large bipartisan majorities in both houses. Yet the larger issue could not be wished or pontificated away. With each passing month, the impending insolvency of the Social Security trust fund became more apparent. By the fall of 1981, projections showed the program running $1.5 trillion deficit over the next seventy-five years.[63] Recognizing the paralysis that enveloped the government over Social Security, Ronald Reagan announced in September the formation of a bipartisan National Commission on Social Security Reform, to be headed by Alan Greenspan. The fifteen-member panel would be composed of five members named by the president, five named by Tip O'Neill, and five by Senate Majority Leader Howard Baker (R-Tenn.). Although the commission would make little progress over the next fifteen months, it would ultimately prove to be the vehicle for legitimizing an unpopular compromise.

The Social Security issue was dormant through the early part of 1982, although Democrats continued to bash Republicans with it in fundraising for the upcoming elections. One successful letter to potential contributors stated, "the Republican party has raised millions of dollars to press for deep cuts in Social Security." The letter netted the Democratic National Committee over a million dollars in just a few weeks.[64] Meanwhile, the U.S. economy was sliding into recession while budget deficits mushroomed. As unemployment approached 10 percent, payroll tax collections sagged, and benefit payments continued to grow. Even Democrats who had minimized the Social Security crisis the year before were forced to admit the gravity of the problem. What was equally clear was the political reality that nothing could be done before the 1982 elections as congressional campaigns further politicized the issue. The "bipartisan" Social Security commission could do little but spin its wheels, because the commission itself was split down partisan political lines. Democratic members opposed benefit cuts; Republicans opposed large payroll tax increases. Despite the lack of progress, Greenspan hoped to break the deadlock after the November 2 elections; he scheduled a three-day brainstorming session to begin on November 11.[65]

It became clear that the commission could not do it alone. For more than a year, its members had done little other than compare and criticize each other's alternatives for achieving solvency. After their three-day parley failed to achieve compromise, Greenspan announced that the direct participation of the two main protagonists—O'Neill and Reagan—was essential if any real progress was to be made. Congress could have returned in a lame-duck session to resolve the crisis, but this did not happen. The commission adjourned on December 10, reporting nothing but the fact that by mid-1983, the government would not be able to cover its Social Security checks.

The National Commission had failed, but it would ultimately serve as a cover in early 1983 for the real negotiations. With the president's blessing, secret meetings between Stockman, Moynihan, and O'Neill's personal representative opened the door to a smaller group who would negotiate in private.[66] In selecting the so-called "gang of nine," the most outspoken partisans on both sides, such as Claude Pepper, were excluded. Out of the spotlight, the tough give-and-take progressed for two weeks. The Democrats agreed to some COLA reductions, and the Republicans agreed to some tax increases. Finally, a deal was struck. The negotiators took their package back to the commission to give the compromise a bipartisan blessing before Reagan and O'Neill publicly gave final approval. Neither side liked it but, recognizing the gravity of the situation, held their noses and approved the plan. Now it had to be sold to the rank and file of both parties in Congress.

What factors led to the extraordinary resolution of this policy deadlock? Ultimately, the impending bankruptcy forced an agreement. The compromise plan bailed out Social Security by raising revenues and lowering benefits. Revenues were enhanced by expanding coverage of the program to include new federal employees and preventing state and local employees from withdrawing. Half of the benefits for taxpayers earning over $25,000 per year were made subject to federal income tax. Both payroll tax rates and the amount of earnings subject to the tax were increased annually through 1990. COLAs were delayed six months, saving billions of dollars. The package was not popular with either party, but most recognized that something had to be done. Final congressional approval was bipartisan, although the tenuous compromise nearly unraveled on several occasions. SOS and other groups opposed the bailout plan, but amendments that would have destroyed the fragile balance were defeated in both houses. On March 24, the House approved the plan by a vote of 243 to 102, while the Senate accepted it by a 58 to 14 vote in the early morning of March 25.[67] Representative Barber Conable (R-N.Y.), one of the key players among the gang of nine, commented, "It may not be a work of art, but it is artful work. It will do what it was supposed to do: It will save the nation's basic social insurance system from imminent disaster."[68]

What were the results of the bailout agreement? Despite the deadlock and divisiveness, the Social Security bailout clearly worked. By the 1990s, the trust fund was running huge surpluses such that some members were actually proposing a payroll tax cut. Demographic trends continued to show that in the future, when the baby boomers begin to retire after 2010, Social Security could face another crisis. Although the use of extraordinary means to resolve deadlocks may often look chaotic and desperate, the results can be satisfactory when a solution is finally hammered out.

CONCLUSION

Interbranch relations in the arena of social welfare policy have shifted over time. Between the 1930s and the 1960s, when poverty and social programs were prominent on the agenda, most of the leadership came from the presidency. Since then, Congress has been a more equal player with the president and occasionally has been able to lead policymaking. After the Republican takeover of Congress in 1994, Congress has been even more assertive in offering policy initiatives. Roosevelt and Johnson were able to gain approval for their proposals from supportive Democratic majorities in Congress; Clinton had no success with Democratic majorities when it came to health care reform. In the case of catastrophic health care insurance, where Presidents Reagan and Bush stayed on the sidelines, Congress was able to play a dominant role in shaping the policy. In reforming welfare in 1996, a policy priority for both branches, Congress took the lead in policymaking, but the president was able to use his veto and veto threats to make major changes.

Interbranch conflict and deadlock frequently occur in social welfare policy. After the defeat of Nixon's Family Assistance Plan, welfare reform efforts were futile for over two decades. Underlying ideological differences about individual responsibility and the role of government made for heated disputes. Only the impending collapse of the Social Security trust fund forced the two sides to resort to extraordinary means—a bipartisan commission fronting for secret negotiations—to break the impasse.

Since the 1960s, presidential leadership has been relatively rare in social welfare policy. Dominance by the legislature is also uncommon, although Congress regularly plays the larger role in formulating the details of policy. Most often, policies either get cooperatively resolved or simply die because of stalemate. Social welfare policy shares some common characteristics with economic and budget policy, in terms of partisanship and the frequency of interbranch conflict. It differs significantly, however, in the absence of a forcing mechanism such as the budget process. Congress has to meet through the night to reach a budget compromise to keep the government from shutting down, but deadlocked social welfare policies often have to wait for years to be resolved.

ENDNOTES

1. Gilbert Fite and Jim Reese, *An Economic History of the United States* (New York: Houghton Mifflin, 1965): 148.

2. Ibid.: 149.

3. See Louis M. Hacker, *The Course of American Growth and Development* (New York: Wiley, 1970): 10–11.

4. Robert Hunter, *Poverty* (New York: Harper and Row, 1965): 62–65.

5. Sidney Lens, *Poverty: America's Enduring Paradox* (New York: Crowell, 1971): 4.

6. Edward Berkowitz and Kim McQuaid, *Creating the Welfare State* (New York: Praeger, 1980): 99.

7. Dorothy B. James, *Poverty, Politics, and Change* (Englewood Cliffs, N.J.: Prentice-Hall, 1972): 51.

8. Michael Harrington, *The Other America* (Baltimore: Penguin, 1963).

9. See Eugene Feingold, *Medicare: Policy and Politics* (San Francisco: Chandler, 1966).

10. Congressional Budget Office, *Economic and Budget Outlook,* FY1991–95 (February 1990).

11. See David Stockman, *The Triumph of Politics* (New York: Harper & Row, 1986).

12. Theda Skocpol, *Boomerang: Health Care Reform and the Turn against Government* (New York: Norton, 1997).

13. League of Women Voters, *Human Needs: Unfinished Business on the Nation's Agenda* (1981): 2.

14. U.S. Bureau of the Census, *March Current Population Survey* (U.S. Census Bureau Internet site, September 26, 1996).

15. Congressional Budget Office, *Economic and Budget Outlook,* FY1991–95 (February 1990).

16. Alison Mitchell, "Two Clinton Aides Resign to Protest New Welfare Law," *New York Times,* September 12, 1996: A1.

17. Aage R. Clausen, *How Congressmen Decide: A Policy Focus* (New York: St. Martin's, 1973).

18. Charles Murray, *Losing Ground: American Policy 1950–1980* (New York: Basic Books, 1984).

19. Michael Harrington, "Crunched Numbers," *New Republic* (January 28, 1985): 7–10.

20. John E. Schwartz, *America's Hidden Success: A Reassessment of Twenty Years of Public Policy* (New York: Norton, 1984).

21. Congressional Budget Office, *Long-Term Budgetary Pressures and Options* (March 1997): xix.

22. John C. Donovan, *The Politics of Poverty* (Indianapolis, Ind.: Bobbs-Merrill, 1973):17.

23. Ibid., 26.

24. Ibid., 29.

25. Ibid.

26. See Anthony Downs, *Inside Bureaucracy* (Boston: Little, Brown, 1967).

27. *Congressional Quarterly Weekly Report* (May 27, 1964): 1037–1042.

28. Title II, Section 202, Economic Opportunity Act of 1964.

29. See Richard F. Fenno, *Congressmen in Committee* (Boston: Little, Brown, 1973).

30. Donovan (note 22): 34.

31. *Congressional Quarterly Weekly Report* (July 24, 1964): 1533.

32. Donovan, (note 22): 37.

33. John F. Bibby and Roger B. Davidson, *On Capitol Hill* (New York: Holt, 1967): 238.

34. *Congressional Quarterly Weekly Report* (January 31, 1987): 207.

35. Ibid., 296.

36. *Congressional Quarterly Weekly Report* (February 8, 1987): 274.

37. *Congressional Quarterly Almanac* (1988): 282.

38. *Congressional Quarterly Weekly Report* (October 31, 1987): 2692.

39. *Congressional Quarterly Weekly Report* (March 26, 1988): 777.

40. *Congressional Quarterly Weekly Report* (December 3, 1988): 3450–3452.

41. *Congressional Quarterly Weekly Report* (June 4, 1988): 1494.

42. *Congressional Quarterly Almanac* (1988): 281.

43. *Congressional Quarterly Weekly Report* (December 3, 1988): 3451.

44. *Congressional Quarterly Weekly Report* (September 9, 1989): 2317.

45. *Congressional Quarterly Weekly Report* (October 14, 1989): 2713–2714.

46. Ibid.

47. *Congressional Quarterly Weekly Report* (November 25, 1989): 3239.

48. Ibid.

49. *Congressional Quarterly Weekly Report* (September 21, 1996): 2696.

50. *Congressional Quarterly Almanac* (1995): 7–36.

51. Ibid., 7–40.

52. Ibid., 7–48.

53. The "Byrd" rule, named after its author, Senator Robert Byrd (D-W.Va.), prohibits nongermane amendments and provisions that do not reduce the deficit.

54. *Congressional Quarterly Almanac* (1995): 7–52.

55. *Congressional Quarterly Weekly Report* (August 31, 1996): 2445.

56. Jason DeParle, "A Sharp Decrease in Welfare Cases Is Gathering Speed," *The New York Times* (February 2, 1997): A1.

57. Ibid.

58. Paul C. Light, *Artful Work: The Politics of Social Security Reform* (New York: Random House, 1985).

59. Stockman (note 11).

60. *Congressional Quarterly Weekly Report* (May 16, 1981): 842–843.

61. Ibid., 842.

62. *Congressional Quarterly Weekly Report* (May 23, 1981): 896.

63. *Congressional Quarterly Weekly Report* (November 28, 1981): 2333.

64. Light (note 58): 139.

65. *Congressional Quarterly Weekly Report* (October 9, 1982): 2615.

66. Light (note 58): Chapter 15.

67. *Congressional Quarterly Weekly Report* (March 26, 1983): 596.

68. Ibid.

9

PATTERNS AND CONSEQUENCES: CAN NATIONAL POLICYMAKING BE IMPROVED?

> *History shows that for government to be effective in solving problems the mode must be cooperation rather than legalistic adversary confrontation.* —*PAUL M. BATOR (1988)*

In the preceding pages, we have seen stunning victories and ignominious defeats; constructive collaboration and bitter combat. Congress and the president may work together in harmony; one may defer to the other; or they may engage in no-holds-barred political warfare. The sixteen cases reflect just a small sample of the diversity of policymaking patterns. In this concluding chapter, we review three questions: (1) How do the four cases of each pattern compare to each other? (2) What factors explain the occurrence of different patterns? (3) Are there any common policy consequences or results common to each pattern? Michael Mezey, who developed criteria to assess policy results, suggests that:

> *. . . the more that legislative institutions were involved in the formulation of public policy, the more likely it was to meet democratic criteria; the more that executive institutions were involved in its formulation, the more likely it was to meet managerial criteria.[1]*

We will attempt to assess this hypothesis for all four patterns of policymaking using the criteria suggested in Chapter 1: timeliness and responsiveness, representativeness, substantiveness, accountability, nature of benefits, consistency and coherence, and effectiveness. Looking at consequences raises a fourth question: Can the policymaking relationships between Congress and the president be improved? What reforms, if any, might promote the most positive patterns, help avoid deadlock, and foster more effective policy results?

Our approach to analyzing Congress and the presidency was characterized by a separationist, tandem institutions perspective, a policy focus, and a belief that the best way to understand congressional-presidential relationships is by systematically observing how they make policy. The policy focus entailed developing a typology of policymaking patterns and case analysis. Rather than the presidency-centered approach, we believe the evidence suggests that the two branches are nearly coequal partners legislating together. Initiatives spring from both ends of Pennsylvania Avenue, and in most cases, each branch helps shape the result.[2] We have contrasted different policymaking patterns across the four substantive policy areas, observing how they are shaped by the political environment and the nature of the times, institutional capacity and decision-making processes, personal leadership, and the nature of the policy agenda. The policy focus not only encompasses the politics of interbranch relations but, in this chapter, leads us to pay special attention to the linkage between process and outcomes. In particular, we are concerned with democratic and managerial criteria: Do policies resulting from the various patterns differ in effectiveness?

Figure 9.1 compares and locates the sixteen cases, based on our judgment of how the cases relate to each other across the two dimensions of relative leadership

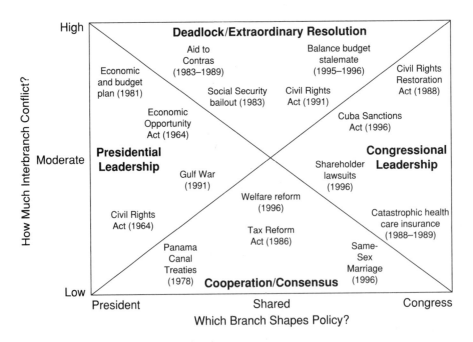

FIGURE 9.1   **Patterns of Presidential-Congressional Policymaking**

and conflict. Of course, these placements are approximate at best; we lack the ability to differentiate precisely between cases. One of the cases, the 1964 Civil Rights Act, was reclassified from our earlier work from consensus/cooperation to presidential leadership. Other cases are on the border between two patterns. More important than the precise location is the opportunity the typology provides to compare and contrast cases to better understand the dynamics of policymaking involving Congress and the president. It focuses attention on how much each branch shapes policy, and whether interbranch combat produces deadlock or can be moderated enough to produce a collaborative solution. The array of the sixteen cases reinforces our assertion that *no single pattern characterizes policymaking today* and that *different patterns can occur across different policy areas at the same point in time.* In the following sections, we review each of the four patterns in terms of their characteristics, determinants, and consequences.

PRESIDENTIAL LEADERSHIP

Characteristics

The defining characteristic of the pattern of presidential leadership is that the presidency plays a greater role in shaping policy; Congress follows the president, regardless of whether congressional policy preferences are in conflict or congruent. This *leadership* is significantly different from "domination" of Congress, which suggests a zero-sum contest. Presidential leadership is also different from the presidential "support" or "success" measures, since presidents may take a position on a roll-call vote that represents a policy largely shaped in Congress. Presidential leadership does not depend on which branch initiates the policy, although in most cases it reflects White House initiatives. Even in such cases, Congress has some degree of influence on the result.

Presidential leadership of the policymaking partnership with Congress occurs at varying levels of interbranch conflict. The degree of conflict often reflects differences in policy preferences between the president and congressional majorities but also can be primarily political or based on constitutional issues. The Civil Rights Act of 1964 probably better fits as an example of presidential leadership than consensus/cooperation because the administration played the leading role in shaping the content of the legislation. The Justice Department played a key role in developing innovative proposals to avoid constitutional issues that derailed civil rights laws a century earlier. Certainly the president could not have succeeded without bipartisanship and the assistance of congressional leadership. It is a case where the cooperation of Congress allowed the presidency to lead the policy process.

In a case with high stakes for the nation, the Persian Gulf War of 1991 generated greater conflict between branches. President Bush initially received strong bipartisan support from Congress for his decision to commit U.S. troops to Saudi Arabia, but that support became weaker on the question of using force. There were calls for a congressional debate and demands that the president respect Congress's constitutional power to declare war. That debate occurred soon after the 102nd Congress convened in January 1991, when the president asked for congressional authorization for the use of force. House and Senate Democratic leaders urged that economic sanctions be given more time to work before military action was taken. However, the debate was characterized by its restraint and lack of recrimination, despite the severe differences between the two sides. Although the margins were close, enough Democrats in both houses crossed over to support the president that authorization was approved. While this cross-partisan vote allowed the president to conduct the war, Bush implicitly acknowledged Congress's war-making power by asking for legislative approval. The legitimacy of the war was enhanced immeasurably by the House and Senate votes. Bush might have pursued military force even without approval from Congress, but the level of interbranch conflict would have escalated and national unity diminished.

The level of interbranch conflict over President Johnson's Economic Opportunity Act in 1964 was also moderate; majorities in Congress shared the president's general objectives. Johnson enjoyed strong support from his own party members, and many Republicans were reluctant to oppose a popular antipoverty program with elections just around the corner. The environment was ripe for enactment. However, criticism and controversy over the War on Poverty was greater in years after its passage than during its formulation and adoption. LBJ proved more attentive to passage than to implementation.

The case of Reagan's 1981 economic and budget plan stands apart from the other cases in that it demonstrates presidential leadership in a highly conflictive, partisan environment. This case was unusual in recent decades for several reasons. The budget and economic plan overwhelmed the policy agenda, pushing other issues to the sidelines. The administration was able to win, without significant compromise, despite the concerted and organized opposition of the House Democratic leadership, who brought all their resources to bear. The work of the standing committees and leadership was discarded in favor of a substitute crafted by the administration and its legislative agents. They were able to prevail repeatedly and to maintain the coalition over a number of months. Reagan's prevailed because two dozen or so Democratic defectors gave him a working cross-partisan majority. But the sharp polarization of parties was as close to a partisan pattern as can exist under divided government. The presidential leadership case that compares most closely with 1981 was President Clinton's 1993 deficit reduction plan briefly described in Chapter 7. Clinton prevailed under unified control of government, and the pattern was strict partisanship, gaining not a single Republican vote for his plan.

Ronald Reagan's successful leadership of Congress in 1981 provides an interesting comparison to Lyndon Johnson's achievements in gaining legislative approval of the Economic Opportunity Act. In both cases, strong presidential leadership helped shepherd a major policy change through Congress. The cases differ in the intensity of conflict and the nature of legislative coalitions. Under unified party control of government, LBJ worked through the regular Democratic congressional leaders. In 1981, however, under divided control of government, the Reagan administration was actively opposed by the regular House Democratic leaders. Their coalition was built from a floor majority outside the normal leadership channels. This case had repercussions for Congress and interbranch relations throughout the 1980s.

What Leads to Presidential Leadership?

The presidency-centered literature contains extensive empirical studies of the conditions that lead to presidential success on Capitol Hill, and some of the findings are useful here. In the cases of the Civil Rights Act, the Economic Opportunity Act, the 1981 budget and tax plan, and the Gulf War, the political environment was highly conducive to decisive action and presidential leadership. Kennedy's death, LBJ's honeymoon, and growing popular concern with poverty and civil rights provided an opportunity for Johnson to move his domestic agenda quickly. President Reagan capitalized on his claims of a conservative electoral mandate, his survival of an assassination attempt, his popularity, and strong public support for both a defense buildup and tax cuts. President Bush's position was strengthened by the strong public support for military action in the Persian Gulf and heightened by Saddam Hussein's inflammatory rhetoric and intransigence. Johnson, Reagan, and Bush all used their personal prestige and the public relations apparatus of the presidency effectively to manage the media. Reagan's 1981 budget and economic plan is the case most directly related to election results and changing majorities in Congress. The 1980 elections produced a solid Republican majority in the Senate and reduced the Democratic majority in the House.

Personal leadership and institutions play a key role in cases of presidential leadership of the policy process. In all four cases, presidents had clearly defined goals and used the institutionalized presidency to achieve these goals. Wanting a bold new antipoverty program, Johnson created a special task force to write the legislation and used his congressional liaison team to get it through Congress. Facing the same Congress that had thwarted Kennedy, Johnson was able to fashion a major domestic legislative victory. In the case of the civil rights bill, the Justice Department and White House had formulated a bold plan to go far beyond previous legislative attempts. The Reagan administration focused the agenda and used skillful timing, institutional innovation (reconciliation), effective lobbying, and public relations to carry the day. George Bush also acted quickly and decisively from the moment Iraq invaded Kuwait. He set definitive goals; explained them to Congress, the nation, and the international community; and gained the support of all.

Although it can occur in any policy area, presidential leadership is not equally prevalent in all areas. Despite the enhanced congressional role since Vietnam, and more recently the end of the cold war, presidential leadership is still more likely to occur in foreign affairs than in domestic policy. Even with strong congressional opposition to many free trade measures, President Clinton was able to get "fast track" authority and convince Congress to approve NAFTA and GATT (the General Agreement on Tariffs and Trade). As the case of the Helms-Burton Act showed, however, Congress can sometimes lead as well. Today, the more normal pattern is one of shared responsibility in a policymaking partnership. Trade, defense procurement, military construction, base closings, immigration, and foreign aid are all characterized by intense congressional involvement. In general, strong presidential leadership is contingent on a special combination of circumstances: effective presidential action matched with a favorable political environment.

Policy Consequences

Were there any common characteristics in the results of these four cases? Were they, as Mezey suggests, more managerially sound if less democratic? Policymaking led by the president appears to be more timely, nonroutine, and responsive than the other three patterns. In all four cases we examined, presidents responded to clearly defined needs and gained favorable congressional action in a period of months rather than years. In moving with dispatch, it may be unavoidable that policy is less representative, ignoring certain interests. For example, the entire purpose of fast-track authority for presidents to negotiate trade agreements is to curtail the representation of interests in Congress by prohibiting amendments. The Economic Opportunity Act of 1964 overlooked many alternatives and potential problems with its approach. The Reagan strategy in 1981 was explicitly designed to overcome opposition to budget cuts from various interest groups by forcing a single yes-or-no vote for the entire budget package.

In these cases, presidency-led policymaking produced outcomes that were more substantive than symbolic.[3] The Reagan economic and budget plan had a dramatic and immediate effect on taxing and spending trends throughout the decade. The antipoverty program adopted in 1964 created a new agency and a host of new programs. The Gulf War achieved its main objective of driving Iraq out of Kuwait and weakening Saddam Hussein's military might. The Civil Rights Act of 1964 is still the most important legislation in the history of civil rights and the basis for continued interpretation and debate today. It had profound impacts on everything from opening up thousands of hotels and restaurants to blacks to dramatically increasing opportunities for women athletes in universities. Based on these cases, presidency-led policymaking also seems to emphasize collective national benefits rather than more particularistic or regional benefits. Of course, each case also had important symbolic components as well, and there are many cases in which presidents have pursued policies that are more symbolic than substantive.

Despite a number of positive characteristics, the verdict on the managerial criteria of consistency, coherence, and long-term effectiveness of policies dominated by the presidency is mixed. Two cases in particular suggest the main danger of presidential leadership: the possibility that timely and decisive actions may prove to be hasty and ill-conceived. The Economic Opportunity Act was a disappointment, even to its most loyal adherents. Although there is insufficient evidence to support the claim that the War on Poverty actually made the poor worse off, it is hard to find significant improvements that are attributable to the Economic Opportunity Act. Its most controversial creation, the community action programs (CAPs), resulted in power struggles across the nation's cities instead of improvements in the situation of society's have-nots.

The Reagan economic and budget plan has come under intense criticism for initiating a decade of chronic deficits that threatened the long-term prosperity of the nation. To further its relentless push for the tax cuts and military buildup, the administration chose to use unrealistic economic assumptions that it knew to be faulty. David Stockman, chief architect of the Reagan plan, later called it a "willful act of ignorance and grotesque irresponsibility."[4] In the decade that followed, the national debt of the United States increased from $1 trillion to over $4 trillion. In a matter of just a few years in the mid-1980s, the United States went from the world's largest creditor nation to the largest debtor nation and found itself saddled with a massive trade deficit.

National security decisions dominated by the White House are particularly susceptible to the demands for quick action, and the results can sometimes be disastrous. Irving Janis has documented a series of policy fiascoes that stemmed from the phenomenon of "groupthink" within the presidency—when presidents do not seek diversity of opinion but focus prematurely on a single policy alternative.[5] The ill-fated Bay of Pigs invasion of Cuba in 1961 and the decision to escalate the war in Vietnam are two prime examples. Even though the Gulf War succeeded in achieving its main short-term objectives, its long-term consequences were less clear. Eight years later, Saddam Hussein was still in power, hiding weapons of mass destruction and thwarting UN inspectors.

Over the years, many presidential programs, such as Social Security in 1935, have been judged a success. In times of foreign or domestic crisis, the presidency is best equipped to respond quickly, but there are attendant risks. Although the pattern of presidential leadership usually leads to policies that are timely, responsive, and national in scope, they are not always coherent, consistent, or effective. In some cases, they may move the nation precipitously down a detrimental path.

CONGRESSIONAL LEADERSHIP

Characteristics

Congressional leadership is the pattern in which Congress plays a dominant role in shaping public policy—whether with the support of or over the objections of the president. As with presidency-led policy, *leadership* is not the same as *domination* (in the sense that Congress winning means the president loses). Of the cases we have examined, only the Civil Rights Restoration Act of 1988 resembles that situation. Leadership is also not dependent on which branch initiates policy; Congress may lead the policy process even if the original proposal was the president's. As Figure 9.1 suggests, the degree of interbranch conflict can vary considerably under the domain of congressional leadership. The amount of presidential involvement also varies but is generally less than in the other three patterns.

Although President Reagan first proposed catastrophic health care coverage, the process was led by Congress. Preoccupied with other matters, Reagan did nothing to resolve deep divisions within his administration; he let Congress carry the ball. Although he threatened to veto the bill if it was not to his liking, the level of interbranch conflict was moderate to low by the standards of most social welfare bills. Because he supported the concept, Reagan was happy to take some credit for the proposal when it was signed into law. President Bush's involvement in the process was even less when catastrophic coverage was repealed in 1989. Sensing that the issue carried political risks, the administration took a hands-off approach and let Congress solve a problem it had created for itself.

The Helms-Burton Act is unique among the cases in that a single external event—the shooting down of the airplane carrying Cuban Americans—allowed Congress to have its way by undercutting administration opposition. It is clear that the administration still thought the bill was a bad idea, would damage relations with allies, and might have been against international law. However, the incident simply made the political costs too high to oppose harsher sanctions on Cuba any longer. The president was limited to administrative actions to delay enforcement of the law.

The two cases of congressional leadership that have a common characteristic are the Civil Rights Restoration Act of 1988 and the Shareholder Lawsuits Act in 1995. In both cases, Congress mustered a two-thirds majority to override a presidential veto. In 1988, with a presidential election approaching, both parties felt civil rights was a critical issue: Democrats in Congress to show their continued support and the administration to highlight its opposition to "quotas," reverse discrimination, and intrusive bureaucracy. The result was an acrimonious fight. The House and Senate ultimately overrode President Reagan's veto, making the Civil Rights Restoration Act law without the president's signature. In 1995, Clinton's first veto override was also based on political calculations as much as on policy considerations. The shareholder lawsuits bill was of lower visibility and interbranch conflict and was the subject of intense special interest lobbying. In the end, President Clinton felt he had to shore up his political support among the trial lawyers more than high-tech businesses. Bipartisan majorities in Congress quickly and decisively overrode the veto, as the administration surely suspected it would. Nonetheless, the difficulty of getting a two-thirds majority in both houses over the active opposition of the president makes this type of congressional leadership relatively rare.

What Leads to Congressional Leadership?

Congressional leadership of the policy process is much more common than the presidency-centered literature would suggest. It often involves issues that have local or regional implications, generating more interest in Congress than in the White House. Congressional-led policymaking often involves routine or low-visibility policies, and inside-the-beltway politics heavy on interest group participation, such as the shareholder lawsuits bill. Congressional leadership is not restricted to low-visibility or regional concerns, however. The Civil Rights Act of 1988 and catastrophic health care insurance were national in scope. Helms-Burton had important international and foreign policy implications. But all were policies that were much higher on the congressional agenda than on the presidential agenda.

Except in cases of veto overrides, congressional leadership is predicated on at least mild support or general disinterest on the part of the administration. In two of the cases, the president was content to let Congress work its will, within certain parameters. The cost of opposition was seen as greater than going along and taking some credit for the result. The political environment must also be right for congressional leadership of policymaking, and sometimes a weaker president improves the chances for congressional leadership. For example, it is unlikely that Congress could have enacted the Civil Rights Restoration Act over Reagan's veto before 1987, when the Democrats recaptured the Senate and the lame-duck president was weakened by the Iran–Contra scandal. Congressional leadership can occur under unified control of government because of pressure from factions within the president's party in Congress, but is more prevalent under divided government. The 1994 elections probably did more to promote congressional leadership of policymaking than any other in the century, propelling the Republicans to power with an articulated national agenda. Two of the cases of congressional leadership come from the 104th Congress. But a number of other cases of congressional attempts at leadership since the Republican takeover fall in the category of deadlock or cooperation. The Republicans learned that even under the most favorable of conditions, it is difficult to run the country from Capitol Hill.

Public support for the Congress appears only marginally related to legislative leadership of policymaking. Much more important is the size and cohesion of congressional majorities. Conversely, presidential popularity can be an obstacle. The Republican Congress was not able to dominate President Clinton and force him to accept their balanced budget proposal in 1995. Congress's declining popularity and Clinton's surging approval strengthened his resolve. Despite large Democratic majorities, Congress was unable to override any of the vetoes cast by then highly popular George Bush in his first three years in office.

Enhanced institutional capability promotes congressional leadership of the policy process. More majoritarian processes, the strengthening of party leaders, the use of omnibus legislation written by the leadership, and the use of restrictive rules in the House all facilitated congressional policy leadership in the late 1980s and 1990s. When Republicans did take over in 1995, they took advantage of new rules and procedures, especially in the budget process. In terms of negotiating with presidents over budget priorities, Congress today has the ability to deliver and enforce a deal, as with the balanced budget agreement in 1997.

Congress's ability to lead the policy process also depends on individual leaders and their skills. Newt Gingrich, despite his ethical and political problems after just one term, represented a dramatic departure from most of the previous speakers. His strategy of nationalizing the 1994 elections with the Contract with America gave him the opportunity to define a Rooseveltlike "100 days" to vote on the congressional agenda. His ability to hand-pick committee chairs, weaken committees vis-à-vis the leadership, and control the process was unprecedented in recent times, even if it did not last for long. More than anything, Gingrich and the Republicans were a reminder of the potential of congressional leadership under the right political situation. Their failures also were a reminder of how quickly the political environment can change and the difficulties of dominating policymaking in a separated system.

Although the party leaders are instrumental in facilitating the legislative process, policy leadership often comes from committees and policy entrepreneurs. Catastrophic health insurance was maneuvered through Congress by leaders such as Ways and Means Chairman Dan Rostenkowski and a handful of other representatives who had a special interest in the issue. Bipartisan cooperation within Congress makes enactment easier and reduces the likelihood of a presidential veto. Support from Minority Leader Robert Michel helped ensure passage of the catastrophic health care insurance bill. The Helms-Burton Act was largely the result of Jesse Helms's hatred of Castro and determination to use the big stick against him. The Civil Rights Restoration Act was masterminded by a coalition of legislators led by Edward Kennedy in the Senate and the Black Caucus in the House.

Congressional leadership of policymaking is less dramatic than the highly visible legislative successes of a Roosevelt, Johnson, or Reagan. Newt Gingrich brought more visibility to Congress and the congressional agenda than any leader in memory. But even before Gingrich, the legislative branch sometimes set the agenda, balanced the diverse interests, and crafted the legislation. Congressional leadership becomes less likely as the political stakes increase and the level of interbranch conflict escalates, but in rare cases, congressional majorities may be strong enough to override the president. More commonly, presidential cooperation or indifference, the persistence of party leaders, and procedures that facilitate majority rule make it possible for Congress to lead.

Consequences

Compared with policymaking led by the president, the legislative process is often careful, slow, deliberative, and less timely. Congress can settle a rail strike or pass a continuing resolution in twenty-four hours when the pressure is on, but in most cases, major legislation takes many months or years to become law. Delay is tolerable in cases such as catastrophic health care or shareholder lawsuits, although the problems may worsen in the interim. In crucial decisions on the budget and foreign policy, however, deliberation and delay can cause serious problems and blunt the effectiveness of policy.

Congressional policymaking generally rates well on democratic criteria. It tends to represent a wide variety of organized interests, ideologies, and regional concerns—sometimes to a fault. The fragmented nature of the legislative process provides many access points with opportunities for amendment, logrolling, compromise, and modification. Narrow interests may dominate the cozy iron triangles of specialized groups, agencies, and subcommittees, but in major legislation, a broader array of organized interests usually are represented.[6] This tends to produce legislation that is more consensus-oriented, modest in nature, and incremental in approach. Congressional policymaking is undermined, however, when legislators prove timid in the face of powerful interests. The rapid repeal of catastrophic health care insurance is an example of Congress's abandonment of an important policy when challenged by a vocal minority.

The representativeness of congressional policymaking is reflected in the nature of benefits. As representatives of states and districts, members of Congress have a fondness for tangible district benefits and pork-barrel projects. There is a tendency to distribute benefits widely, rather than targeting them to regions or groups of individuals that have the greatest need. Although this may provide a measure of geographical equity, it often dilutes and diminishes the impact of policy. Revenue sharing is often cited as an example of a policy that gave states and cities benefits whether their need was great or nonexistent.[7]

Despite these well-known proclivities, the penchant of Congress for distributive politics is often overemphasized.[8] Pork-barrel spending on district projects constitutes only a tiny fraction of federal outlays, and its proportion has been dropping in recent years.[9] Congress deals with issues that are national in scope—ranging from defense to tax policy to civil rights—and it can resolve regional disputes in areas such as immigration or energy policy.

Perhaps a more serious flaw in policy dominated by Congress is a tendency to promote symbolism over substance. This can also occur in cases of consensus where Congress leads in shaping policy, such as the Same-Sex Marriage Act. When the political implications of legislation become as important as the policy implications, members act to protect themselves by adopting "motherhood" legislation, avoiding "dangerous" votes, and sidestepping tough issues. Such gestures may seem harmless or even politically useful, but they reinforce public cynicism about the Congress and congressional leadership.

Congressional influence in foreign policy is a two-edged sword. It can safeguard the country from dangerous entanglements or simply confuse and fragment U.S. policy. Helms-Burton has caused problems with many allies and brought scorn and ridicule among the international community for trying to impose America's ideas about how to deal with Cuba on everyone else. Helms-Burton is a real threat to important allies such as Canada. It has brought threats of retaliation and action in the World Court for violating international law. This delights some of the law's most ardent supporters, but hardly gives Helms-Burton high scores for elements of good policy.

Representation of diverse interests, localized benefits, and emphasis on symbols rather than substance can have a negative impact on the consistency, coherence, and effectiveness of policies shaped by Congress. That explains in part why the federal government still subsidizes tobacco growers at the same time as it spends hundreds of millions of dollars on cancer research and "stop smoking" campaigns. Because coalitions are unstable, policies may be contradictory. Because the political environment changes quickly, congressional policymaking is often repetitive and redundant. Many issues return again and again without final resolution. This may be a necessary consequence of democracy, but it can have damaging consequences on the effectiveness of policy.

Despite these problems, policies shaped by Congress are not inherently less effective or less coherent than presidential policies. Because all policies are administered by the executive branch, Congress-led policies do not appear to differ significantly in managerial effectiveness from policies dominated by the president. Presidents, too, engage in symbolic exercises, change directions, and produce results that are less than optimal at times. Congressional action tends to be slow, and the legislative process often appears chaotic and messy. However, when congressional leaders act responsibly, working carefully through difficult issues, the resulting policies can effectively balance diverse and competing interests in society.

CONSENSUS/COOPERATION

Characteristics

Consensus/cooperation is a pattern characterized by moderate to low levels of interbranch conflict and a constructive mutual engagement in shaping the content of policy. As Figure 9.1 suggests, responsibility is not necessarily shared equally, but one branch does not lead the other as much as in the two previous patterns. Cases of cooperation often share common traits with congressional or presidential leadership at lower levels of interbranch conflict. In cases of consensus, there is no real opposition. In cases of cooperation, policy preferences diverge and conflict exists, but the two branches work in collaboration to achieve an acceptable outcome. Among our cases, the Same-Sex Marriage Bill comes closest to consensus. This was a case of both branches responding to a hot-button issue with the American people. Despite Clinton's support for gay rights, in the face of overwhelming public opposition to homosexual marriages, both branches and both parties came together to enact a largely symbolic act.

Despite the media emphasis on conflict and deadlock, cooperation is probably the most prevalent pattern of presidential-congressional policymaking today. Initiatives may develop in either branch, from the thousands of bills submitted in Congress to the president's legislative agenda. Many congressional initiatives end up on the presidential agenda, such as tax reform and welfare reform. Others may be administration proposals, such as the Panama Canal Treaties and the 1964 Civil Rights Act. Wherever the proposals originate, in cases of cooperation both branches perceive significant stakes and participate in the process.

The approval of the Panama Canal treaties is close to being a case of presidential leadership. The administration negotiated the treaties and then used all its resources to gain Senate ratification. However, this case involves significant differences from the Persian Gulf War and other instances of presidential leadership in foreign policy. First, the Senate's constitutional legitimacy in ratifying treaties is less ambiguous than the dispute between congressional war powers and the president's powers as commander-in-chief. Second, the Senate made important substantive revisions in the treaties, forcing the White House to accept a number of reservations. Finally, although ratification represented a significant victory for President Carter, capping one of his administration's more effective lobbying campaigns, final approval was made possible only by the bipartisan efforts of Majority Leader Robert Byrd and Minority Leader Howard Baker.

Despite President Clinton's promise during the 1992 campaign to "end welfare as we know it," Congress was the initiator and played the more significant role in shaping the Welfare Reform Act of 1996. Congress had been the leading force in enacting modest reforms in the Family Support Act of 1988, but that legislation had done little to change the underlying structure of welfare. The 1994 elections were critical for creating an environment leading to the enactment of the far-reaching welfare reform package agreed to in 1996. Yet this case had all the ingredients for deadlock under divided government. In general, the Republicans wanted to go much further in eliminating the federal entitlement for welfare than the Clinton administration, which had to deal with hostility from the liberal wing of the Democratic Party. Clinton used his veto twice to force Republicans to make important concessions. The issue could have remained in deadlock, but both sides decided a deal was both good policy and good politics. Congress generally shaped the overall dimensions of the bill, but the administration won many critical concessions on Medicaid and other issues. Despite serious differences, both branches worked out a compromise that made historic and far-reaching changes in public policy.

The Tax Reform Act of 1986 is also a good example of the pattern of interbranch cooperation in making a significant policy change. It was all the more remarkable given the hostility between Congress and the president over taxing and spending issues in the mid-1980s. The presidency and Congress shared responsibility nearly equally: The Treasury had drafted two detailed plans, and the House and Senate each adopted their own versions. All sides participated in shaping the final bill. Not only was bipartisanship essential, but suspension of interbranch combat and adoption of new policymaking ground rules were required. Despite concerted opposition from interest groups to virtually every part of the bill, cooperation between the two branches made it possible to do what most observers had thought impossible.

What Leads to Consensus/Cooperation?

In the simplest terms, cooperation occurs when neither branch has the ability to dominate the other, and both partners place higher value on passing a bill than gaining a political advantage. Some degree of bipartisanship or cross-partisanship is essential to cooperation under divided government. Tax reform was considered impossible by political experts, because of the potential political costs of eliminating tax preferences that benefited a diverse array of interest groups. However, both parties believed they had much to gain: The Republicans wanted lower rates and a tax system that did not distort investment decisions, and Democrats wanted a fairer system and an end to many of the loopholes enjoyed by the rich. In this and other cases of cooperation, collaboration took place in an environment conducive to accommodation and reciprocity. Cooperation in welfare reform occurred because the Democratic president moved significantly toward the Republican position in accepting the end of the federal entitlement, requiring work from all beneficiaries, and lifetime limits on benefits. Despite this movement, the bill easily could have resulted in a third veto, with welfare reform becoming a campaign issue. It did not because both sides believed they were better off claiming credit for the policy rather than pointing blame for its failure.

Interbranch consensus and cooperation can occur with or without supportive public opinion. In the case of the Same-Sex Marriage bill, public opinion was paramount, eclipsing whatever policy differences may have existed between branches. The same was true for the congressional-led proposals to reform the Internal Revenue Service in 1997 and 1998. Although party differences were significant in these cases, strong public support for tax reform, balancing the budget, sanctioning IRS, and ending welfare was instrumental in leading to action. In contrast, support for the Panama Canal treaties was soft with a plurality opposed in most polls. In that case, cooperation occurred because a two-thirds majority of senators agreed with the president that it was the right thing to do, regardless of public opinion.

The clearest example of the importance of manipulating institutions was tax reform. In both houses, public sessions produced political posturing, special-interest amendments, and a steady erosion of the goals of each party. One of the key elements that allowed tax reform to pass was the new rules adopted in 1985 under the Gramm-Rudman deficit reduction plan, which required all amendments to be "revenue neutral." When the bill got to the Senate in 1986, any amendment that reduced revenue was ruled out of order unless offset with a provision that correspondingly increased revenue. This procedure and other new restrictions, unprecedented in nearly 200 years of Senate history, helped tax reform succeed. Welfare reform succeeded in 1996 in a Congress with more centralized leadership than had occurred in decades. That made it possible for the Republicans to negotiate with the administration and to deliver the deal when it was struck.

Individual leadership, particularly bipartisanship leadership, was a crucial factor in all four cases. President Jimmy Carter worked extremely hard and effectively with congressional leaders to get the Panama Canal Treaties enacted. Senate Majority Leader Robert Byrd's personal leadership also played an important role in the ratification of the outcome.[10] Although Clinton was more reactive than proactive in shaping welfare reform, his previous vetoes established his credentials as a tough negotiator on this issue. By not only demanding concessions but also making concessions, Clinton and congressional leaders allowed welfare reform to pass. Creative leadership by Senate Finance Committee chairman Robert Packwood helped make tax reform a reality. His tactic of challenging committee members in a closed-door session to throw out their previous votes to get the top rate below 30 percent had a profound impact on the process.

Most of the instances of cooperation that we examined concerned policies that had percolated in the political system for many years. These issues had been carefully studied, explored, and debated inside and outside of government. Change was finally possible when both branches agreed that it was time to act. One of the most interesting questions concerns why some issues deadlock and others are resolved through negotiation and compromise. Why, for example, in 1995–1996 was welfare reform resolved but the balanced budget negotiations ended in standoff, when the political environment and key actors appeared to be the same? The differences between the two sides were not notably greater in balancing the budget than in reforming welfare. It came down to political calculations over policy concerns; the budget issues were perceived as more potent in the upcoming election than finger-pointing over welfare reform. We will look more closely at this question when deadlock and extraordinary resolution is discussed in the next section.

Consequences

Because both branches are involved in the process, policies emerging from a pattern of interbranch cooperation tend to represent diverse interests and perspectives. As tax reform suggests, however, representativeness is not the same as catering to special interests or taking the lowest common denominator. Because of the long process of building coalitions to reach a policy consensus, this pattern is rarely quick or timely. Tax reform and welfare reform took years before they were finally enacted. Under some circumstances, however, consensus/cooperation can be timely. The Panama Canal treaties were debated and ratified under a deadline. The same-sex marriage bill was developed quickly in response to developments in Hawaii and intense media attention.

The cases of cooperation produced policies that were reasonably coherent and effective in comparison with other major legislation. Welfare reform has turned significant authority over to the states. In the first few years, the results have shown a dramatic reduction in welfare rolls in most states. Many of the "workfare" programs in the states seem to be working, helped by the strong national economy. The provision of the law that denied benefits to legal aliens proved very unpopular in the states and was repealed as part of the 1997 balanced budget agreement. The people who have left welfare are the most employable of the welfare recipients. In terms of overall impact, it is still too soon to tell whether in the long term the act will break the cycle of welfare dependency and get the hard-core underclass into the productive work force. The Panama Canal treaties did not solve all the problems in Panama or Central America, but without it, U.S. relations with Latin America would probably be much worse than they are today. The canal has remained open and fully operational.

Tax reform has received mixed reviews in the years since its adoption. The goal of tax simplification was not realized; the tax code is perhaps even more complicated than ever, even though the number of tax brackets was reduced from fifteen to three. Nonetheless, many important accomplishments were achieved. The tax burden on the poor was significantly reduced. Hundreds of billions of dollars of tax expenditures were eliminated, enhancing the integrity of the tax system. Although billions of dollars of tax preferences still remain, the new system promoted efficiency because it eliminated many incentives to make unproductive investments for the sake of sheltering income. Congress and the president have undone much of the Tax Reform Act in subsequent years, adding additional tax brackets in 1990 and 1993, and further complicating the tax system with a host of tax preferences in 1997. Taxes have gotten so complicated again that tax reform is back on the political agenda.

The least substantive case in this category was the same-sex marriage law. Many legal experts argued the ban was unnecessary and duplicated existing state laws. No critical public problem was solved by the legislation. It simply expressed the sentiment of the American people in favor of traditional marriage and against same-sex unions. Symbolic legislation can play a useful social function in some cases but is unlikely to really make a difference in slowing the pace of changing mores and social behavior.

We have seen that many of the policies that emerge from this pattern meet the test of good policy. Perhaps the greatest danger of consensus/cooperation is that to reach an acceptable compromise, policies become watered down and more symbolic than substantive, eroding their impact. Bipartisan cooperation is no guarantee of good policy if it simply papers over differences for the sake of appearing to do something about a problem. Consensus on an issue may ensure a democratic outcome but not necessarily effective public policy.

DEADLOCK/EXTRAORDINARY RESOLUTION

Characteristics

Deadlock occurs when sharp differences on visible issues lead to high levels of interbranch conflict, and neither branch is willing to compromise or able to lead the other. When a forcing mechanism exists (such as the annual budget), or the consequences of inaction are disastrous, deadlock may be resolved by extraordinary means outside the normal policymaking process. Each of the four cases we examined generated unusual animosity between Congress and the presidency. Each took place under divided government (although deadlock can occur with unified control of government) and was characterized by high levels of partisanship. Social Security, aid to the Contras, and the budget conflict were prolonged struggles, evolving through a series of stalemates over many years until finally resolved. The two parties warred over Social Security for years before the 1983 bailout plan. The 1995–1996 budget standoff was preceded by a fifteen-year impasse over how to reduce chronic deficits. Aid to the Contras was a dilemma that the political system seemed incapable of resolving; there were repetitive decisions and inconsistent actions throughout the 1980s.

The 1990 Civil Rights bill remained deadlocked at the end of the 101st Congress but finally was resolved in 1991 as a result of the Clarence Thomas hearings, the David Duke candidacy, and closed-door negotiations between Senate Republicans and the White House. As a case of presidential-congressional policymaking, it is very similar to the Civil Rights Restoration Act of 1988, except for one crucial difference. In 1990, Congress had been just short of the two-thirds majority to override Bush's veto, missing by one vote in the Senate. Perhaps it was the administration's fear that the one-vote margin would not hold that prompted a negotiated settlement. Thus, in this case as in each of the other three, deadlock was resolved by extraordinary means.

The Social Security crisis was resolved by the use of a bipartisan commission, which gave the administration and congressional leaders the political cover they needed to make the unpopular decision to raise taxes and cut benefits. Deadlock over the balanced budget plan in 1995–1996 remained unresolved until after the 1996 elections. Both sides went to the barricades, shutting down the government rather than compromising. Compared with 1990, when the budget crisis was resolved by the use of a summit between branches, there was no extraordinary resolution for Clinton and the 104th Congress.

Aid to the Contras was characterized by a number of extraordinary actions by both sides, intended to outmaneuver the other branch. Congress passed the Boland amendments to handcuff the administration. In frustration, the White House devised the ill-fated plan to channel funds covertly to the Contras through private foreign contributions and diversion of the profits from secret arms sales to Iran. The result was the highly damaging Iran–Contra scandal that marred Ronald Reagan's second term. This issue was not resolved until 1989 when Bush and Congress reached an accord. Finally, the issue became moot when the Sandanistas were defeated in Nicaragua's elections in early 1990.

What Leads to Deadlock?

Deadlock in policymaking often reflects deep divisions in the nation, translated into sharp cleavages in the policy preferences of government officials. Public opinion was divided over the question of aid to the Contras throughout the mid-1980s. The polls showed volatility on this question as the Iran–Contra scandal unfolded. Public opinion on budget questions was also inconsistent. The public strongly opposes big deficits, supports the Republicans' promise not to raise taxes, and at the same time supports Democrats who oppose further cuts in entitlement programs. Conversely, extremely strong public support for Social Security made it difficult for negotiators to raise payroll taxes and cut benefits, both of which had to be accomplished to solve the problem.

The pattern of deadlock emerges in a political environment in which policy differences are great and political stakes are high. The electoral consequences of these issues are extremely important at both the congressional and presidential levels, so compromise becomes even more difficult during an election year. The Social Security bailout became politically possible only after the 1982 midterm elections, and the final resolution of aid to the Contras after the 1988 elections. The deadlock over the 1990–1991 civil rights bill reflected electoral calculations by both parties. The balanced budget plan remained in deadlock during the whole of the 104th Congress. Only the 1996 presidential and congressional election produced the conditions to break the deadlock.

Extraordinary resolution of policy deadlocks involves alternative institutional arrangements or innovative means to break the political impasse. Ad hoc devices such as summits and secret negotiations between branches became more common in the 1980s. Automatic mechanisms such as Gramm-Rudman mandatory deficit reduction were used in an attempt to force a political settlement on the budget conflict, but they restricted the options of both branches. Bipartisan commissions were used successfully in the Social Security dispute and have been employed in other controversial issues, such as military base closings, and have been proposed to deal with Medicare, for example. Restrictive rules limiting amendments in Congress made it possible to preserve unpopular solutions, including both the Social Security and some of the earlier budget compromises.

Deadlock is not confined to any single policy area but has been less common in foreign policy and civil rights. Historically, issues in these areas have more often been characterized by compromise and cooperation, but interbranch conflict in both areas escalated in the 1980s. Economic and budget policy and social welfare policy have been more divisive, partisan, and prone to deadlock in the modern era. In welfare reform, it took a generation to enact meaningful change, and the budget was marked by paralysis throughout the 1980s and 1990s. Although we have seen many instances of constructive policymaking occur under divided government, it is clearly more vulnerable to the intense partisan interbranch combat that leads to deadlock.

Consequences

Unresolved deadlock can result in drift and inaction in the face of pressing national problems. The specter of partisan intransigence—epitomized by government shutdowns—leads to public cynicism and disillusionment. Aid to the Contras and the budget paralysis of 1995–1996 are the best examples of the negative consequences of deadlock. U.S. policy in Nicaragua in the 1980s produced the worst of both worlds. It was a policy marked by contradictions—the approval of aid to the rebels one year, the denial of aid the next. It led Congress to adopt means that may have been unconstitutional in its quest to handcuff the executive branch. Likewise, the administration reacted to the deadlock by breaking the law to achieve its objectives. The resulting policy failed to meet the objectives of either branch or to serve national interests.

Stalemate over the budget after 1981 led to the largest deficits in history. The national debt quadrupled despite the fact that both branches decried the sorry state of affairs. The history of budget negotiations between Congress and the president in the 1980s and 1990s is a combination of deadlock, negotiation, and extraordinary resolution. Significant progress was made in reducing the deficits in the 1990s. In terms of size, the 1990 and 1993 deficit reduction agreements actually were larger than the eventual budget agreement in 1997.[11] In 1995, the Republican Congress attempted to impose a partisan plan on the administration, and the result was stalemate. Unlike after previous budget deadlocks, with strong economic growth, the deficits continued to fall. When a balanced budget agreement was finally reached two years later, it needed to save only $204 billion over five years. Both branches were actually able to balance the budget in fiscal year 1998 and deliver to constituencies in terms of lower taxes and more spending.

Deadlock per se and extraordinary resolution of deadlocks are not always disastrous for the nation. Some deadlocks simply mean temporary delay, which can improve the policy in the long run. Other stalemates may be frustrating but not disastrous. Despite its importance, the failure to pass the civil rights bill of 1990 had nowhere near the negative impact of inconsistent policy in Central America or chronic deficits. In addition, resolution by extraordinary means can sometimes produce very satisfactory results. The 1983 Social Security bailout ensured the solvency of the Social Security Trust fund well into the twenty-first century. In fact, it created such large surpluses in the trust fund that afterwards, some suggested cutting payroll taxes. Gramm-Rudman initially succeeded in forcing a declining trend in deficits, although it ultimately failed to reach targeted levels. Because the deficits were declining, the balanced budget standoff in 1995–1996 was less disastrous than earlier ones.

Deadlock, by its very nature, fails many of the tests of good policy. It blunts the responsiveness of policymaking and fails to take action in a timely manner. Extraordinary resolution of deadlocks is often achieved only by limiting the participation and representation of competing interests. Summits and bipartisan commissions centralize policymaking in the hands of a few key decision makers in both branches. The rank-and-file members of Congress and cabinet officials often bristle at being cut out of the process, denied the right to amend or alter policy. Moreover, summits do not guarantee that issues will be resolved. The 1989 budget summit agreement between Bush and Congress, for example, simply papered over differences; it was an exercise in "least common denominator" bipartisanship. Deadlock usually fails the tests of consistency, coherence, and effectiveness. Inconsistent policy in Nicaragua had costs, both in Nicaraguan lives and in the diminished international credibility for the

United States. Because of a decade of deficits, despite a healthy economy in the 1980s, a growing portion of federal outlays in the 1990s must be devoted to paying interest on the debt, diverting resources from pressing domestic needs. Extraordinary resolution of deadlocks can ultimately solve problems, but the political system pays a price in terms of public confidence, international credibility, civility in government, and national unity.

Collaboration and Combat

Table 9.1 summarizes the sixteen cases that have been examined. Based on the conclusions to each of the substantive chapters, we suggest, in simplified form, which patterns are most prevalent by policy area. Based on the discussion in this chapter, Table 9.1 also suggests some of the policy consequences associated with each pattern of presidential-congressional policymaking. Of course, it must be remembered

TABLE 9.1   Cases of Presidential-Congressional Policymaking, by Pattern and Policy Area

	Pattern of Interaction	
Policy Area	Presidential Leadership	Congressional Leadership
Foreign Policy	Gulf War (1991)	Cuba Sanctions Act (1996)
Civil rights policy	Civil Rights Act (1964)	Civil Rights Restoration Act (1988)
Economic and budget policy	Economic and budget plan (1981)	Shareholder Lawsuits Act (1995)
Social welfare policy	Economic Opportunity Act (1964)	Catastrophic health care insurance (1988–1989)
Policy Consequences	Timely and decisive but can be hasty or ill-conceived; responsive if not always representative; nonroutine, major change	Often slow but representative; favors local and dispersed benefits; often more symbolic than substantive; modest and major changes

that the prevalence, causes, and consequences of these policymaking patterns defy simple conclusions.

What can we conclude about the policymaking strengths and weaknesses of Congress and the presidency? Perhaps most important, no single pattern guarantees good policy, although some patterns seem more promising than others. Michael Mezey's hypothesis about the inherent characteristics of Congress and the president as policymakers is partially right but provides only part of the picture. The presidency does have certain advantages of dispatch and clarity, but presidential-led policymaking does not always result in well-managed, effective policies (or, conversely, in less democratic policies). The Congress has the advantages of representativeness and openness, but Congress-led policy does not always result in poorly managed, ineffective policies—or in more democratic policies. In addition, two other important patterns reflect a mix of the strengths and weaknesses of both branches as they cooperate or mutually resolve differences.

TABLE 9.1   Continued

Pattern of Interaction		
Consensus/Cooperation	Deadlock/Extraordinary Resolution	Most Prevalent Patterns
Panama Canal Treaties (1978)	Aid to Contras (1983–1989)	Presidential leadership more frequent, but growing congressional role, particularly when domestic implications are substantial
Same-Sex Marriage Act (1996)	Civil Rights Act (1991)	Congress more important in recent years; cooperation diminishing as partisanship and deadlock increase
Tax Reform Act (1986)	Balanced Budget Plan (1995–1996)	Dominance by either branch rare; deadlock common; extraordinary resolution frequently needed
Welfare Reform Act (1996)	Social Security bailout (1983)	Greater congressional leadership; neither branch dominant; periodic deadlocks punctuated by compromise
Not timely but can be decisive; representative and consensus-oriented; generally substantive and effective, but compromise may dilute impact	Inaction in the face of demands; less representative; politics over policy; extraordinary resolution can sometimes be effective but strains system	

What can we conclude about divided government? There is increasing survey evidence that the American people say they want it, taking to heart Madison's view that ambition should counteract ambition.[12] Yet more than 75 percent of voters cast their ballots in 1996 for congressional and presidential candidates of the same party.[13] It is clear that divided government does not preclude policymaking. As David Mayhew's study has shown, much important legislation has emerged under divided party control of government.[14] But it is also clear that divided government does matter. Recent studies have found that major legislation is more controversial and more likely to fail under divided government.[15] It increases the probability for deadlock to occur and often lengthens the time that it takes for problems to be addressed. Issues that lack the urgency of a government shutdown or trust fund bankruptcy may go unresolved indefinitely.

It appears that divided government reduces the probability of either presidential or congressional leadership across policy areas. But that could mean an increase of either cooperation or deadlock under divided government. Under a Democratic president and Republican Congress in the 1990s, there have been vetoes, political attacks, and government shutdowns, but also welfare reform, approval of the line item veto, major trade legislation, and a balanced budget agreement. The record under unified government in recent times is mixed as well. In a case of presidential leadership, President Clinton successfully pushed through a tough and unpopular deficit reduction plan in 1993. But health care reform was one of the major policy failures of the 1990s, and it occurred under Democratic party control of both branches.

We have seen the diversity of patterns across policy areas, shifting factors that affect how separate institutions make policy, and the mix of policy consequences that result. Our final question concerns the policy connection itself: Can anything be done to promote patterns that produce more effective public policy? Our analysis to this point suggests that the key to more effective policymaking is not strengthening either the president's or Congress's role; rather, it is to enhance the ability of both branches to enter into a constructive engagement with each other. This could be accomplished in various ways.

CAN PRESIDENTIAL-CONGRESSIONAL POLICYMAKING BE IMPROVED?

Constitutional Reform

The most outspoken critics of presidential-congressional conflict and the growing prevalence of deadlock in the 1980s proposed a radical solution: changing the basic structure of the Constitution. Constitutional reformers make the case that, however brilliant a solution separation of powers may have been two centuries ago, it is simply inadequate for the governing needs of today. However, over the years, there has been remarkably little sentiment for tinkering with the Constitution. In an attempt to break down resistance to change, a group of scholars and public officials, including

Douglas Dillon, Lloyd Cutler, Charles Hardin, and James Sundquist, formed the Committee on the Constitutional System.[16] Although interest in constitutional reform has peaked for the moment, their proposals are still useful for thinking about improving presidential-congressional policymaking. The checks and balances designed to prevent despotism, in the words of the committee, have led to "government stalemate and deadlock, to indecision and inaction in the face of urgent problems."[17]

Accordingly, the Committee on the Constitutional System drafted a series of proposed constitutional amendments that would fundamentally restructure the way the American political system works. To prevent divided government, they proposed electing candidates for the House, the Senate, and the presidency on a single ticket.[18] To provide greater consultation and collective responsibility in policymaking, they suggested amending the Constitution to allow members of Congress to sit on the president's cabinet. This idea was first introduced in Congress in the 1880s. To achieve a similar result, another proposal called for cabinet secretaries and administration officials to participate in the deliberations in Congress, including floor debate. Other alternatives to avoid divided government included awarding bonus seats in Congress to the party winning the presidency and repealing the Twenty-Second Amendment, which limits the president to two terms.[19]

If deadlock occurs, the constitutional system of the United States provides no method for breaking it, short of waiting for the next election. Even then, elections are rarely decisive. The committee suggested several daring constitutional changes to break deadlocks between Congress and the president. One proposal provided for a congressional vote of no confidence, making it possible to remove the president and call new elections. Conversely, the committee also proposed giving the president the power to dissolve Congress once during his presidential term and call for new legislative elections. Less radical amendments to reduce political deadlock included a one-house veto override, a presidential line item veto, reduced majorities required for treaty ratification, and the establishment of a national referendum to break a stalemate.[20]

These and other dramatic proposals to make the United States more like a parliamentary democracy are interesting and provocative, but constitutional reform is not the answer. There are serious flaws in both the diagnosis and the cure. Scholars have analyzed and criticized the major reforms proposed by the committee and found that each is based on an incorrect diagnosis of the problems or does not match political needs.[21] As we have seen throughout, deadlock is not the only pattern of policymaking that occurs under divided government, nor is unified party control of Congress and the presidency any guarantee that deadlock will be prevented. The patterns of presidential leadership, congressional leadership, and cooperation also occur under divided government and often result in effective policymaking. Even when deadlock occurs, leaders of both branches have increasingly relied on extraordinary means to resolve deadlocks. Administration officials already consult and negotiate with congressional leaders throughout the legislative process, particularly on the most important policy issues.

Constitutional reform is not the solution to improving the policy connection for two main reasons. First, it is not at all clear that the amended system would work as the reformers claim. Much would depend on the party system, the rules and procedures in Congress, and presidential leadership. Second, restructuring government through constitutional amendment is simply unrealistic and counterproductive. In over 200 years, only five amendments dealing with the structure of government have been ratified. Of those, the Twelfth (election of the president and vice president as a ticket), the Twentieth (advancing the date of the president's inauguration), and the Twenty-Fifth (dealing with presidential disability and filling a vacancy in the vice presidency) are peripheral to fundamental structural issues. Only the Seventeenth (direct election of senators) and the Twenty-Second (limiting the president to two terms) seriously altered the nature of Congress and the presidency. It is possible that in the coming century, cataclysmic events may create a constitutional crisis unprecedented in American history. Having an intellectual bank of structural alternatives may yet prove useful.[22] Until that day arrives, however, constitutional reform offers no practical solutions for preventing deadlock, strengthening ties between branches, or improving the effectiveness of policymaking.

Some reformers have proposed changes that attempt to achieve ends similar to those of the Committee on the Constitutional System, but without the necessity of amending the Constitution. Admirers of parliamentary systems have suggested that the United States adopt a practice similar to "question time" in the British government, where the prime minister appears before the House of Commons every week to answer questions submitted in writing by both government-party and opposition-party members. This procedure could be adopted in the United States by mutual consent of Congress and the president. Proponents believe it would improve accountability in government and perhaps encourage consultation. Other suggestions include joint committees comprising officials from both branches to tackle issues such as the declassification or dissemination of government information. Question time and other such reforms would not require constitutional amendment but suffer from some of the same flaws as constitutional reform. Parliamentary practices are not easy to import into the U.S. federal system, and it is unclear what they would accomplish. Presidents are unlikely to reap many benefits from weekly appearances before Congress to face hostile questioning; it could actually damage relations between branches. Nonetheless, given the continuing concern with the policy connection, the search for nonconstitutional changes to strengthen policymaking is a useful one.

One of the most interesting nonconstitutional reforms to be adopted in recent years is the line item veto. Because it was seen as too difficult to pass as a constitutional amendment, it was adopted as a statute that provides an elaborate mechanism for enhanced rescission authority that functions like a line item veto. The Supreme Court upheld the line item veto on technical grounds in 1997 because the parties did not have standing to sue.[23] That opened the door for Bill Clinton to be the only president in history to use this power. As we saw in Chapter 3, in 1997 he used it eighty-two times in tax and spending bills. Despite using it carefully, many Republican members of Congress who had voted for the veto were unhappy with its application and overrode thirty-eight of the item vetoes in 1998. In the unlikely event that it does survive a court challenge in 1998, the line item veto will probably not have much impact on deficits or surpluses but could significantly alter public perception of the relationship between Congress and the president.

Strengthening the Party System

Assuming that improvements must be made within the constitutional system that now exists, the reforms most frequently proposed to bridge the separation of powers are to restructure and strengthen political parties. The notion of disciplined, responsible parties has long held appeal to political scientists.[24] Long-time party reform advocate James MacGregor Burns urges the parties to emphasize their differences. Burns argues that the early Reagan presidency is a good model, "a textbook demonstration of how a leader both mobilizes and engages with his followers, wins office, and works closely with party leadership in governing the nation."[25] He and other critics believe that the American people have for too long been lulled by bland appeals to compromise, centrism, bipartisanship, and national unity. Following the same logic, Nicholas von Hoffman urges the two parties to "politicize, polarize, ignite the rancors of politics, disunite, crack open the one-party state."[26] To accomplish these changes, party reformers advocate a return to old values: party caucuses rather than primaries, uncommitted party convention delegates, laws to strengthen the national parties, and the single-minded pursuit of a partisan agenda.

Variants on the party reform theme abound. Theodore Lowi discounts reforms to strengthen the two-party system, advocating instead the creation of a multiparty system. He believes such a system would throw presidential elections into the House of Representatives or at least require a president to build and maintain a constituency in Congress.[27] He suggests abolishing the electoral college and instituting a presidential runoff election between the two top vote-getters to accommodate third parties even more. Third-party candidate Ross Perot won 19 percent of the vote in 1992, but fell off to 7 percent in 1996. So far, nothing like a multiparty system seems to be emerging.

Mainstream party reformers are more circumspect about the path to party renewal to strengthen ties between legislative and executive branches. Larry Sabato argues that unless our parties become stronger, PACs, celebrity candidates, incumbents, television news, and political consultants will dominate the political system.[28] To achieve stronger political parties, he advocates increased party services to members, expanded party fund-raising, better education of the public, party sponsorship of presidential primaries, and more uncommitted delegates at national conventions. Government-assisted reforms would include state deregulation of parties; legislation to make the parties the main conduit of campaign funds; free media time for parties; and requirements for party registration, party labels on ballots, and the option of voting a straight party ticket in all states. While ambitious, Sabato's agenda for party reform is clearly within the bounds of existing American political life. The question is: Would such reforms make a difference?

Party reform is not the answer to governing problems. It is ironic that as voter loyalty and attachment to the parties weakens, partisanship and party voting have increased sharply in Congress. This is more a function of divided government and changes in the ideological composition of congressional parties than of party reform. Traditional appeals for a more responsible two-party system have changed little since the Roosevelt era, whereas the political system has changed dramatically. These wistful longings for a bygone era are simply irrelevant to the Congress and presidency of today. Party government, although it occasionally reappears, simply cannot sustain effective governing coalitions today, even under unified party control. Clinton's mixed record with unified government in 1993–1994 is an example. Under divided government, increased party differences, sharper divisions, greater conflict, and a rejection of compromise may result in paralysis. Proposals to create a multiparty system are also based more on wishful thinking than on hard political analysis. It is unclear how such a system would come about. Even if it did, it is doubtful that it would accomplish anything more than further fragmentation and divisiveness in policymaking.

More moderate proposals for party reforms, such as Sabato's, are certainly possible, but the broader contention that the decline of parties can be reversed is dubious. Party organizations have become more about fund-raising than anything else. Even if political parties become more visible and important in the electoral process, the fact remains that in the media age, people do not find parties necessary when deciding which candidates to vote for. Even Sabato's own research indicated that a candidate's party label was the least important factor of ten included in a postelection survey.[29] Party reform proposals do have appeal for people who are concerned about the institutional combat that has developed in recent decades, but such proposals are not responsive to the political needs and governing problems of the current era.

Collaborative Policymaking

The party government model is no longer the yardstick by which the performance of Congress and the president should be gauged. The fact is that over the past thirty years, Congress has greatly enhanced its capacity to shape the policy agenda, formulate and enact legislation, and hence, negotiate as an equal partner with the president. Even when the Democrats had two years of unified government after twelve years of divided government, common partisan bonds did not eliminate interbranch conflict or fundamentally change different institutional perspectives. The 1993 deficit reduction package was one of the few pieces of major legislation that followed the party government script. Arguably, Clinton has had as much success negotiating with a hostile Republican Congress as he did with a friendly but independent Democratic Congress. Unified Republican or Democratic control of government is possible in 2001. If it is the Republicans, it would be the first time since 1952 and only the second time in seventy years. That fact alone would likely make it a more productive unified party partnership for a while. But even in this case, the president will still have to enter into a partnership with Congress and build coalitions between branches. Under current political conditions, successful policymaking coalitions usually must have some support from members of both parties. As one Democratic senator noted, "We have coalition government now. It only works when both sides are on board."[30]

Collaborative cross-party coalition building and bipartisan compromise as a mode of operation raises the hackles of party reformers such as Burns and von Hoffman. It draws the jeers of the most partisan ideologues in both parties, who wonder how they will be able to win the next election if both parties work together. Although bipartisan coalitions can blur party differences, the cases suggest that cooperation tends to produce more satisfactory policy outcomes. If deadlocks occur, extraordinary means of resolution can be sought. They may prove useful in dealing with tough issues, such as the growth of Medicare and Social Security before baby boomers begin to retire. In the final analysis, arriving at effective foreign and domestic policies, which respond to the rapidly changing environment, is more important than clarifying party differences. Cooperation may obscure accountability, but it increases the collective responsibility of the government as a whole.

Coalition government based on accommodation, negotiation, and mutual cooperation is not the same as the one-party state. Bipartisanship—majority support in both parties—will not always result. Cross-partisanship means that enough support from one party is gained to produce a majority and enhance legitimacy. A majority of one party may still oppose a majority of the other party. Both parties can establish a record to run on based on their negotiating positions and using the media to clarify their differences. For example, after the balanced budget agreement in 1997, Republicans were still talking about lower taxes and spending cuts, while Democrats were promising to protect the elderly and promote fairness in future tax reform. Collaboration does not mean that all issues will take the pattern of consensus/cooperation. If political conditions are right, certain policies may still be led by either Congress or the president, particularly if the other branch believes that the costs of opposition are high. Reform of the IRS in 1997–1998 is an example of congressional leadership with the somewhat reluctant assent of the president. In many areas, issues will remain unresolved if there is insufficient public pressure or urgency to act. However, when critical decisions must be made, it is essential that the political system adopt means to reach a compromise. NAFTA in 1993, welfare reform in 1996, and the balanced budget agreement in 1997 are examples.

What specific steps can be taken to strengthen policymaking between Congress and the president to foster collaborative policymaking? Prior consultation and open lines of communication during the legislative process can help avoid deadlock. Unless an initiative is offered simply to make a political record, understanding the aims and goals of the other side can help frame the context of negotiations. This does not preclude strategic gamesmanship to gain leverage in bargaining but may help establish more realistic parameters from the outset.

Effective bargaining can be encouraged by occasional closed-door negotiations— away from the media spotlights, PACs and interest groups, and potential looking for partisan advantage. Sunshine laws are intrinsically appealing in a free society, but openness must be balanced with other values. The importance of secrecy was recognized by the founders in 1787, when they closed their sessions to the public. Public posturing can lead to deadlock. However, congressional negotiators must keep the rank-and-file members informed and on board. The comparison between the 1990 and 1997 budget agreements is instructive. In 1990, the small group of White House and congressional negotiators did not sufficiently keep in touch with the membership. The deal was perceived as too detailed, infringing on the domain of committees. As a result, the initial agreement was defeated by a majority of both parties. In contrast, the 1997 balanced budget agreement kept members of both parties better apprised of the deals that were being made. It set broad parameters rather than specifics, allowing the committees to retain their options. In the end, despite the opposition of the Democratic leader in the House, the agreement was approved by a majority of both parties.

Congress has become more capable as a policymaker. Reducing fragmentation and increasing decision-making capability in Congress is also an important ingredient of more effective collaborative policymaking. Trends in the 1980s and 1990s have made significant strides in this direction. Stronger party leaders and key committee chairs, control of the legislative agenda, management of the legislative process through restrictive rules, leadership bills that avoid committee conflicts, and limits on delaying tactics all increase the capacity of Congress to negotiate with the executive. Unlimited amendments, nongermane riders, and procedural delays can cripple the legislative process. Procedural restrictions are not necessary for all bills or even most bills, only for certain essential legislation. Although a more centralized legislative leadership and cohesive majorities may make deadlock more likely when interbranch conflicts are high, such a situation enhances the capability to negotiate and compromise through ad hoc means.

Collaborative policymaking also can be enhanced by better norms of governing—the unwritten rules of the political game. Particularly desirable would be a "truth in budgeting" norm: In recent years, both branches have been guilty of using "cooked" numbers, unrealistic assumptions, and rosy scenarios for political purposes, although some improvement has occurred in the 1990s. Norms that emphasize governing would encourage attempts to depoliticize deadlocked issues. This remains a problem in dealing with Medicare spending over the long run. At critical times, participants at both ends of the avenue would avoid bashing the other institution for short-term political gain, mindful of long-term policy consequences and the necessity of maintaining an ongoing working relationship. Compare the restrained debate about authorizing the use of force in the Persian Gulf in 1991 with the partisan warfare over aid to the Contras in the mid-1980s, or the constructive engagement regarding tax reform in 1986 compared with the accusations hurled during the 1995–1996 budget battle. If warring nations can abide by the Geneva Convention, surely Congress and the president could abide by certain rules of political engagement when dealing with critical decisions that affect the nation's future.

Governing by cross-partisan or bipartisan collaboration in a separated system may be comparable to a multiparty governing coalition in a parliamentary system. It does not equal a depoliticized policy process, and an unhappy party can quit the coalition. It is both undesirable and impossible to take the politics out of policy-making. Each branch must protect its political resources and institutional strength, clarify differences, and attempt to shape public policy as it sees best. However, actions taken by one branch to weaken or undermine the other are counterproductive for the political system. Michael Malbin suggests the balance that is needed:

> *Preserving the power of the office is a top priority to be enforced independently of the specific policy in dispute at the moment. The preceding is not meant to urge political leaders to stop fighting for deeply felt policy convictions. It is not too much to ask, however, that the two branches learn to limit the damage from such fighting. . . . It is best to arrive at an informal, mutual understanding of what constitutes procedural cooperation and then encourage each side to protect its own interest.[31]*

The presidency-centered era of national policymaking is over. The postmodern presidency in the aftermath of the cold war confronts an assertive and capable Congress. Until political conditions change, collaborative policymaking in some form seems inevitable for national policymaking. Recognizing this fact, policymaking will be improved not only by enhancing the competence and capability of both branches, but also by strengthening those mechanisms that allow mutual cooperation and reciprocity between them.

ENDNOTES

1. Michael Mezey, *Congress, the President, and Public Policy* (Boulder, Colo.: Westview Press, 1989): 189.

2. Steven A. Shull, *Domestic Policy Formation: Presidential-Congressional Partnership?* (Westport, Conn.: Greenwood Press, 1983).

3. The major investigation of political symbolism is by Murray Edelman, *Symbolic Uses of Politics* (Urbana: University of Illinois Press, 1964).

4. Quoted in "Debunking the Myth of Decline," *New York Times Magazine* (June 19, 1988): 35.

5. Irving L. Janis, *Victims of Groupthink* (Boston: Houghton Mifflin, 1972).

6. See Randall B. Ripley and Grace R. Franklin, *Congress, the Bureaucracy, and Public Policy* (Homewood, Ill.: Dorsey, 1988).

7. Richard P. Nathan et al., *Monitoring Revenue Sharing* (Washington, D.C.: Brookings Institution, 1976).

8. Theodore Lowi differentiated among distributive, regulatory, and redistributive policies in "American Business, Public Policy, Case Studies, and Political Theory," *World Politics* 16 (July 1964): 677–715. For an empirical treatment using his typology, see Shull (note 2).

9. John Ellwood, "Comments on Shepsle and Weingast," in Gregory B. Mills and John L. Palmer (eds.), *Federal Budget Policy in the 1980's* (Washington, D.C.: Urban Institute Press, 1984).

10. See discussion of Senator Byrd as "trustee" in David Vogler, *The Politics of Congress,* 3d ed. (Boston: Allyn and Bacon, 1980): 82.

11. CBO and Senate Budget Committee estimates, reported in *Congressional Quarterly Weekly Report* (May 17, 1997): 1118.

12. Morris Fiorina, *Divided Government,* (Boston: Allyn and Bacon, 1996): 64–65.

13. Ronald D. Elving, "Partisanship Belies Rhetoric of Peace," *Congressional Quarterly Weekly Report,* Jan. 18, 1997: 198.

14. David Mayhew, *Divided We Govern* (New Haven, Conn.: Yale University Press, 1991). Other critiques of divided government include Morris P. Fiorina, *Divided Government* (New York: Macmillan, 1992); Gary W. Cox and Samuel Kernell (eds.), *Politics of Divided Government* (Boulder, Colo.: Westview Press, 1991); and Steven A. Shull, *Presidential-Congressional Relations* (Ann Arbor: University of Michigan Press, 1997).

15. George C. Edwards III, Andrew Barrett, and Jeffrey Peake, "The Legislative Impact of Divided Government," *American Journal of Political Science,* 41 (1997): 545–563.

16. Donald Robinson (ed.), *Reforming American Government: The Bicentennial Papers of the Committee on the Constitutional System* (Boulder, Colo.: Westview Press, 1985).

17. Ibid., 69.

18. Ibid., 175–188.

19. Authors writing on the Twenty-Second Amendment include Bruce Buchanan, "The Six-Year One-Term Presidency," *Presidential Studies Quarterly* 17 (Winter 1988): 129–142; Thomas E. Cronin, "Two Cheers for the 22nd Amendment," *Presidency Research 9* (Spring 1987): 6; David C. Nice, "In Retreat from Excellence: The Single Six Year Presidential Term," *Congress and the Presidency* 13 (Autumn 1986): 209–220.

20. Robinson (note 16): 254–264; see also John Orman, *Presidential Accountability* (Westport, Conn.: Greenwood Press, 1990).

21. Mark Petraca et al., "Proposals for Constitutional Reform," *Presidential Studies Quarterly,* 20 (Summer, 1990): 503–532.

22. James MacGregor Burns, "Why Think about Constitutional Reform," in Robinson (note 16): 59–60.

23. *Byrd v. Raines,* 956 F.Supp. 25 (1997).

24. The American Political Science Association issued a report entitled "Towards a More Responsible Two-Party System" in 1950.

25. James MacGregor Burns, *The Power to Lead* (New York: Simon and Schuster, 1984): 212.

26. Nicholas van Hoffman, *Make Believe Presidents* (New York: Pantheon, 1978): 213.

27. Theodore J. Lowi, *The Personal Presidency* (Ithaca, N. Y.: Cornell University Press, 1985): 203–209.

28. Larry Sabato, *The Party's Just Begun* (Glenview, Ill.: Scott Foresman, 1988).

29. Ibid., 6–7.

30. *Congressional Quarterly Weekly Report* (December 30, 1989): 3354.

31. Michael Malbin, "Legislative-Executive Lessons from the Iran–Contra Affair," in Lawrence C. Dodd and Bruce I. Oppenheimer (eds.), *Congress Reconsidered,* 4th ed. (Washington, D.C.: Congressional Quarterly Press, 1989): 390–391.

INDEX

Abrams, Elliot, 118
Adams, John, 42, 43
Adams, John Quincy, 148
Adams, Sherman, 74
Adarand Contractors Inc.
v. Pena, 157
Ad hoc arrangements, 18, 113,
254
Administrative presidency, 75
Affirmative action, 153, 154,
155–156, 171
Afghanistan, Soviet invasion of,
122, 123
African Americans. *See* Blacks
Agenda. *See* Policy agenda
Aid the the Blind, 208
Aid to Families with Dependent
Children (AFDC), 208. *See*
also under Welfare
Aid to the Disabled, 208
Albert, Carl, 109
Albright, Madeline, 133
Allen, James, 138
Allison, Graham, 121
American Civil Liberties Union,
166–167
America's Hidden Success
(Schwartz), 217
Anderson, James, 186
Appointment power, 54–55, 64
Appointments, judicial, 55, 56
Armey, Dick, 109, 111, 200
Arms race, 120–121
Articles of Confederation, 34–35,
36
Aspin, Les, 131
Automatic devices, for
extraordinary resolution, 18

Baker, Howard, 25, 138, 139,
232, 249
Baker, James, 142
Baker, Ross, 26
Bakke decision, 154
Balanced Budget and Emergency
Deficit Control Act of 1985,
57–58, 106
Balanced budget standoff,
197–201, 251, 263
Barber, James David, 20, 24
Barger, Howard, 65
Bay of Pigs, 121, 243
Bills. *See* Legislation
Bipartisan commissions, 113, 254

Bipartisanship, 11. *See also*
Consensus/ cooperation
in civil rights policy, 151,
157–158, 158–164
in Clinton administration, 70
collaborative policymaking
and, 263–265
in economic and budget
policy, 194–197
effectiveness of, 113
examples of, 70
in foreign policy, 130–133
in Johnson administration, 70
in Persian Gulf War, 130–132
in social welfare policy,
224–226
Birnbaum, Jeffrey, 194
Bismark, Otto von, 207
Blacks
civil rights for. *See* Civil rights
policy
voting rights for, 149
Boland, Edward, 141
Boland amendments, 126, 141
Bond, Jon, 20, 127, 128
Bork, Robert, 55
Boskin, Michael, 186
Bosnia, 124, 127
Bowen, Otis, 223, 224
Bowsher v. Synar, 57
Bradley, Bill, 195
Breaux, John, 70
Broder, David, 142
Brownlow Report, 71
Brown v. Board of Education, 51,
150
Buchanan, James, 45
Budget and Accounting Act of
1921, 48
Budget and Impoundment
Control Act of 1974, 6, 15,
52, 53, 187
Budget deficit, 179–181, 255–256
reduction measures for, 18,
57–58, 106, 179–181,
182–183, 187–188, 250, 255
Budget Enforcement Act of
1990, 106
Bureau of the Budget (BOB), 71,
176–177, 185–186
Burns, James McGregor, 261, 263
Burr, Aaron, 42
Bush, George, 15, 20, 22, 23, 24,
55, 64, 85, 241, 245

approval ratings for, 67–68, 69
civil rights policy of, 148, 155,
157, 158, 163–164,
167–170
communication and selling
skills of, 75
congressional lobbying by, 73
economic and budget policy
of, 179, 183, 186
foreign policy of, 63–64, 126,
127, 130–133, 144
leadership skills of, 241
legislative success of, 82
management style of, 74
Nicaraguan Contras and, 142
101st Congress and, 2–3
Persian Gulf War and, 3, 21,
63–64, 130–133, 144,
239–240
retrenchment agenda of, 78–79
social welfare policy of, 226,
233, 244
vetoes by, 83, 84, 253
Busing, 153
Byrd, Robert, 25, 138, 139, 166,
249, 250–251

Cabinet, 48, 71–72
in foreign policy, 125–126
inner, 42
rejection of nominees to, 55
removal of members of, 55
Cabinet Council on Economic
Affairs, 186
Calhoun, John C., 5
Campaign finance reform, 17
Campaign financing, of
congressional elections, 97
Canada, 135
Cannon, Joseph, 102
Carter, Jimmy, 9, 20, 22, 24, 52,
57, 190, 194, 230, 231
approval ratings for, 68, 69
civil rights policy of, 154, 157,
158, 170
communication and selling
skills of, 75
consolidation/maintenance
agenda of, 79, 80–81
foreign policy of, 122, 250
legislative agenda of, 26
legislative success of, 73, 127,
128
management style of, 74

267

Legislative branch. *See under*
Congress; Congressional
Legislative-executive relations
ad hoc devices in, 18, 113, 254
bipartisanship in. *See*
Bipartisanship
central clearance and, 72
in civil rights policy, 152–170.
See also Civil rights policy
collaborative policymaking
and, 262–265
congressionalist view of, 5–6
constitutional aspects of, 4–8,
258–261
dimensions of, 12–13
in early Republic, 42–43
foreign policy and, 117–144.
See also Foreign policy
honeymoon period in, 24
from Jackson era to Civil War,
44–45
legislative liaison and, 72–73
in modern era, 50–54
overview of, 238–239
vs. parliamentary system, 4–5
patterns of, 1–4, 13–27
policymaking and. *See*
Policymaking
political parties and, 261–262
presidentialist view of, 6
public-policy perspective on,
12–30. *See also*
Policymaking from
Reconstruction to
Depression, 45–48
separationist view of, 7–11
separation of powers and, 3–8.
See also Separation of
powers
sources of conflict in, 12–13
strategies for improvement of,
258–265
Supreme Court's role in,
54–58
Legislative liaison, 72
Legislative process, 99–102
Legislative Reorganization Act of
1970, 103–104
Legislative success. *See also*
specific presidents
in civil rights policy, 157–158
congressional control and,
69–70
Congressional Quarterly
measures of, 81–83
criteria for, 26–27
in economic and budget
policy, 190–191

environmental factors in,
19–22, 66–70
in foreign policy, 127–130
institutional factors in, 22–23,
70–73
leadership skills and, 73–75
partisanship and, 69–70
personal factors in, 23–26
policy agenda and, 26–27,
75–81
presidential popularity and, 69
public opinion and, 69
vs. support, 82, 83
Legislative support, 82, 83
Legislative veto, 57
Lewinsky, Monica, 22, 58, 69
Lewis, John, 167
LIBERTAD Act, 113, 133–136
Lieberman, Joseph, 131
Light, Paul, 24, 91
Lincoln, Abraham, 15, 45, 46
Lindsay, Bruce, 56
Line item veto, 84, 260–261
Literacy tests, for voting, 149
Lobbying, presidential, 72–73
Lobbyists, 21–22
Locke, John, 35, 37
Loeb, William, 160
Long, Huey, 207
Losing Ground (Murray), 217
Lott, Trent, 94, 109, 110, 126,
166, 229
Lowi, Theodore, 261
Luger, Richard, 126

Madison, James, 4, 37, 39, 42
Major, John, 5
Majority leader
House, 108
Senate, 109
Malbin, Michael, 265
Management style, presidential,
73–74
Mandate for change,
policymaking and, 19–20
Mandatory entitlements. *See*
Entitlements
Mansfield, Mike, 25, 160
Marbury v. Madison, 40
Markup, 100
Marshall Plan, 120
Massive retaliation, 120
Mass media. *See* Media
Mayhew, David, 10, 258
McCarthy, Joseph, 120
McCormack, Mike, 109
McCullough v. Maryland, 40
McCurry, Mike, 167

McGovern, George, 216
Media
influence of, 21–22
in political environment,
21–22, 103–104, 263–264
presidential use of, 64, 69
Medicaid, 210
costs of, 218
Medicare, 183, 210, 224, 263
catastrophic health insurance
and, 223–226, 244, 245,
246
costs of, 218
Medicare Act of 1965, 51, 209
Medicare Catastrophic Coverage
Act, 223–226
Mexico, 136
Mezey, Michael, 27, 237, 242,
257
Michel, Robert, 225, 246
Military spending, post–Cold
War, 123–124
Mills, Wilbur, 210
Minority leader
House, 109
Senate, 109
Missouri Compromise, 148
Mitchell, George, 25, 94, 131,
132, 169, 226
Modified-closed rules, 101, 105
Mondale, Walter, 139, 194
Monetarism, 178–181
Monroe, James, 42, 148
Montgomery bus boycott,
150–151
Morrill Act, 46
Morrison vs. Olsen, 58
Motor Voter law (1993), 18
Moynihan, Daniel Patrick, 221,
231, 232
Multiparty system, 67, 261
Murray, Alan, 194
Murray, Charles, 217
Mutually assured destruction,
120
Myers v. United States, 55, 56

Nathan, Richard, 75
National Aeronautics and Space
Act of 1958, 16
National Association for the
Advancement of Colored
People (NAACP), 49, 150
National Bank Act, 46
National Committee to Preserve
Social Security, 225, 226
National Emergencies Act of
1976, 53

273